After ten years, can two old flam

False Memories

Story & Art by Isaku **Natsume**

Although they were best friends in high school, Nakano and Tsuda haven't talked in ten years. Which may have a little something to do with the fact that not only were they more than best friends, but also that Tsuda broke Nakano's heart, leaving him to pick up the pieces. Now that they've been thrown back together thanks to a work project, Nakano is determined to put the past behind him, and both men decide to keep their relationship strictly professional. The question is, can they?

MATURE

On sale now at
SuBLimeManga.com
Also available at your local
bookstore or comic book store.

SuBLIME

© 2012 Isaku Natsume/SHINSHOKAN

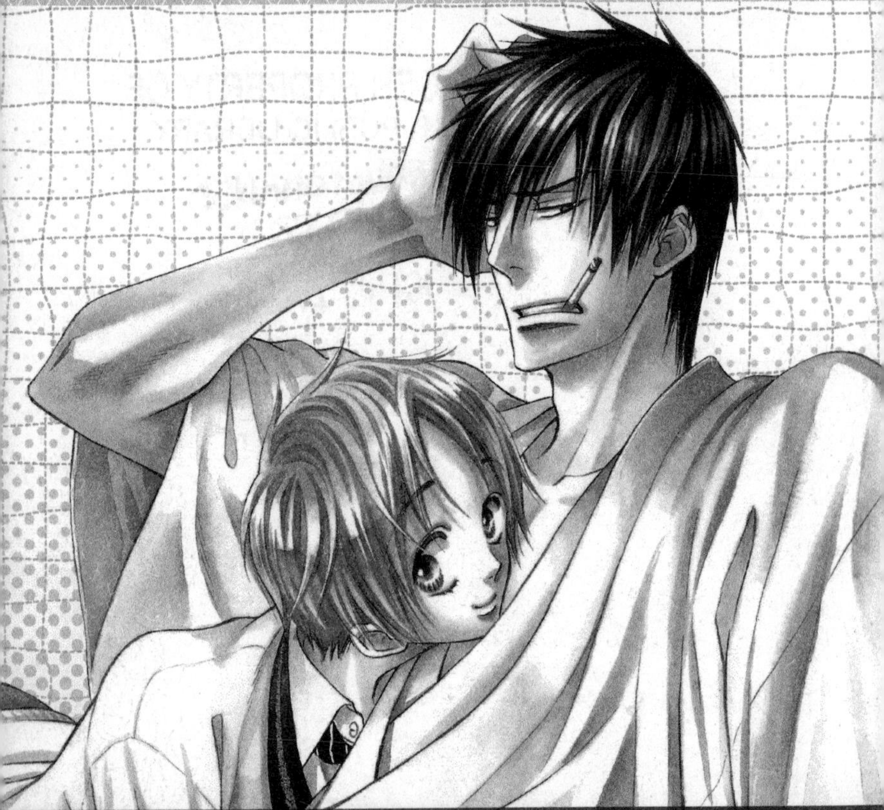

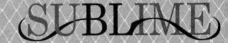

Downloading is as easy as:

1

2

3

For more information

on all our products, along with the most up-to-date news on releases, series announcements, and contests, please visit us at:

 SuBLimeManga.com

 twitter.com/**SuBLimeManga**

 facebook.com/**SuBLimeManga**

 SuBLimeManga.tumblr.com

Love Stage!!
Volume 6
SuBLime Manga Edition

Story by **Eiki Eiki**
Art by **Taishi Zaou**

Translation—**Adrienne Beck**
Touch-up Art and Lettering—**Mara Coman**
Cover and Graphic Design—**Sarah Richardson**
Editor—**Jennifer LeBlanc**

LOVE STAGE!! Volume 6
©Eiki EIKI 2015
©Taishi ZAOU 2015
Edited by KADOKAWA SHOTEN
First published in Japan in 2015
by KADOKAWA CORPORATION, Tokyo.
English translation rights arranged
with KADOKAWA CORPORATION, Tokyo.

ASUKA
COMICS
CL D X

Printed in the U.S.A.

Published by SuBLime Manga
P.O. Box 77010
San Francisco, CA 94107

10 9 8 7 6 5 4 3 2 1
First printing, December 2016

www.SuBLimeManga.com

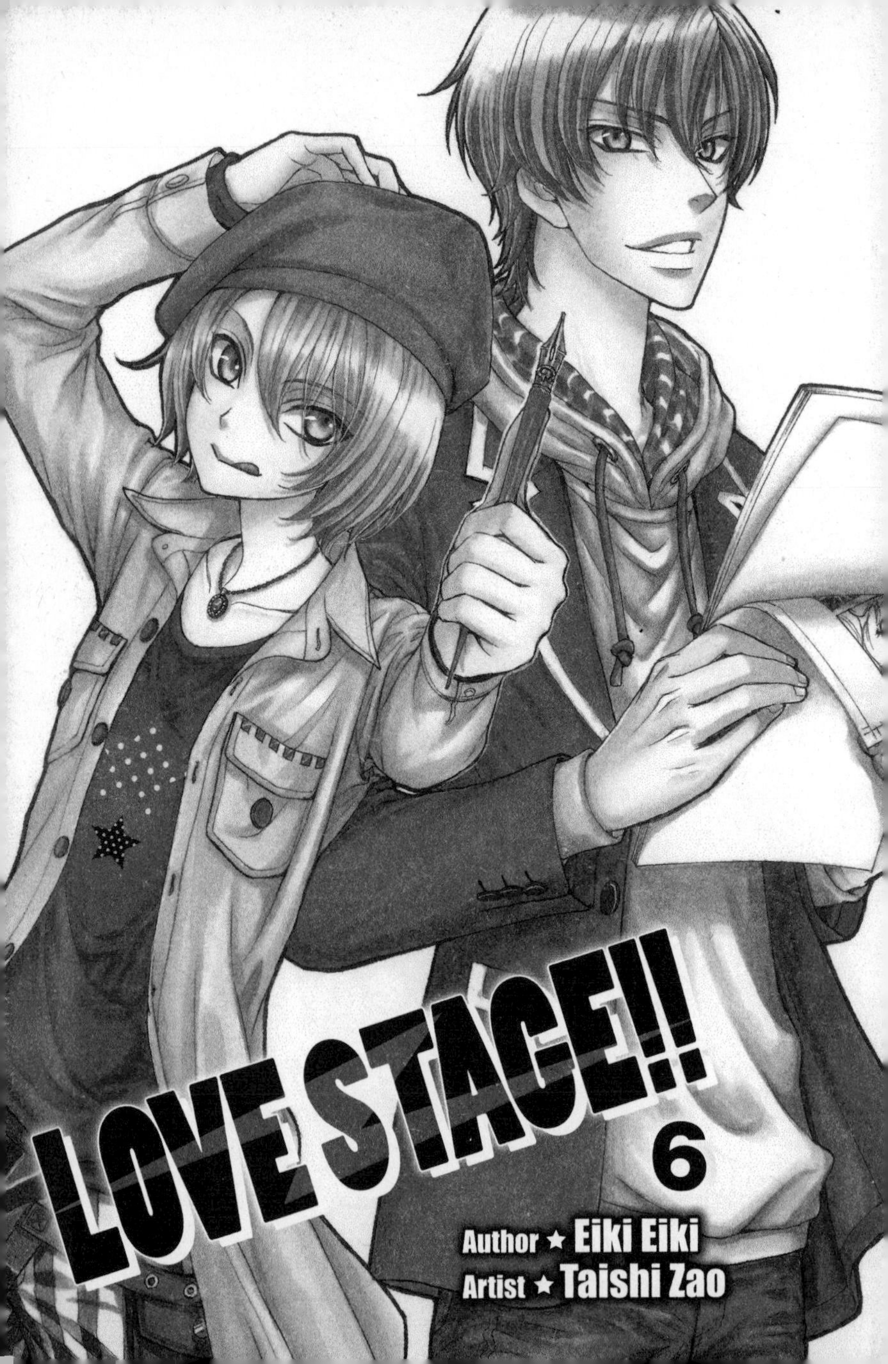
LOVE STAGE!!
6
Author ★ Eiki Eiki
Artist ★ Taishi Zao

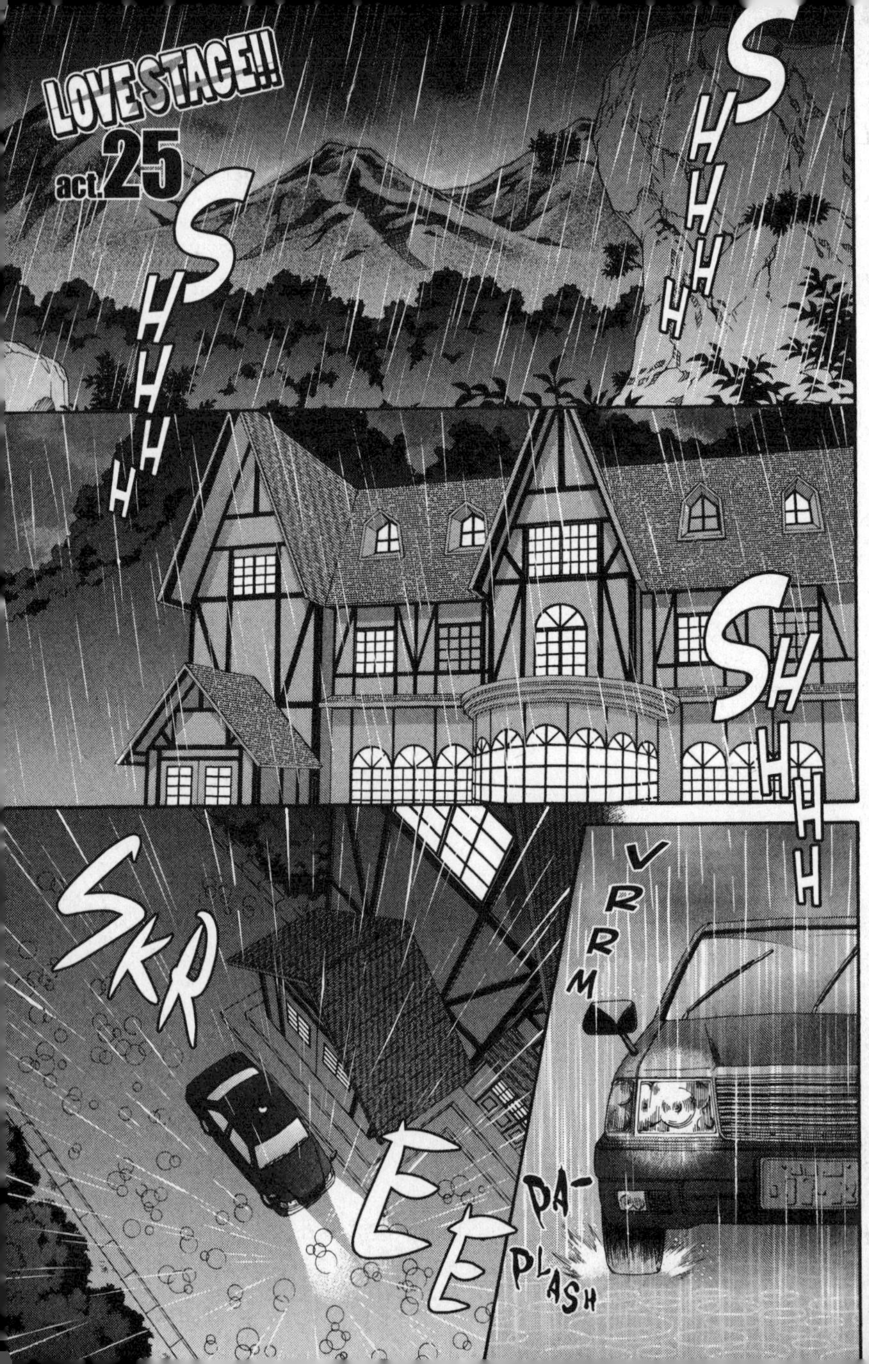
SHHHHHH
LOVE STAGE!!
act.25
SHHHHHH
SHHHHHH
VRRRM
PA-PLASH
SKREE

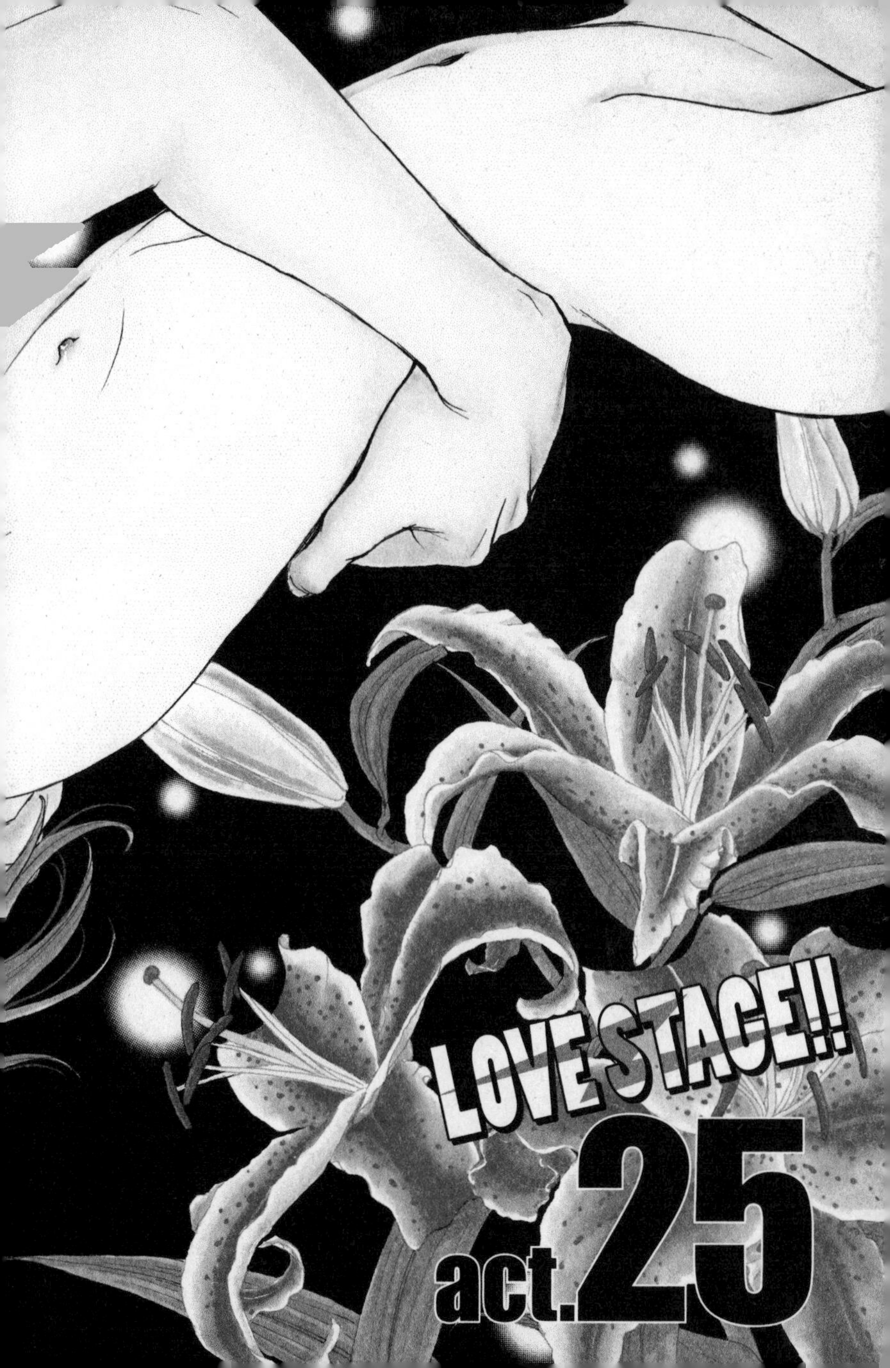
LOVE STAGE!!
act.25

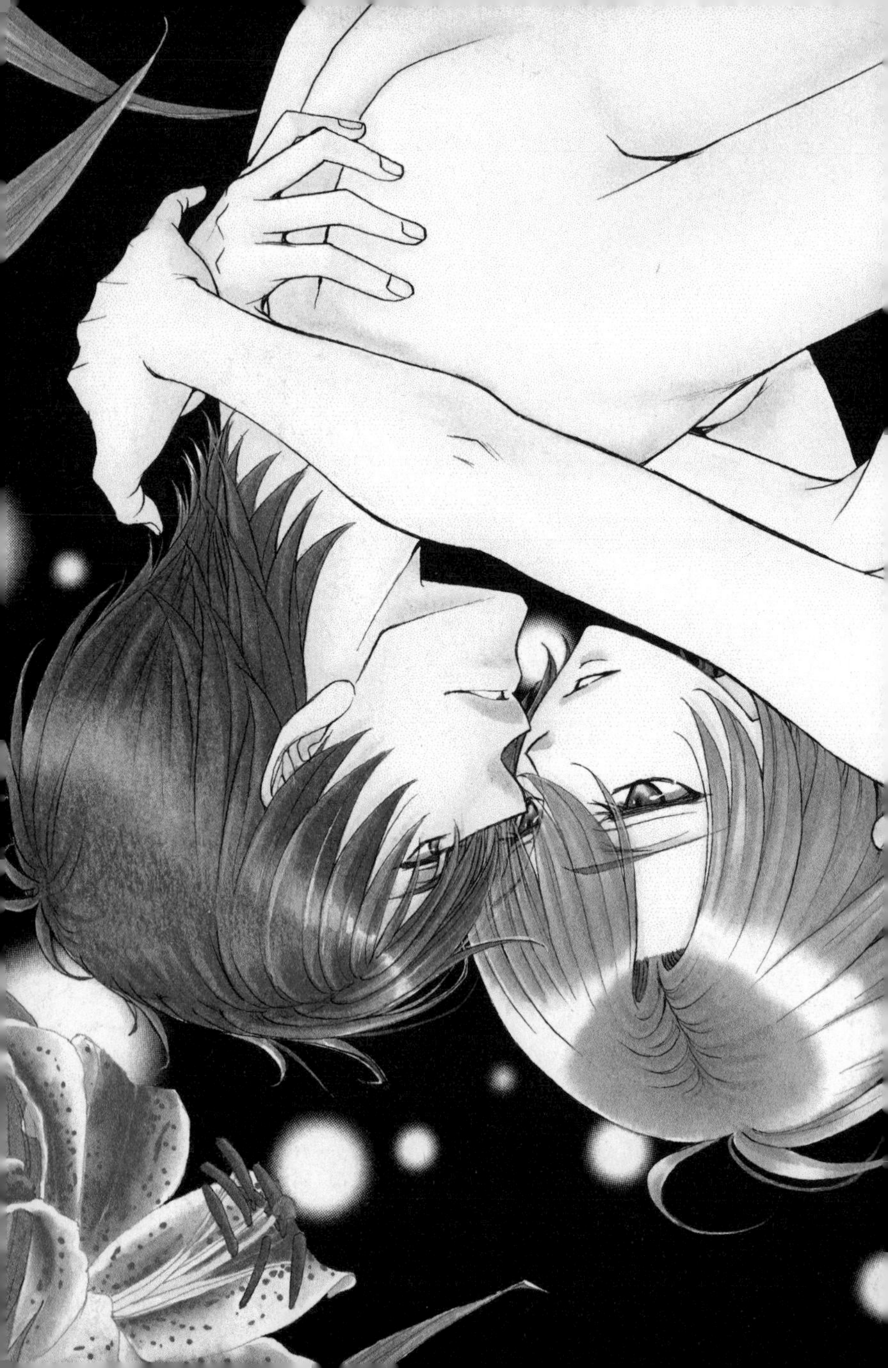

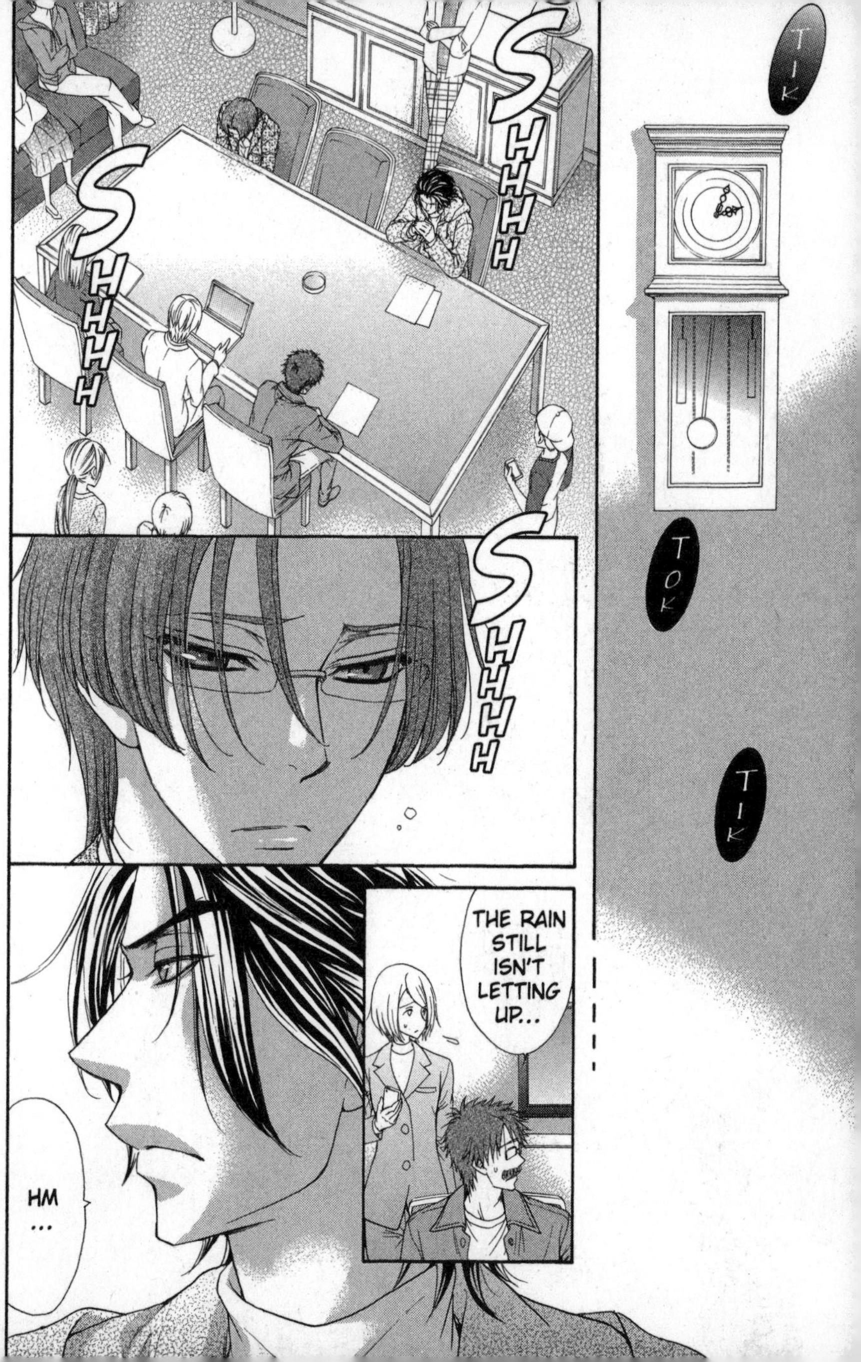
TIK
TOK
TIK
SHHHHH
SHHHHH
SHHHHH
SHHHHH
THE RAIN STILL ISN'T LETTING UP...
HM...

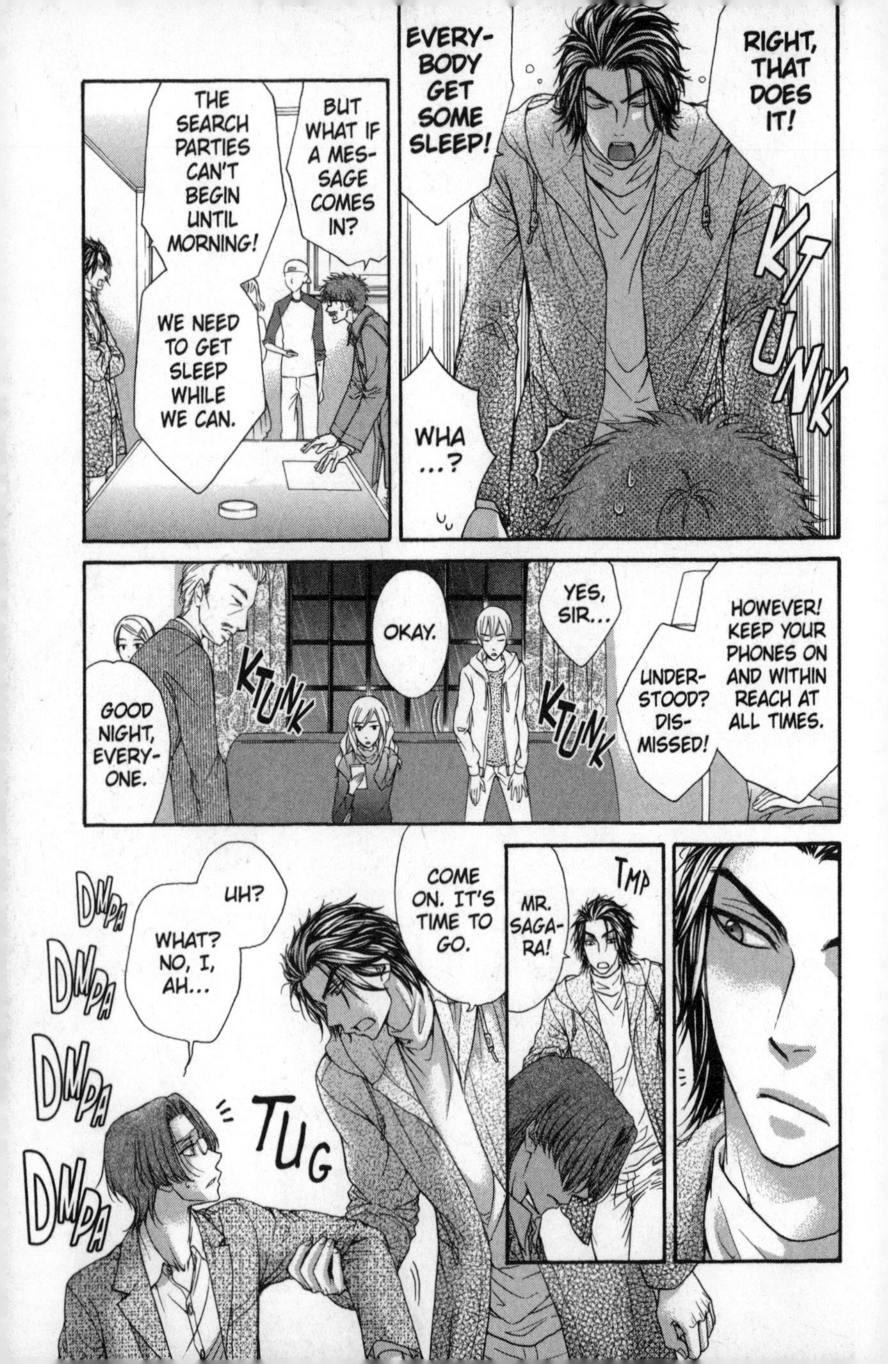

RIGHT, THAT DOES IT!
EVERY-BODY GET SOME SLEEP!
KT UNK
WHA ...?
BUT WHAT IF A MES-SAGE COMES IN?
THE SEARCH PARTIES CAN'T BEGIN UNTIL MORNING!
WE NEED TO GET SLEEP WHILE WE CAN.
HOWEVER! KEEP YOUR PHONES ON AND WITHIN REACH AT ALL TIMES.
UNDER-STOOD? DIS-MISSED!
YES, SIR...
KTUNK
OKAY.
KTUNK
GOOD NIGHT, EVERY-ONE.
TMP
MR. SAGA-RA!
COME ON. IT'S TIME TO GO.
UH?
WHAT? NO, I, AH...
TUG
DMPA
DMPA
DMPA
DMPA

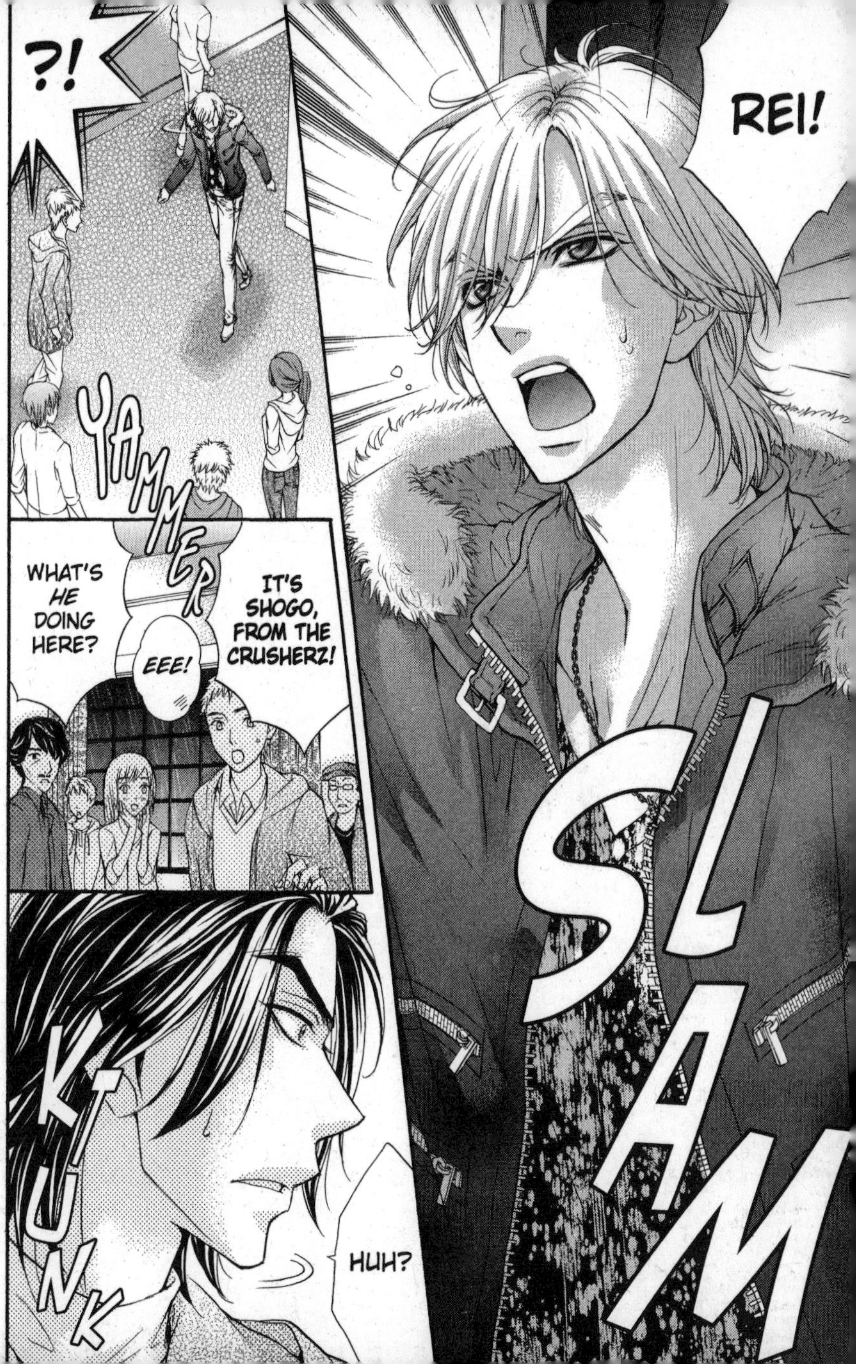
REI!
SLAM
?!
YAMMER
IT'S SHOGO, FROM THE CRUSHERZ!
EEE!
WHAT'S HE DOING HERE?
HUH?
KTUNK

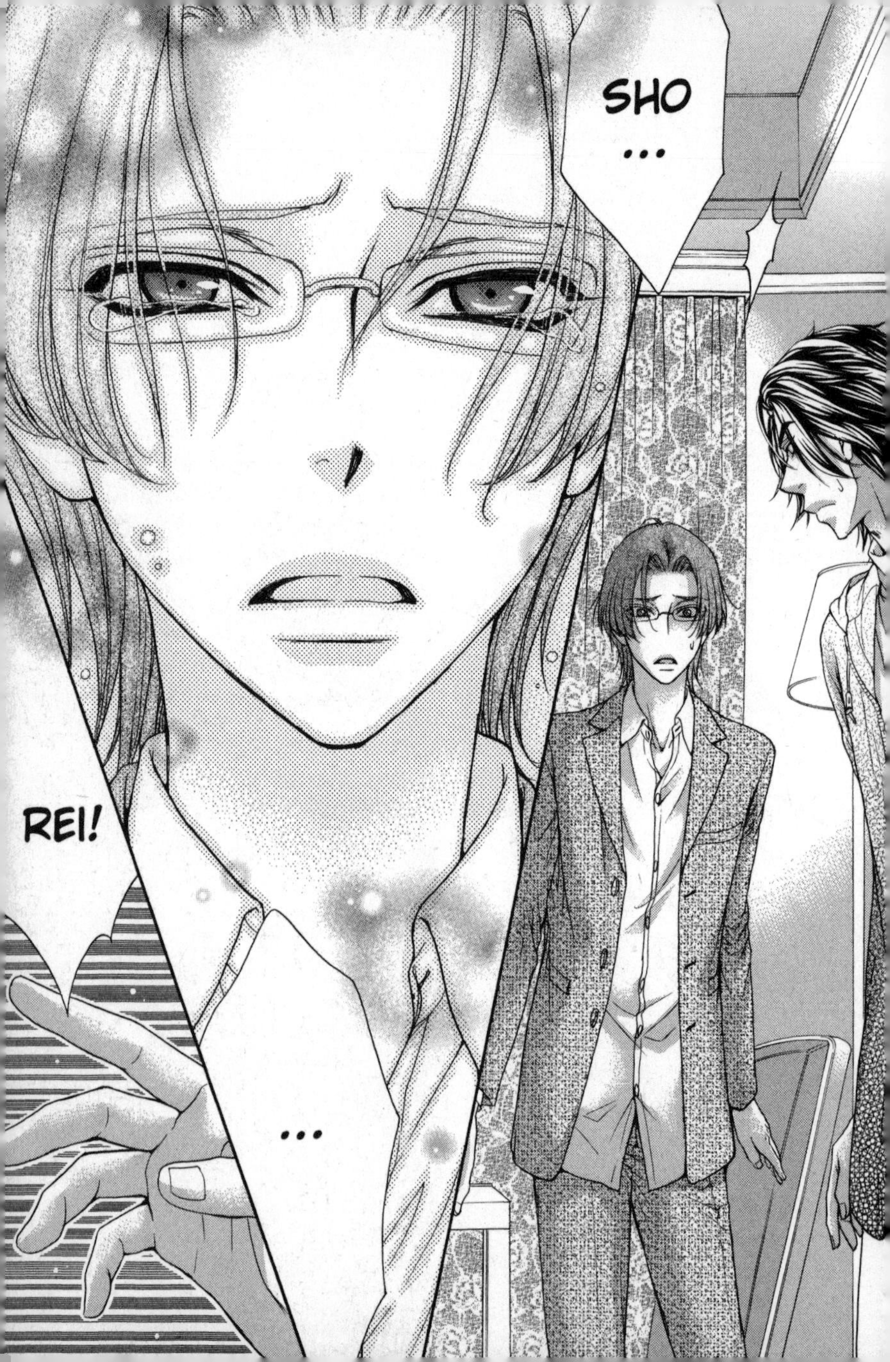
SHO ...
...
REI!

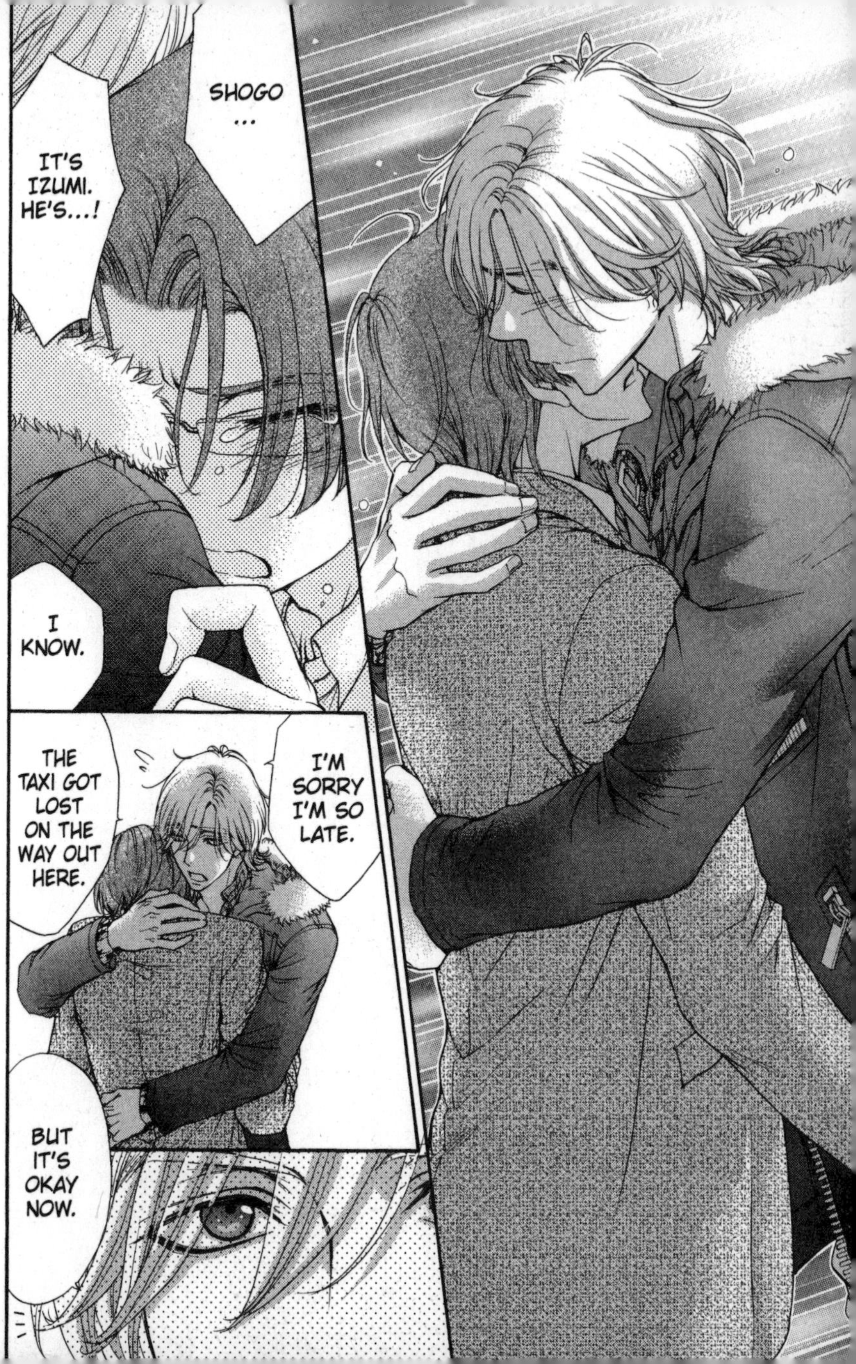
SHOGO ...
IT'S IZUMI. HE'S...!
I KNOW.
I'M SORRY I'M SO LATE.
THE TAXI GOT LOST ON THE WAY OUT HERE.
BUT IT'S OKAY NOW.

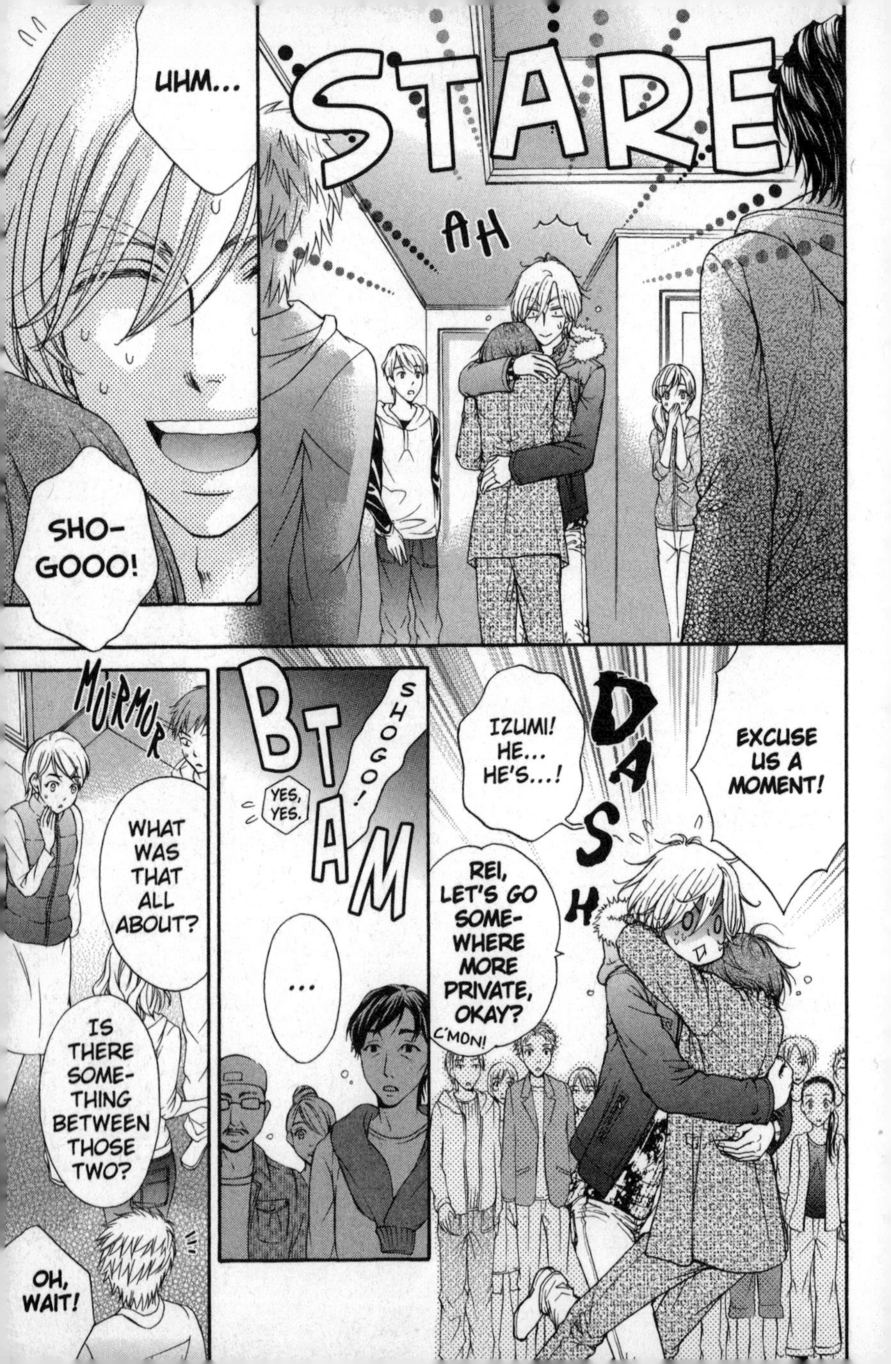
STARE
AH
UHM...
SHO-GOOO!
EXCUSE US A MOMENT!
IZUMI! HE... HE'S...!
DASH
REI, LET'S GO SOME-WHERE MORE PRIVATE, OKAY?
C'MON!
BTAM
SHOGO!
YES, YES.
...
MURMUR
WHAT WAS THAT ALL ABOUT?
IS THERE SOME-THING BETWEEN THOSE TWO?
OH, WAIT!

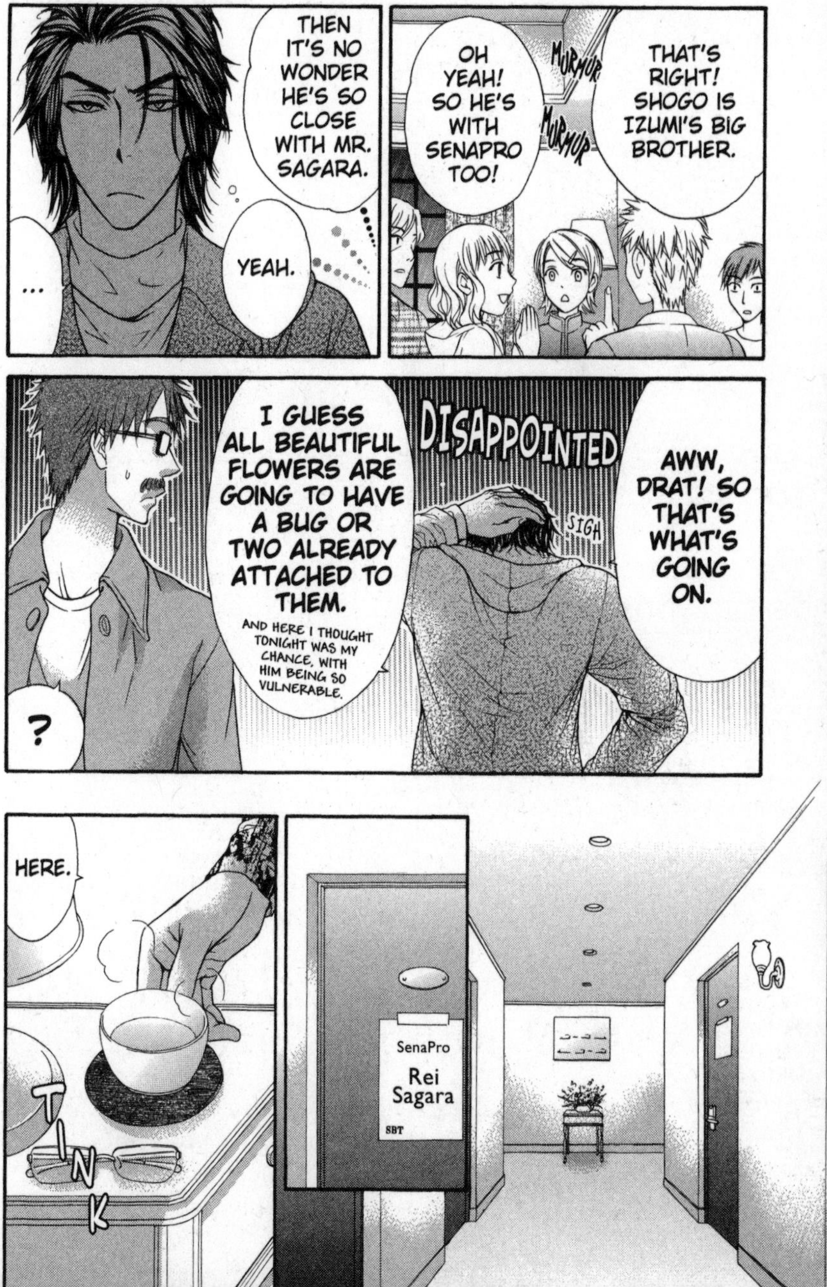
THAT'S RIGHT! SHOGO IS IZUMI'S BIG BROTHER.
MURMUR
MURMUR
OH YEAH! SO HE'S WITH SENAPRO TOO!
THEN IT'S NO WONDER HE'S SO CLOSE WITH MR. SAGARA.
YEAH.
...
AWW, DRAT! SO THAT'S WHAT'S GOING ON.
SIGH
DISAPPOINTED
I GUESS ALL BEAUTIFUL FLOWERS ARE GOING TO HAVE A BUG OR TWO ALREADY ATTACHED TO THEM.
AND HERE I THOUGHT TONIGHT WAS MY CHANCE, WITH HIM BEING SO VULNERABLE.
?
SenaPro
Rei Sagara
SBT
HERE.
TINK

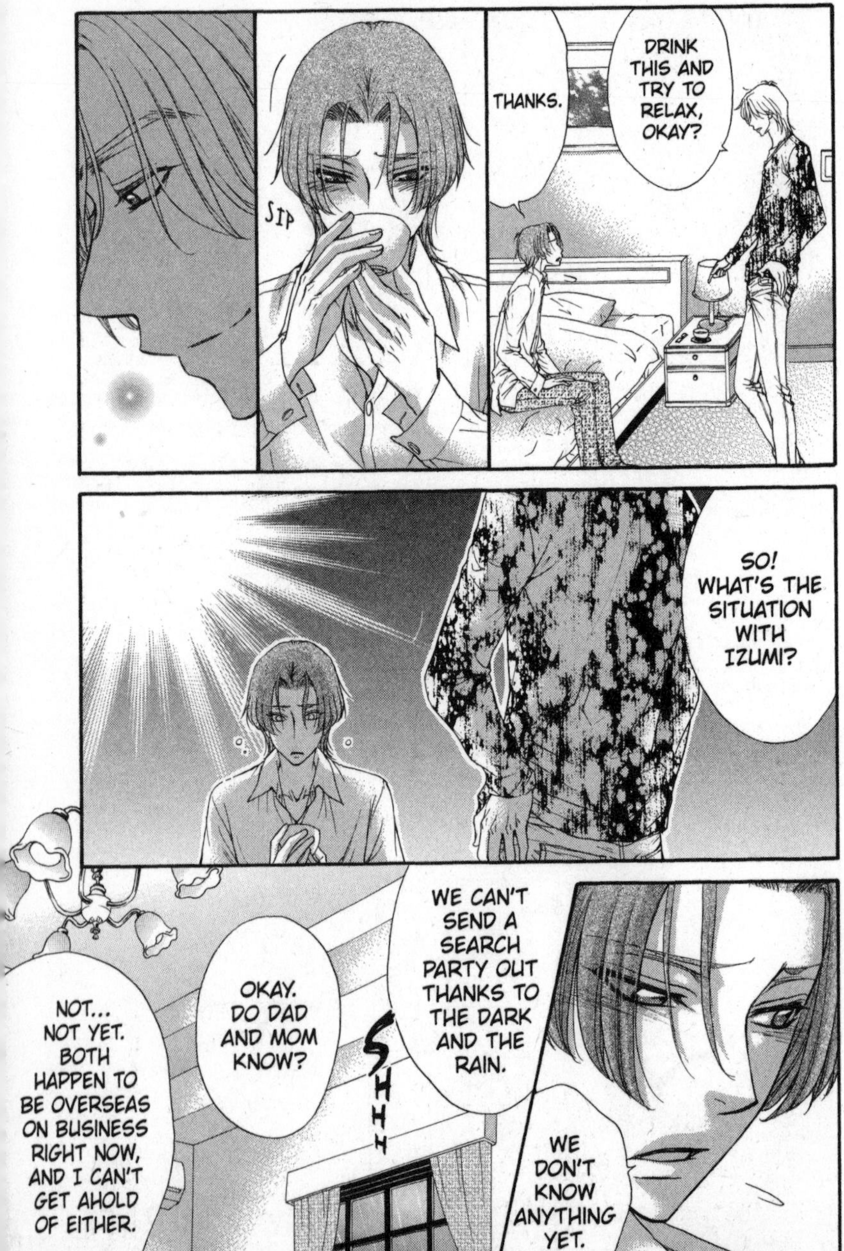
DRINK THIS AND TRY TO RELAX, OKAY?
THANKS.
SIP
SO! WHAT'S THE SITUATION WITH IZUMI?
WE DON'T KNOW ANYTHING YET.
WE CAN'T SEND A SEARCH PARTY OUT THANKS TO THE DARK AND THE RAIN.
SHHHH
OKAY. DO DAD AND MOM KNOW?
NOT... NOT YET. BOTH HAPPEN TO BE OVERSEAS ON BUSINESS RIGHT NOW, AND I CAN'T GET AHOLD OF EITHER.

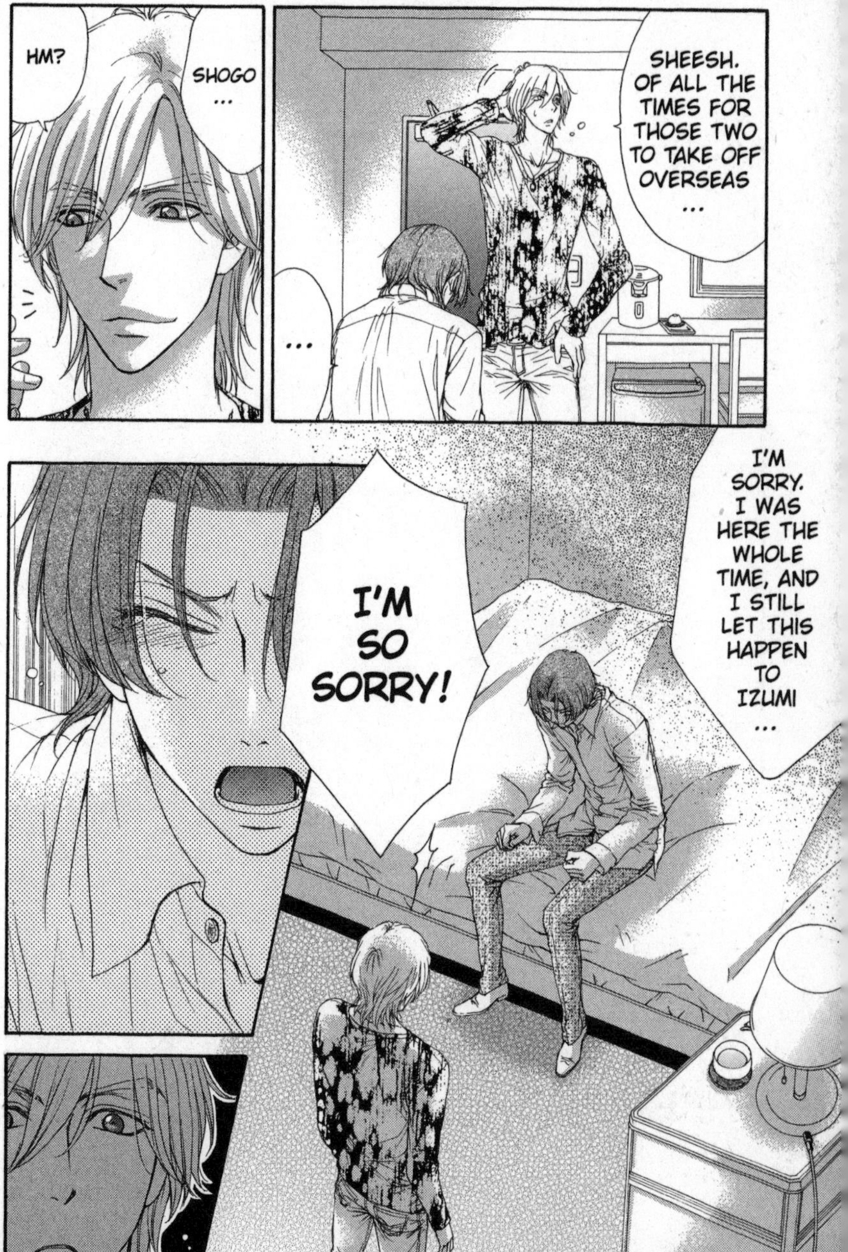
SHEESH. OF ALL THE TIMES FOR THOSE TWO TO TAKE OFF OVERSEAS ...
...
SHOGO ...
HM?
I'M SORRY. I WAS HERE THE WHOLE TIME, AND I STILL LET THIS HAPPEN TO IZUMI ...
I'M SO SORRY!

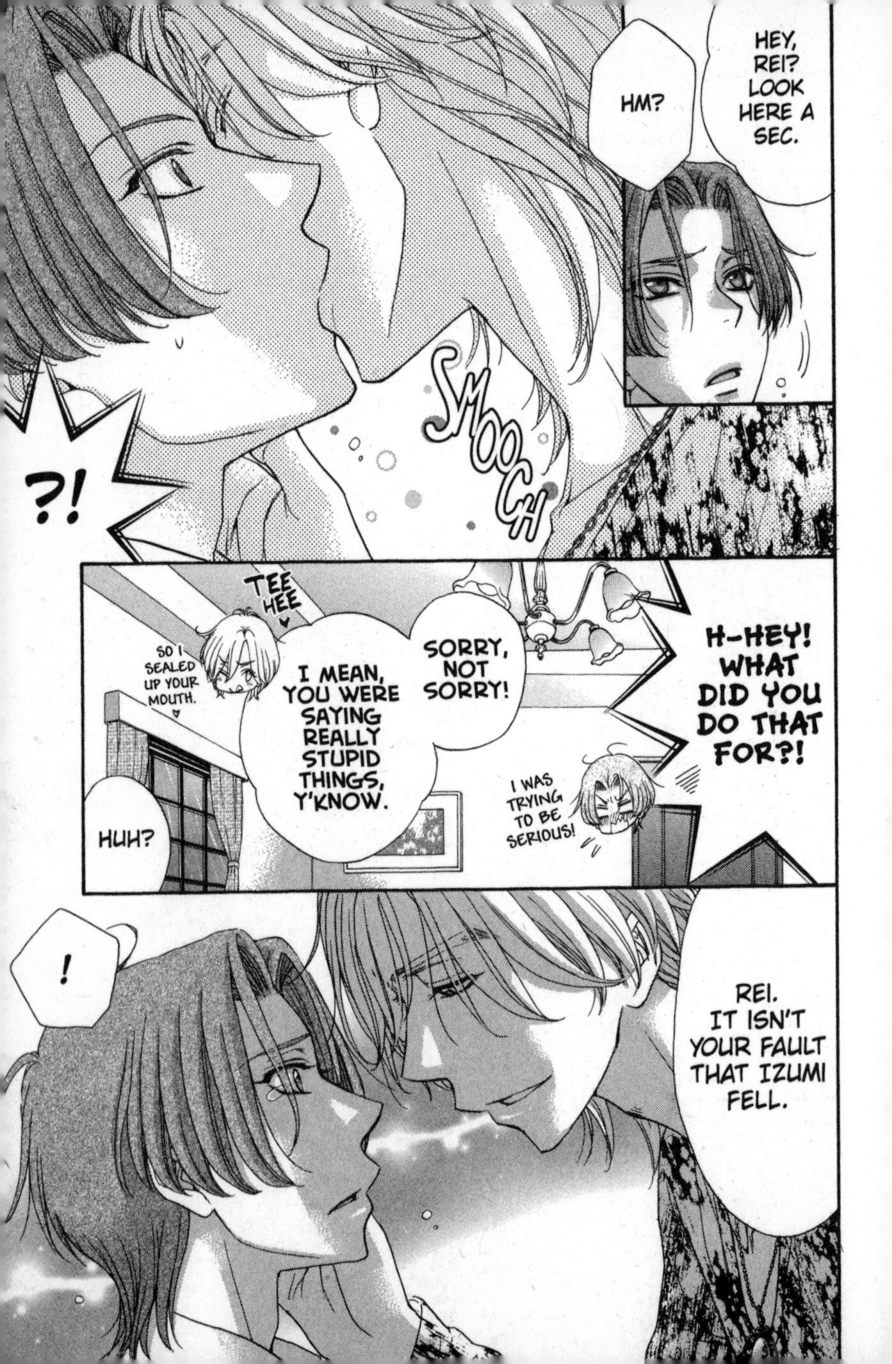
HEY, REI? LOOK HERE A SEC.
HM?
SMOOCH
?!
H-HEY! WHAT DID YOU DO THAT FOR?!
I WAS TRYING TO BE SERIOUS!
SORRY, NOT SORRY!
I MEAN, YOU WERE SAYING REALLY STUPID THINGS, Y'KNOW.
TEE HEE
SO I SEALED UP YOUR MOUTH.
HUH?
REI. IT ISN'T YOUR FAULT THAT IZUMI FELL.
!

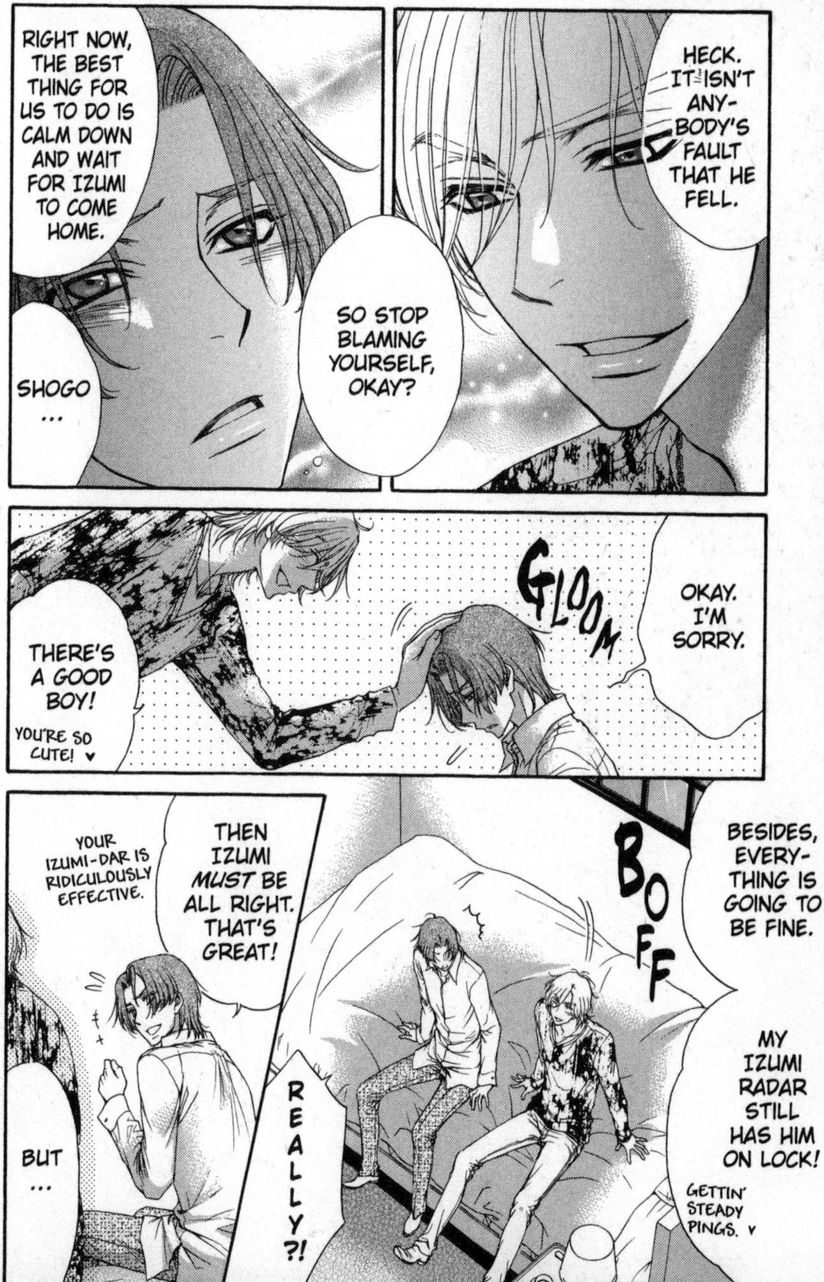
HECK. IT ISN'T ANY-BODY'S FAULT THAT HE FELL.
SO STOP BLAMING YOURSELF, OKAY?
RIGHT NOW, THE BEST THING FOR US TO DO IS CALM DOWN AND WAIT FOR IZUMI TO COME HOME.
SHOGO ...
OKAY. I'M SORRY.
GLOOM
THERE'S A GOOD BOY!
YOU'RE SO CUTE! ♥
BESIDES, EVERY-THING IS GOING TO BE FINE.
BOFF
MY IZUMI RADAR STILL HAS HIM ON LOCK!
GETTIN' STEADY PINGS. ♥
REALLY?!
THEN IZUMI *MUST* BE ALL RIGHT. THAT'S GREAT!
YOUR IZUMI-DAR IS RIDICULOUSLY EFFECTIVE.
BUT ...

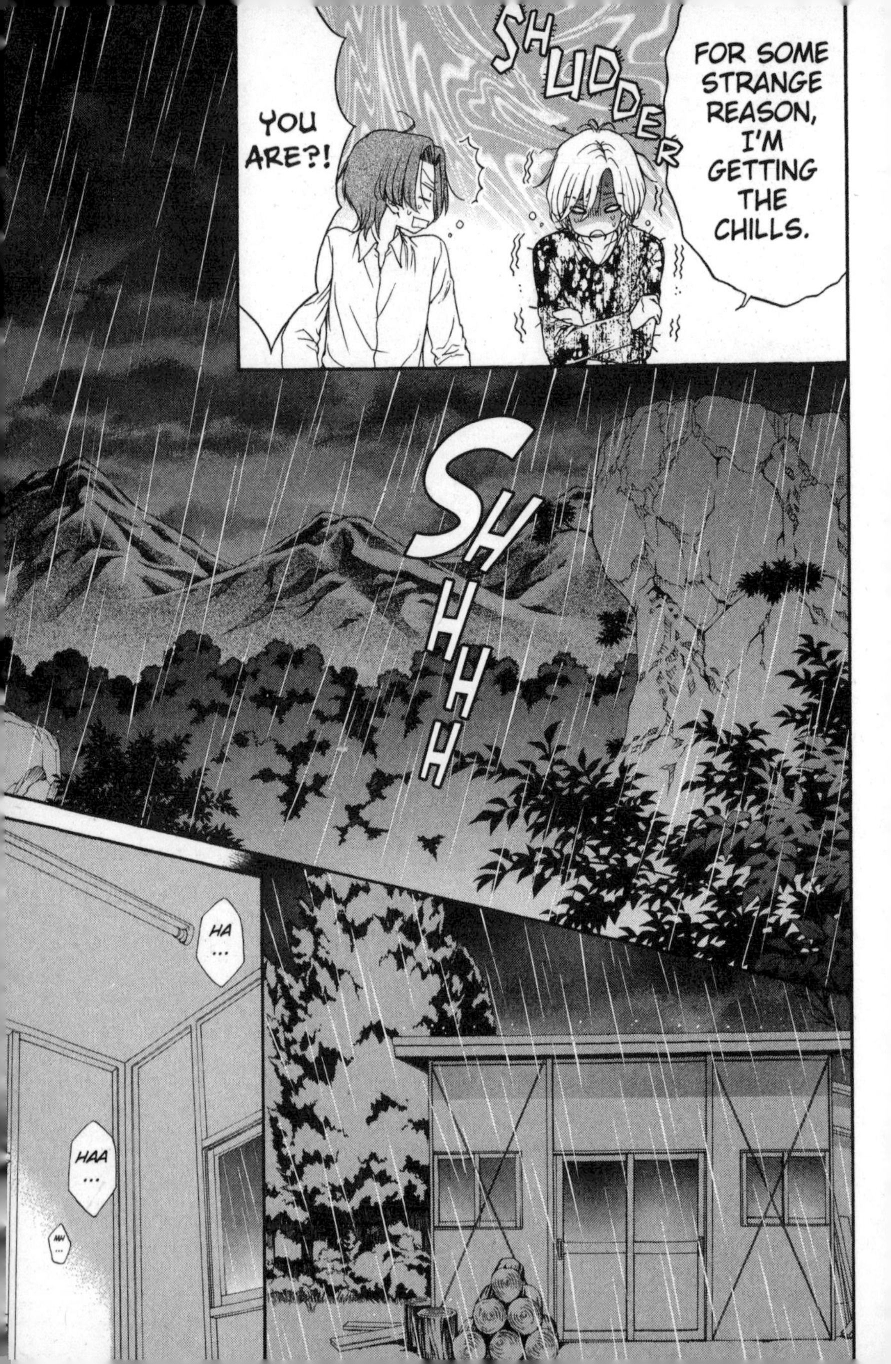
FOR SOME STRANGE REASON, I'M GETTING THE CHILLS.
SHUDDER
YOU ARE?!
SHHHHH
HA ...
HAA ...
MH ...

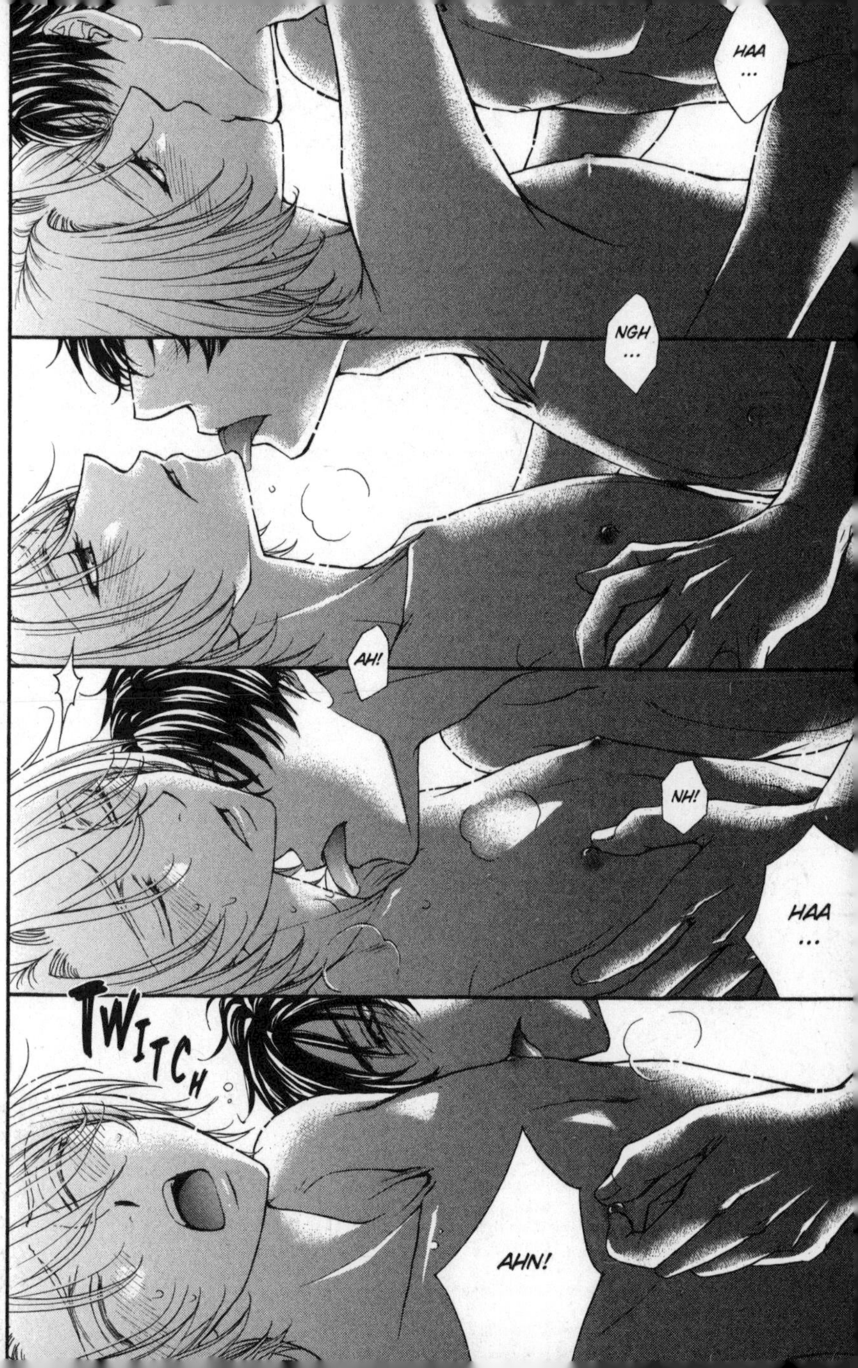
HAA ...
NGH ...
AH!
NH!
HAA ...
TWITCH
AHN!

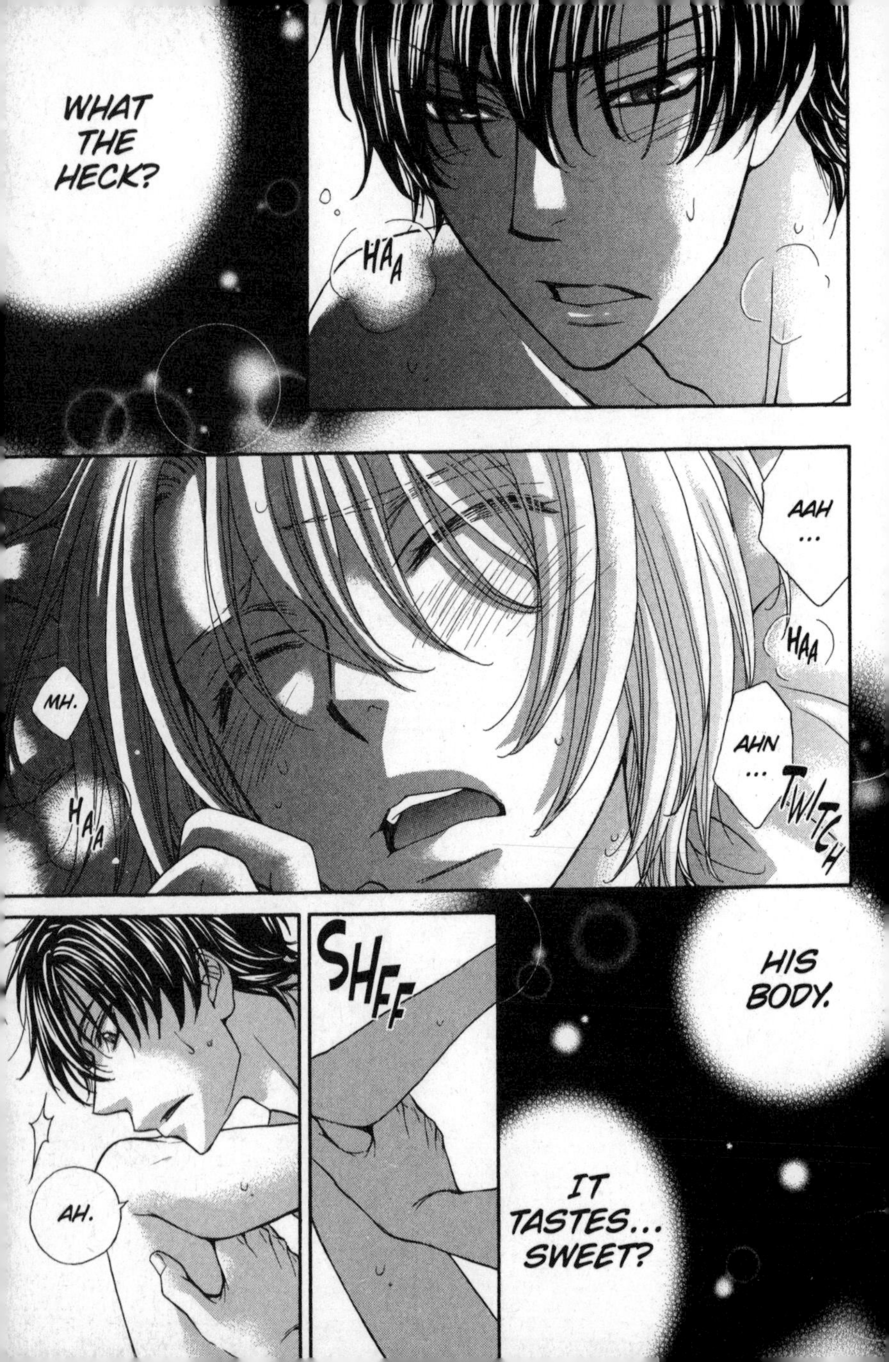
HAA
WHAT THE HECK?
AAH...
HAA
AHN...
TWITCH
MH.
HAA
HIS BODY.
IT TASTES... SWEET?
SHFF
AH.

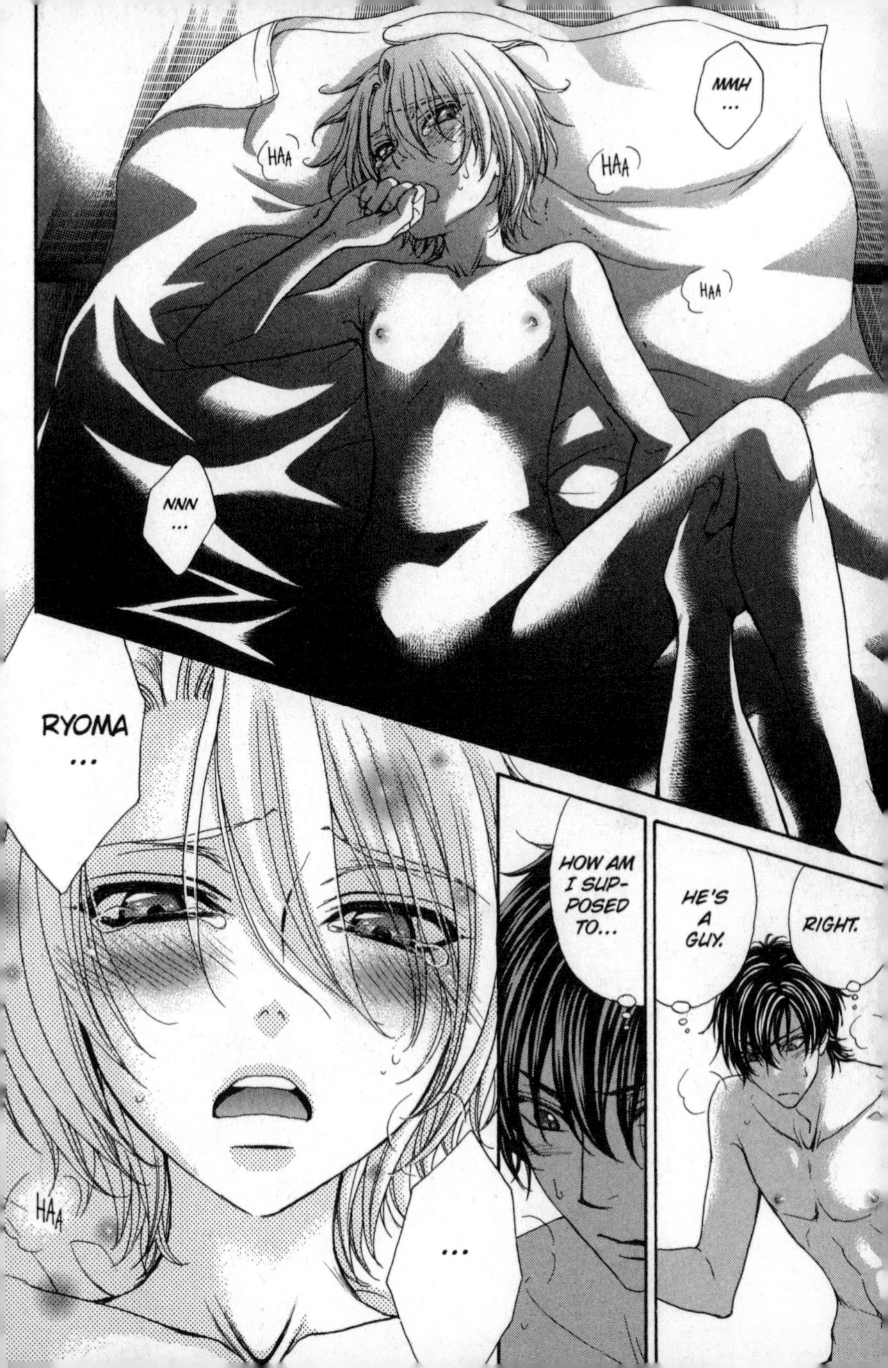
MMH …
HAA
HAA
HAA
NNN …
RIGHT.
HE'S A GUY.
HOW AM I SUP-POSED TO…
RYOMA …
…
HAA

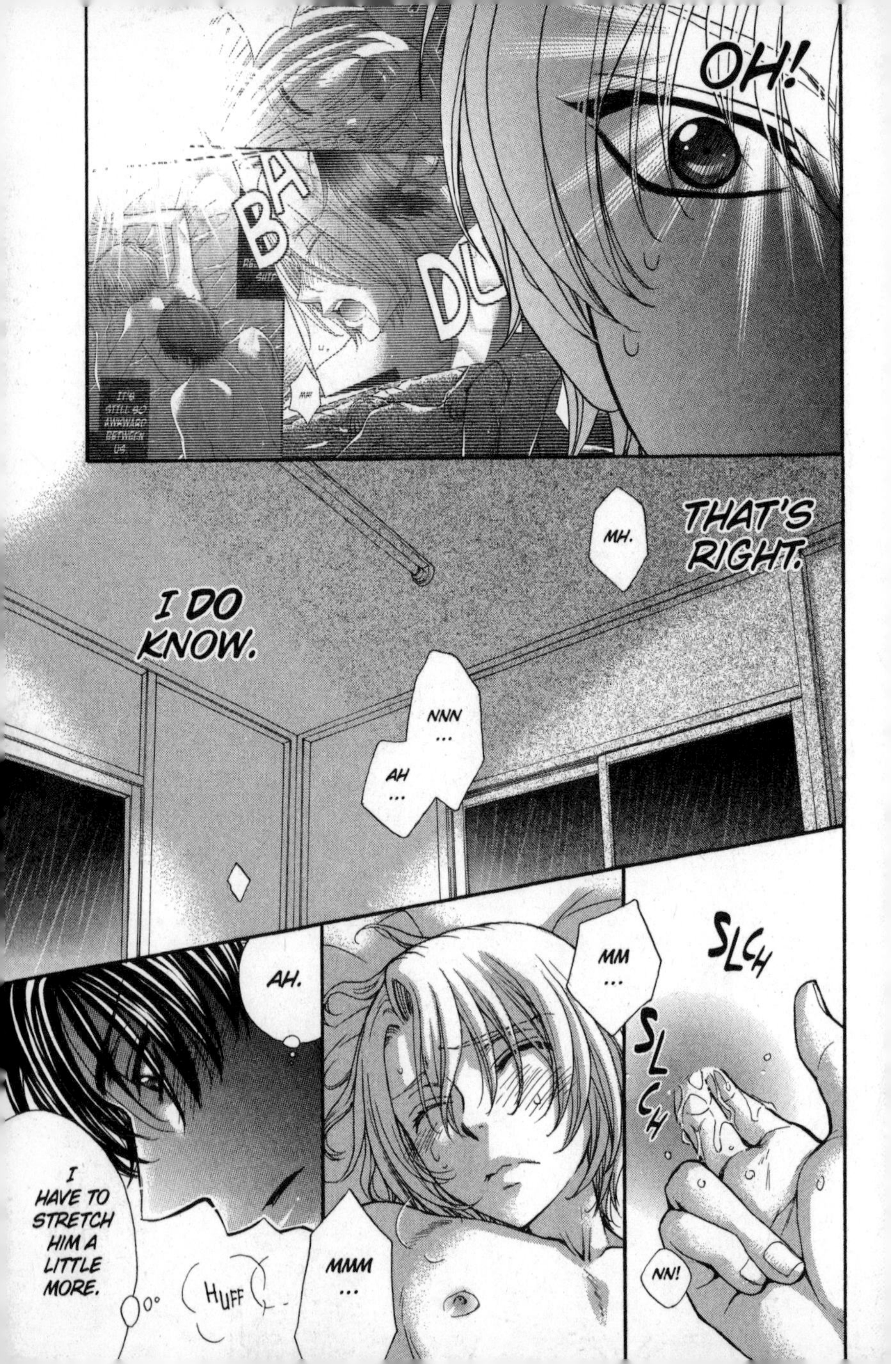
OH!
BA
DU
IT'S STILL SO AWKWARD BETWEEN US.
THAT'S RIGHT.
MH.
I DO KNOW.
NNN...
AH...
SLCH
SLCH
NN!
MM...
MMM...
AH.
I HAVE TO STRETCH HIM A LITTLE MORE.
HUFF

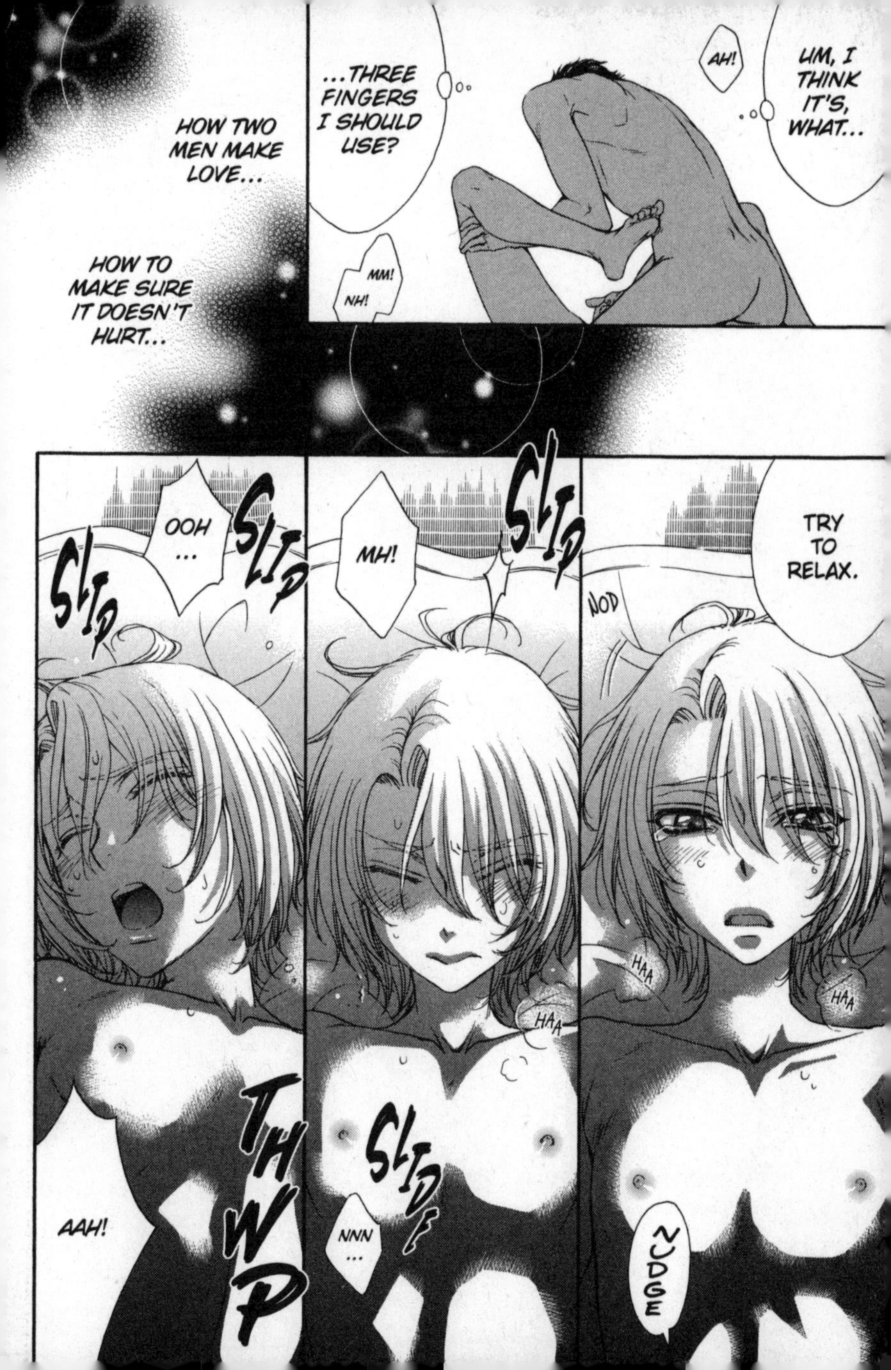
UM, I THINK IT'S, WHAT...
AH!
...THREE FINGERS I SHOULD USE?
MM!
NH!
HOW TWO MEN MAKE LOVE...
HOW TO MAKE SURE IT DOESN'T HURT...
TRY TO RELAX.
NOD
HAA
HAA
NUDGE
SLIP
MH!
HAA
SLIDE
NNN ...
SLIP
OOH ...
SLIP
THWP
AAH!

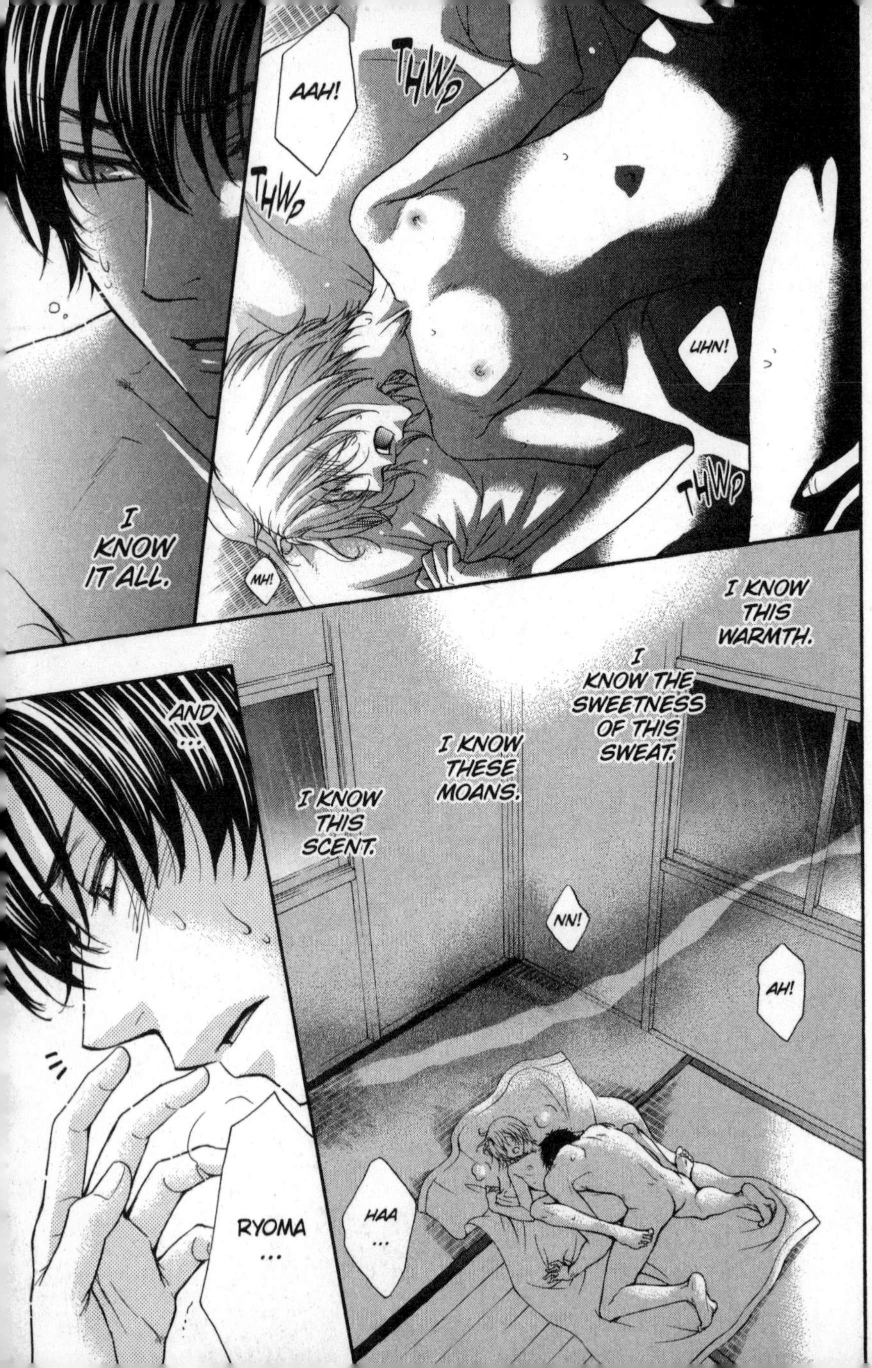
THWP
AAH!
THWP
UHN!
THWP
MH!
I KNOW IT ALL.
I KNOW THIS WARMTH.
I KNOW THE SWEETNESS OF THIS SWEAT.
I KNOW THESE MOANS.
I KNOW THIS SCENT.
NN!
AH!
HAA ...
AND ...
RYOMA ...

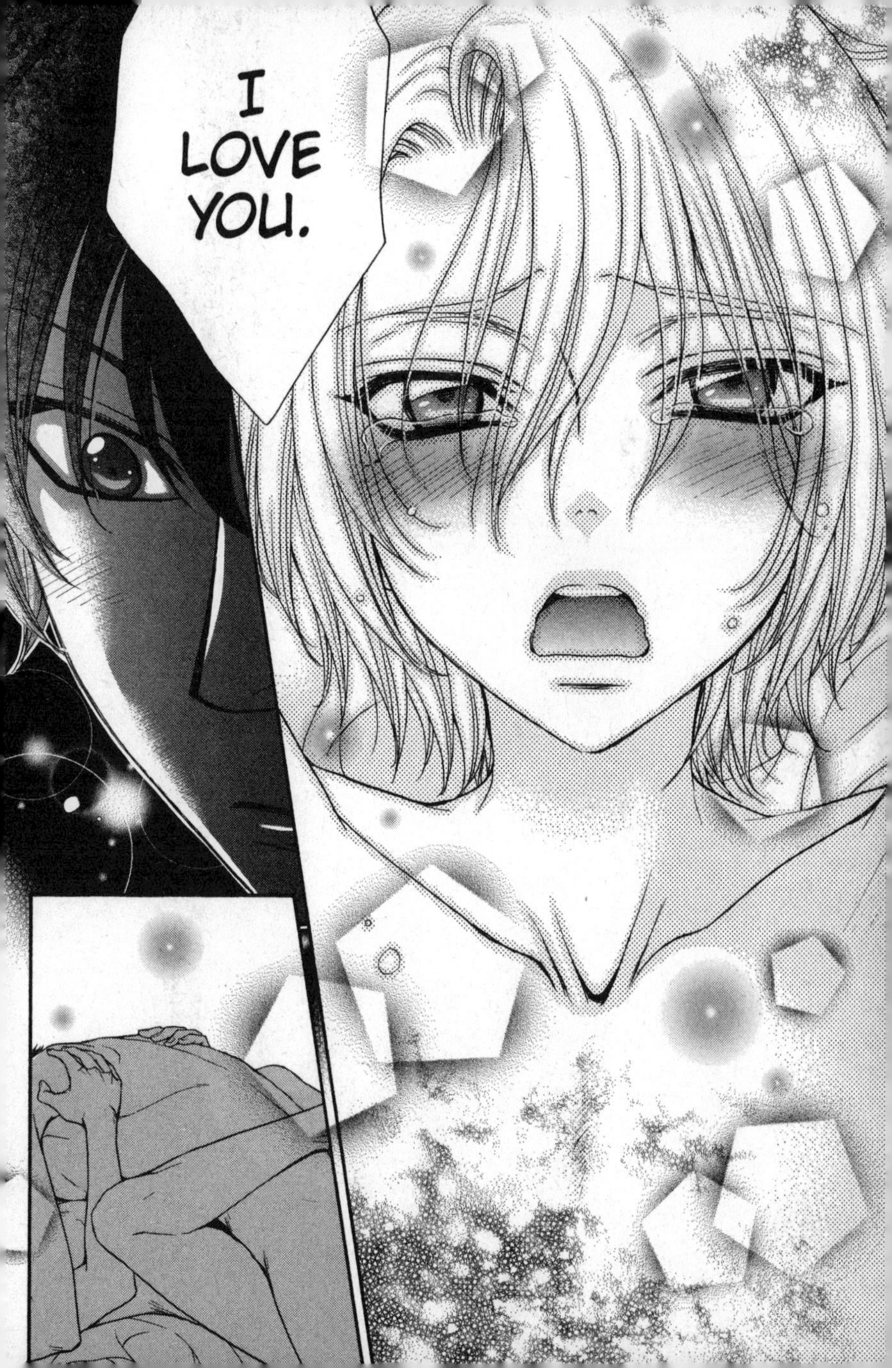
I LOVE YOU.

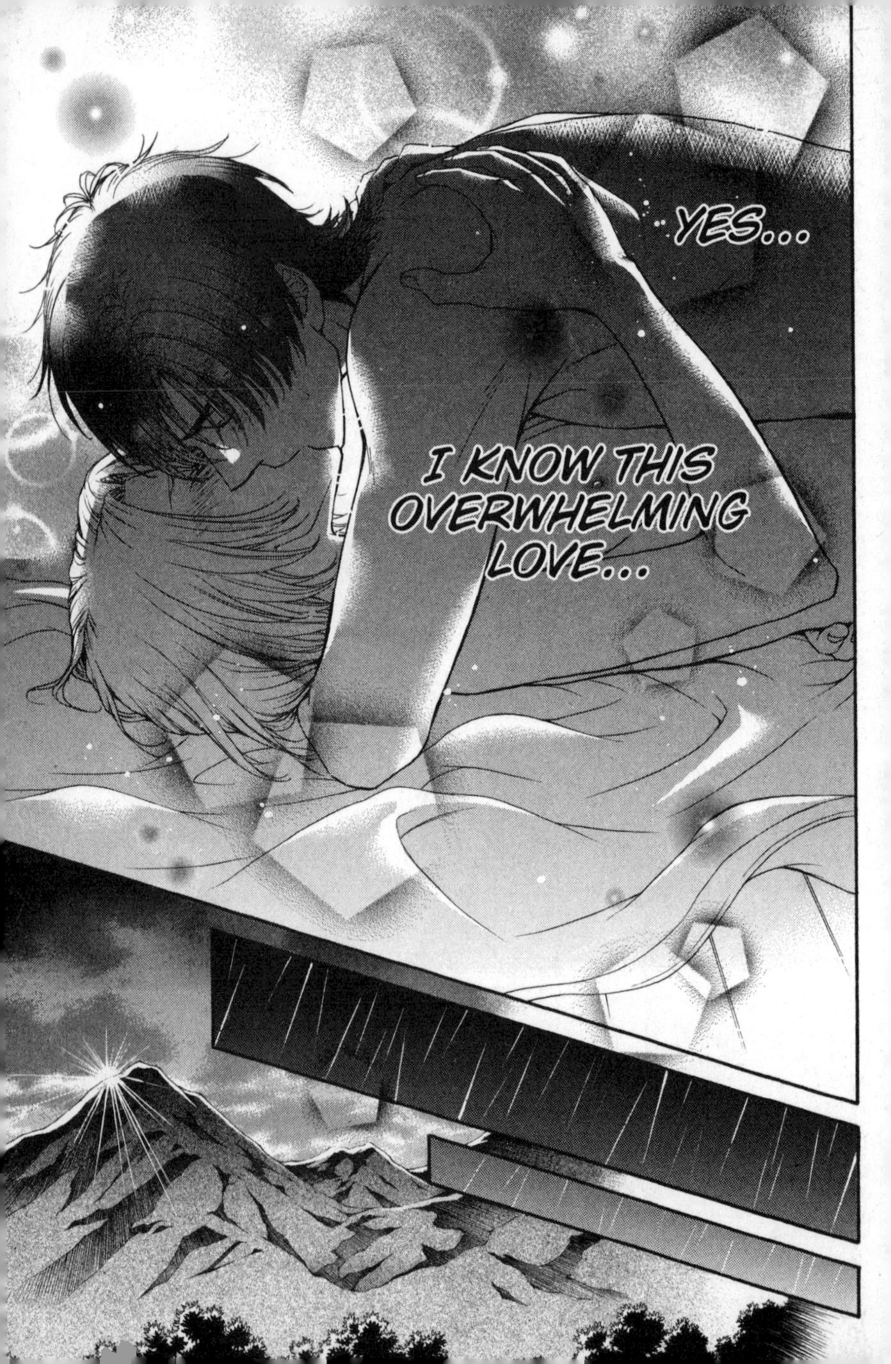
YES...
I KNOW THIS OVERWHELMING LOVE...

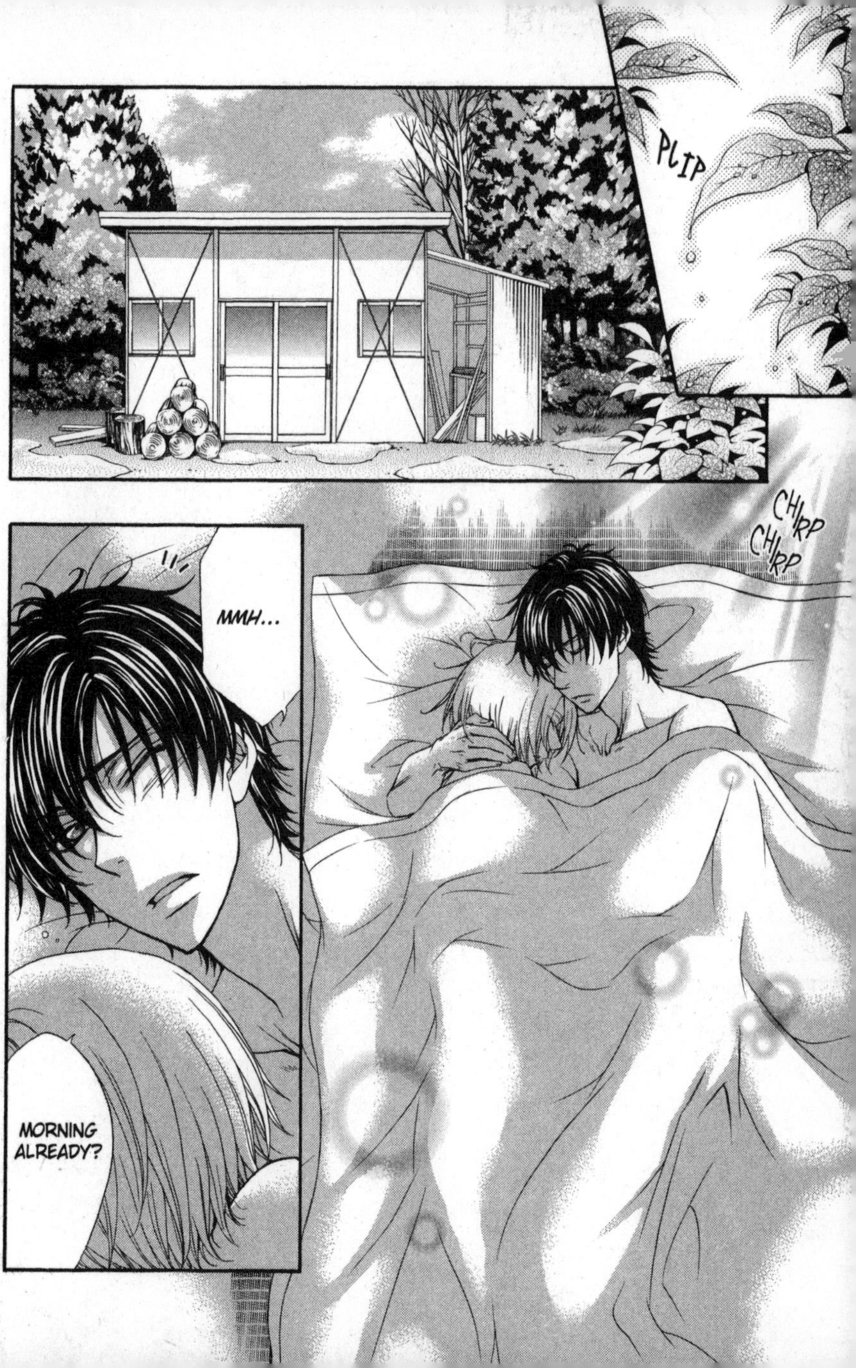
PLIP
CHIRP CHIRP
MMH...
MORNING ALREADY?

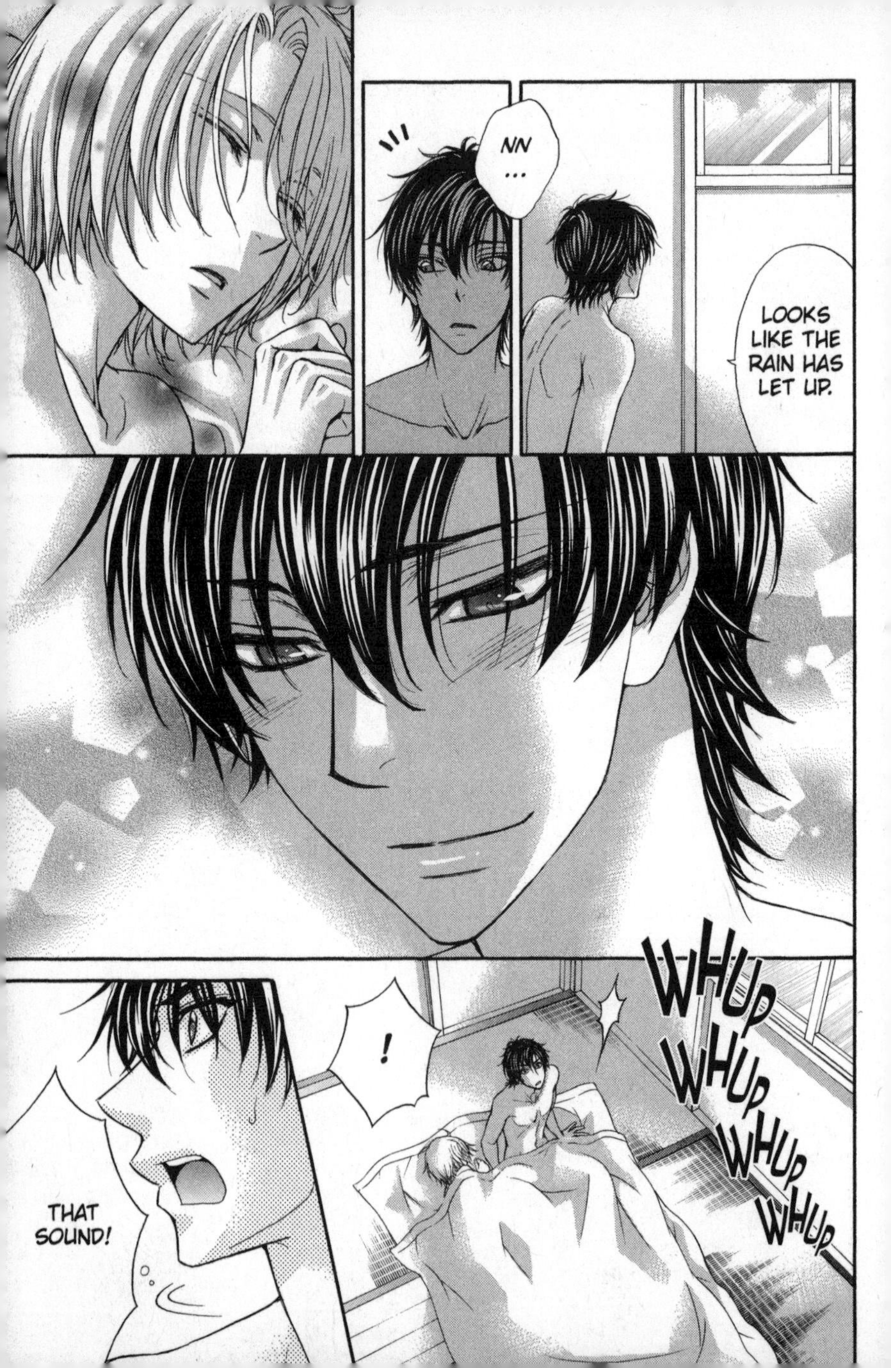
LOOKS LIKE THE RAIN HAS LET UP.
NN ...
WHUP WHUP WHUP WHUP WHUP
!
THAT SOUND!

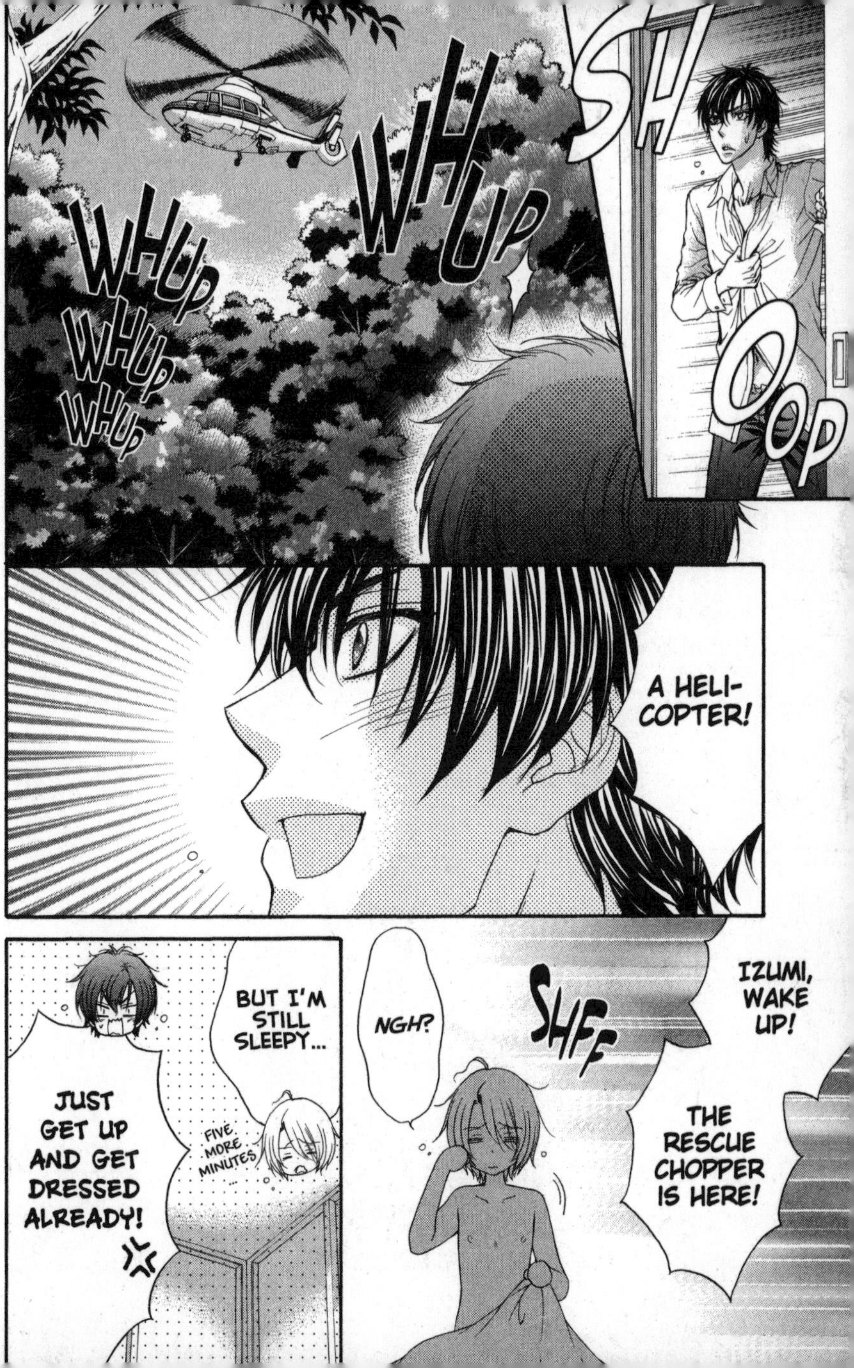
SHOOP
WHUP
WHUP WHUP WHUP WHUP
A HELI-COPTER!
IZUMI, WAKE UP!
THE RESCUE CHOPPER IS HERE!
SHFF
NGH?
BUT I'M STILL SLEEPY...
FIVE MORE MINUTES...
JUST GET UP AND GET DRESSED ALREADY!

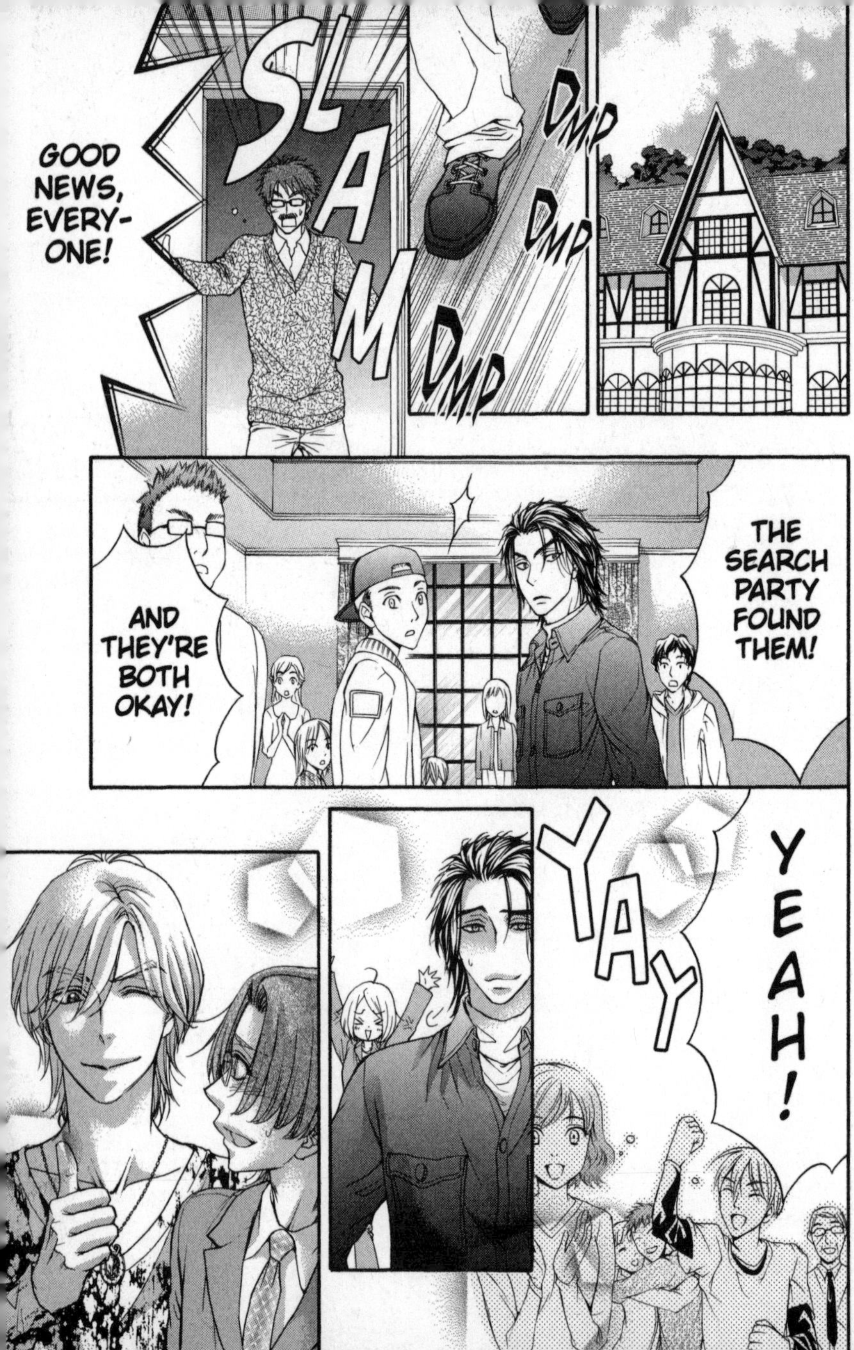
DMP
DMP
DMP
SLAM
GOOD NEWS, EVERYONE!
THE SEARCH PARTY FOUND THEM!
AND THEY'RE BOTH OKAY!
YEAH!
YAY

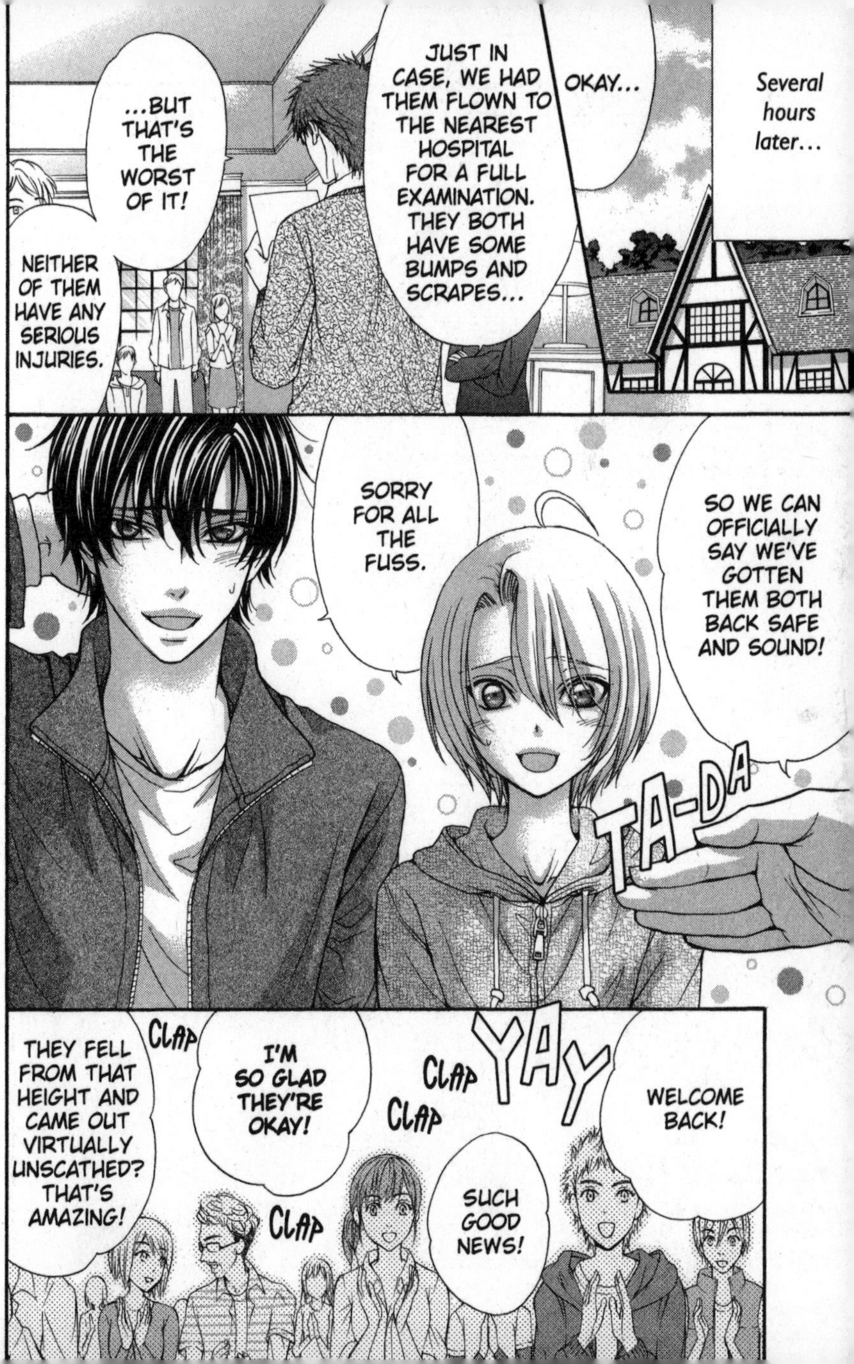
Several hours later…
OKAY…
JUST IN CASE, WE HAD THEM FLOWN TO THE NEAREST HOSPITAL FOR A FULL EXAMINATION. THEY BOTH HAVE SOME BUMPS AND SCRAPES…
…BUT THAT'S THE WORST OF IT!
NEITHER OF THEM HAVE ANY SERIOUS INJURIES.
SO WE CAN OFFICIALLY SAY WE'VE GOTTEN THEM BOTH BACK SAFE AND SOUND!
TA-DA
SORRY FOR ALL THE FUSS.
WELCOME BACK!
YAY
CLAP
CLAP
I'M SO GLAD THEY'RE OKAY!
CLAP
THEY FELL FROM THAT HEIGHT AND CAME OUT VIRTUALLY UNSCATHED? THAT'S AMAZING!
SUCH GOOD NEWS!
CLAP

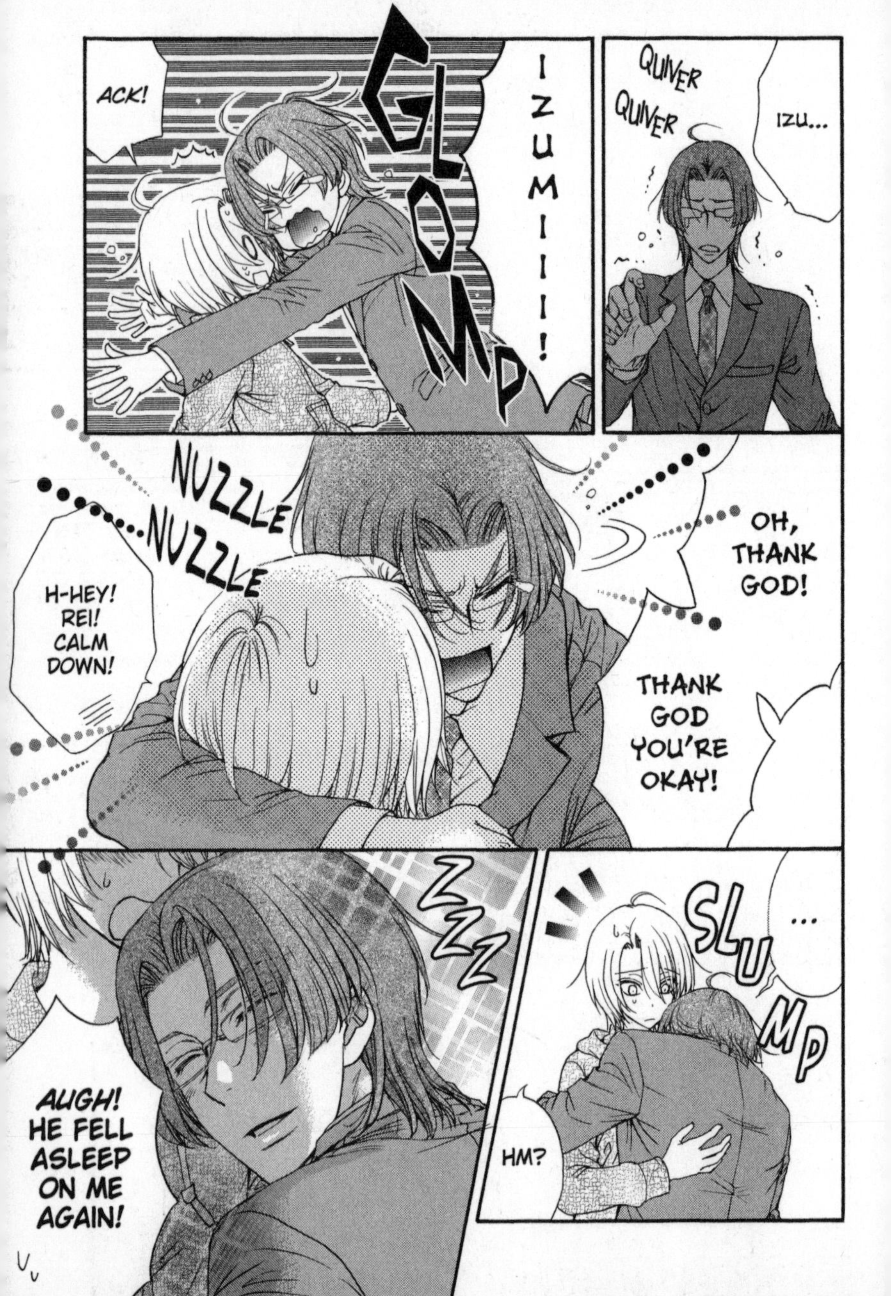
QUIVER
QUIVER
IZU...
IZUMIIII!
GLOMP
ACK!
OH, THANK GOD!
THANK GOD YOU'RE OKAY!
NUZZLE
NUZZLE
H-HEY! REI! CALM DOWN!
...
SLUMP
HM?
ZZZ
AUGH! HE FELL ASLEEP ON ME AGAIN!

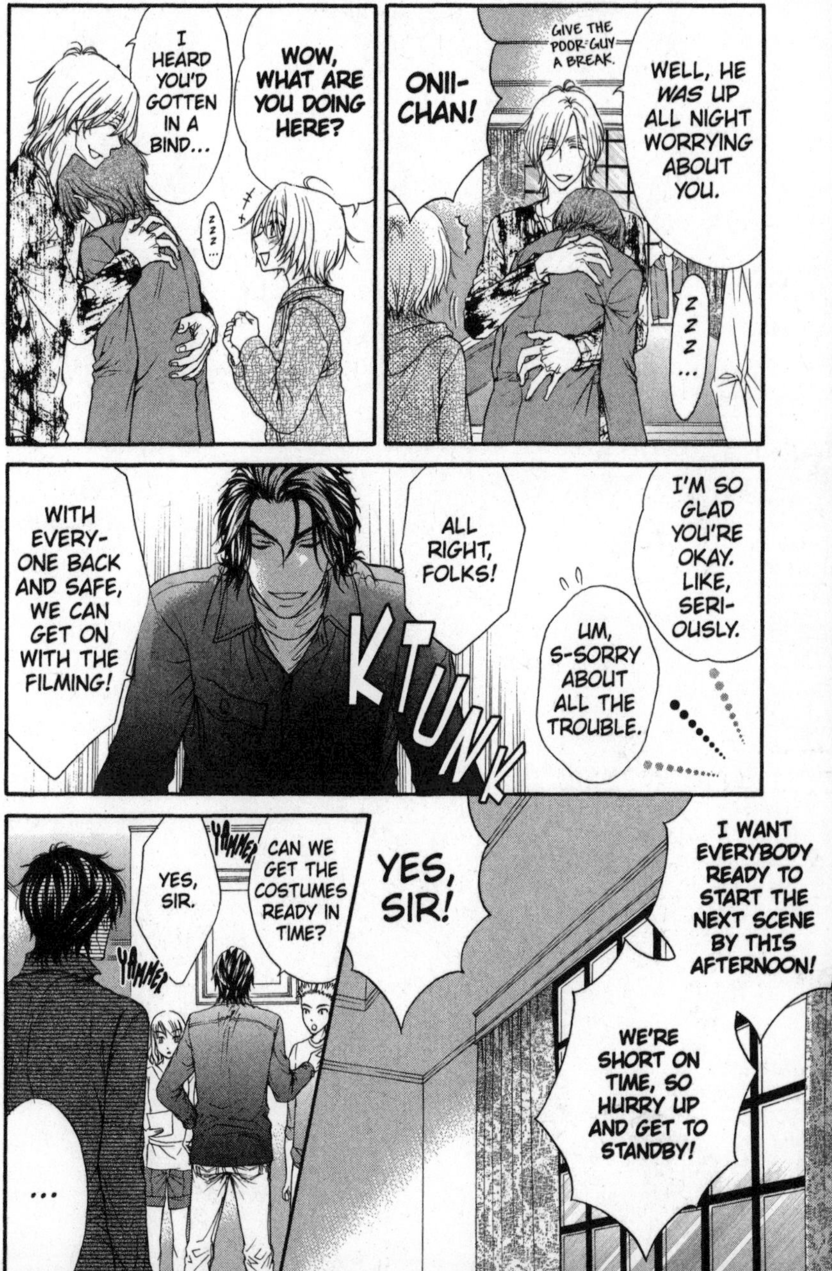
WELL, HE WAS UP ALL NIGHT WORRYING ABOUT YOU.
GIVE THE POOR GUY A BREAK.
ONII-CHAN!
ZZZ...
WOW, WHAT ARE YOU DOING HERE?
I HEARD YOU'D GOTTEN IN A BIND...
ZZZ...
I'M SO GLAD YOU'RE OKAY. LIKE, SERIOUSLY.
UM, S-SORRY ABOUT ALL THE TROUBLE.
ALL RIGHT, FOLKS!
KTUNK
WITH EVERYONE BACK AND SAFE, WE CAN GET ON WITH THE FILMING!
I WANT EVERYBODY READY TO START THE NEXT SCENE BY THIS AFTERNOON!
WE'RE SHORT ON TIME, SO HURRY UP AND GET TO STANDBY!
YES, SIR!
CAN WE GET THE COSTUMES READY IN TIME?
YAMMER
YES, SIR.
YAMMER
...

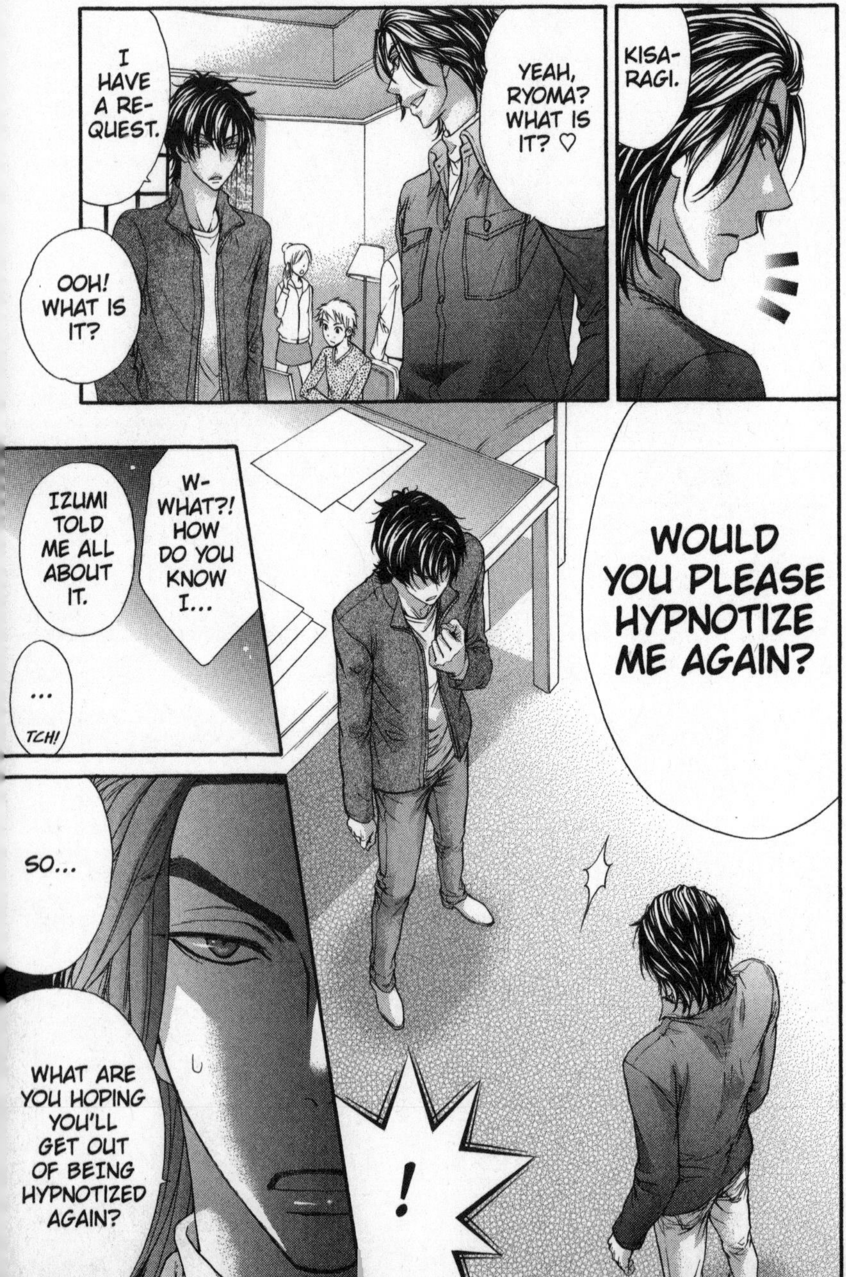
KISA-RAGI.
YEAH, RYOMA? WHAT IS IT? ♡
I HAVE A RE-QUEST.
OOH! WHAT IS IT?
WOULD YOU PLEASE HYPNOTIZE ME AGAIN?
!
W-WHAT?! HOW DO YOU KNOW I...
IZUMI TOLD ME ALL ABOUT IT.
...
TCH!
SO...
WHAT ARE YOU HOPING YOU'LL GET OUT OF BEING HYPNOTIZED AGAIN?

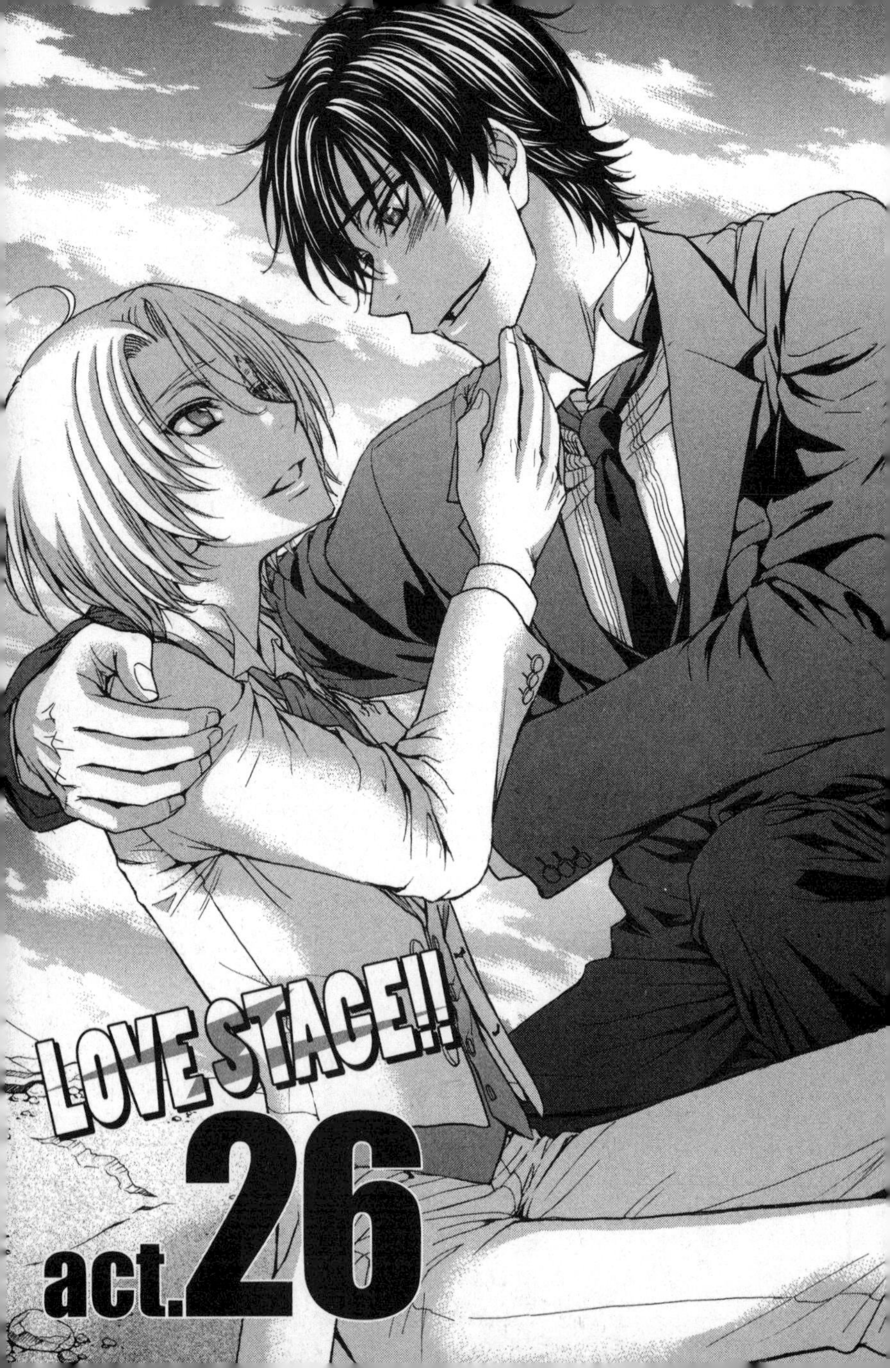
LOVE STAGE!!
act.26

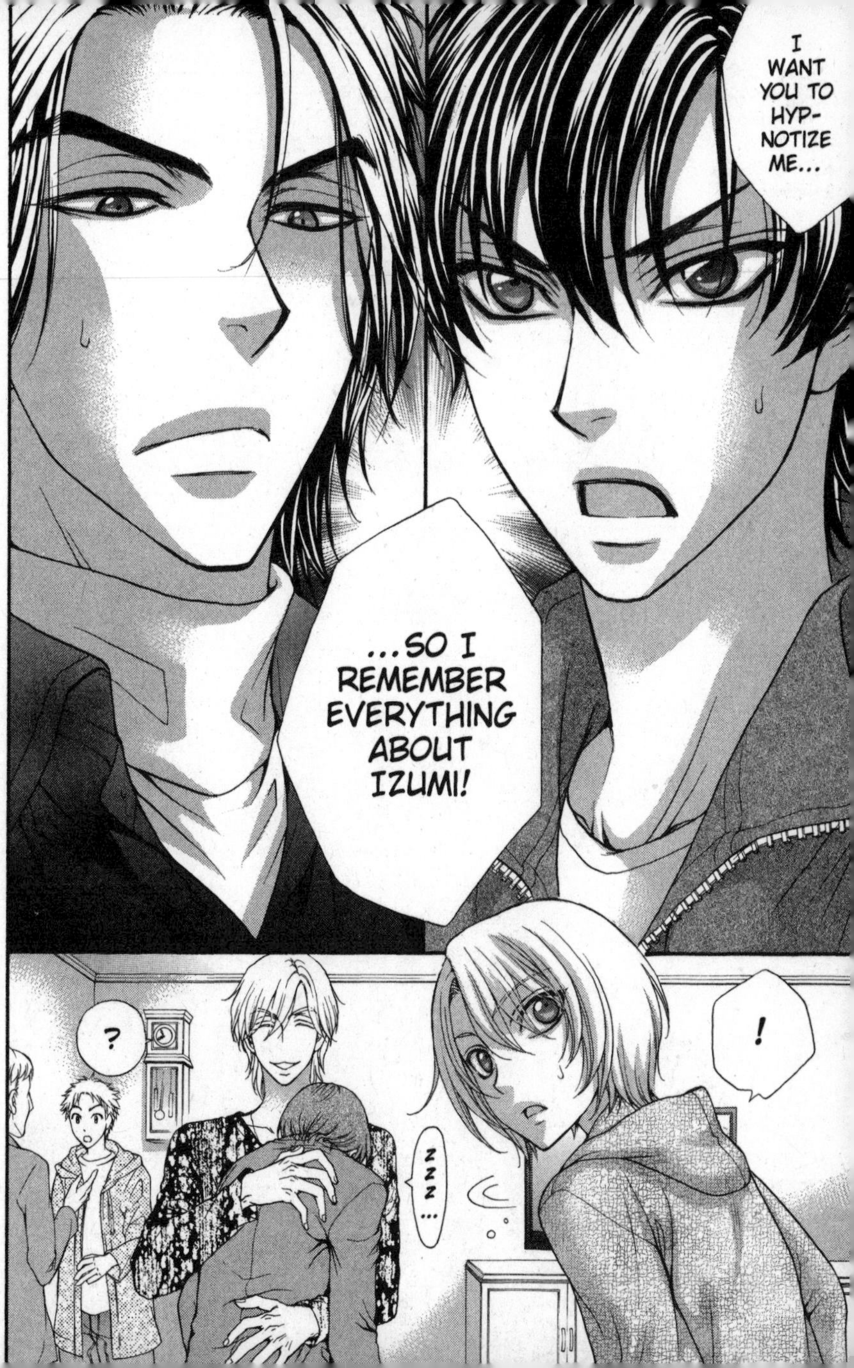
I WANT YOU TO HYP-NOTIZE ME...
...SO I REMEMBER EVERYTHING ABOUT IZUMI!
!
ZZZ...
?

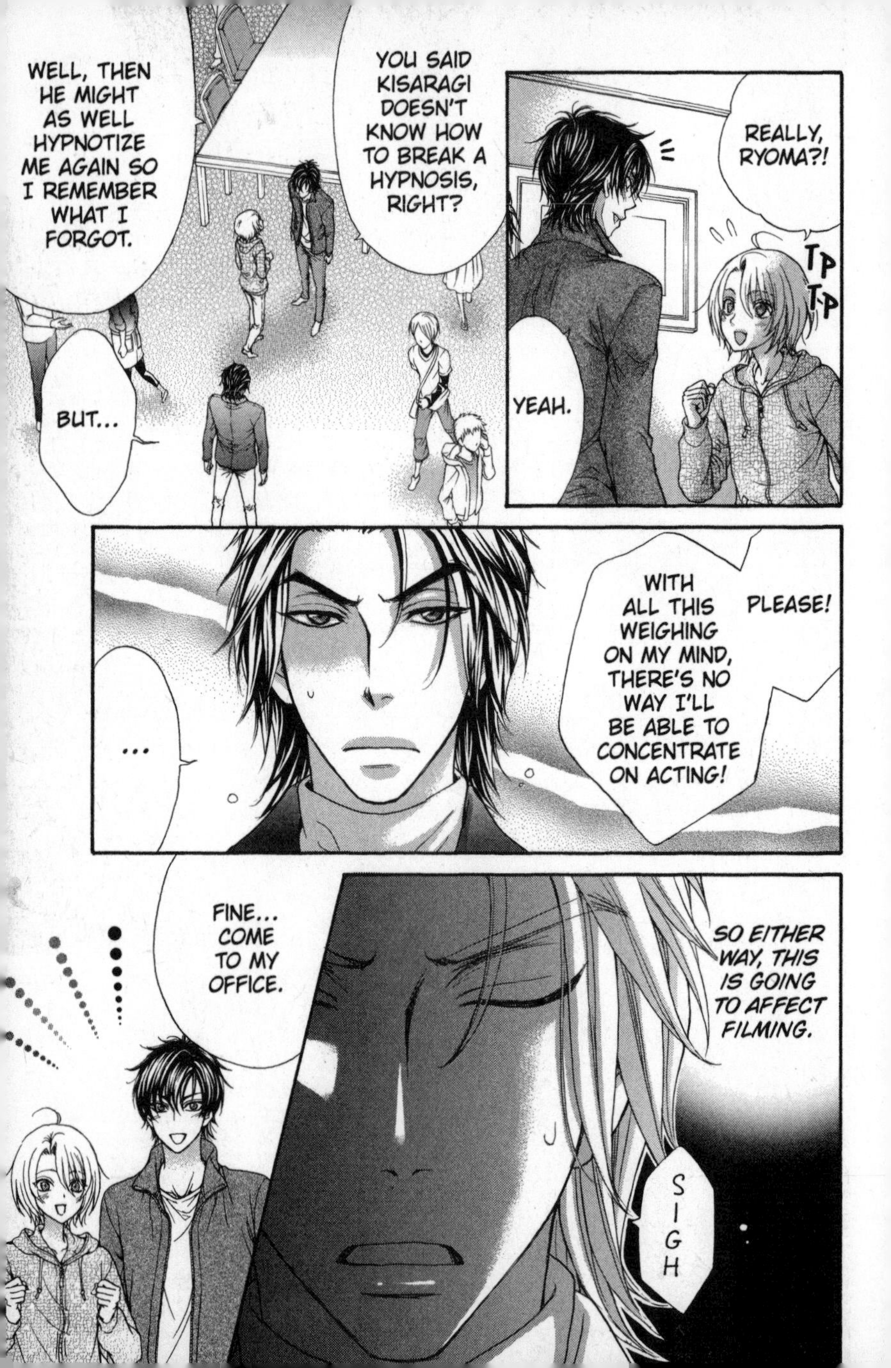
REALLY, RYOMA?!
TP TP
YEAH.
YOU SAID KISARAGI DOESN'T KNOW HOW TO BREAK A HYPNOSIS, RIGHT?
WELL, THEN HE MIGHT AS WELL HYPNOTIZE ME AGAIN SO I REMEMBER WHAT I FORGOT.
BUT...
PLEASE!
WITH ALL THIS WEIGHING ON MY MIND, THERE'S NO WAY I'LL BE ABLE TO CONCENTRATE ON ACTING!
...
SO EITHER WAY, THIS IS GOING TO AFFECT FILMING.
SIGH
FINE... COME TO MY OFFICE.

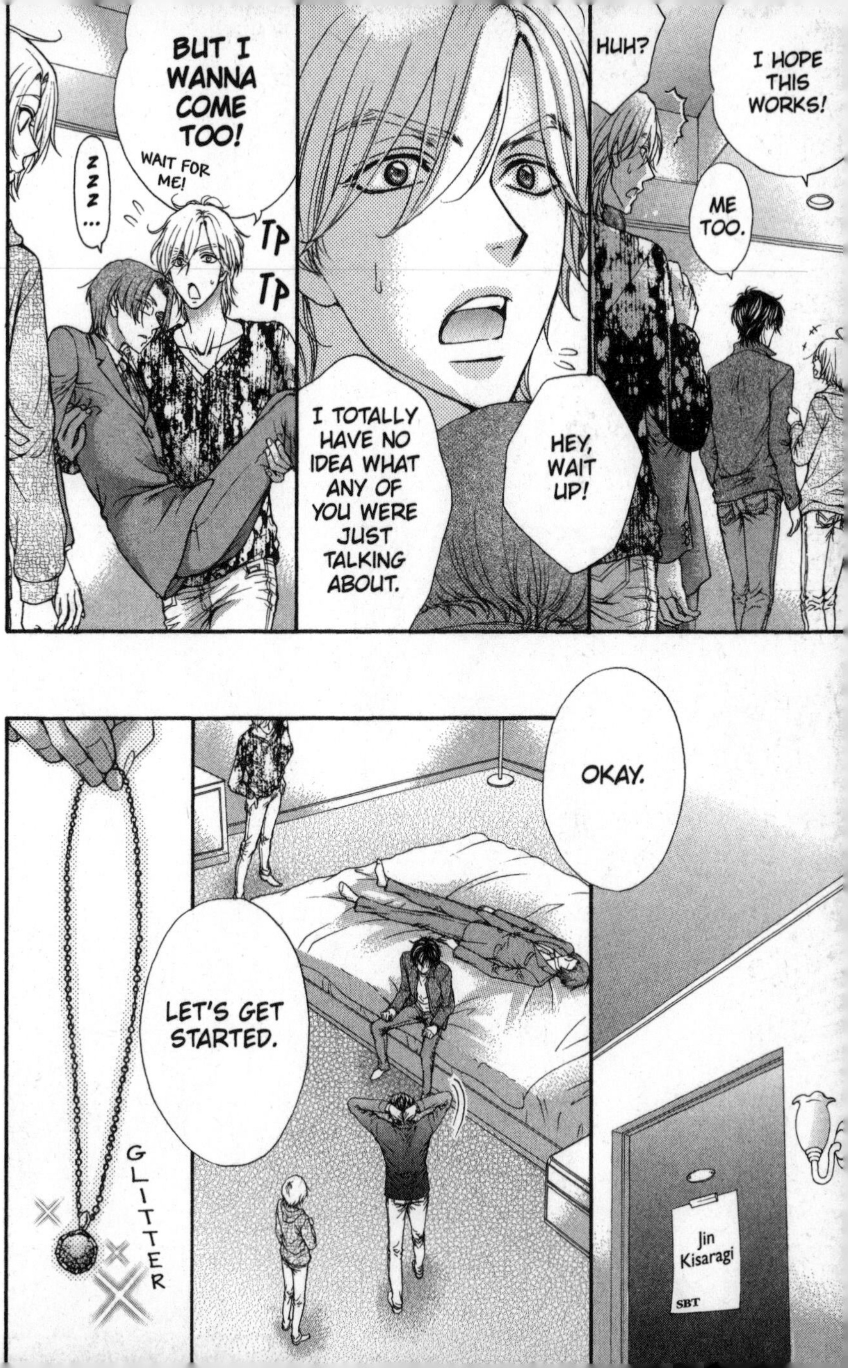
I HOPE THIS WORKS!
HUH?
ME TOO.
HEY, WAIT UP!
I TOTALLY HAVE NO IDEA WHAT ANY OF YOU WERE JUST TALKING ABOUT.
BUT I WANNA COME TOO!
WAIT FOR ME!
TP TP
ZZZ...
OKAY.
Jin Kisaragi
SBT
LET'S GET STARTED.
GLITTER

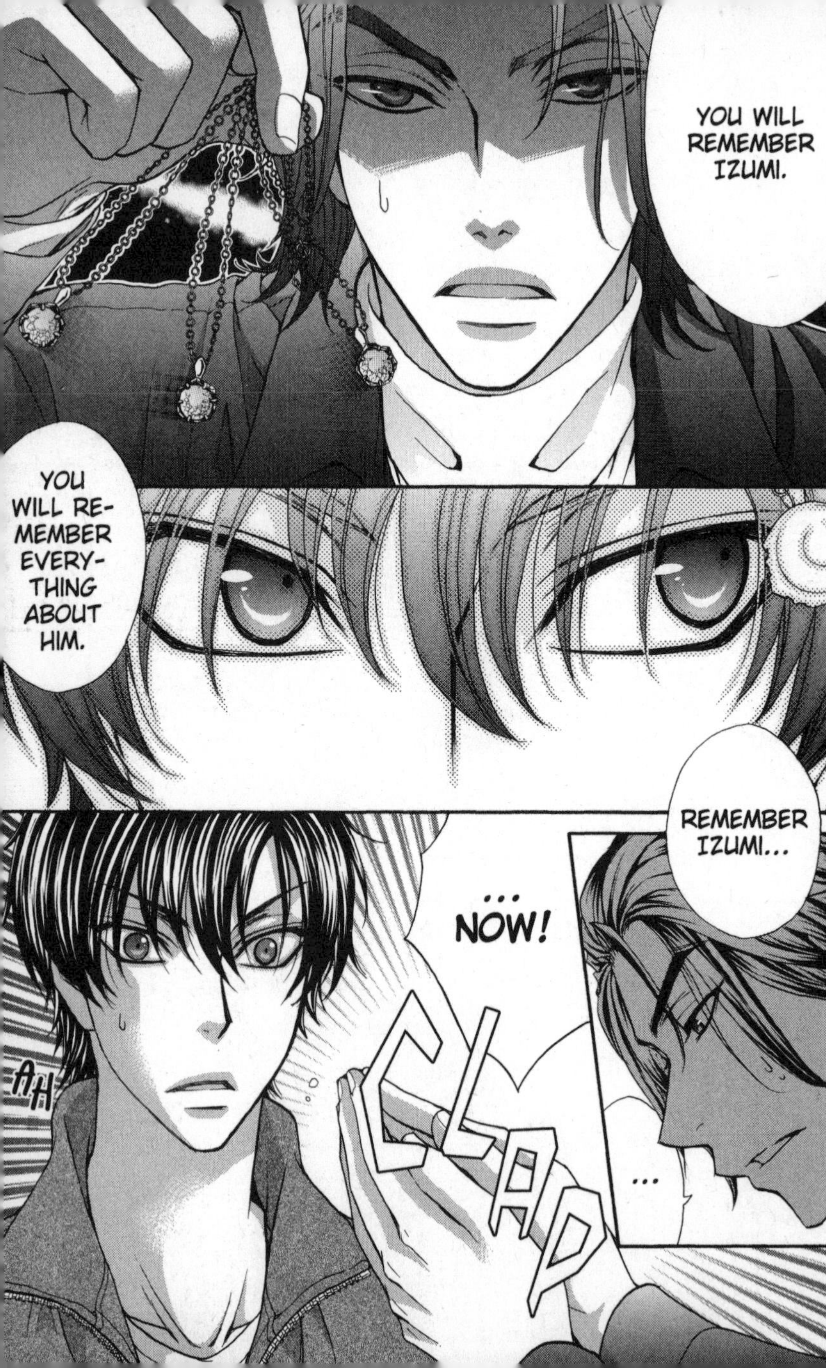
YOU WILL REMEMBER IZUMI.
YOU WILL RE-MEMBER EVERY-THING ABOUT HIM.
REMEMBER IZUMI...
...
... NOW!
CLAP
AH

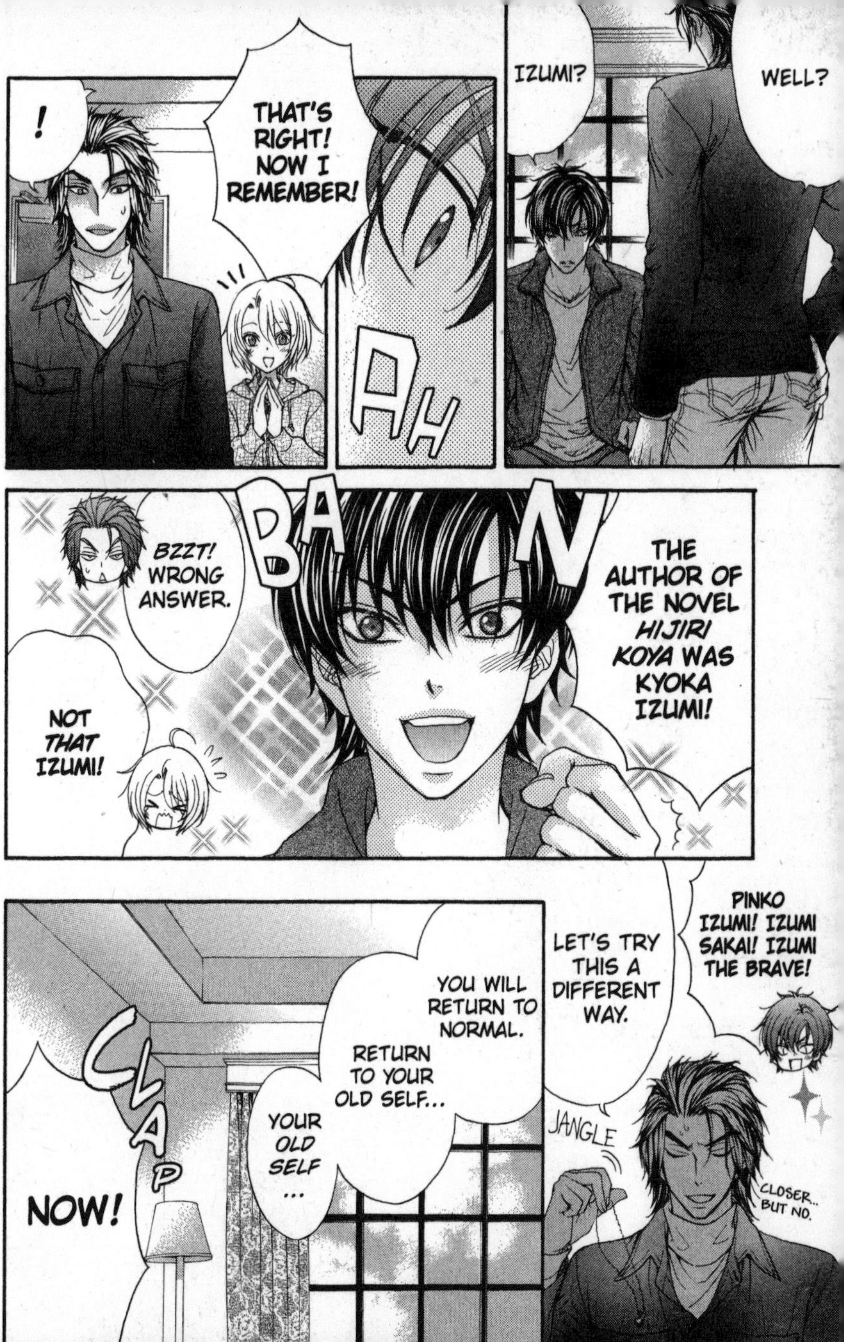
WELL?
IZUMI?
THAT'S RIGHT! NOW I REMEMBER!
AH
!
BAN
THE AUTHOR OF THE NOVEL HIJIRI KOYA WAS KYOKA IZUMI!
BZZT! WRONG ANSWER.
NOT THAT IZUMI!
PINKO IZUMI! IZUMI SAKAI! IZUMI THE BRAVE!
CLOSER... BUT NO.
LET'S TRY THIS A DIFFERENT WAY.
JANGLE
YOU WILL RETURN TO NORMAL.
RETURN TO YOUR OLD SELF...
YOUR OLD SELF...
CLAP
NOW!

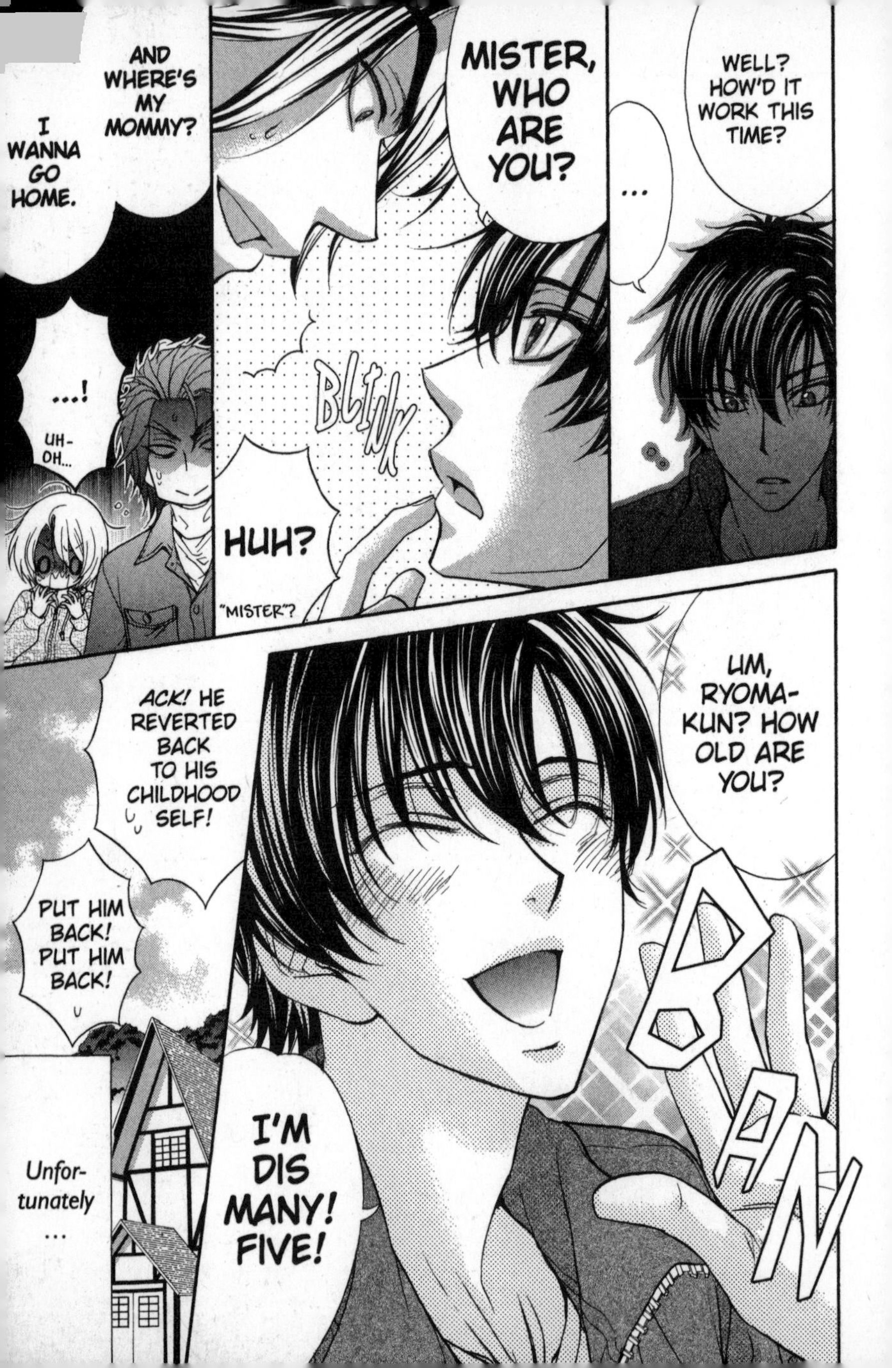
WELL? HOW'D IT WORK THIS TIME?
...
MISTER, WHO ARE YOU?
BLINK
HUH?
"MISTER"?
AND WHERE'S MY MOMMY?
I WANNA GO HOME.
...!
UH-OH...
UM, RYOMA-KUN? HOW OLD ARE YOU?
BAN
I'M DIS MANY! FIVE!
ACK! HE REVERTED BACK TO HIS CHILDHOOD SELF!
PUT HIM BACK! PUT HIM BACK!
Unfortunately ...

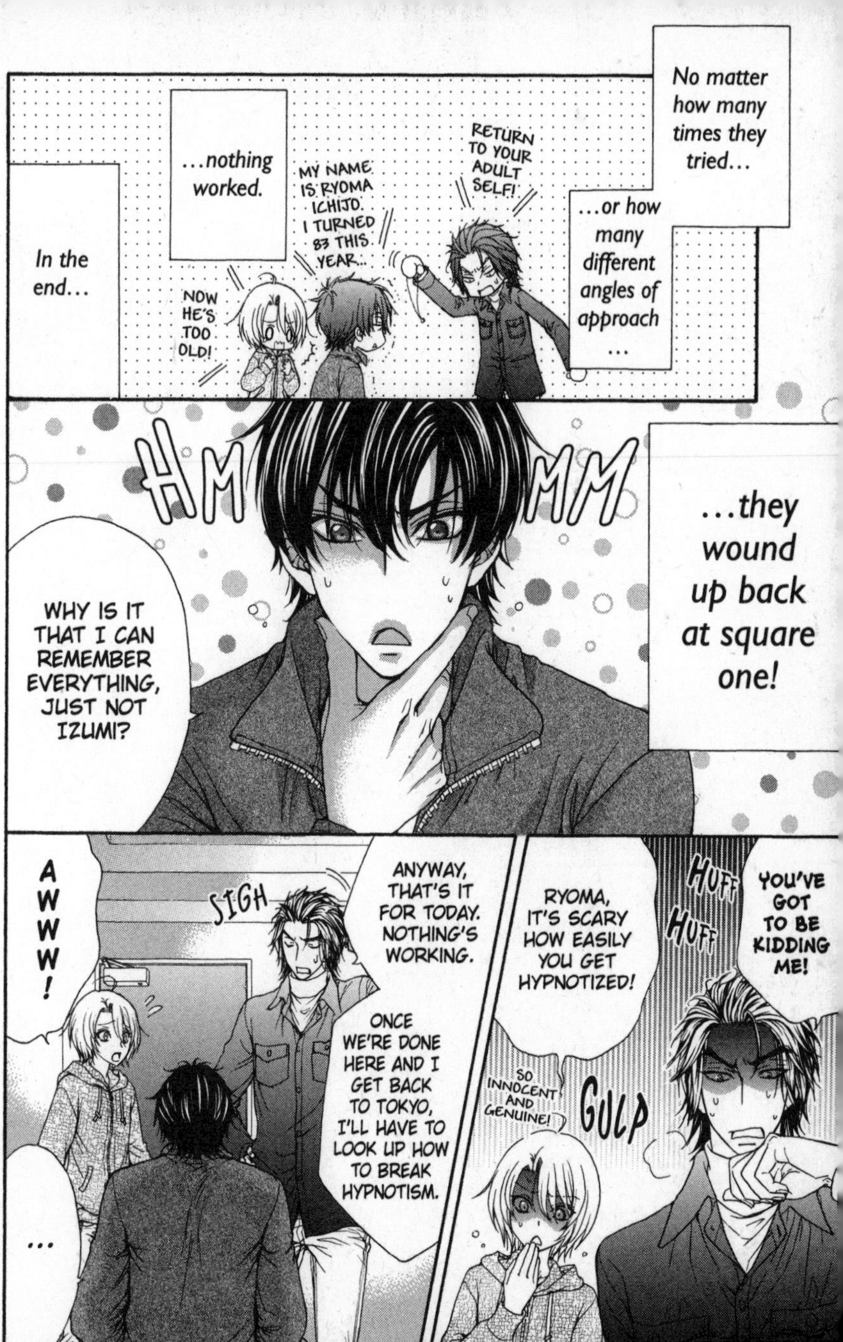
No matter how many times they tried…
…or how many different angles of approach …
RETURN TO YOUR ADULT SELF!
MY NAME IS RYOMA ICHIJO. I TURNED 83 THIS YEAR…
…nothing worked.
NOW HE'S TOO OLD!
In the end…
…they wound up back at square one!
HMMMM
WHY IS IT THAT I CAN REMEMBER EVERYTHING, JUST NOT IZUMI?
YOU'VE GOT TO BE KIDDING ME!
HUFF HUFF
RYOMA, IT'S SCARY HOW EASILY YOU GET HYPNOTIZED!
SO INNOCENT AND GENUINE!
GULP
ANYWAY, THAT'S IT FOR TODAY. NOTHING'S WORKING.
SIGH
ONCE WE'RE DONE HERE AND I GET BACK TO TOKYO, I'LL HAVE TO LOOK UP HOW TO BREAK HYPNOTISM.
AWWWW!
…

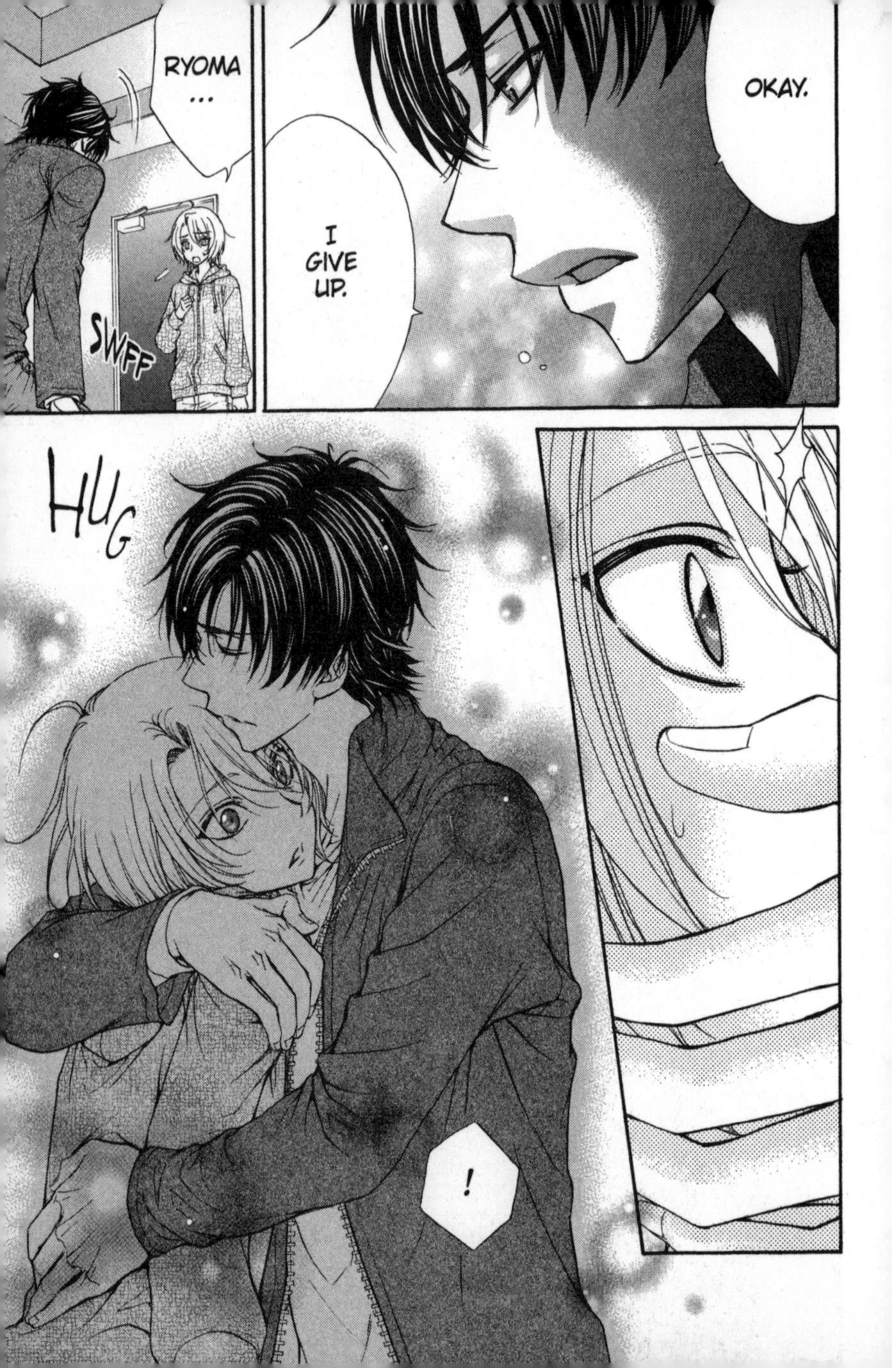
OKAY.
I GIVE UP.
RYOMA...
SWFF
HUG
!

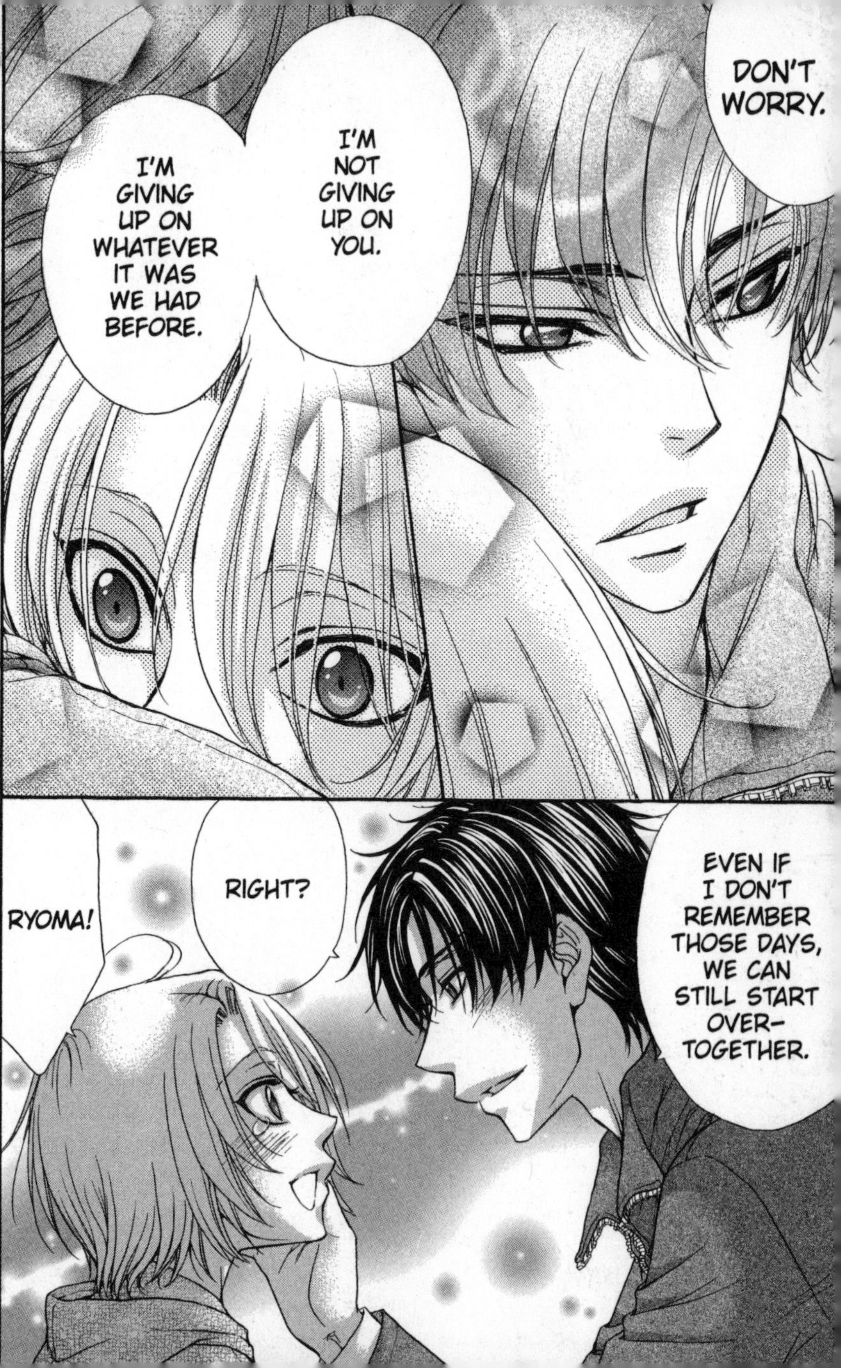
DON'T WORRY.
I'M NOT GIVING UP ON YOU.
I'M GIVING UP ON WHATEVER IT WAS WE HAD BEFORE.
EVEN IF I DON'T REMEMBER THOSE DAYS, WE CAN STILL START OVER—TOGETHER.
RIGHT?
RYOMA!

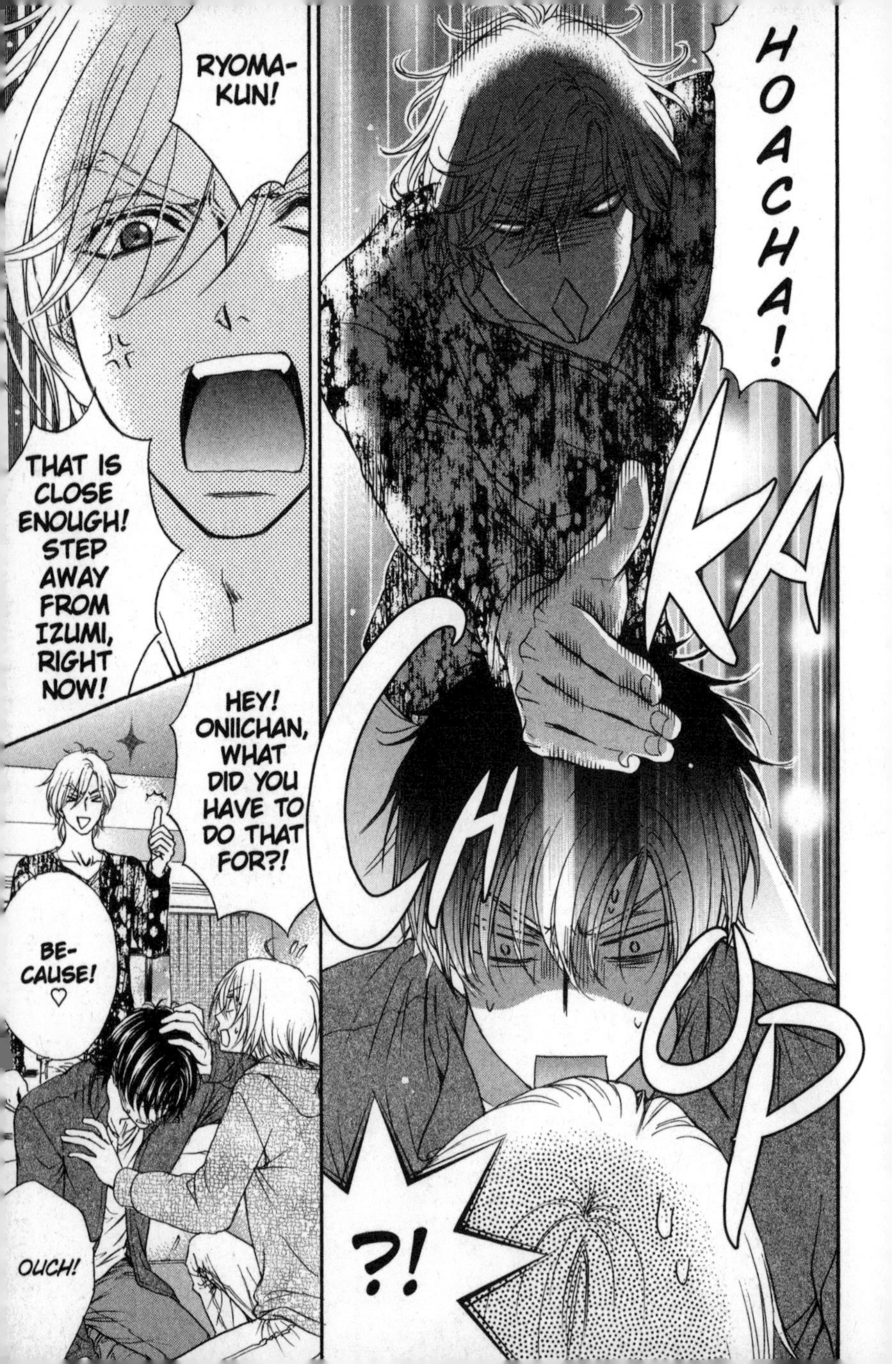
HOACHA!
KA CHOP
?!
RYOMA-KUN!
THAT IS CLOSE ENOUGH! STEP AWAY FROM IZUMI, RIGHT NOW!
HEY! ONIICHAN, WHAT DID YOU HAVE TO DO THAT FOR?!
BE-CAUSE! ♡
OUCH!

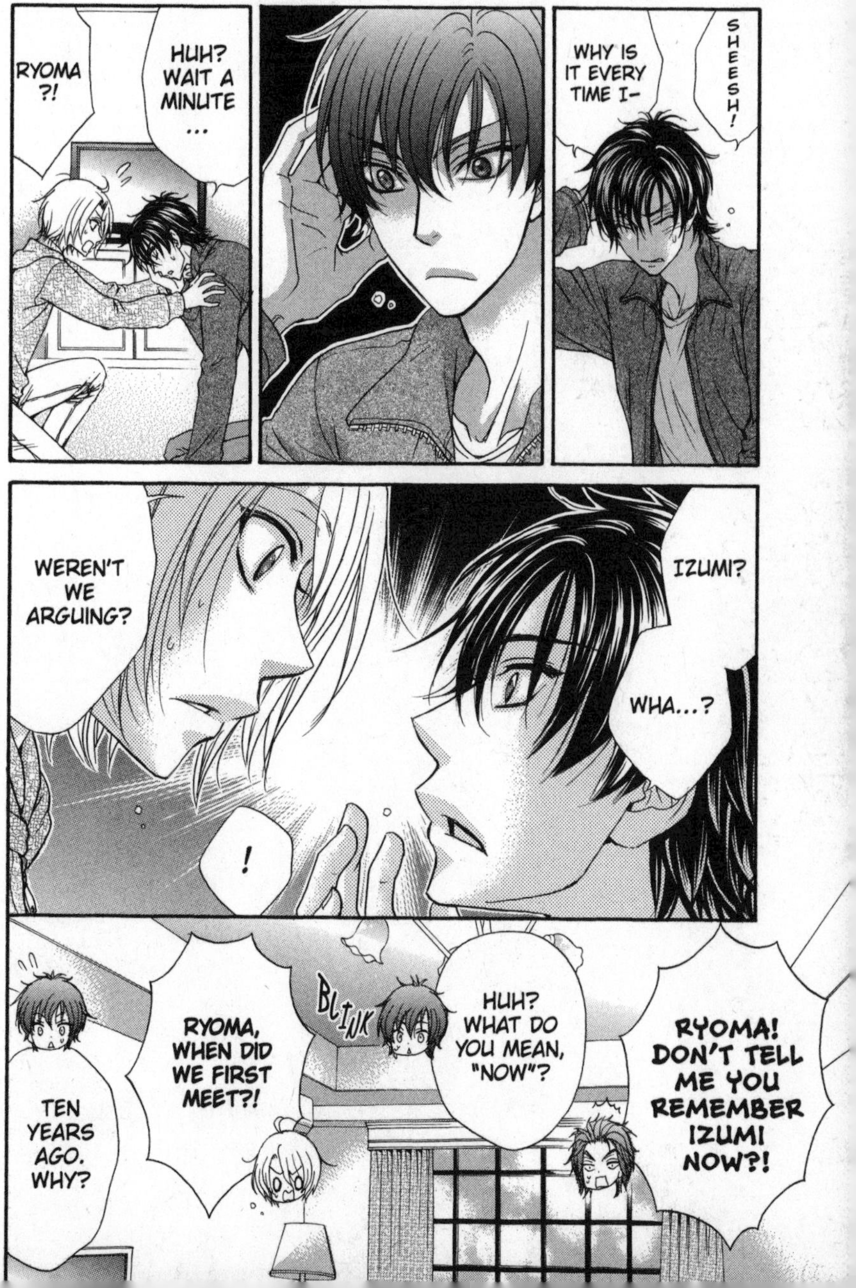
SHEESH!
WHY IS IT EVERY TIME I-
HUH? WAIT A MINUTE ...
RYOMA ?!
IZUMI?
WHA...?
WEREN'T WE ARGUING?
!
RYOMA! DON'T TELL ME YOU REMEMBER IZUMI NOW?!
HUH? WHAT DO YOU MEAN, "NOW"?
BLINK
RYOMA, WHEN DID WE FIRST MEET?!
TEN YEARS AGO. WHY?

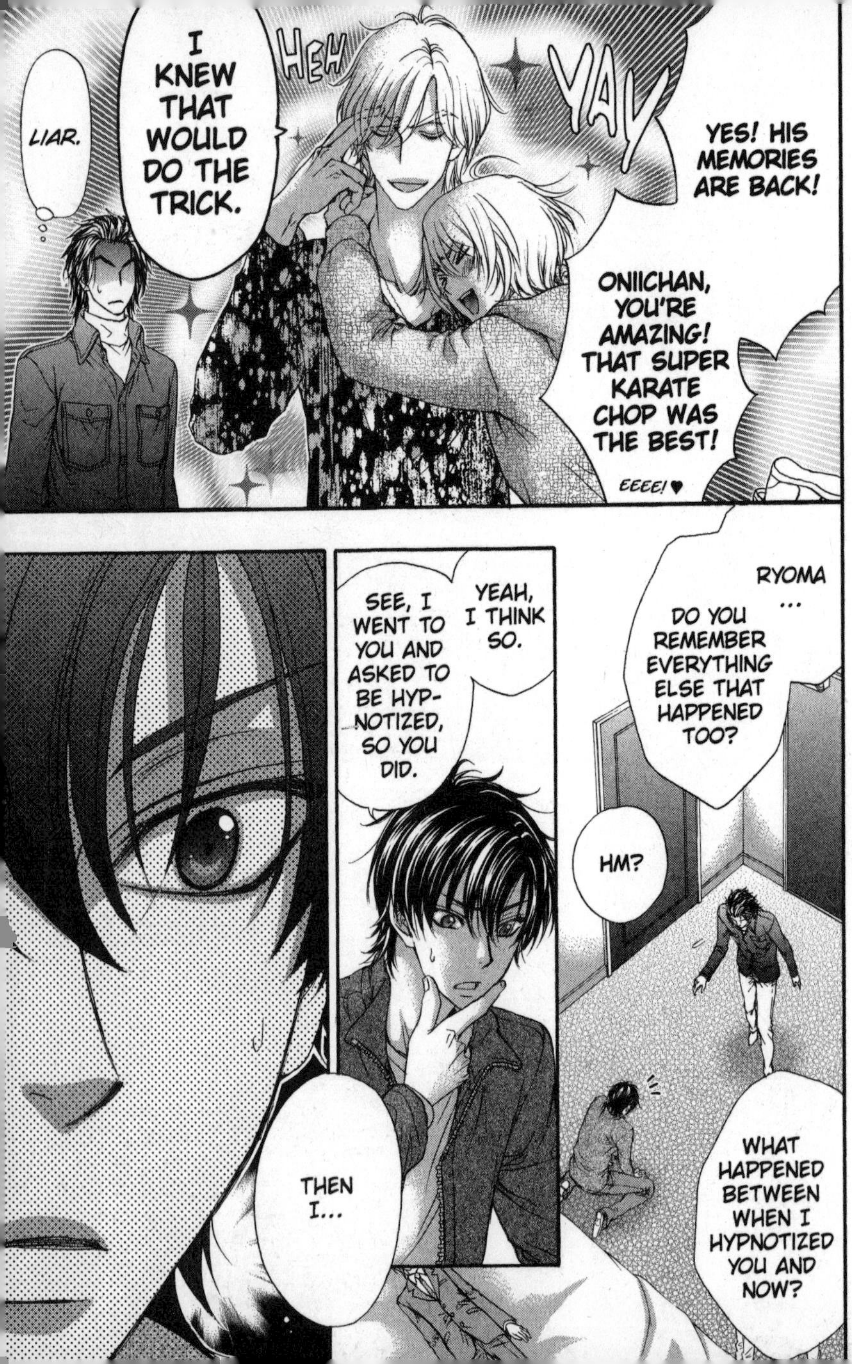
YAY
YES! HIS MEMORIES ARE BACK!
ONIICHAN, YOU'RE AMAZING! THAT SUPER KARATE CHOP WAS THE BEST!
EEEE! ♥
HEH
I KNEW THAT WOULD DO THE TRICK.
LIAR.
RYOMA ...
DO YOU REMEMBER EVERYTHING ELSE THAT HAPPENED TOO?
HM?
WHAT HAPPENED BETWEEN WHEN I HYPNOTIZED YOU AND NOW?
YEAH, I THINK SO.
SEE, I WENT TO YOU AND ASKED TO BE HYP-NOTIZED, SO YOU DID.
THEN I...

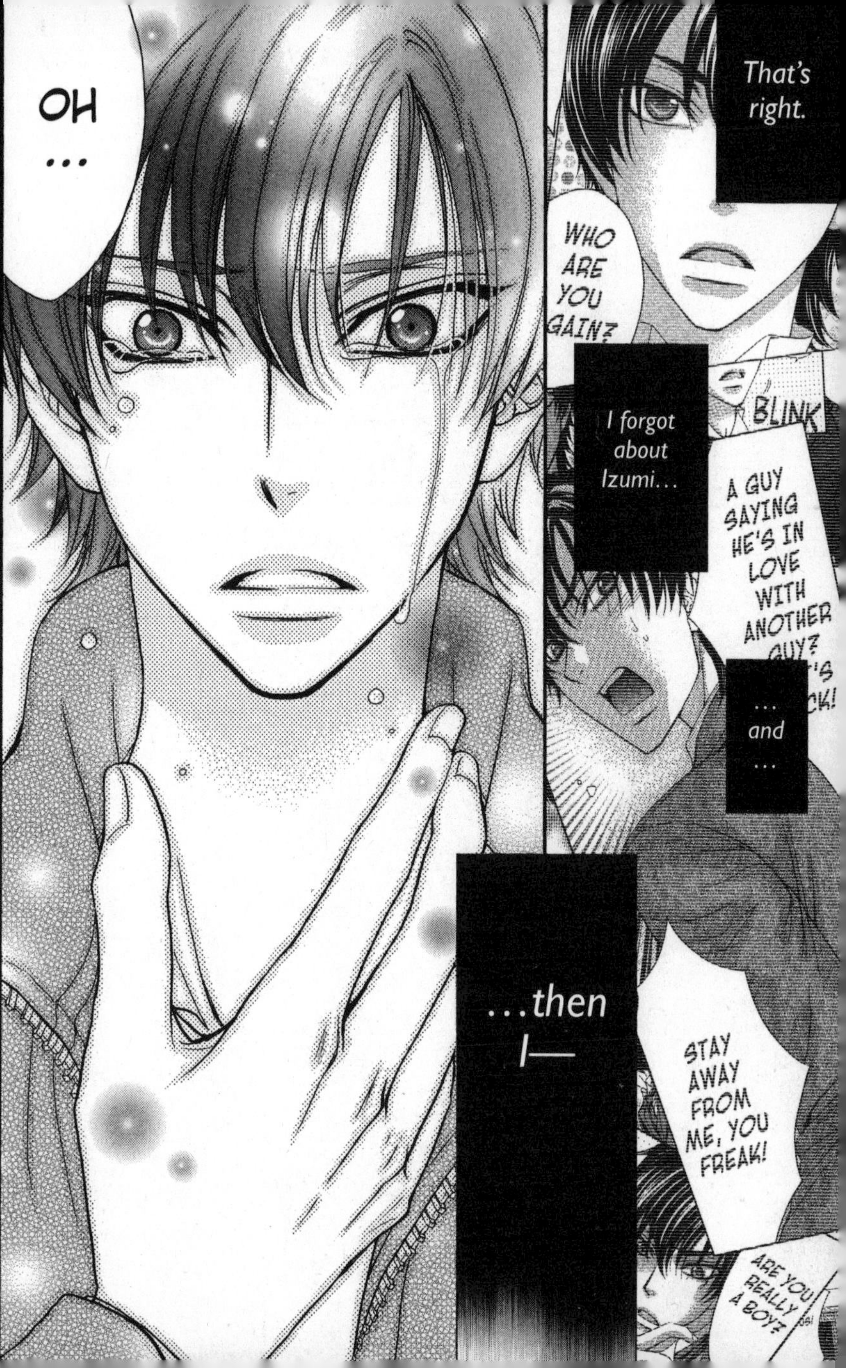

That's right.
WHO ARE YOU GAIN?
I forgot about Izumi...
BLINK
A GUY SAYING HE'S IN LOVE WITH ANOTHER GUY?
... and ...
STAY AWAY FROM ME, YOU FREAK!
ARE YOU REALLY A BOY?
...then I—
OH ...

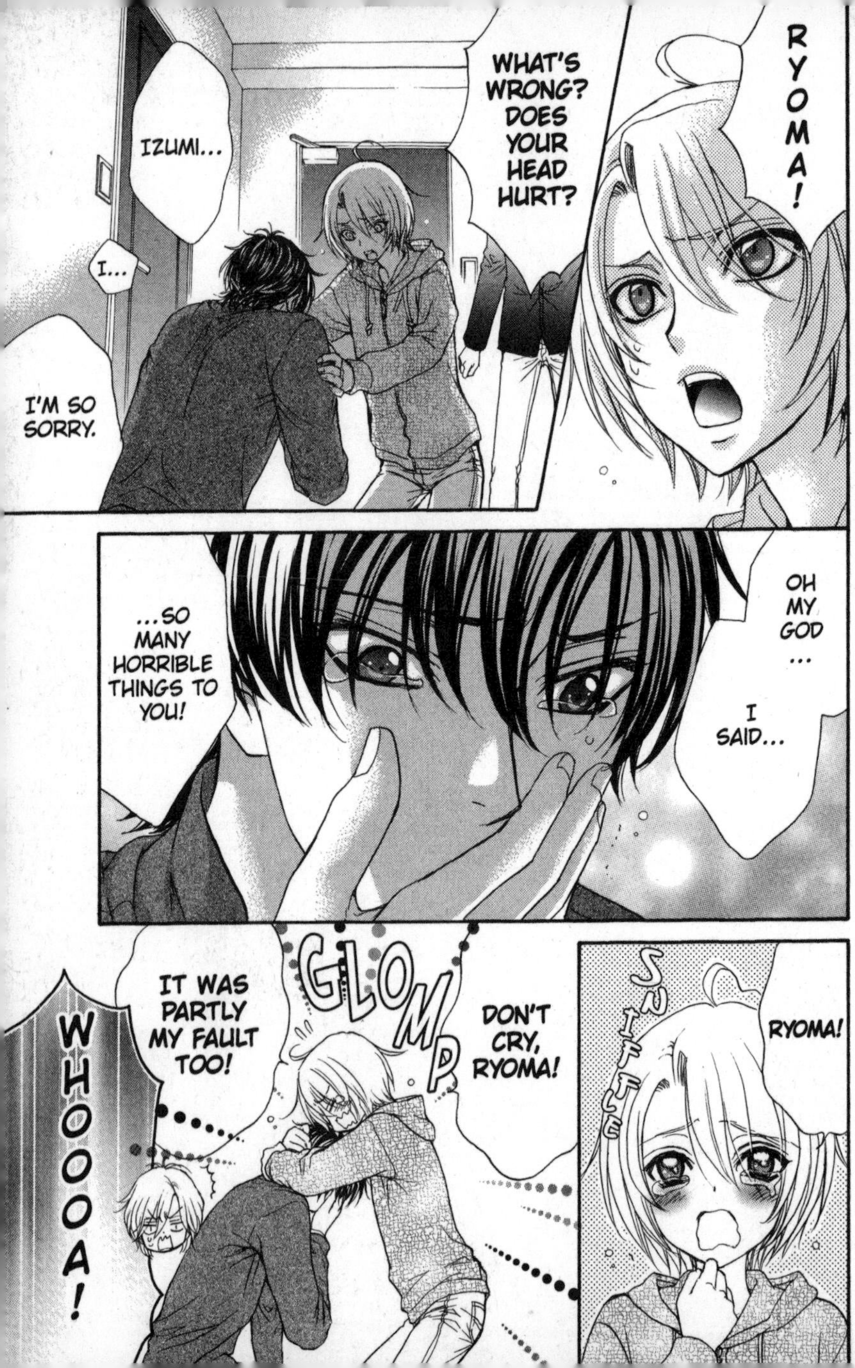
RYOMA!
WHAT'S WRONG? DOES YOUR HEAD HURT?
IZUMI...
I...
I'M SO SORRY.
OH MY GOD... I SAID...
...SO MANY HORRIBLE THINGS TO YOU!
SNIFFLE
RYOMA!
DON'T CRY, RYOMA!
GLOMP
IT WAS PARTLY MY FAULT TOO!
WHOOOOA!

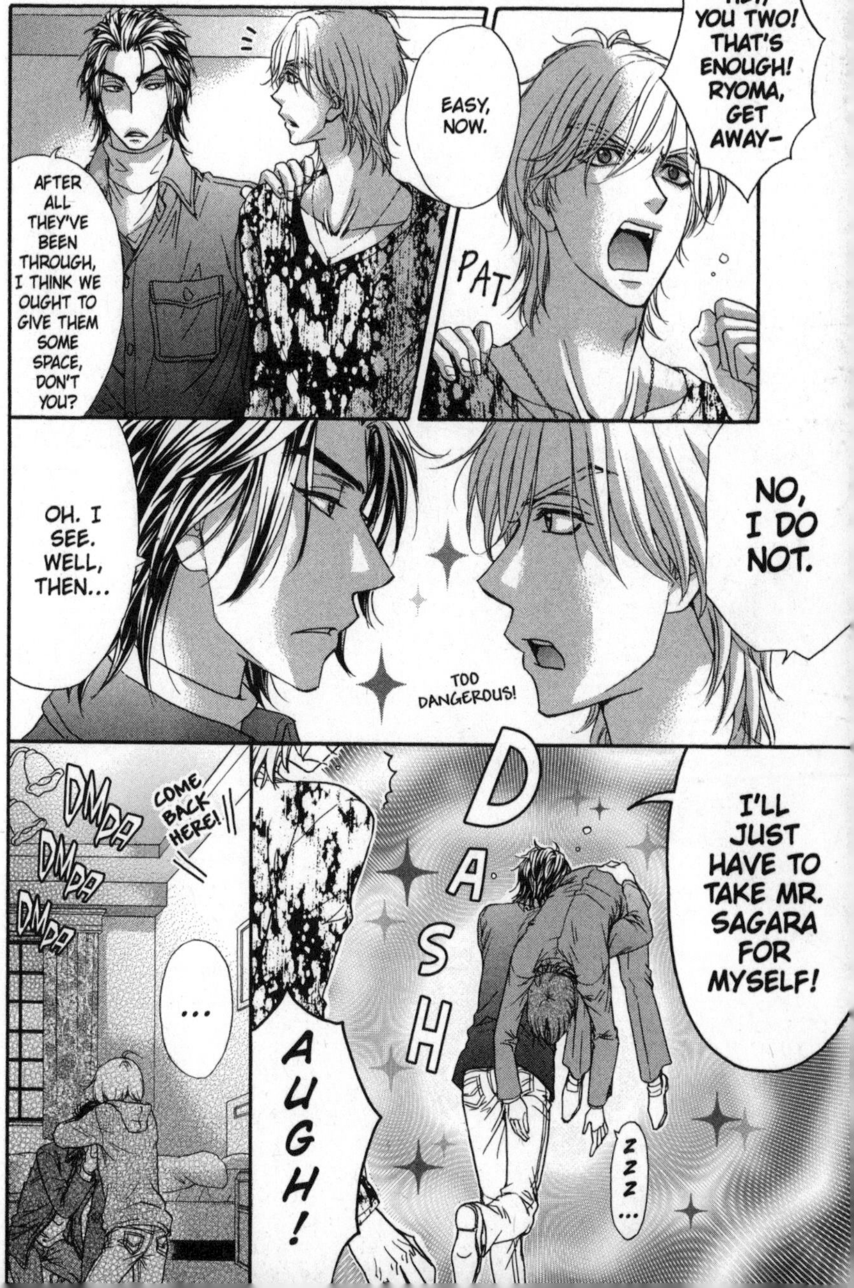
HEY, YOU TWO! THAT'S ENOUGH! RYOMA, GET AWAY–
PAT
EASY, NOW.
AFTER ALL THEY'VE BEEN THROUGH, I THINK WE OUGHT TO GIVE THEM SOME SPACE, DON'T YOU?
NO, I DO NOT.
TOO DANGEROUS!
OH. I SEE. WELL, THEN...
I'LL JUST HAVE TO TAKE MR. SAGARA FOR MYSELF!
DASH
ZZZ...
AUGH!
COME BACK HERE!
DMDA
DMDA
DMDA
...

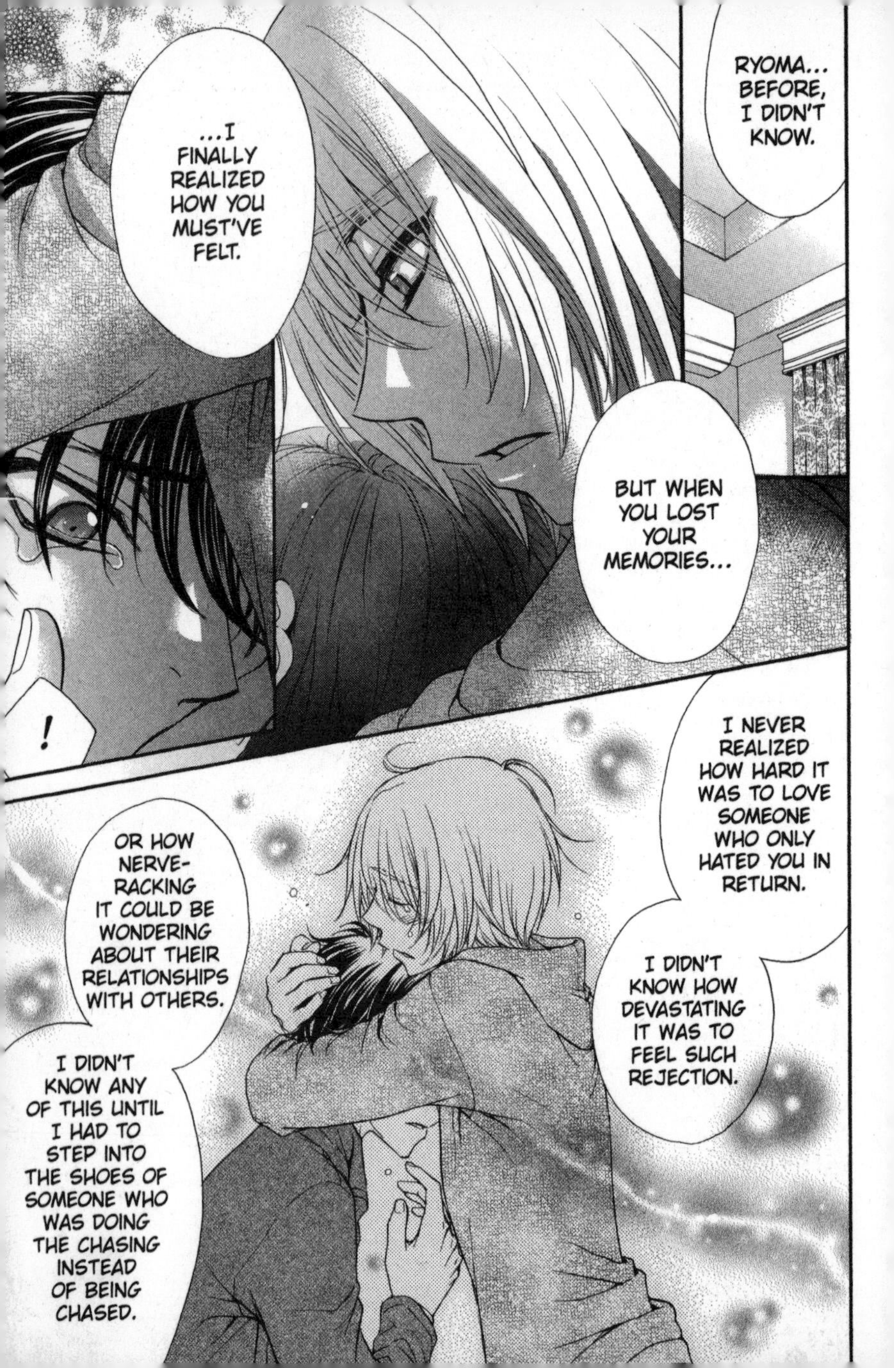
RYOMA... BEFORE, I DIDN'T KNOW.
BUT WHEN YOU LOST YOUR MEMORIES...
...I FINALLY REALIZED HOW YOU MUST'VE FELT.
!
I NEVER REALIZED HOW HARD IT WAS TO LOVE SOMEONE WHO ONLY HATED YOU IN RETURN.
I DIDN'T KNOW HOW DEVASTATING IT WAS TO FEEL SUCH REJECTION.
OR HOW NERVE-RACKING IT COULD BE WONDERING ABOUT THEIR RELATIONSHIPS WITH OTHERS.
I DIDN'T KNOW ANY OF THIS UNTIL I HAD TO STEP INTO THE SHOES OF SOMEONE WHO WAS DOING THE CHASING INSTEAD OF BEING CHASED.

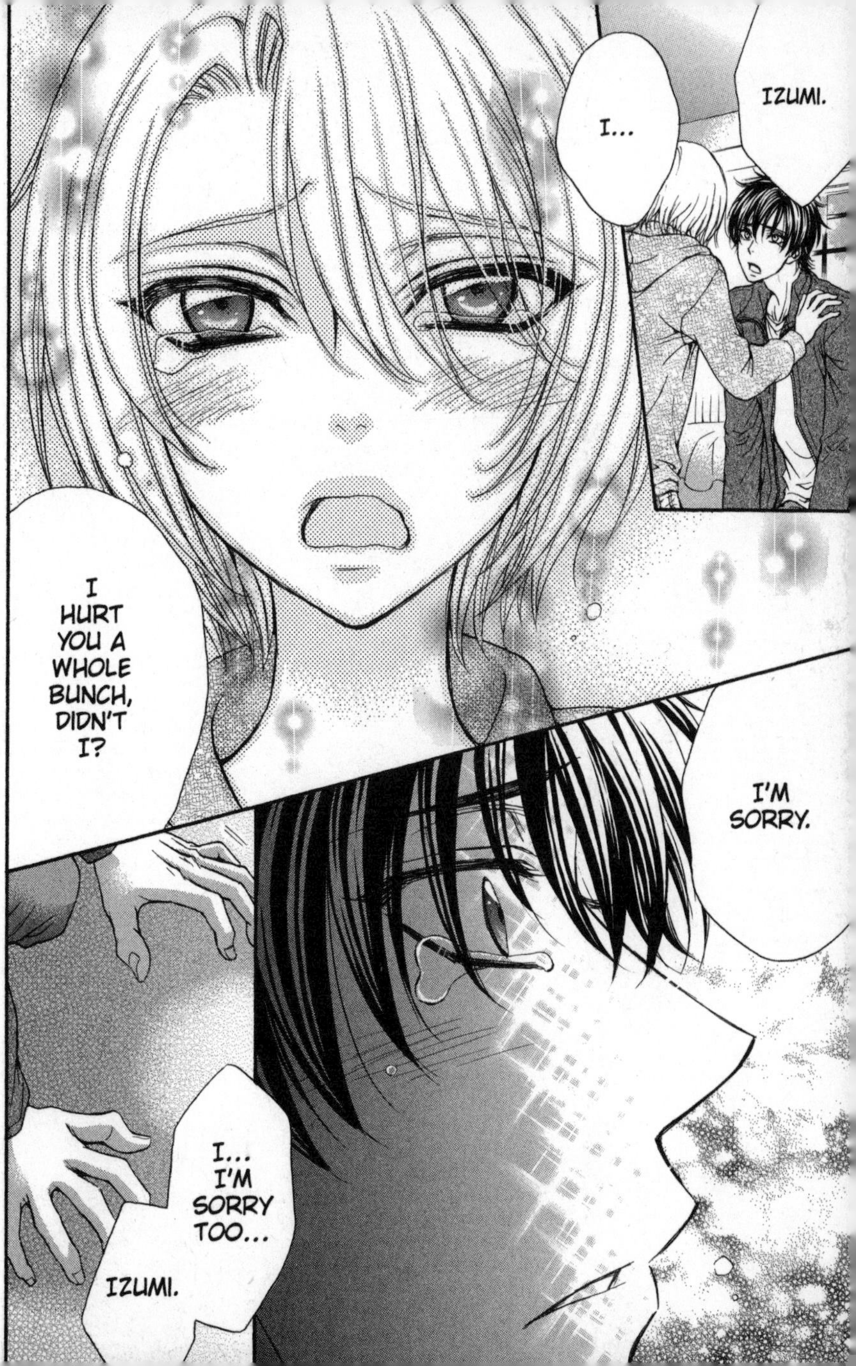
IZUMI.
I...
I HURT YOU A WHOLE BUNCH, DIDN'T I?
I'M SORRY.
I... I'M SORRY TOO...
IZUMI.

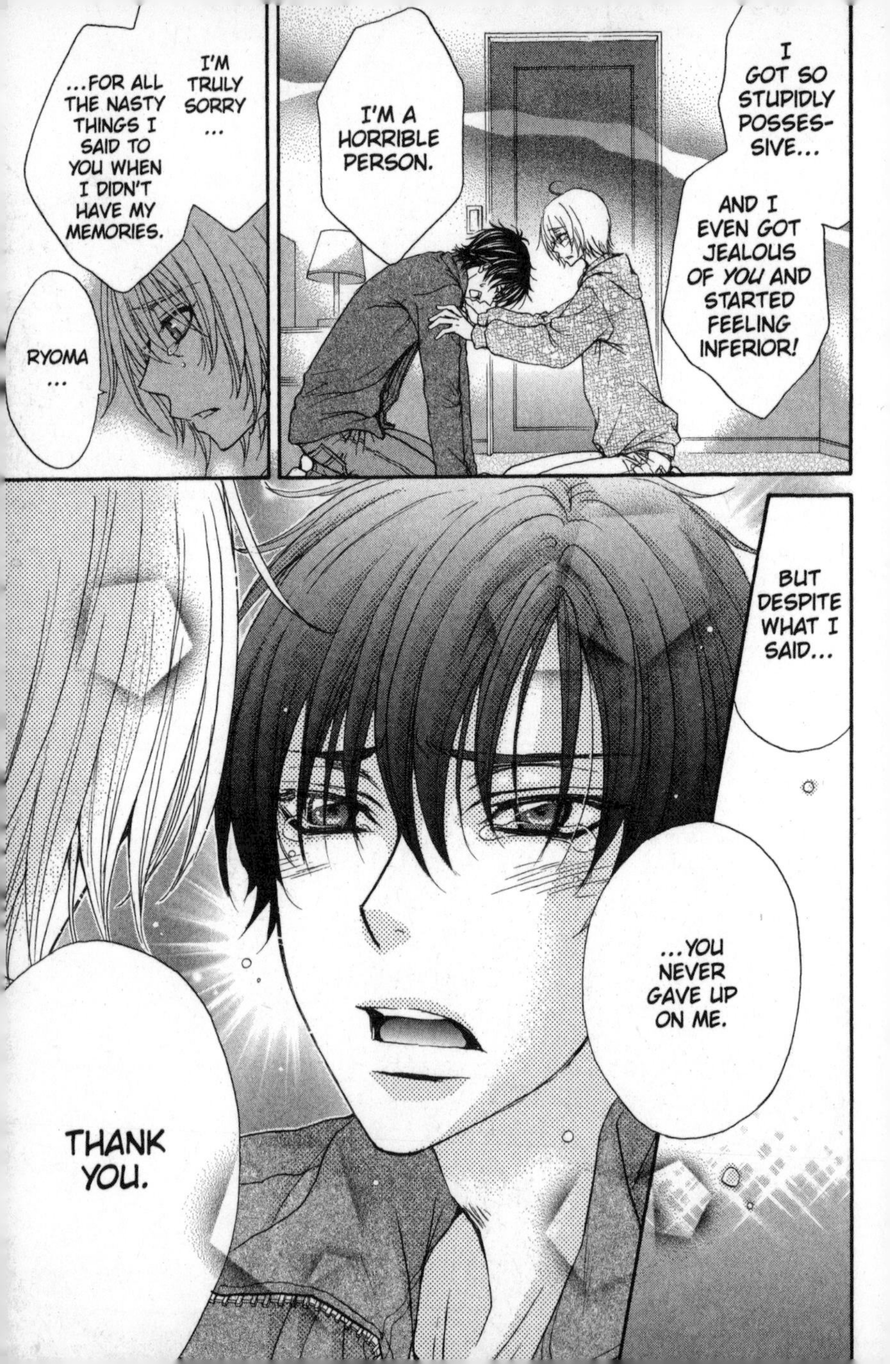
I GOT SO STUPIDLY POSSES-SIVE...
AND I EVEN GOT JEALOUS OF *YOU* AND STARTED FEELING INFERIOR!
I'M A HORRIBLE PERSON.
I'M TRULY SORRY...
...FOR ALL THE NASTY THINGS I SAID TO YOU WHEN I DIDN'T HAVE MY MEMORIES.
RYOMA...
BUT DESPITE WHAT I SAID...
...YOU NEVER GAVE UP ON ME.
THANK YOU.

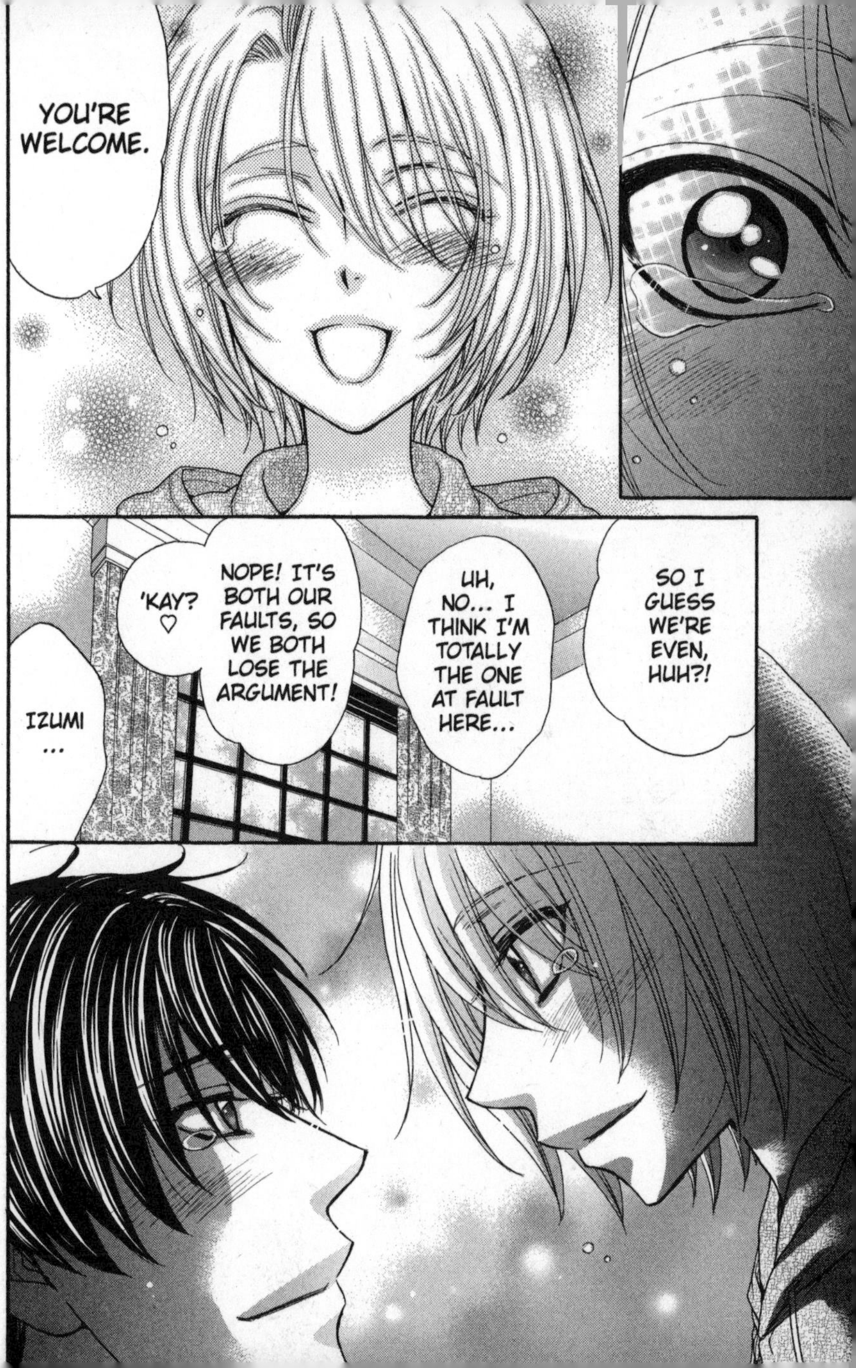
YOU'RE WELCOME.
SO I GUESS WE'RE EVEN, HUH?!
UH, NO... I THINK I'M TOTALLY THE ONE AT FAULT HERE...
NOPE! IT'S BOTH OUR FAULTS, SO WE BOTH LOSE THE ARGUMENT!
'KAY? ♡
IZUMI ...

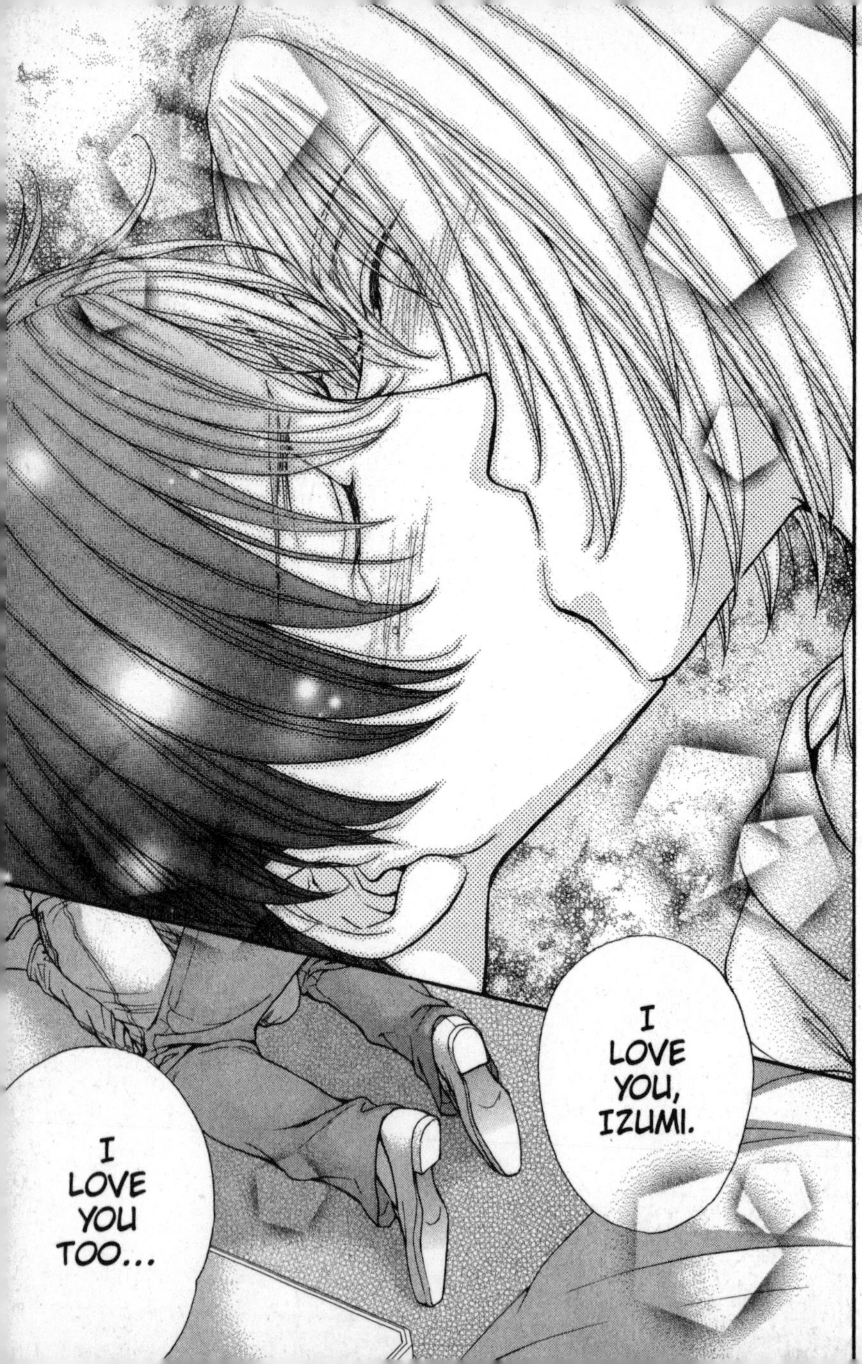
I LOVE YOU, IZUMI.
I LOVE YOU TOO...

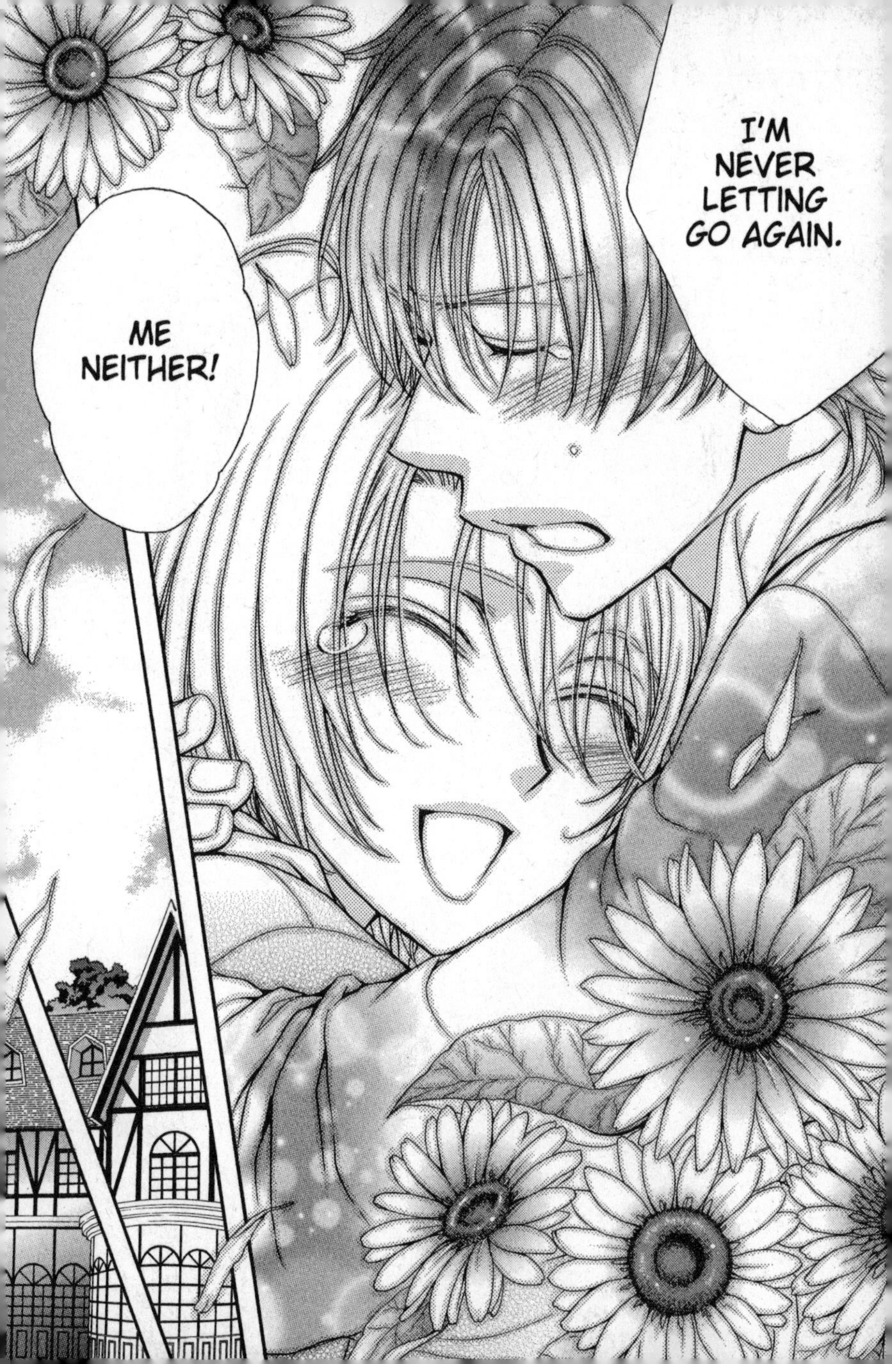
I'M NEVER LETTING GO AGAIN.
ME NEITHER!

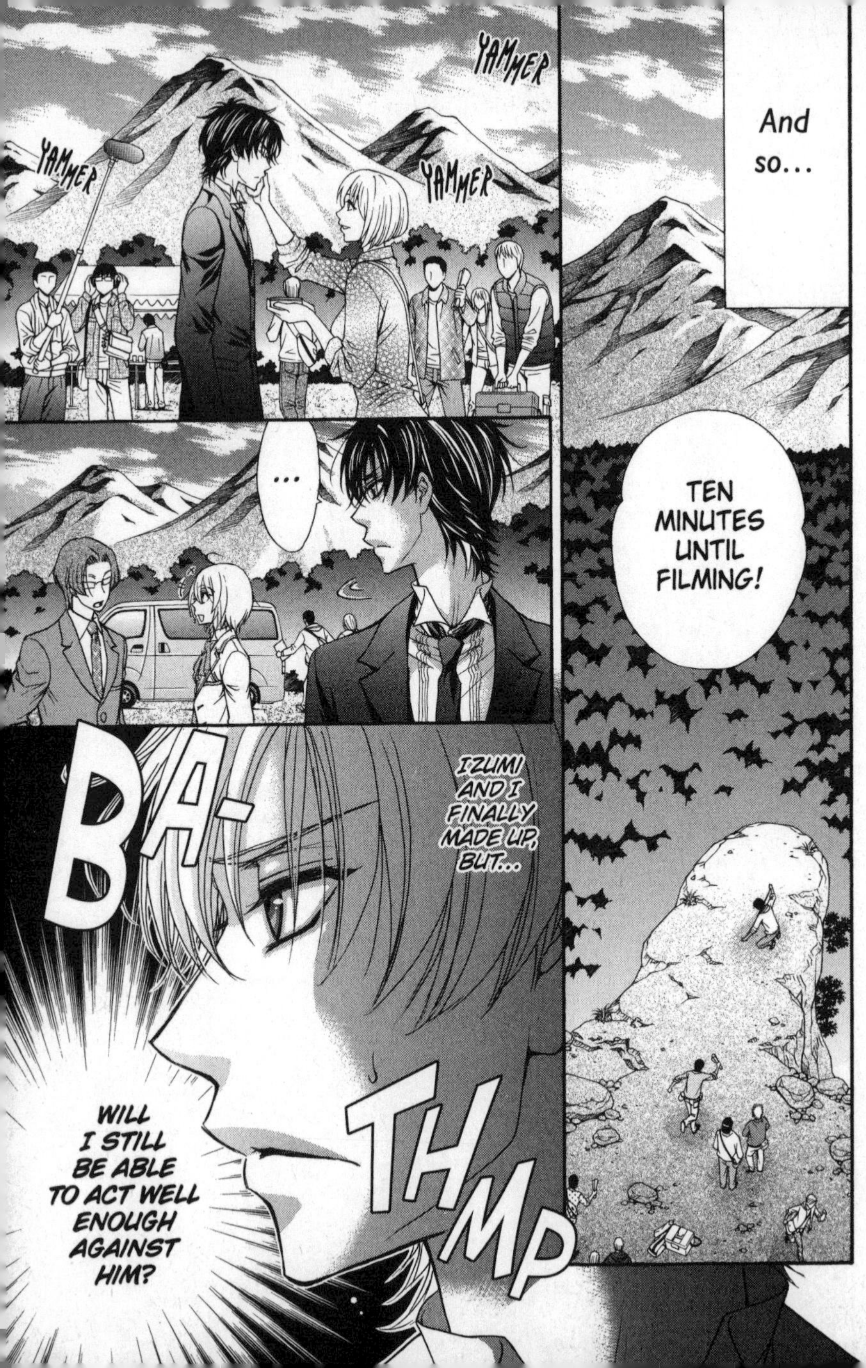

And so…
TEN MINUTES UNTIL FILMING!
YAMMER
YAMMER
YAMMER
…
IZUMI AND I FINALLY MADE UP, BUT…
BA-
THMP
WILL I STILL BE ABLE TO ACT WELL ENOUGH AGAINST HIM?

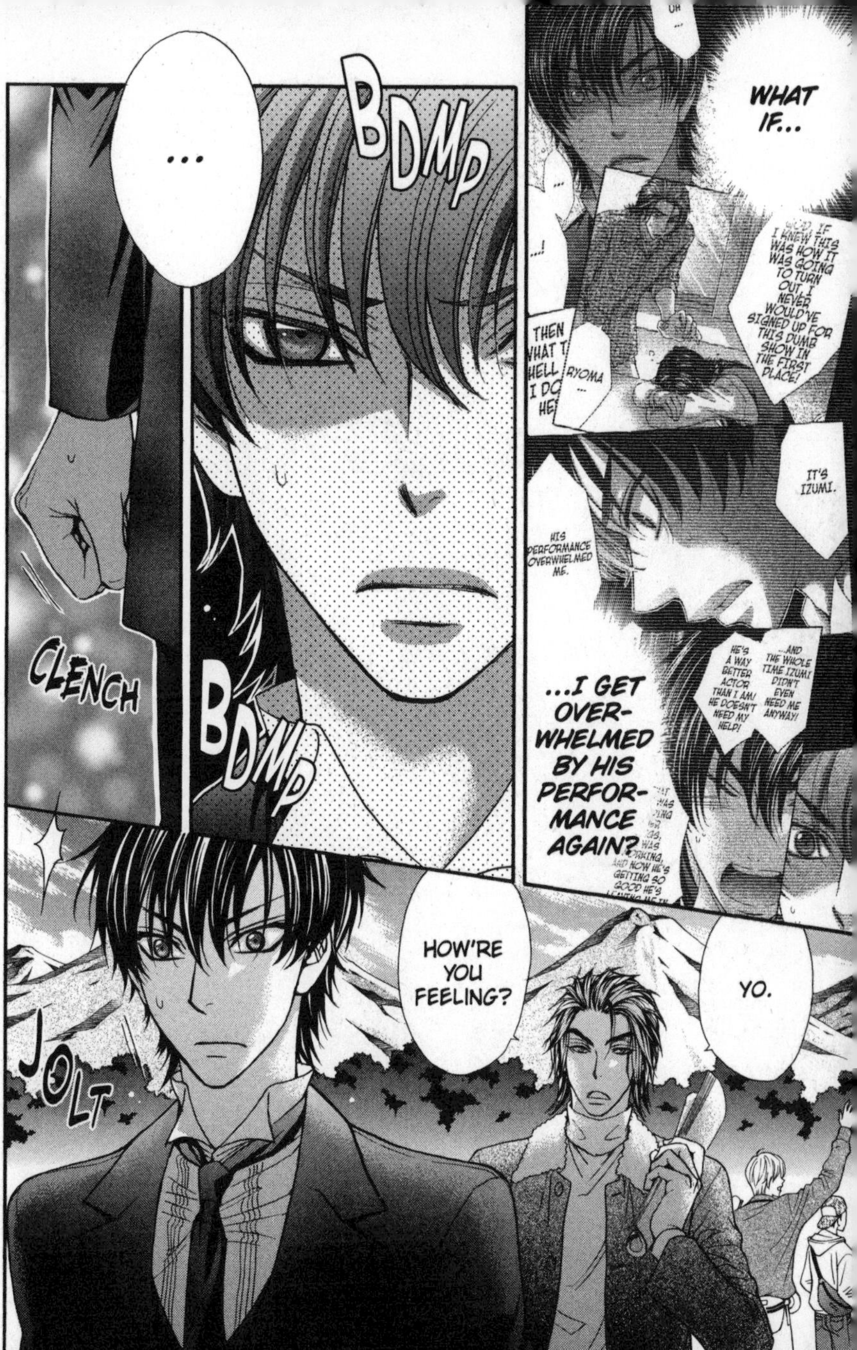
UH ...
WHAT IF...
...
...!
GOD, IF I KNEW THIS WAS HOW IT WAS GOING TO TURN OUT, I NEVER WOULD'VE SIGNED UP FOR THIS DUMB SHOW IN THE FIRST PLACE!
RYOMA ...
IT'S IZUMI.
HIS PERFORMANCE OVERWHELMED ME.
...AND THE WHOLE TIME IZUMI DIDN'T EVEN NEED ME ANYWAY!
HE'S A WAY BETTER ACTOR THAN I AM! HE DOESN'T NEED MY HELP!
...I GET OVER-WHELMED BY HIS PERFOR-MANCE AGAIN?
BDMP
BDMP
...
CLENCH
YO.
HOW'RE YOU FEELING?
JOLT

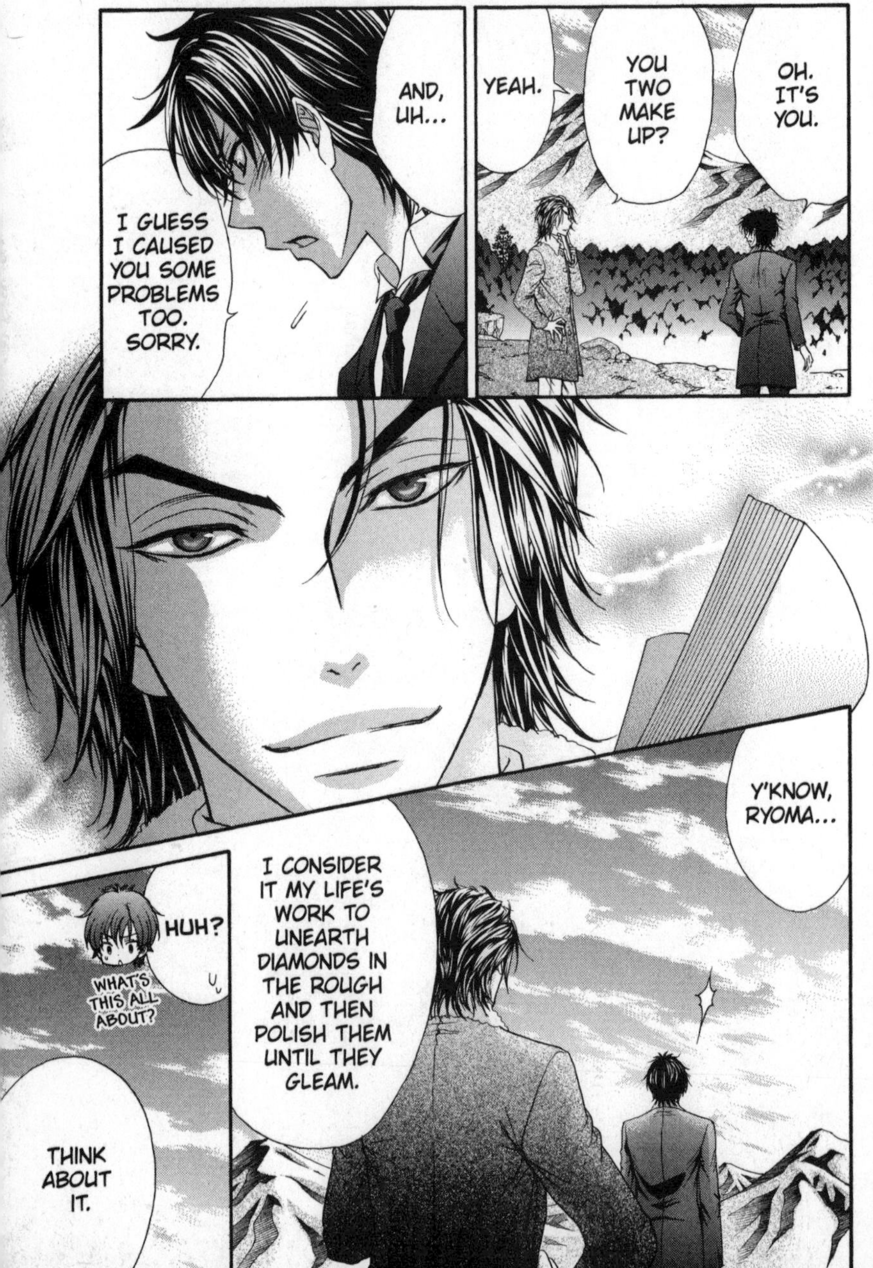
OH. IT'S YOU.
YOU TWO MAKE UP?
YEAH.
AND, UH...
I GUESS I CAUSED YOU SOME PROBLEMS TOO. SORRY.
Y'KNOW, RYOMA...
I CONSIDER IT MY LIFE'S WORK TO UNEARTH DIAMONDS IN THE ROUGH AND THEN POLISH THEM UNTIL THEY GLEAM.
HUH?
WHAT'S THIS ALL ABOUT?
THINK ABOUT IT.

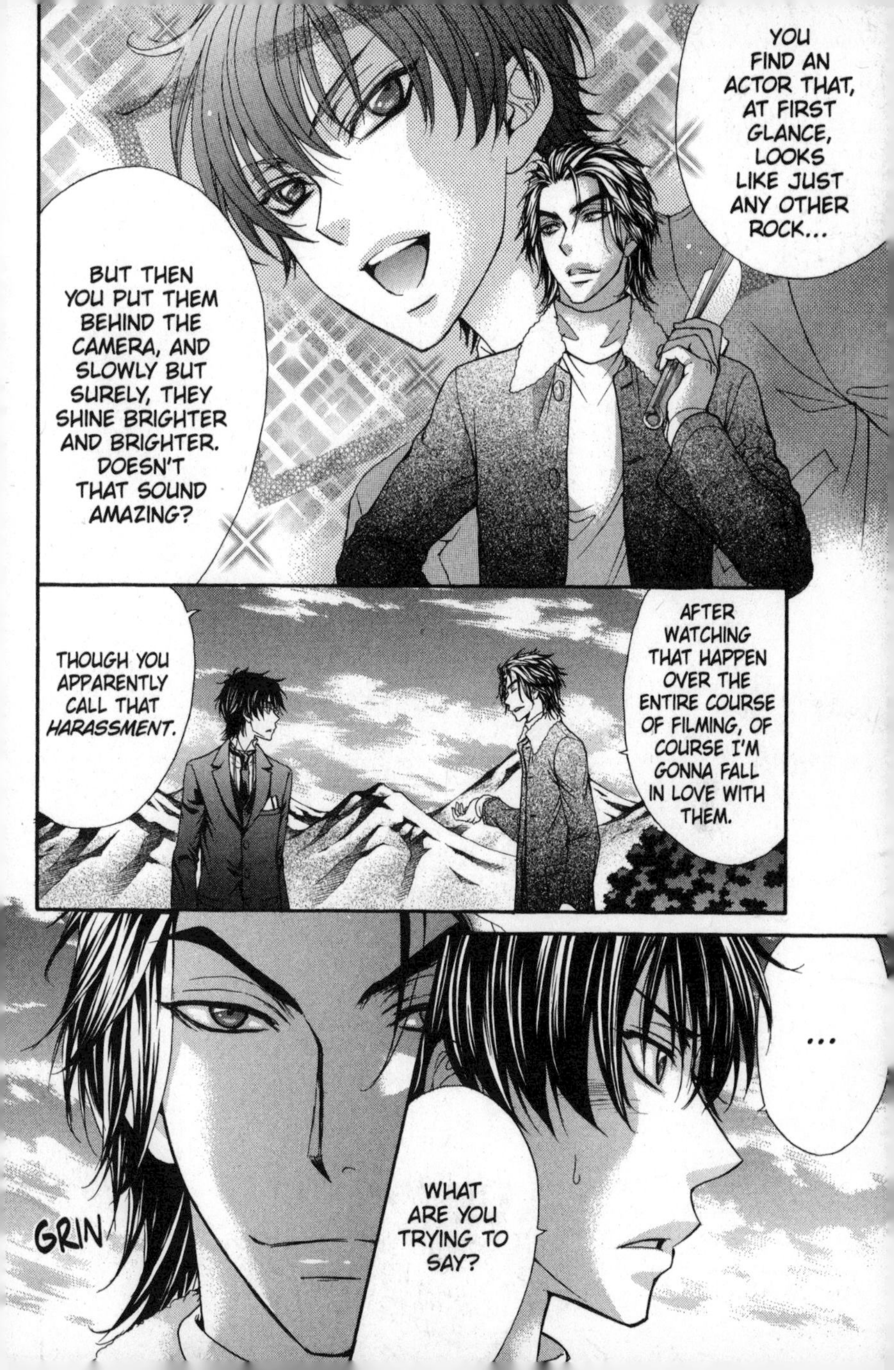
YOU FIND AN ACTOR THAT, AT FIRST GLANCE, LOOKS LIKE JUST ANY OTHER ROCK...
BUT THEN YOU PUT THEM BEHIND THE CAMERA, AND SLOWLY BUT SURELY, THEY SHINE BRIGHTER AND BRIGHTER. DOESN'T THAT SOUND AMAZING?
AFTER WATCHING THAT HAPPEN OVER THE ENTIRE COURSE OF FILMING, OF COURSE I'M GONNA FALL IN LOVE WITH THEM.
THOUGH YOU APPARENTLY CALL THAT *HARASSMENT*.
...
WHAT ARE YOU TRYING TO SAY?
GRIN

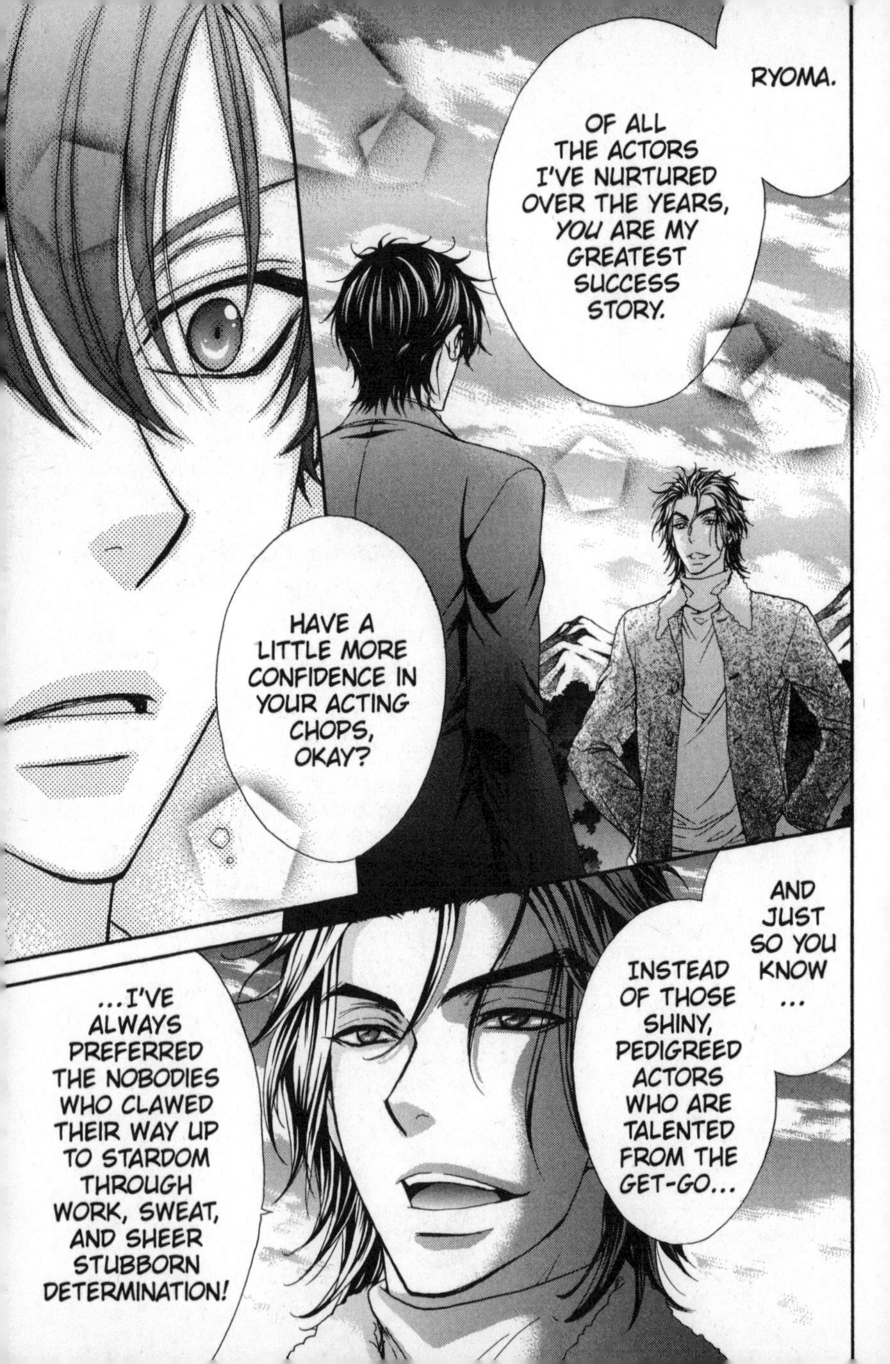
RYOMA.
OF ALL THE ACTORS I'VE NURTURED OVER THE YEARS, *YOU* ARE MY GREATEST SUCCESS STORY.
HAVE A LITTLE MORE CONFIDENCE IN YOUR ACTING CHOPS, OKAY?
AND JUST SO YOU KNOW...
INSTEAD OF THOSE SHINY, PEDIGREED ACTORS WHO ARE TALENTED FROM THE GET-GO...
...I'VE ALWAYS PREFERRED THE NOBODIES WHO CLAWED THEIR WAY UP TO STARDOM THROUGH WORK, SWEAT, AND SHEER STUBBORN DETERMINATION!

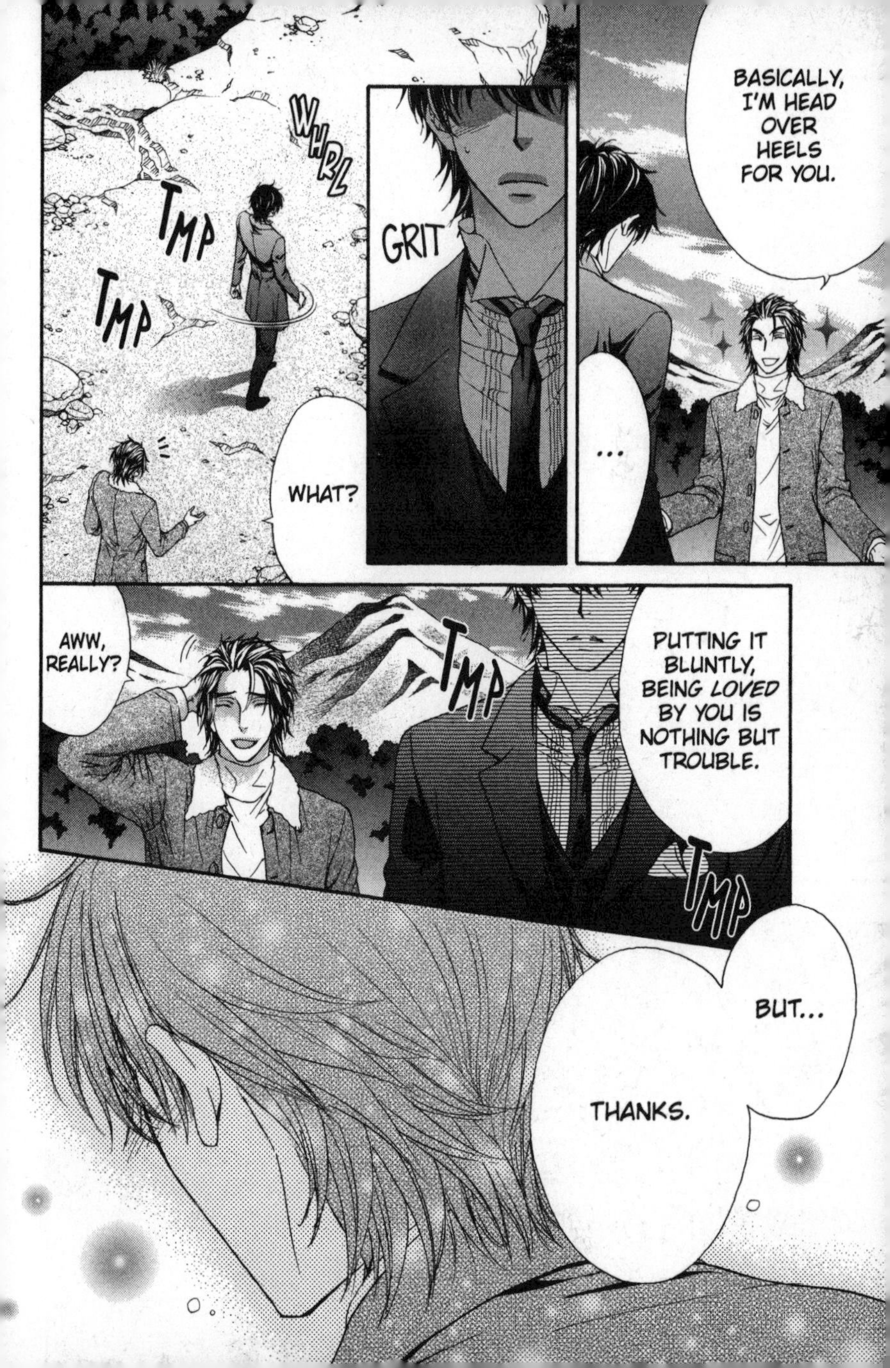
BASICALLY, I'M HEAD OVER HEELS FOR YOU.
...
GRIT
WHRL
TMP
TMP
WHAT?
PUTTING IT BLUNTLY, BEING *LOVED* BY YOU IS NOTHING BUT TROUBLE.
TMP
AWW, REALLY?
TMP
BUT...
THANKS.

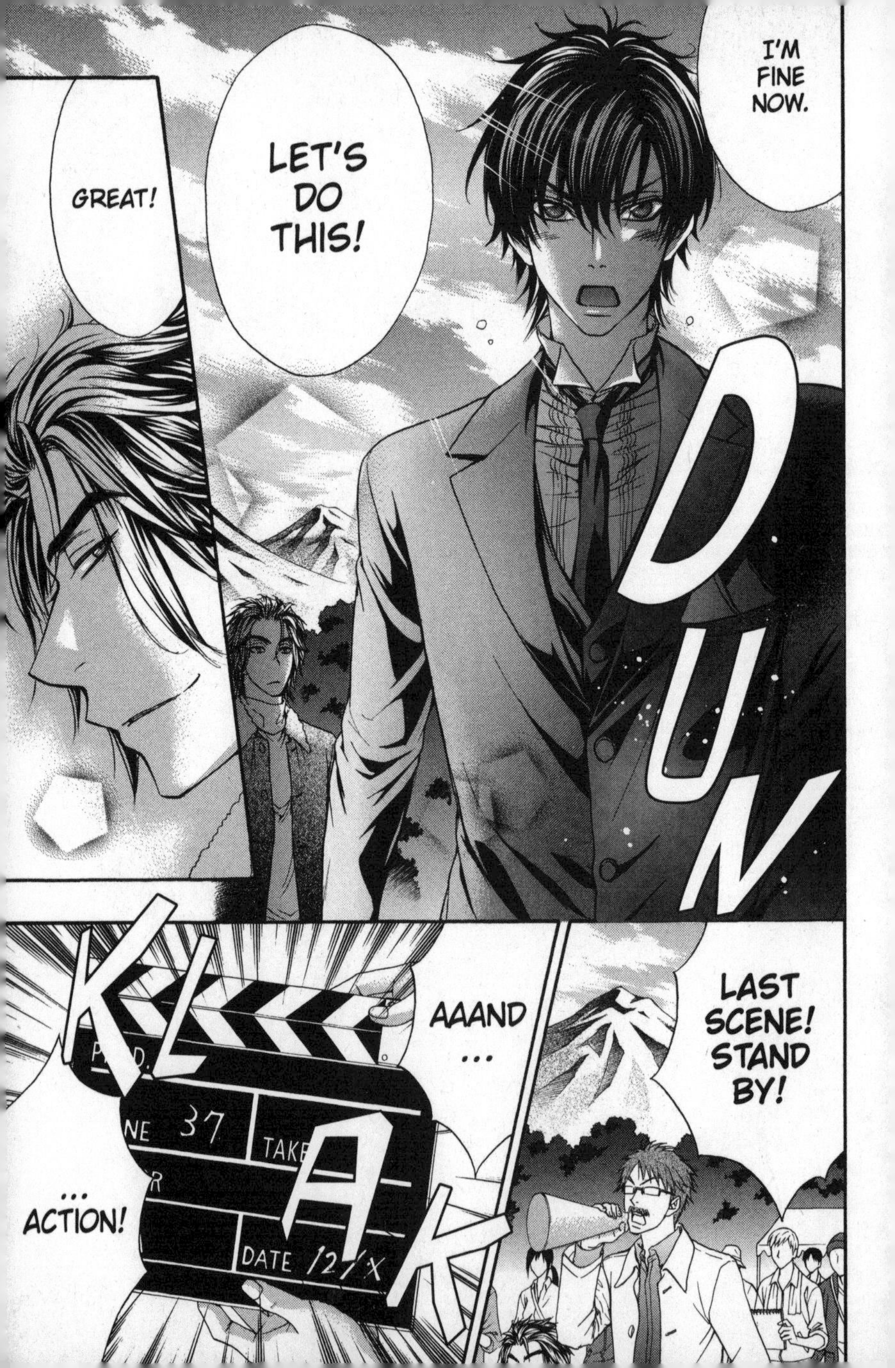
I'M FINE NOW.
DUN
LET'S DO THIS!
GREAT!
LAST SCENE! STAND BY!
AAAND ...
... ACTION!
KLAK
37
TAKE
DATE 12/X

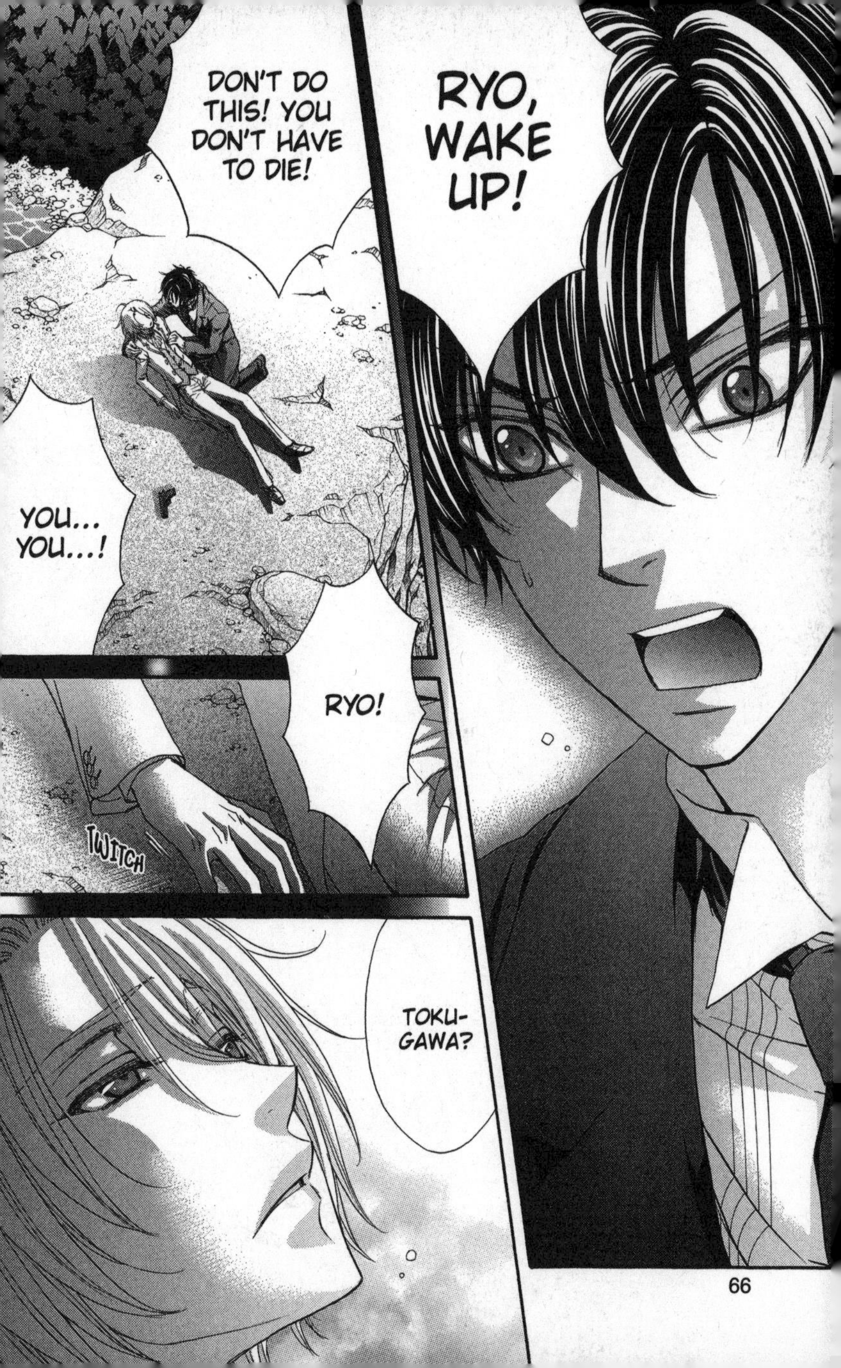
RYO, WAKE UP!
DON'T DO THIS! YOU DON'T HAVE TO DIE!
YOU... YOU...!
RYO!
TWITCH
TOKU-GAWA?

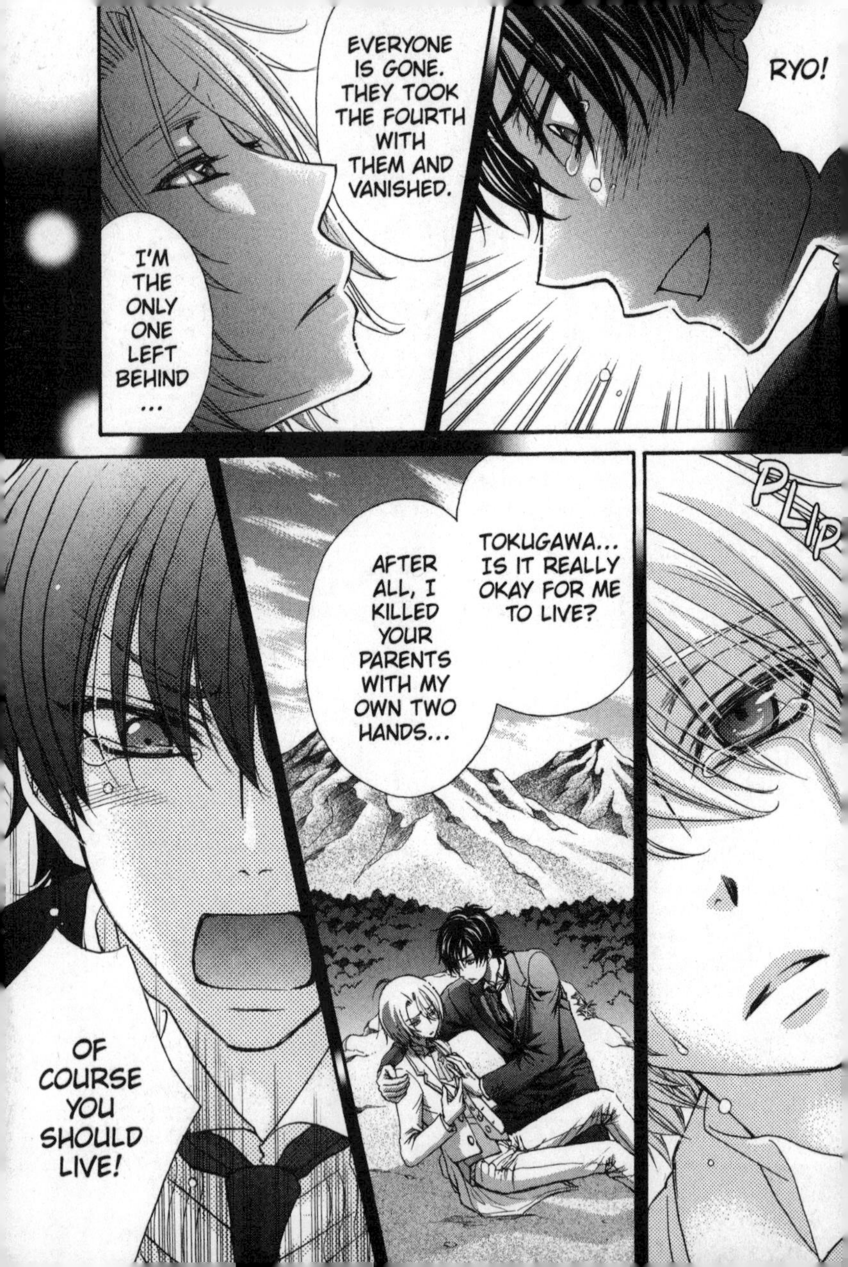
RYO!
EVERYONE IS GONE. THEY TOOK THE FOURTH WITH THEM AND VANISHED.
I'M THE ONLY ONE LEFT BEHIND...
PLIP
TOKUGAWA... IS IT REALLY OKAY FOR ME TO LIVE?
AFTER ALL, I KILLED YOUR PARENTS WITH MY OWN TWO HANDS...
OF COURSE YOU SHOULD LIVE!

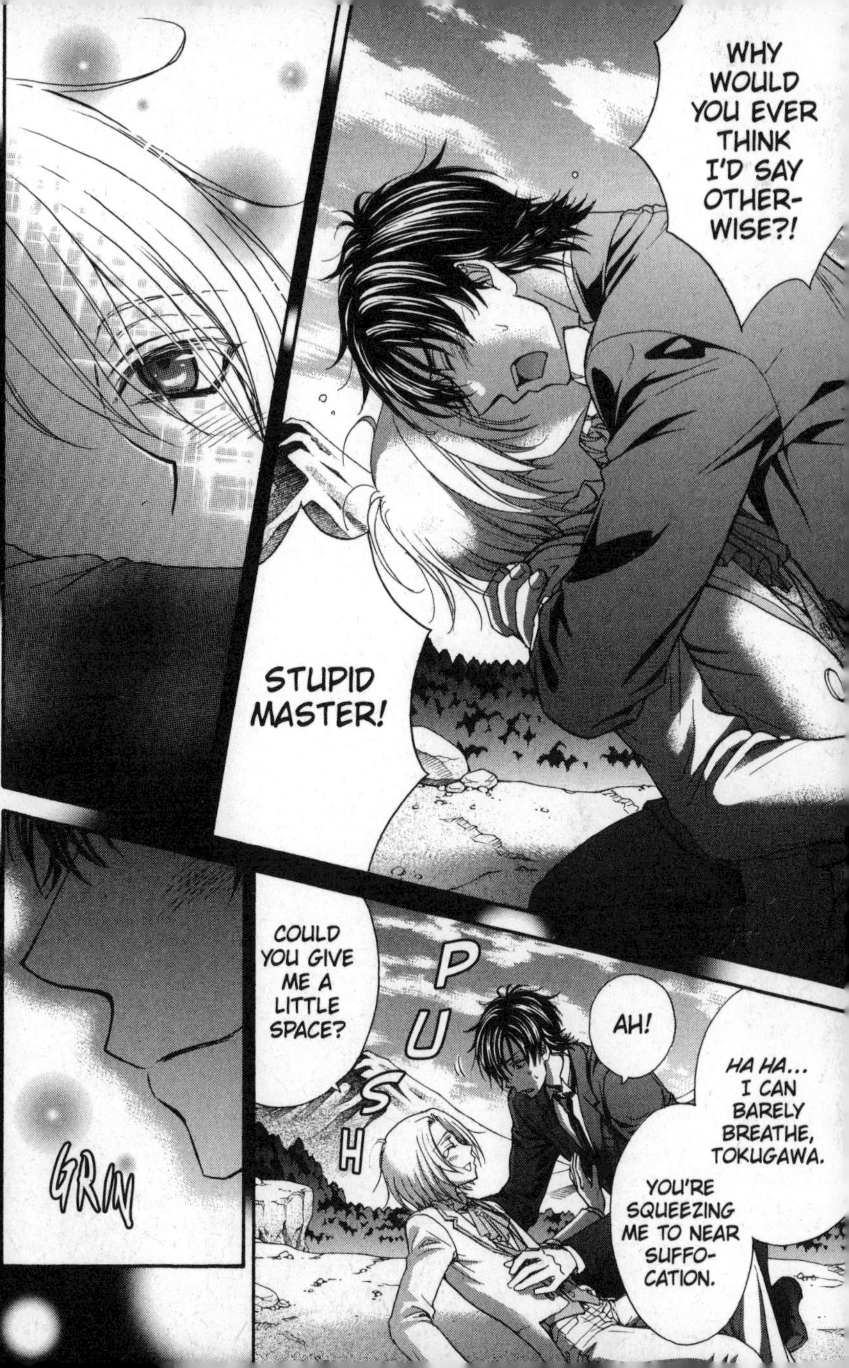
WHY WOULD YOU EVER THINK I'D SAY OTHER-WISE?!
STUPID MASTER!
HA HA... I CAN BARELY BREATHE, TOKUGAWA.
YOU'RE SQUEEZING ME TO NEAR SUFFO-CATION.
AH!
PUSH
COULD YOU GIVE ME A LITTLE SPACE?
GRIN

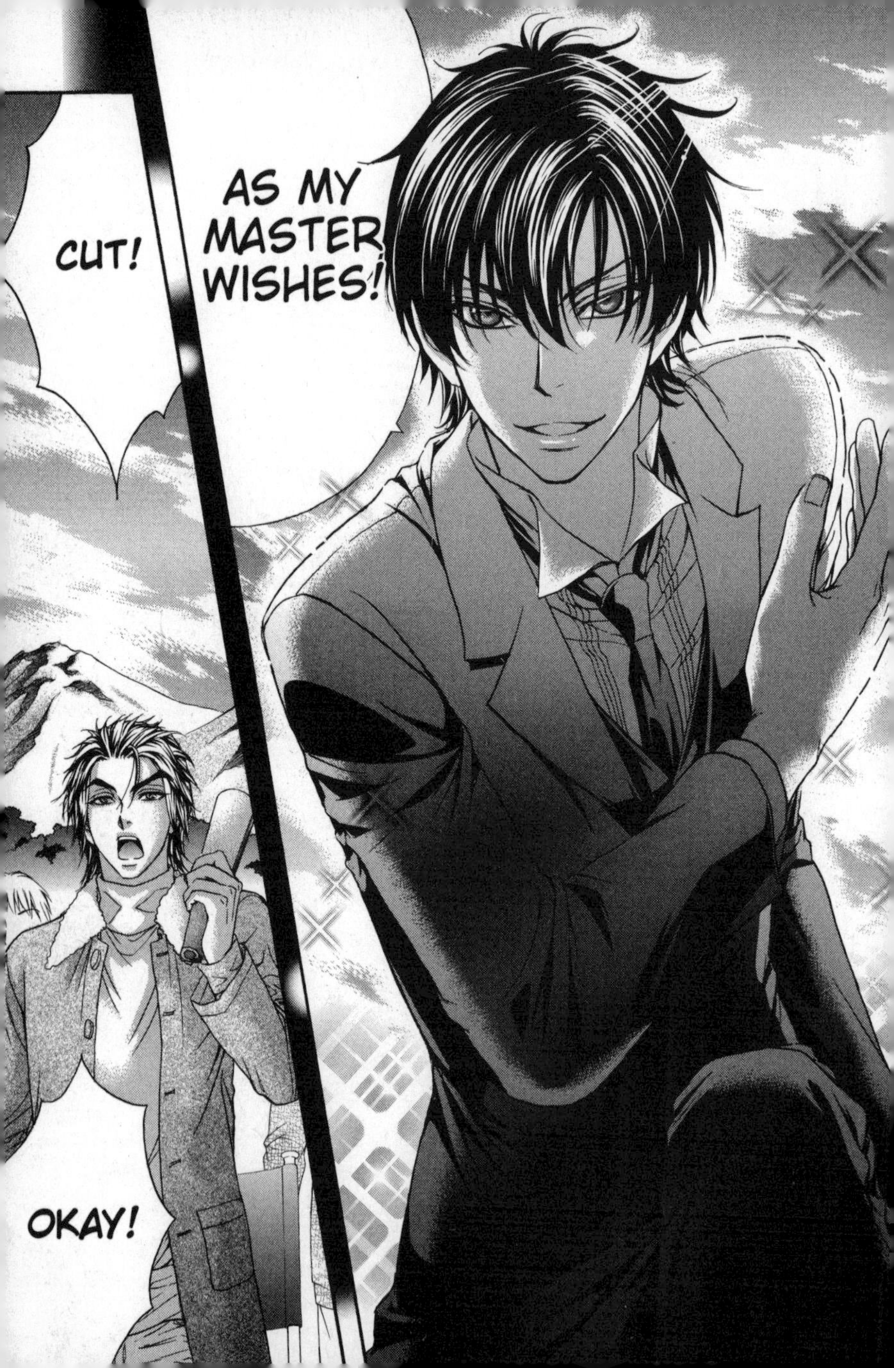
AS MY MASTER WISHES!
CUT!
OKAY!

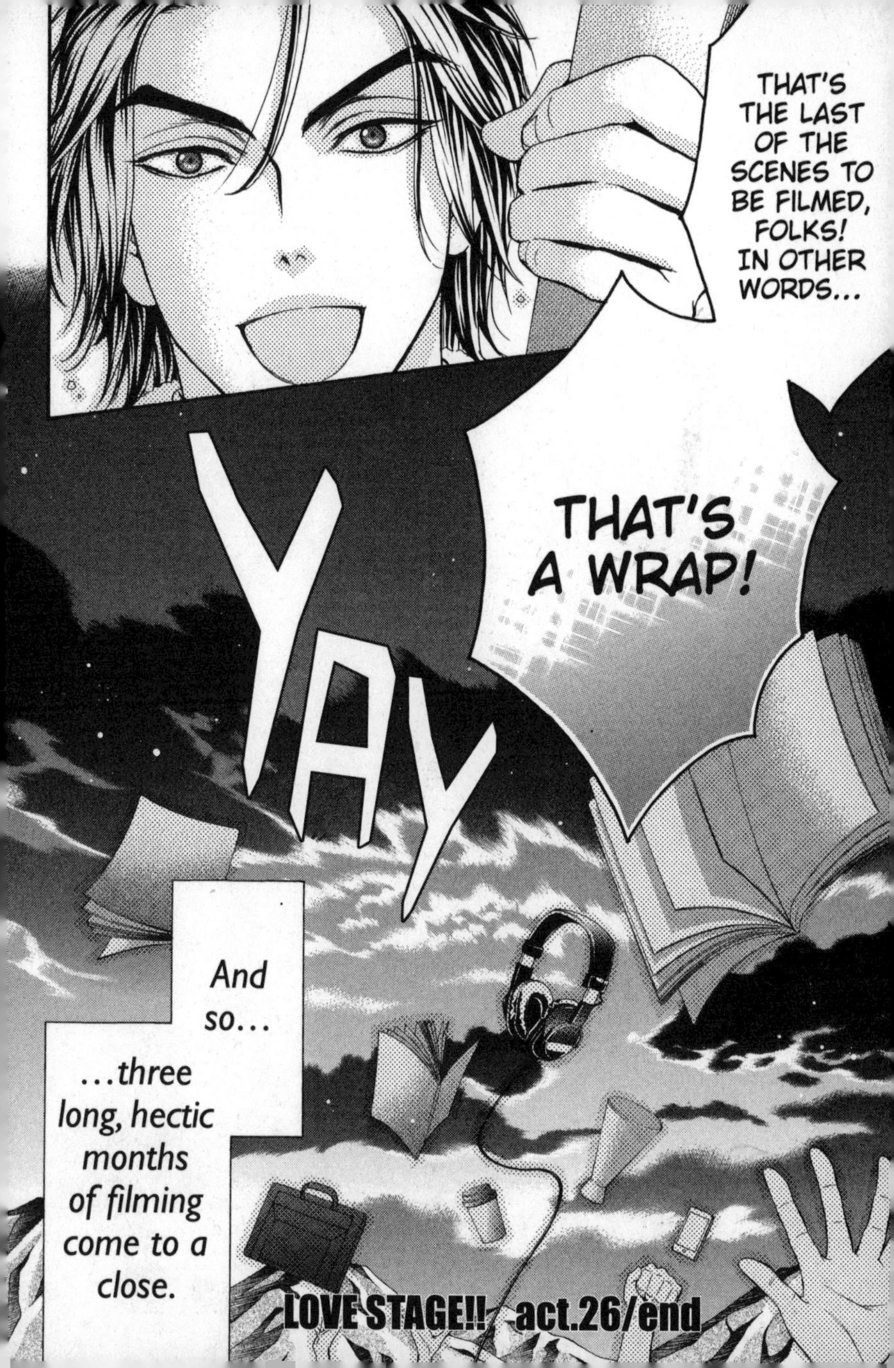
THAT'S THE LAST OF THE SCENES TO BE FILMED, FOLKS! IN OTHER WORDS...
THAT'S A WRAP!
YAY
And so...
...three long, hectic months of filming come to a close.
LOVE STAGE!! act.26/end

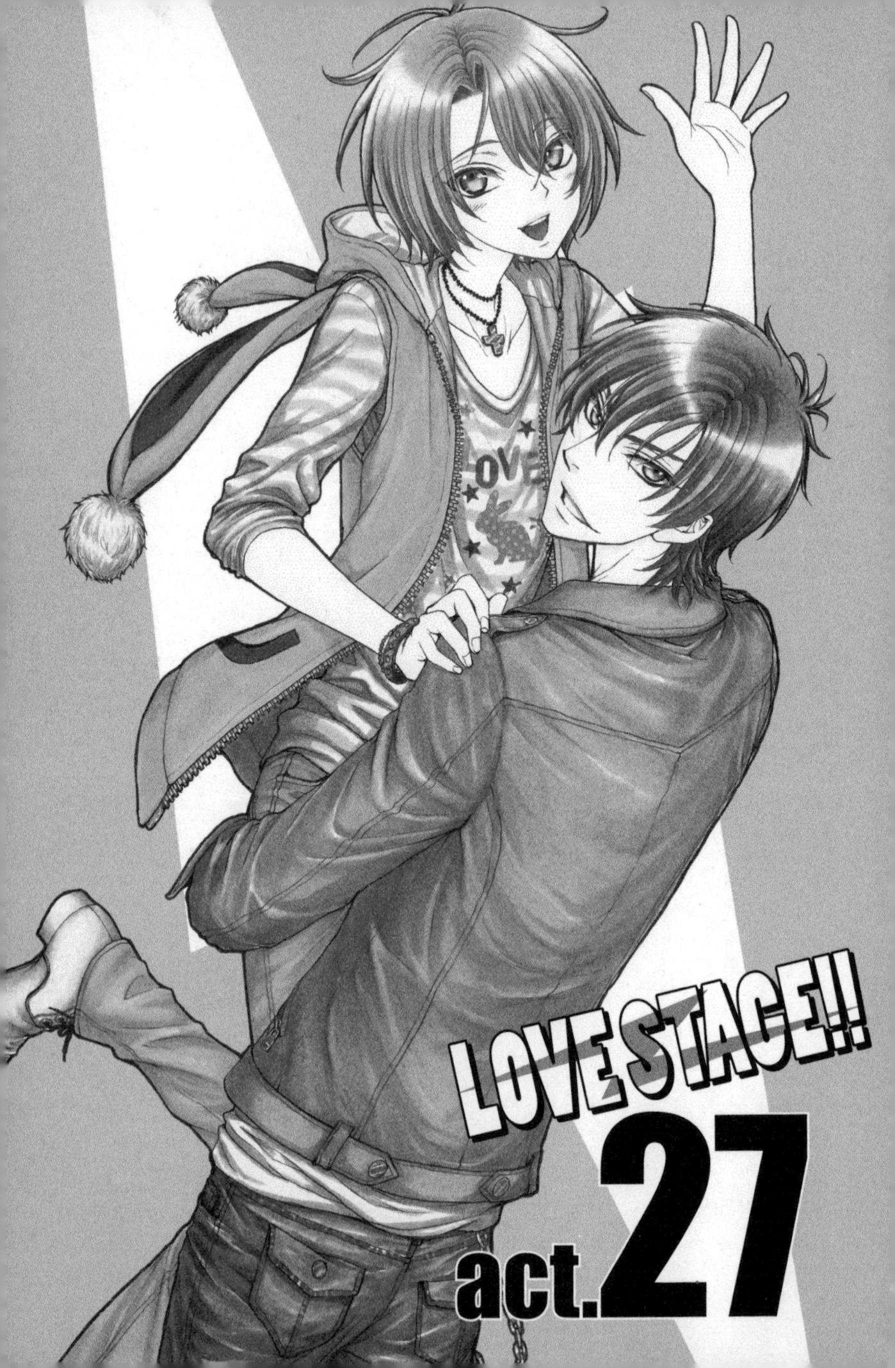
LOVE STAGE!!
act.27

LOVE STAGE!!

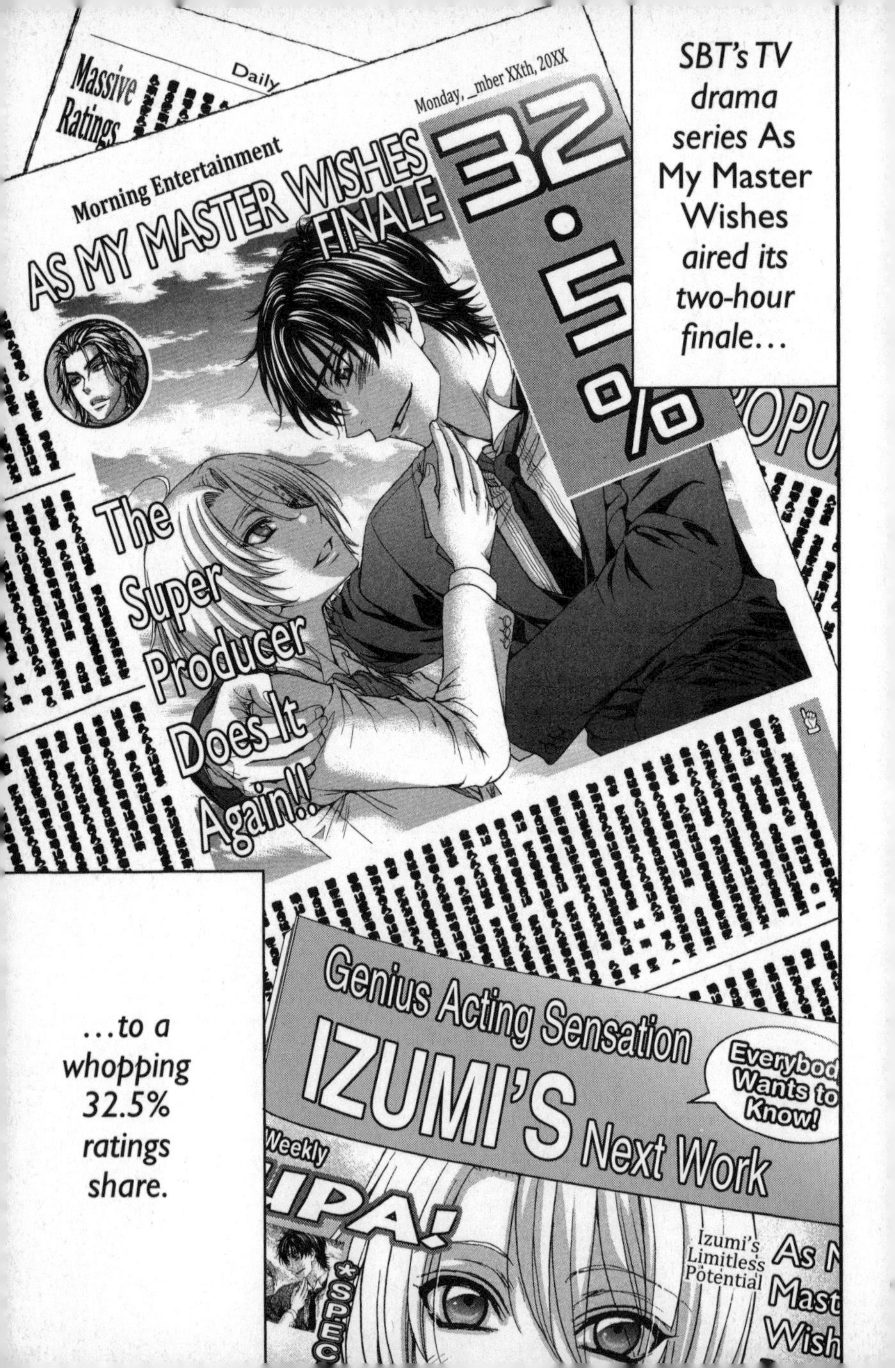
SBT's TV drama series As My Master Wishes aired its two-hour finale...
Massive Ratings
Daily
Monday, _mber XXth, 20XX
Morning Entertainment
AS MY MASTER WISHES FINALE
32.5%
POPU
The Super Producer Does It Again!!
...to a whopping 32.5% ratings share.
Genius Acting Sensation IZUMI'S Next Work
Everybod Wants to Know!
Weekly
IPA!
*SPEC
Izumi's Limitless Potential
As M Mast Wish

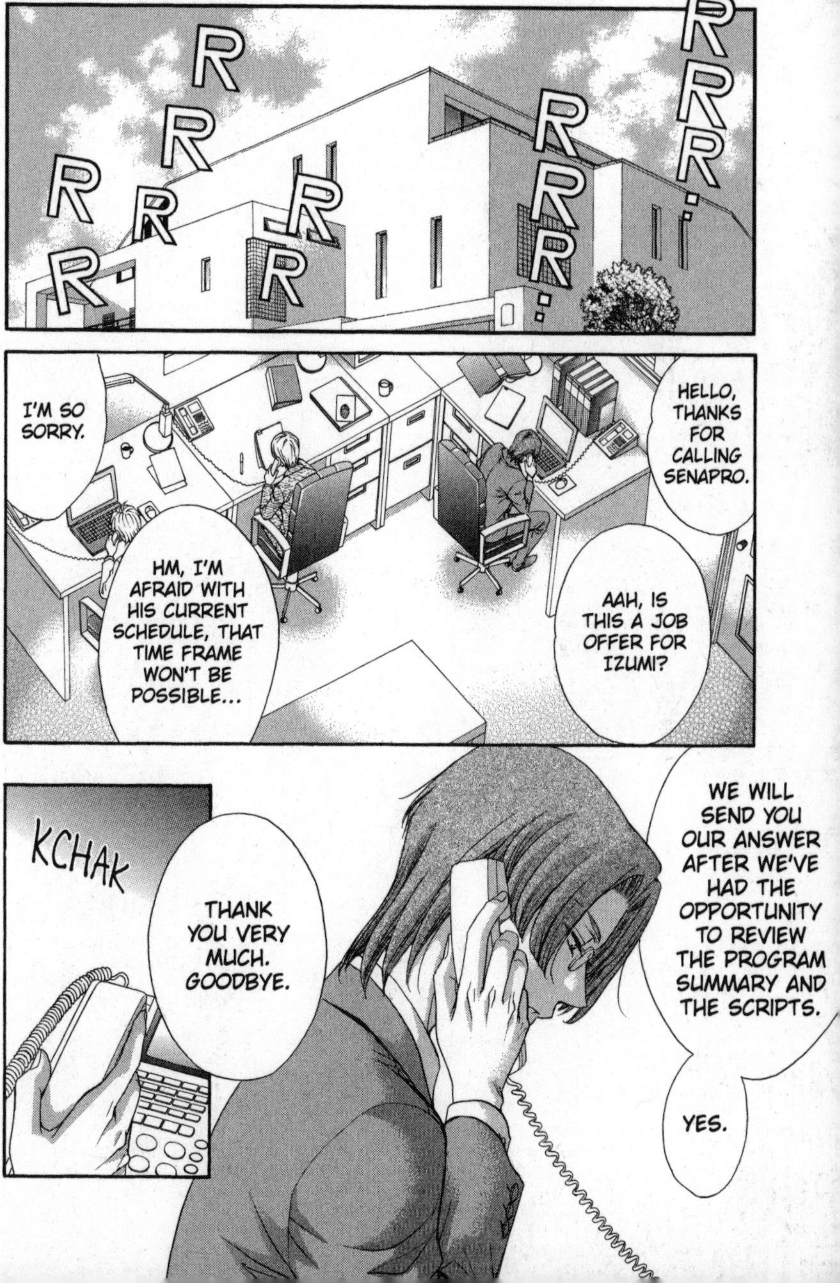
RRR...
RRR...
RRR
RRR
HELLO, THANKS FOR CALLING SENAPRO.
AAH, IS THIS A JOB OFFER FOR IZUMI?
HM, I'M AFRAID WITH HIS CURRENT SCHEDULE, THAT TIME FRAME WON'T BE POSSIBLE...
I'M SO SORRY.
WE WILL SEND YOU OUR ANSWER AFTER WE'VE HAD THE OPPORTUNITY TO REVIEW THE PROGRAM SUMMARY AND THE SCRIPTS.
YES.
THANK YOU VERY MUCH. GOODBYE.
KCHAK

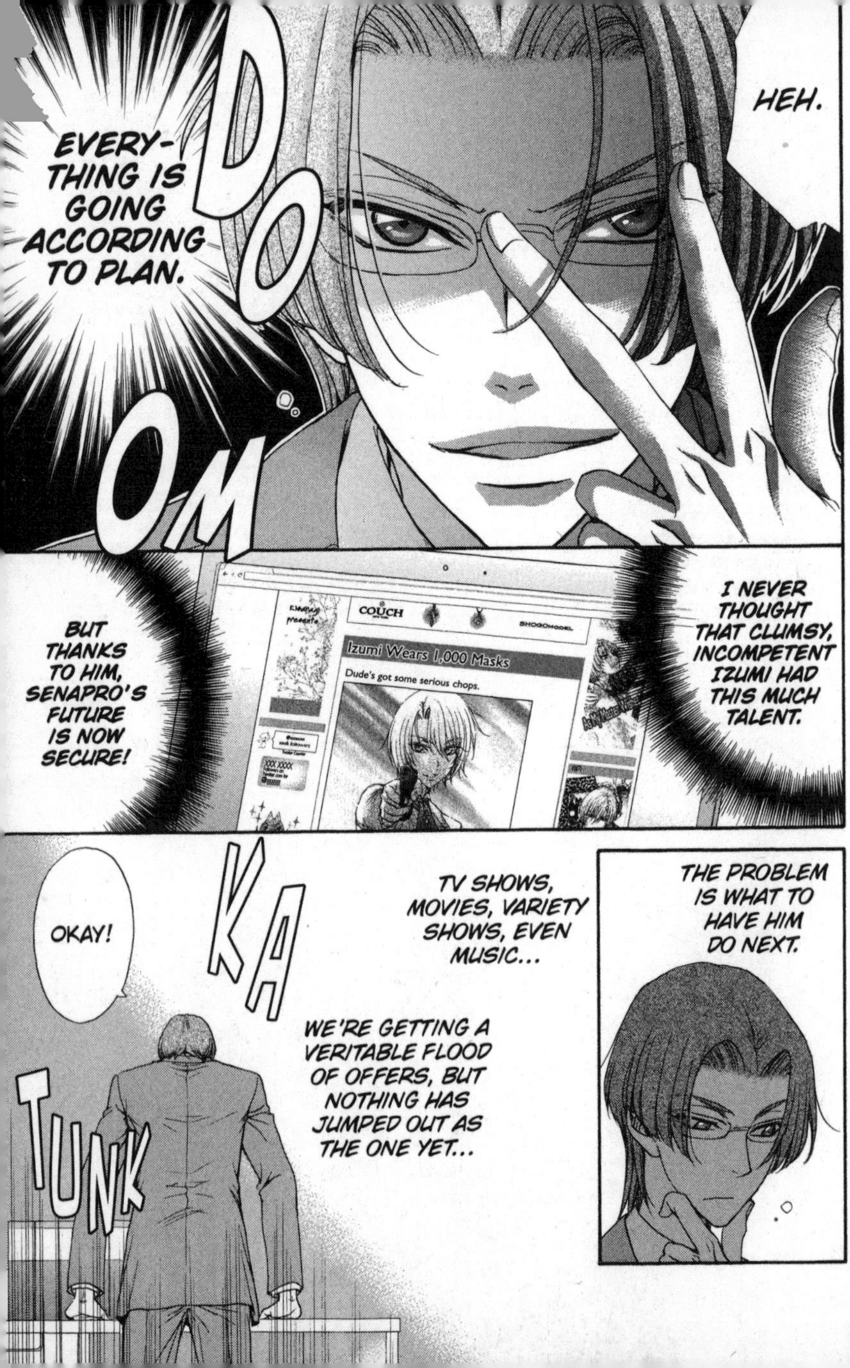
HEH.
EVERY-THING IS GOING ACCORDING TO PLAN.
DOOOM
I NEVER THOUGHT THAT CLUMSY, INCOMPETENT IZUMI HAD THIS MUCH TALENT.
COUCH
SHOGOMODEL
Izumi Wears 1,000 Masks
Dude's got some serious chops.
BUT THANKS TO HIM, SENAPRO'S FUTURE IS NOW SECURE!
THE PROBLEM IS WHAT TO HAVE HIM DO NEXT.
TV SHOWS, MOVIES, VARIETY SHOWS, EVEN MUSIC...
WE'RE GETTING A VERITABLE FLOOD OF OFFERS, BUT NOTHING HAS JUMPED OUT AS THE ONE YET...
KA
OKAY!
TUNK

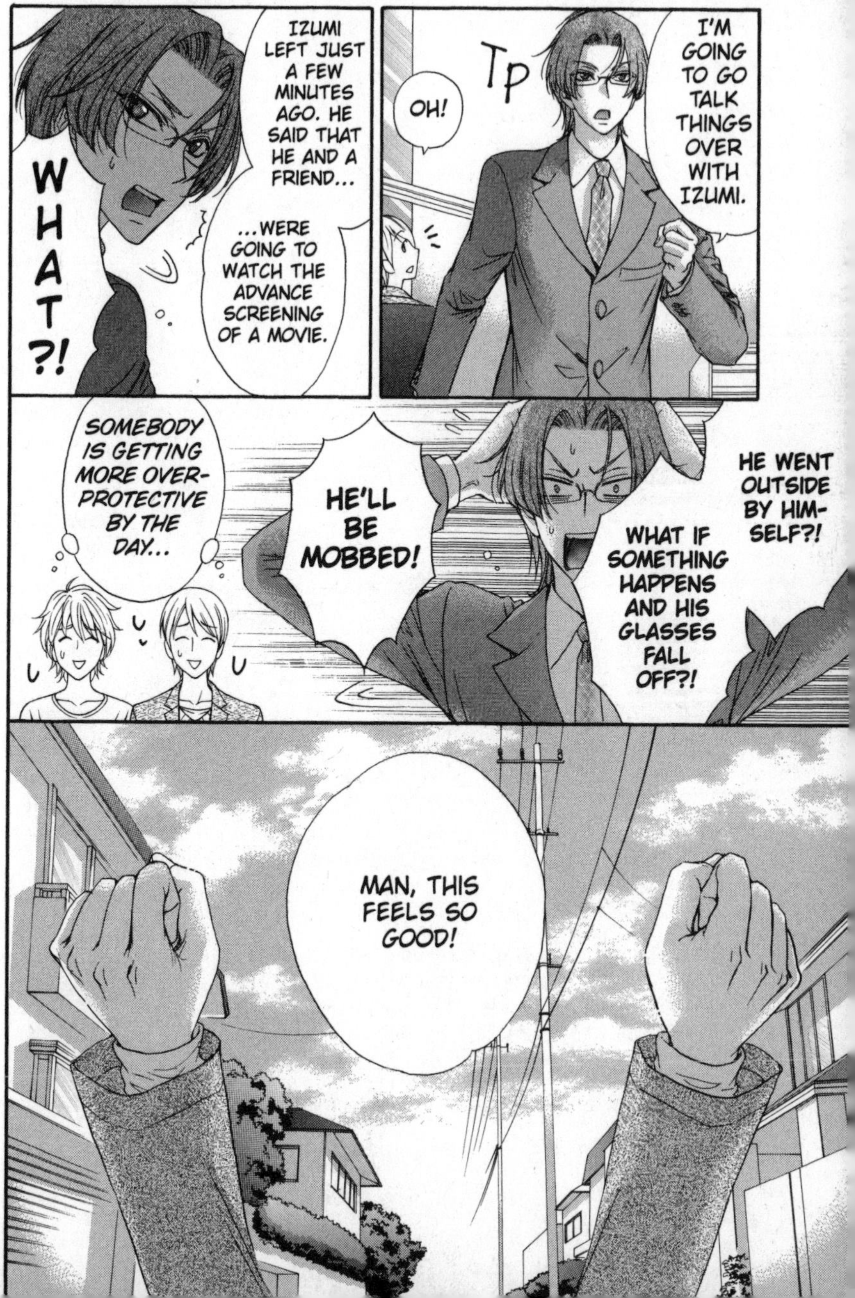
I'M GOING TO GO TALK THINGS OVER WITH IZUMI.
Tp
OH!
IZUMI LEFT JUST A FEW MINUTES AGO. HE SAID THAT HE AND A FRIEND...
...WERE GOING TO WATCH THE ADVANCE SCREENING OF A MOVIE.
WHAT?!
HE WENT OUTSIDE BY HIM-SELF?!
WHAT IF SOMETHING HAPPENS AND HIS GLASSES FALL OFF?!
HE'LL BE MOBBED!
SOMEBODY IS GETTING MORE OVER-PROTECTIVE BY THE DAY...
MAN, THIS FEELS SO GOOD!

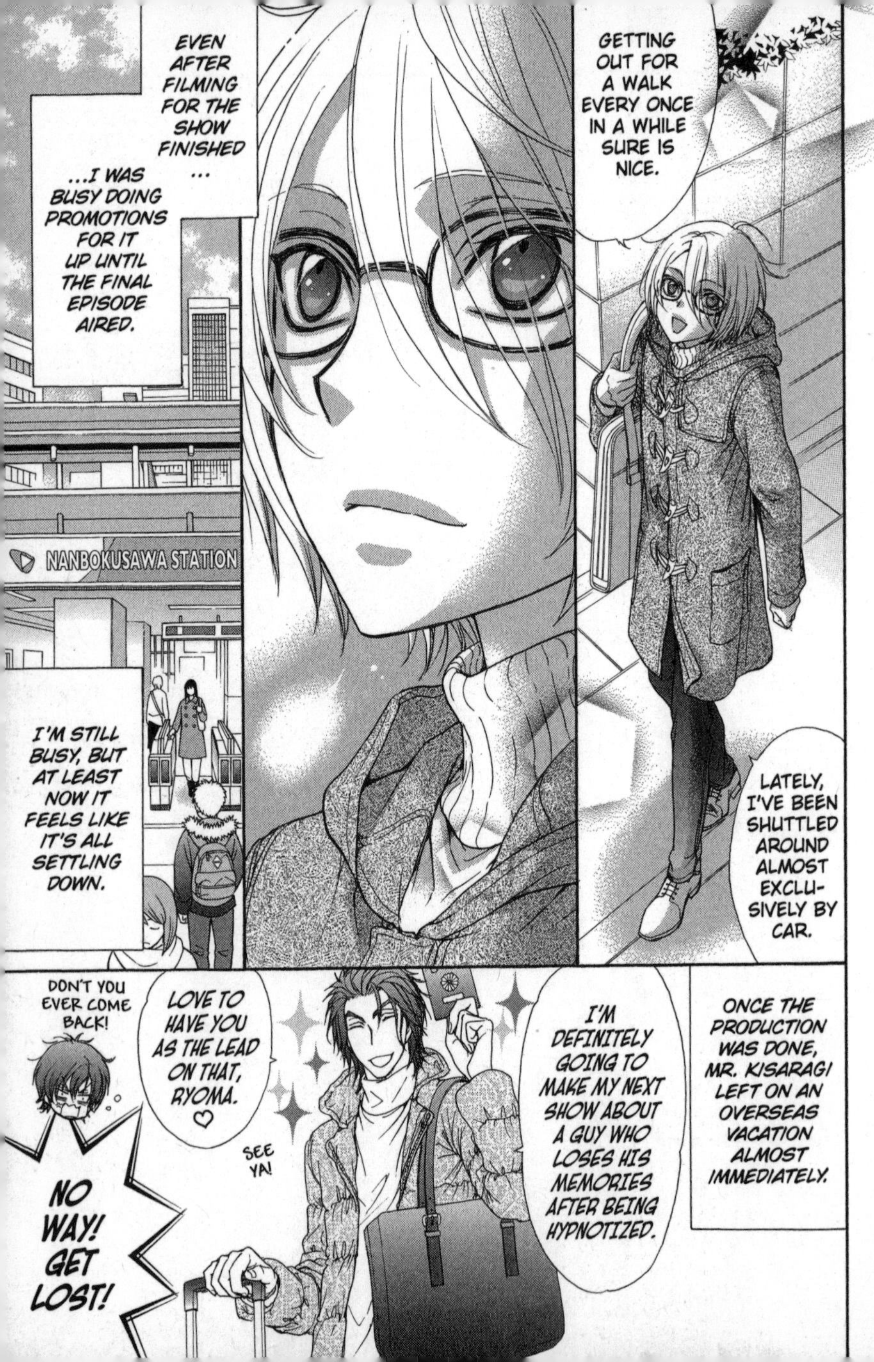
GETTING OUT FOR A WALK EVERY ONCE IN A WHILE SURE IS NICE.
LATELY, I'VE BEEN SHUTTLED AROUND ALMOST EXCLU-SIVELY BY CAR.
EVEN AFTER FILMING FOR THE SHOW FINISHED...
...I WAS BUSY DOING PROMOTIONS FOR IT UP UNTIL THE FINAL EPISODE AIRED.
NANBOKUSAWA STATION
I'M STILL BUSY, BUT AT LEAST NOW IT FEELS LIKE IT'S ALL SETTLING DOWN.
ONCE THE PRODUCTION WAS DONE, MR. KISARAGI LEFT ON AN OVERSEAS VACATION ALMOST IMMEDIATELY.
I'M DEFINITELY GOING TO MAKE MY NEXT SHOW ABOUT A GUY WHO LOSES HIS MEMORIES AFTER BEING HYPNOTIZED.
LOVE TO HAVE YOU AS THE LEAD ON THAT, RYOMA. ♡
SEE YA!
DON'T YOU EVER COME BACK!
NO WAY! GET LOST!

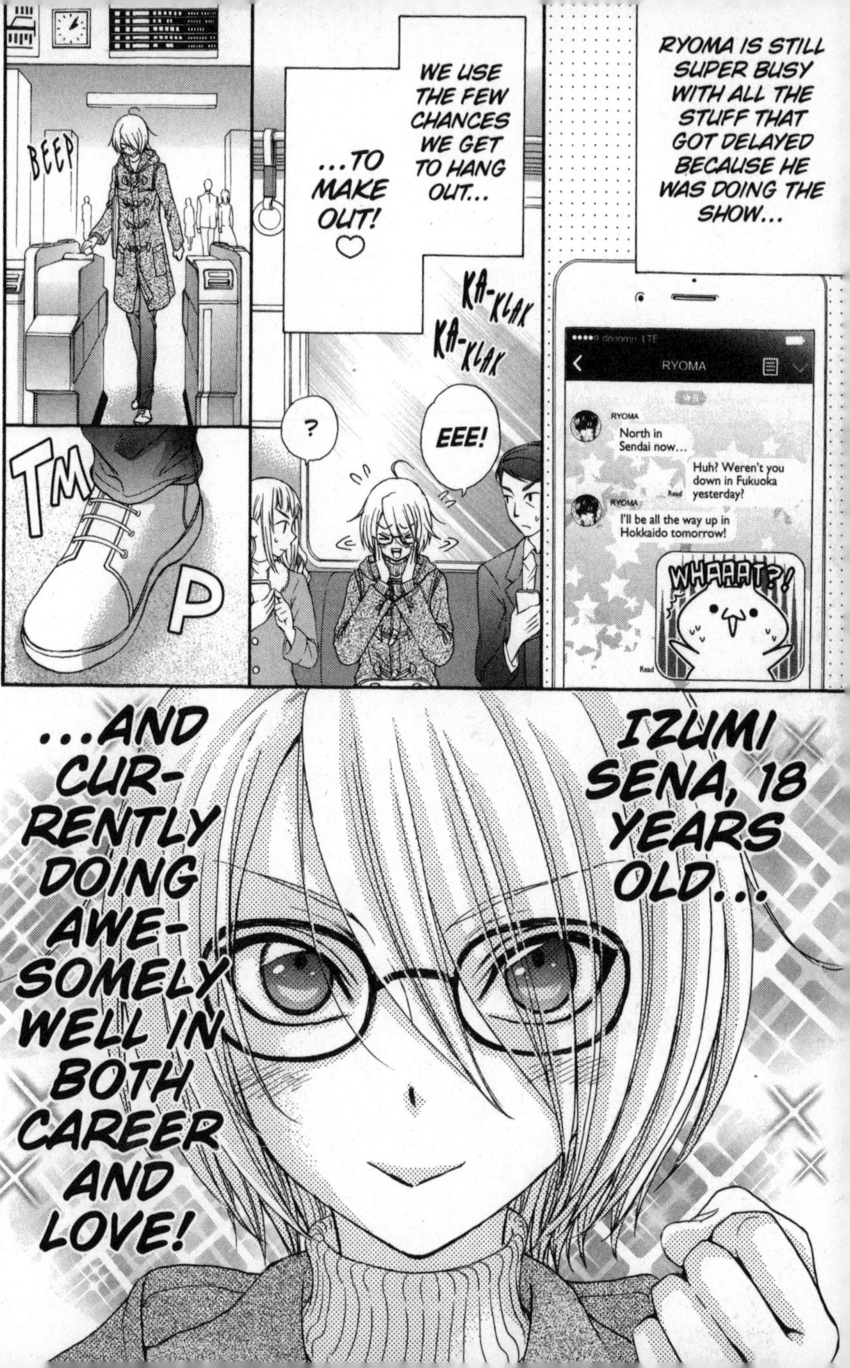
RYOMA IS STILL SUPER BUSY WITH ALL THE STUFF THAT GOT DELAYED BECAUSE HE WAS DOING THE SHOW...
RYOMA
RYOMA
North in Sendai now...
Huh? Weren't you down in Fukuoka yesterday?
Read
RYOMA
I'll be all the way up in Hokkaido tomorrow!
WHAAAT?!
Read
WE USE THE FEW CHANCES WE GET TO HANG OUT...
...TO MAKE OUT! ♡
KA-KLAK
KA-KLAK
BEEP
EEE!
?
TMP
IZUMI SENA, 18 YEARS OLD...
...AND CUR-RENTLY DOING AWE-SOMELY WELL IN BOTH CAREER AND LOVE!

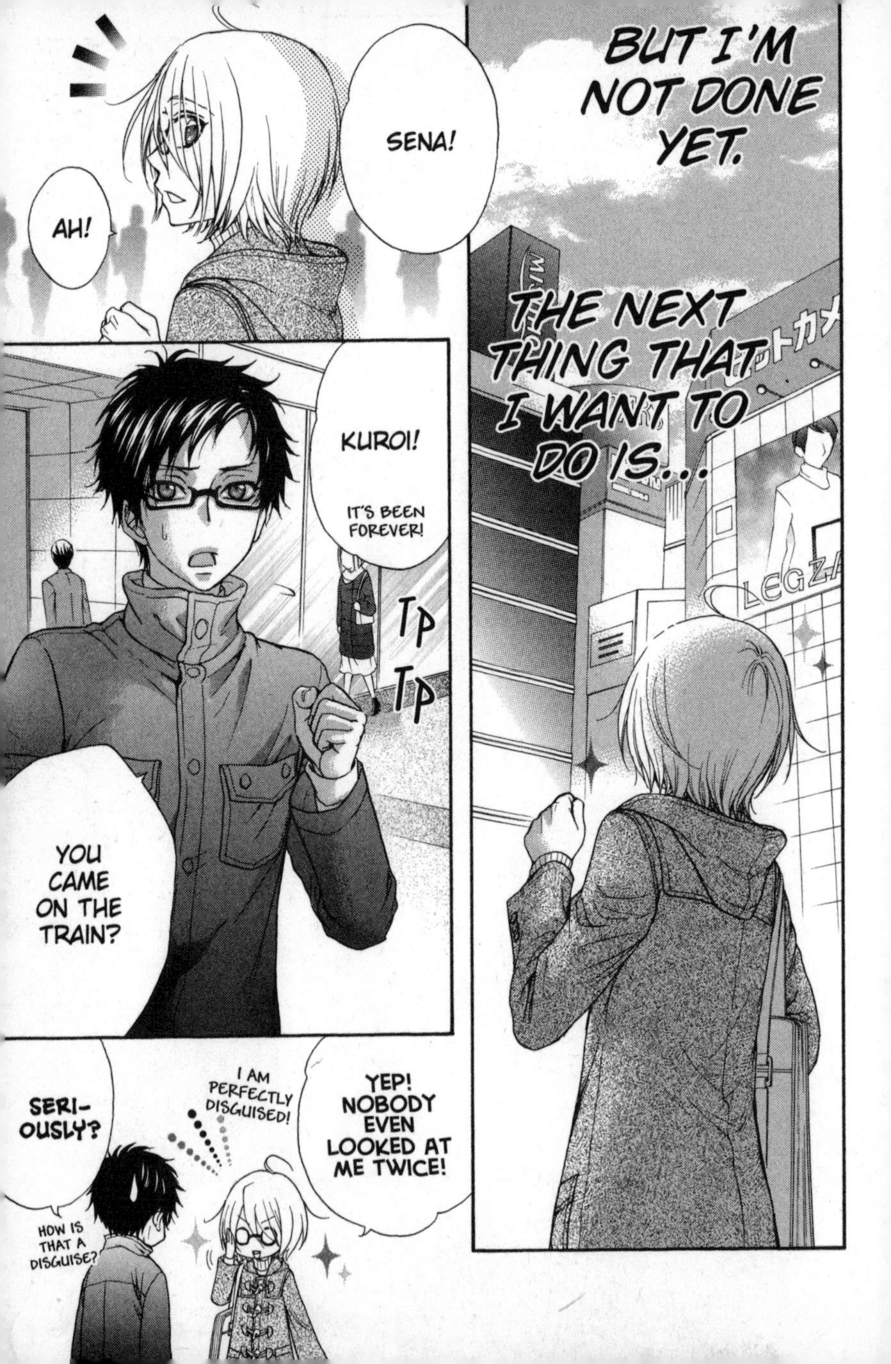
BUT I'M NOT DONE YET.
THE NEXT THING THAT I WANT TO DO IS...
SENA!
AH!
KUROI!
IT'S BEEN FOREVER!
TP TP
YOU CAME ON THE TRAIN?
YEP! NOBODY EVEN LOOKED AT ME TWICE!
I AM PERFECTLY DISGUISED!
SERI-OUSLY?
HOW IS THAT A DISGUISE?

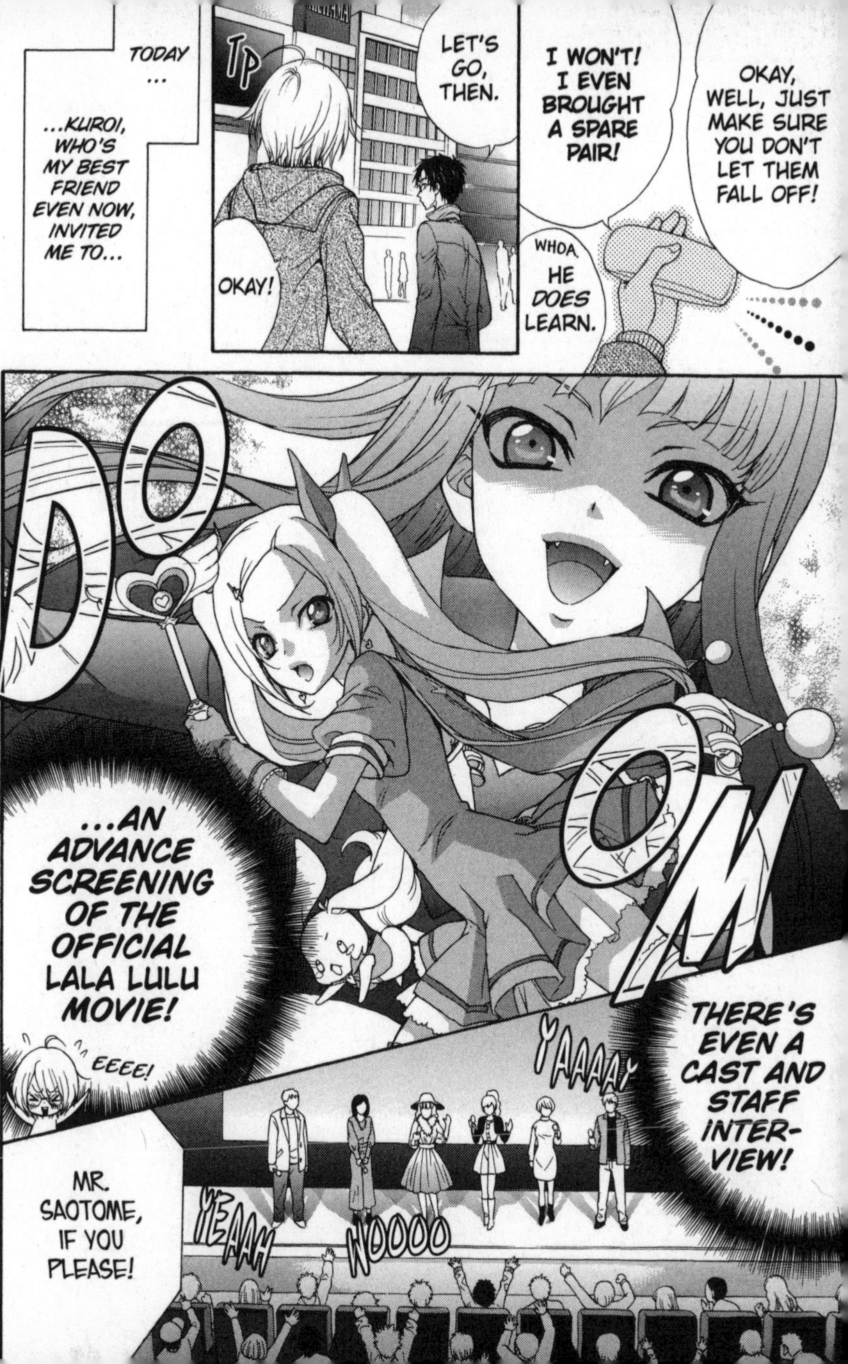
OKAY, WELL, JUST MAKE SURE YOU DON'T LET THEM FALL OFF!
I WON'T! I EVEN BROUGHT A SPARE PAIR!
WHOA. HE DOES LEARN.
LET'S GO, THEN.
OKAY!
TODAY ...
...KUROI, WHO'S MY BEST FRIEND EVEN NOW, INVITED ME TO...
DOOM
...AN ADVANCE SCREENING OF THE OFFICIAL LALA LULU MOVIE!
THERE'S EVEN A CAST AND STAFF INTERVIEW!
YAAAAY
EEEE!
YEAAH
WOOOO
MR. SAOTOME, IF YOU PLEASE!

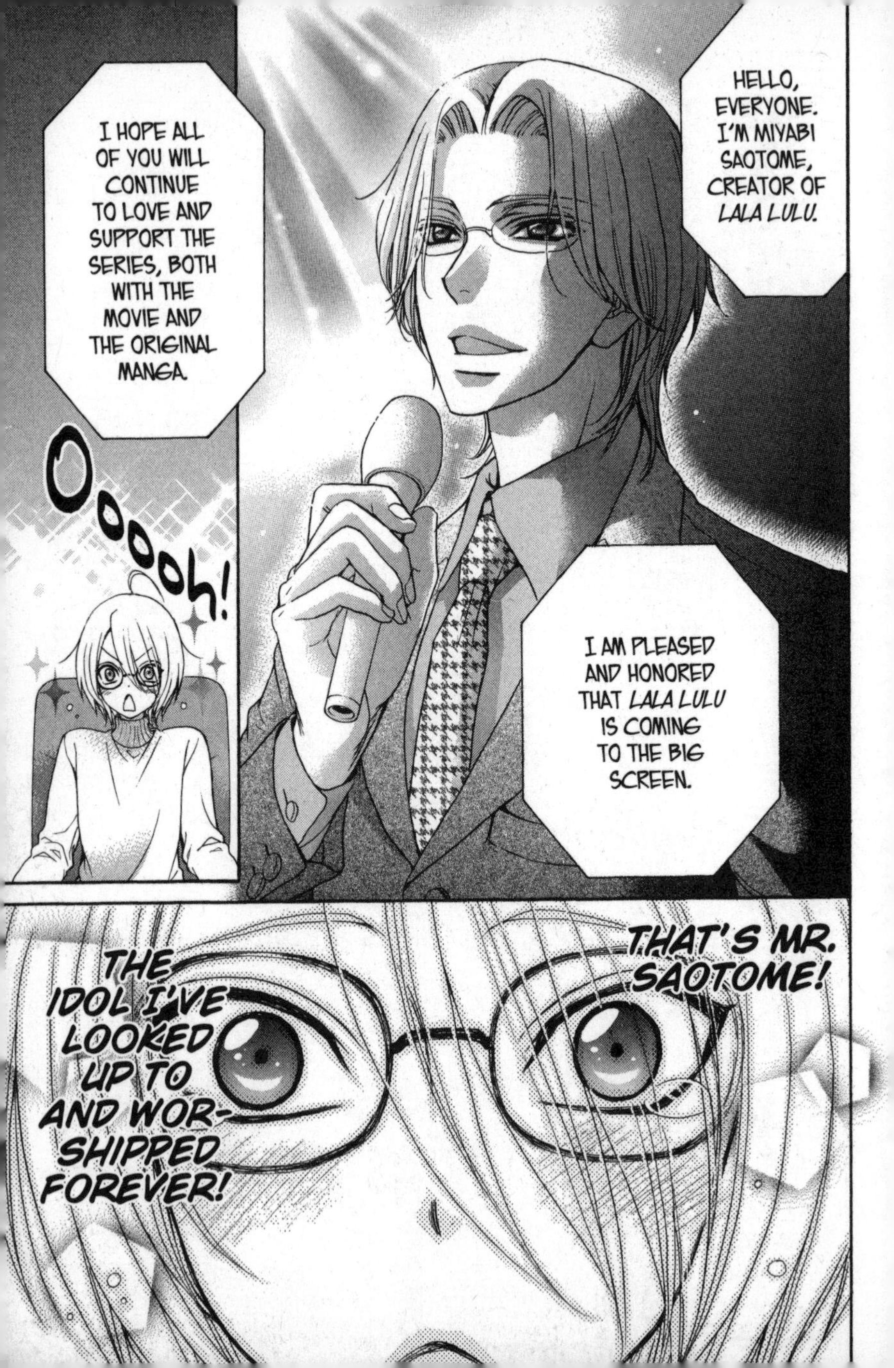
HELLO, EVERYONE. I'M MIYABI SAOTOME, CREATOR OF *LALA LULU.*
I AM PLEASED AND HONORED THAT *LALA LULU* IS COMING TO THE BIG SCREEN.
I HOPE ALL OF YOU WILL CONTINUE TO LOVE AND SUPPORT THE SERIES, BOTH WITH THE MOVIE AND THE ORIGINAL MANGA.
Ooooh!
THAT'S MR. SAOTOME!
THE IDOL I'VE LOOKED UP TO AND WOR-SHIPPED FOREVER!

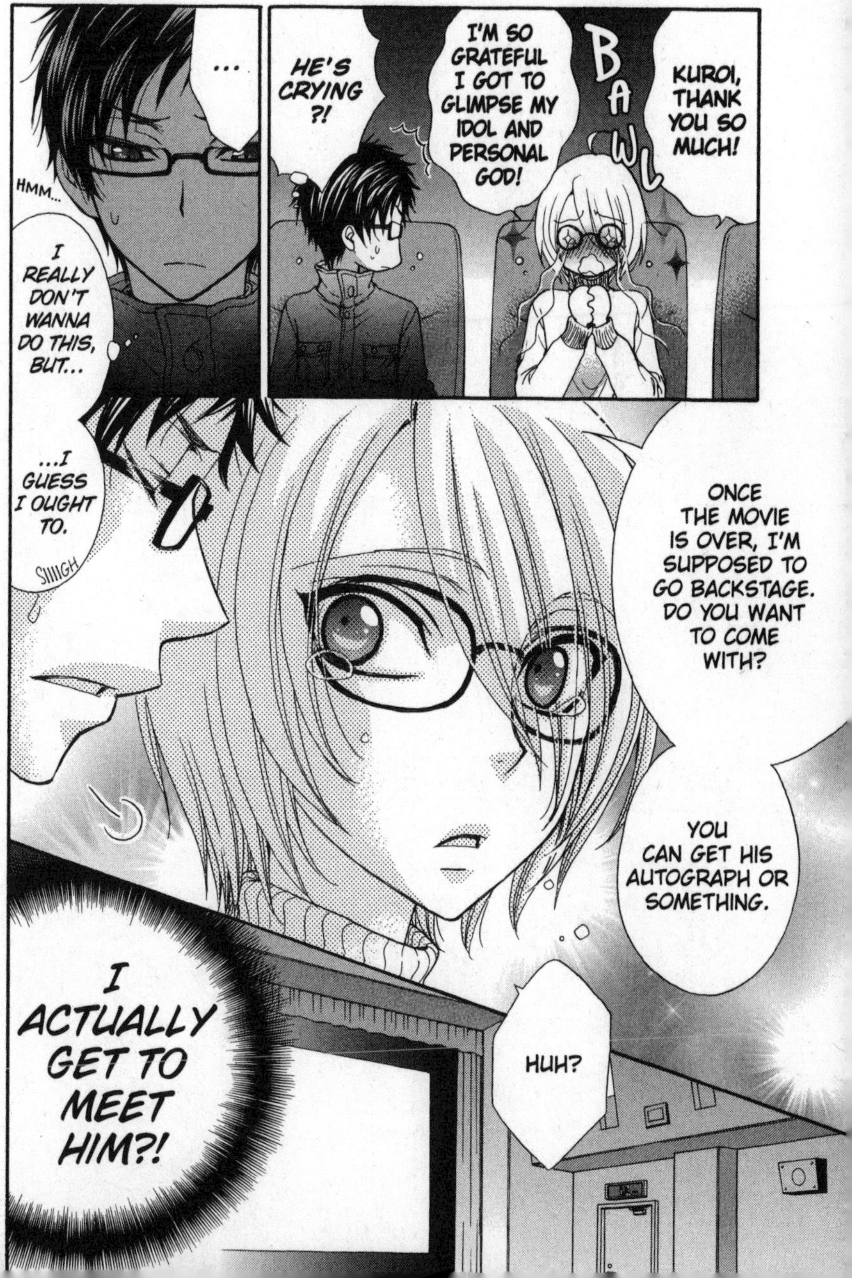
KUROI, THANK YOU SO MUCH!
BAWL
I'M SO GRATEFUL I GOT TO GLIMPSE MY IDOL AND PERSONAL GOD!
HE'S CRYING?!
...
HMM...
I REALLY DON'T WANNA DO THIS, BUT...
ONCE THE MOVIE IS OVER, I'M SUPPOSED TO GO BACKSTAGE. DO YOU WANT TO COME WITH?
YOU CAN GET HIS AUTOGRAPH OR SOMETHING.
...I GUESS I OUGHT TO.
SIIIGH
HUH?
I ACTUALLY GET TO MEET HIM?!

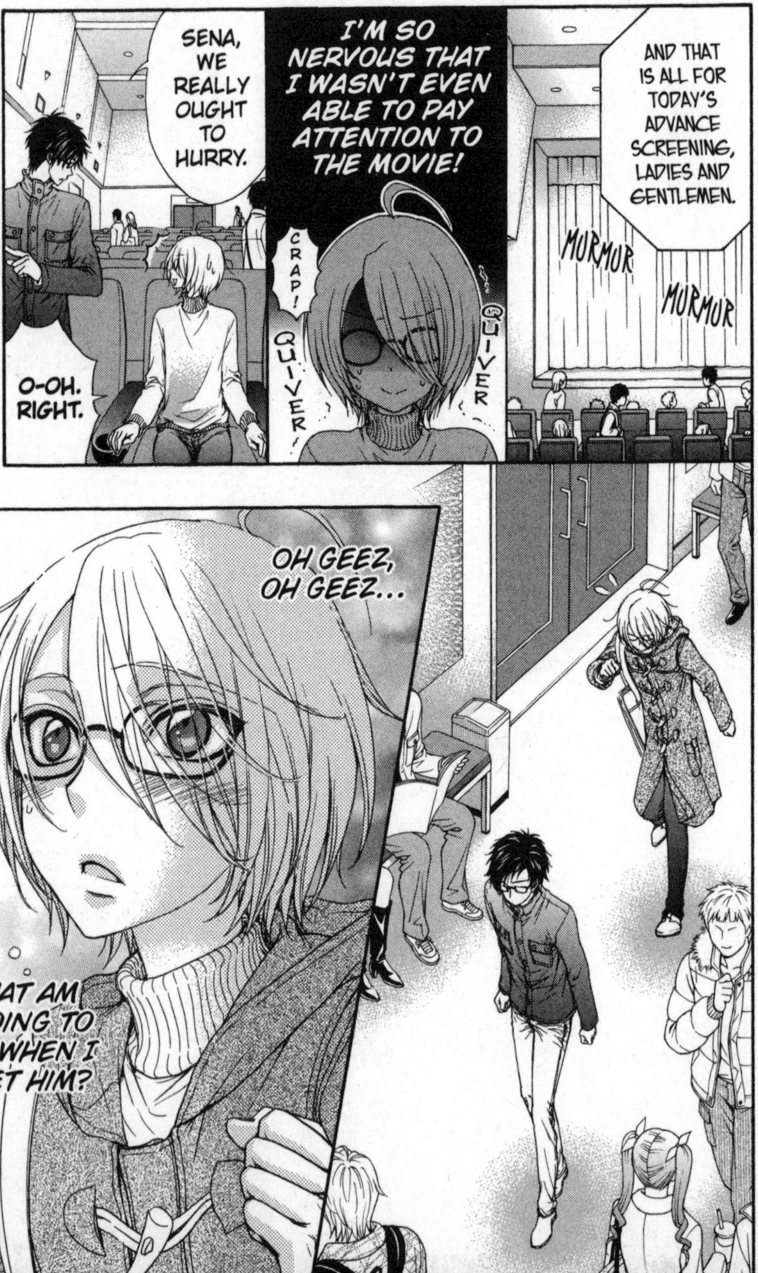
AND THAT IS ALL FOR TODAY'S ADVANCE SCREENING, LADIES AND GENTLEMEN.
MURMUR
MURMUR
I'M SO NERVOUS THAT I WASN'T EVEN ABLE TO PAY ATTENTION TO THE MOVIE!
QUIVER
CRAP!
QUIVER
SENA, WE REALLY OUGHT TO HURRY.
O-OH. RIGHT.
OH GEEZ, OH GEEZ...
WHAT AM I GOING TO SAY WHEN I MEET HIM?

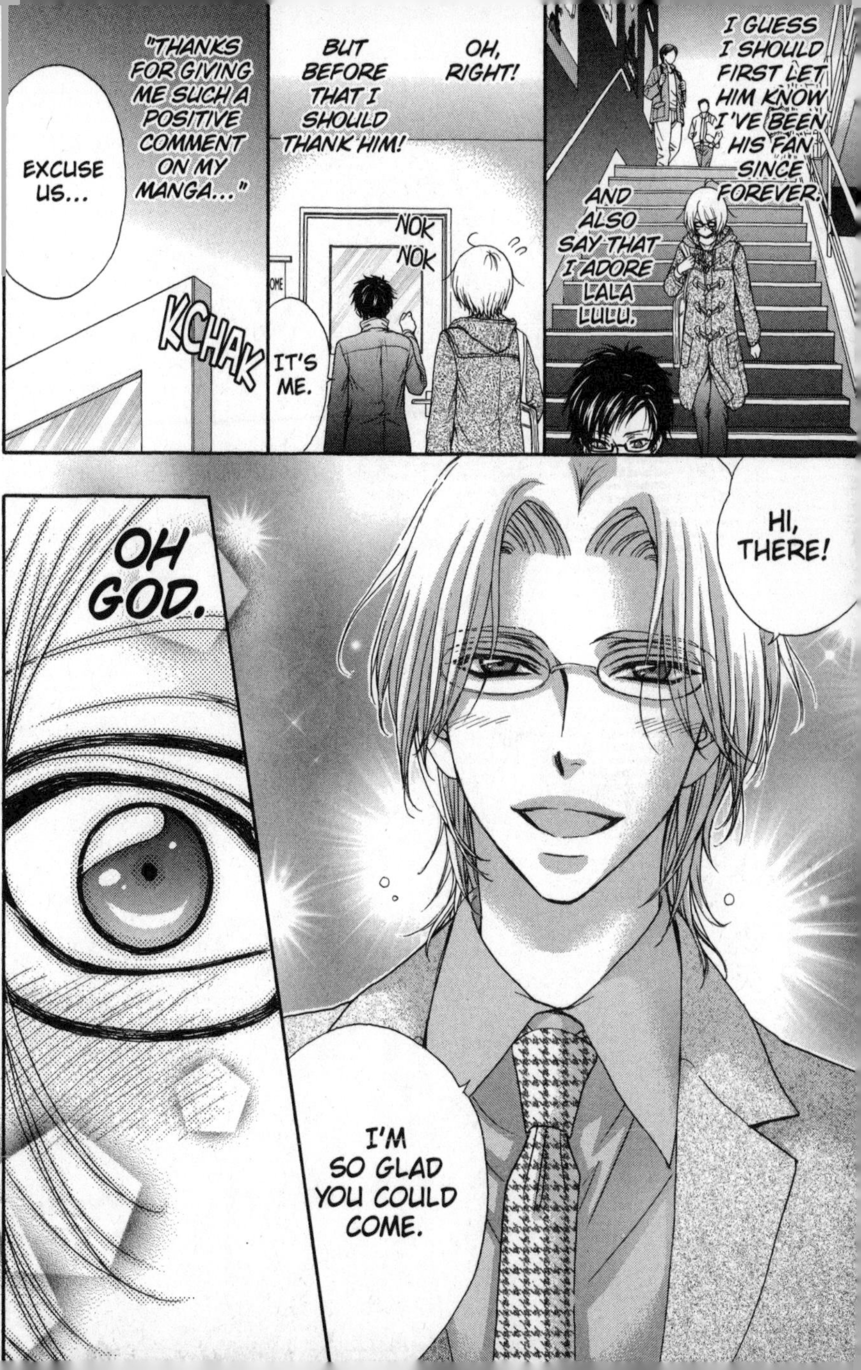
I GUESS I SHOULD FIRST LET HIM KNOW I'VE BEEN HIS FAN SINCE FOREVER.
AND ALSO SAY THAT I ADORE LALA LULU.
OH, RIGHT!
BUT BEFORE THAT I SHOULD THANK HIM!
NOK NOK
IT'S ME.
"THANKS FOR GIVING ME SUCH A POSITIVE COMMENT ON MY MANGA..."
EXCUSE US...
KCHAK
HI, THERE!
I'M SO GLAD YOU COULD COME.
OH GOD.

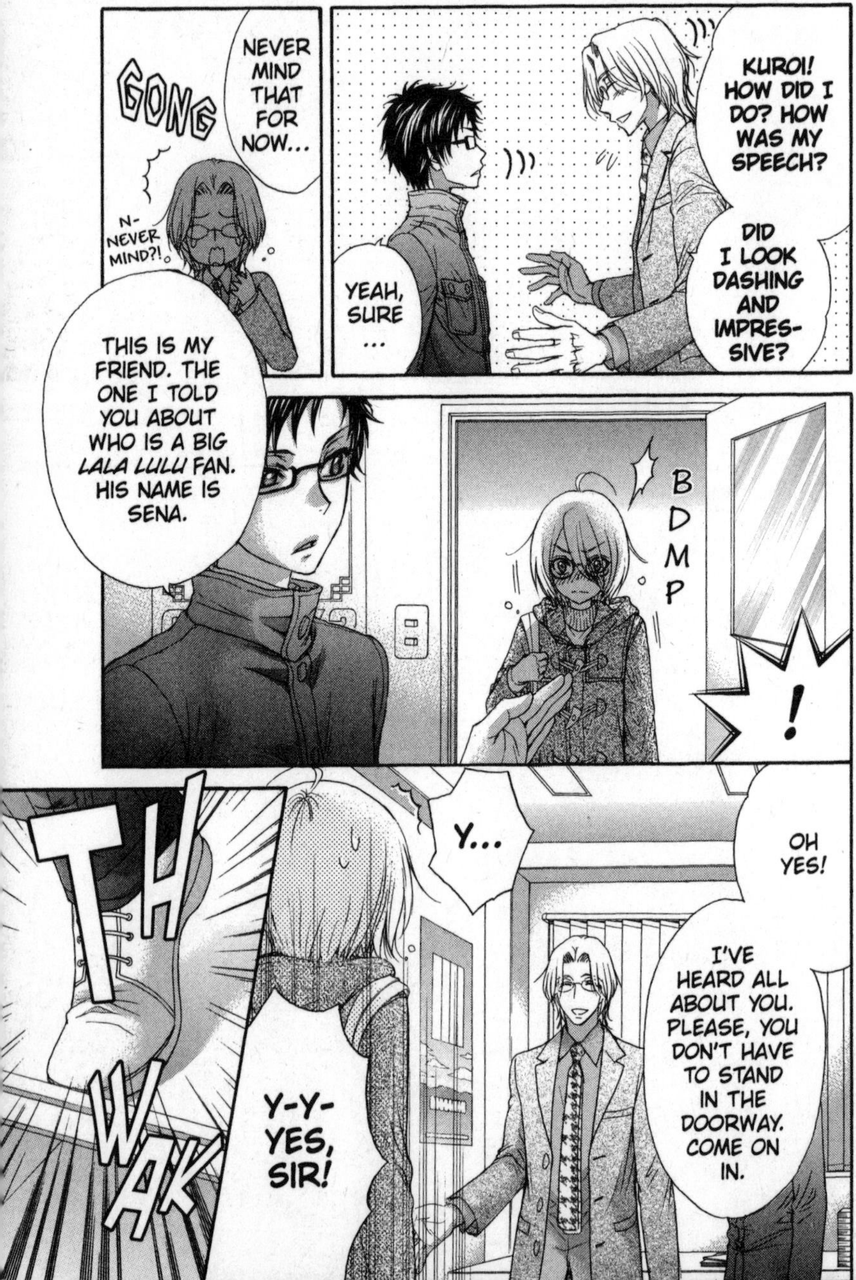
KUROI! HOW DID I DO? HOW WAS MY SPEECH?
DID I LOOK DASHING AND IMPRES-SIVE?
YEAH, SURE...
NEVER MIND THAT FOR NOW...
GONG
N-NEVER MIND?!
BDMP
!
THIS IS MY FRIEND. THE ONE I TOLD YOU ABOUT WHO IS A BIG *LALA LULU* FAN. HIS NAME IS SENA.
OH YES!
I'VE HEARD ALL ABOUT YOU. PLEASE, YOU DON'T HAVE TO STAND IN THE DOORWAY. COME ON IN.
Y...
Y-Y-YES, SIR!
THWAK

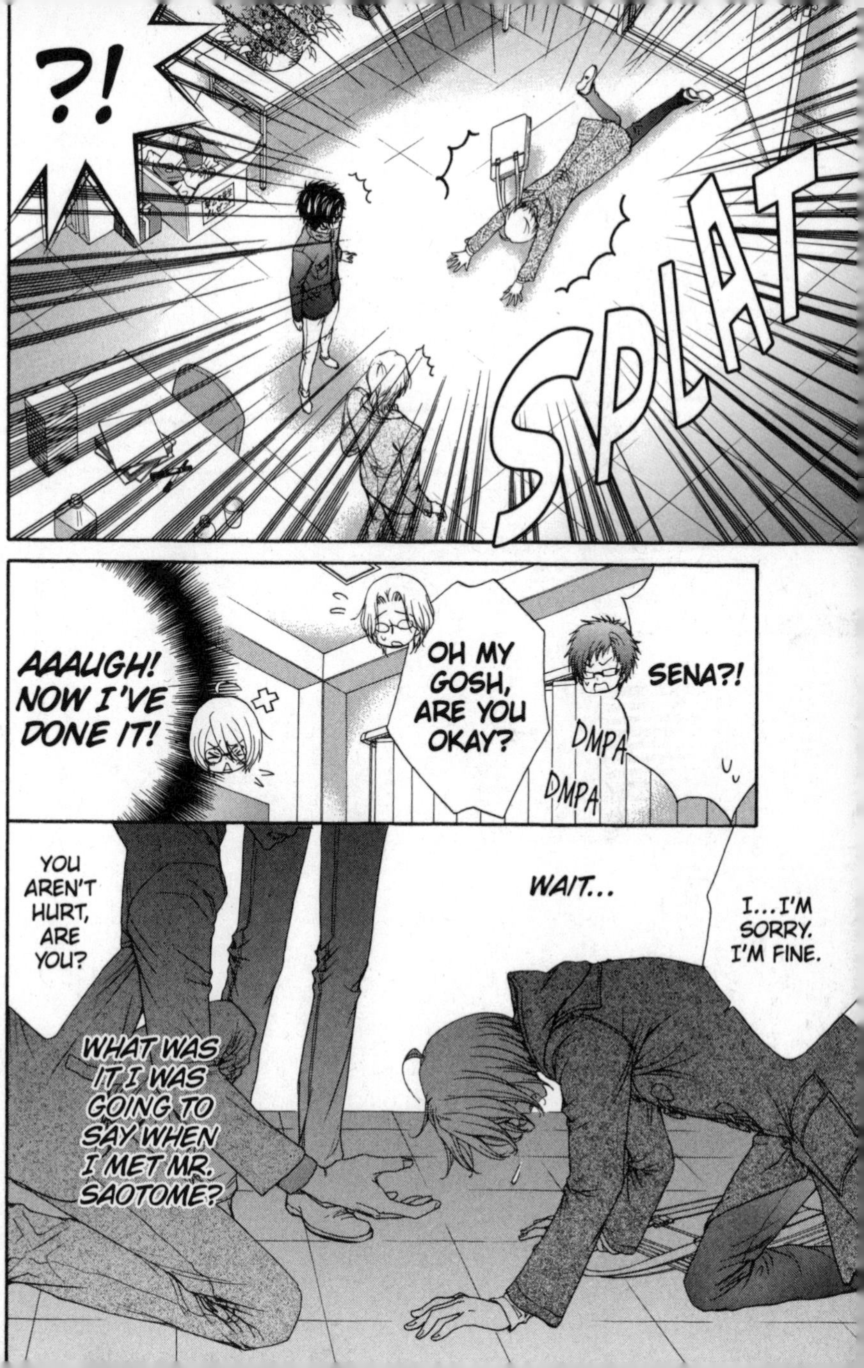
SPLAT
?!
SENA?!
DMPA
DMPA
OH MY GOSH, ARE YOU OKAY?
AAAUGH! NOW I'VE DONE IT!
I...I'M SORRY. I'M FINE.
WAIT...
YOU AREN'T HURT, ARE YOU?
WHAT WAS IT I WAS GOING TO SAY WHEN I MET MR. SAOTOME?

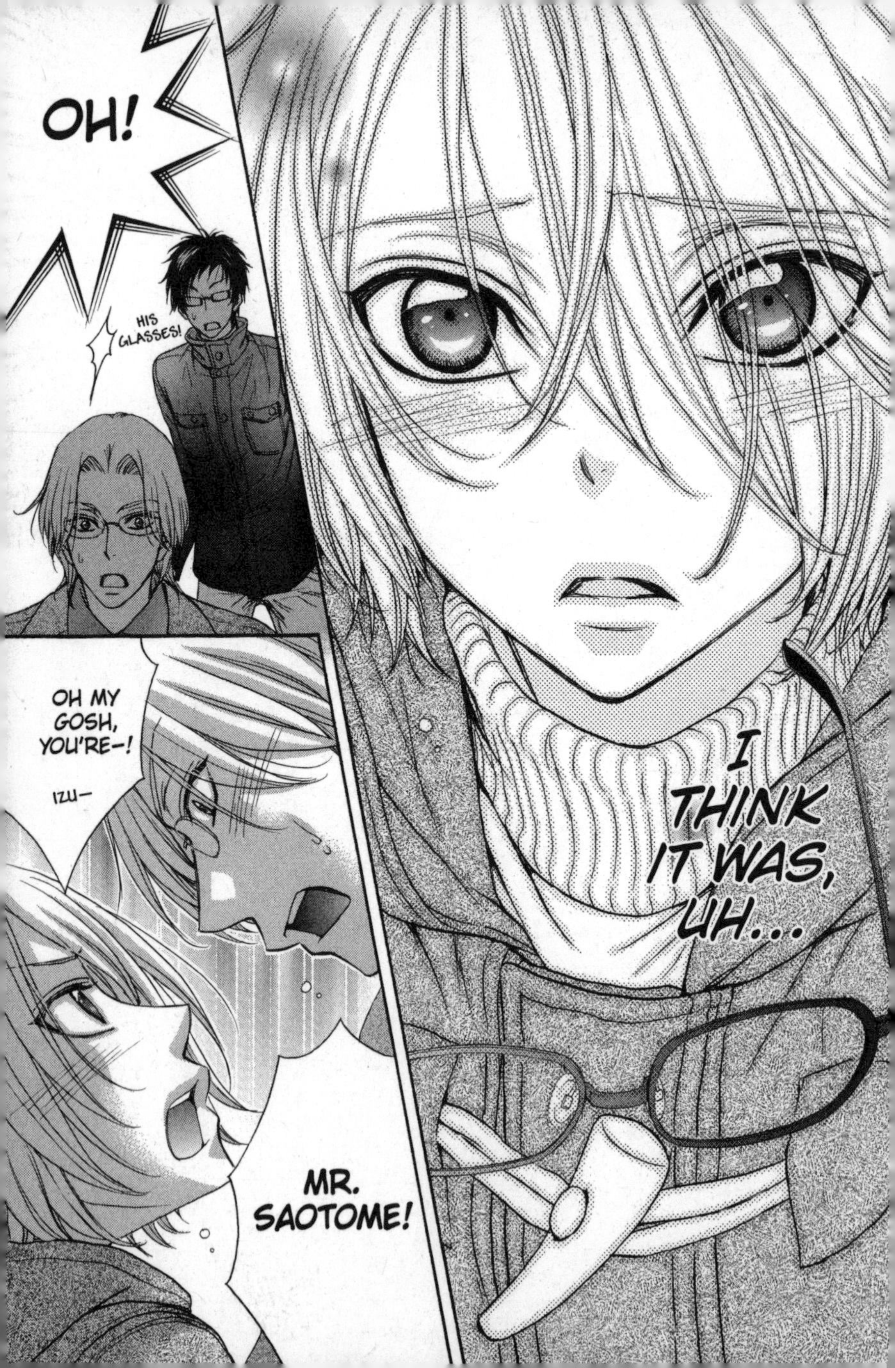
I THINK IT WAS, UH...
OH!
HIS GLASSES!
OH MY GOSH, YOU'RE-!
IZU-
MR. SAOTOME!

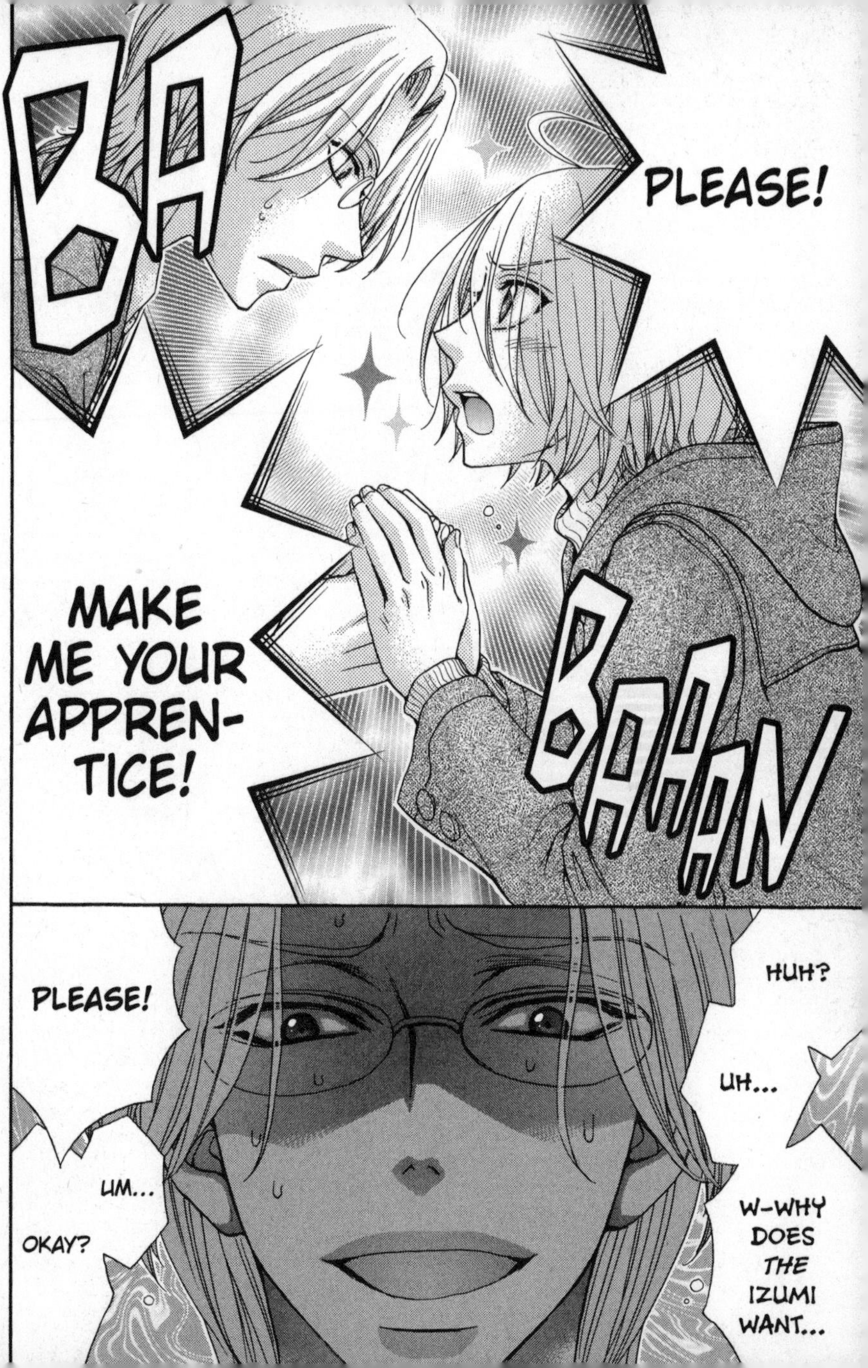
PLEASE!
BA
MAKE ME YOUR APPREN-TICE!
BAAAN
HUH?
UH...
W-WHY DOES THE IZUMI WANT...
PLEASE!
UM...
OKAY?

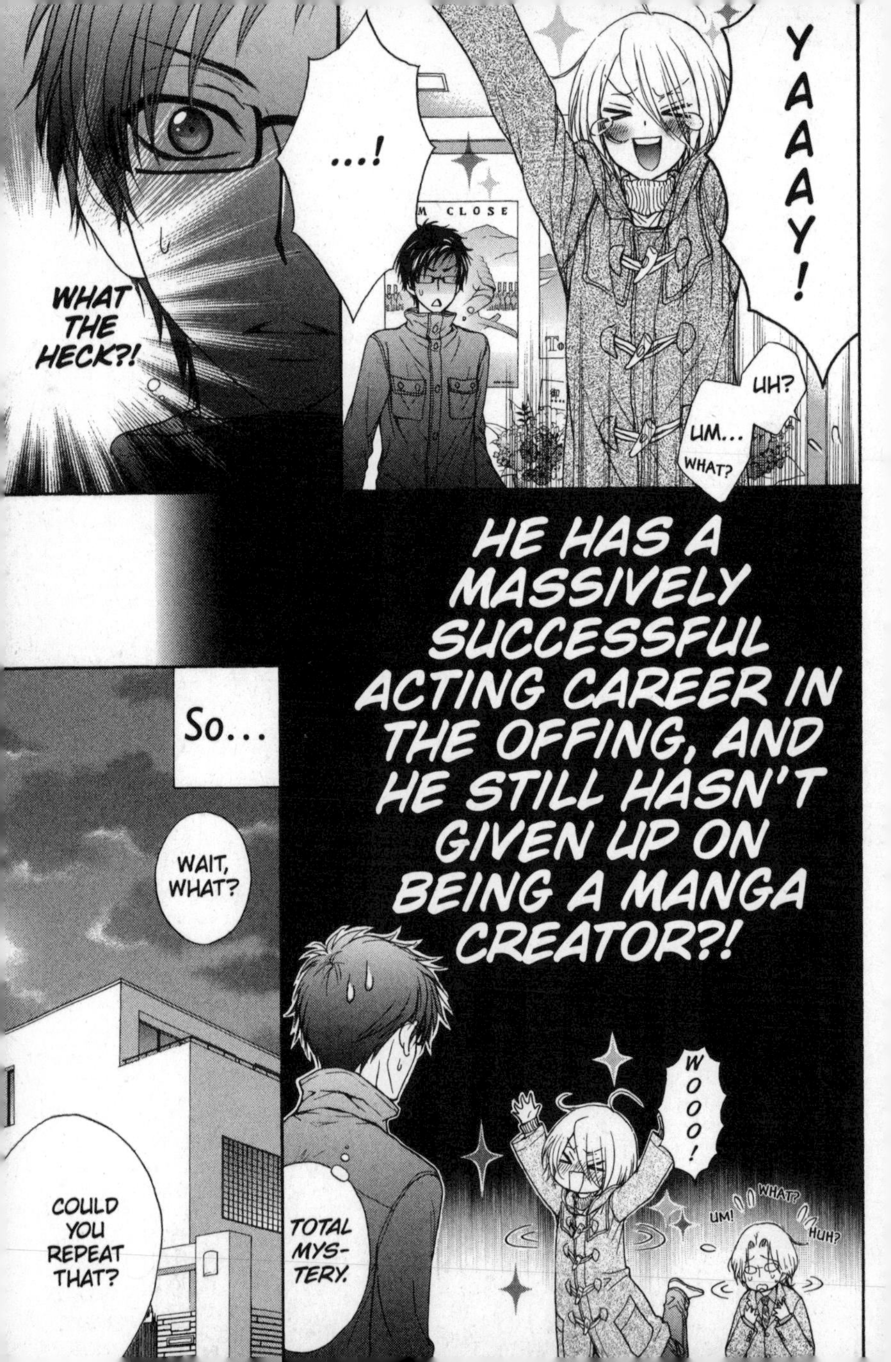
YAAAAY!
...!
UH?
UM... WHAT?
WHAT THE HECK?!
HE HAS A MASSIVELY SUCCESSFUL ACTING CAREER IN THE OFFING, AND HE STILL HASN'T GIVEN UP ON BEING A MANGA CREATOR?!
WOOOO!
WHAT?
UM!
HUH?
TOTAL MYS- TERY.
So...
WAIT, WHAT?
COULD YOU REPEAT THAT?

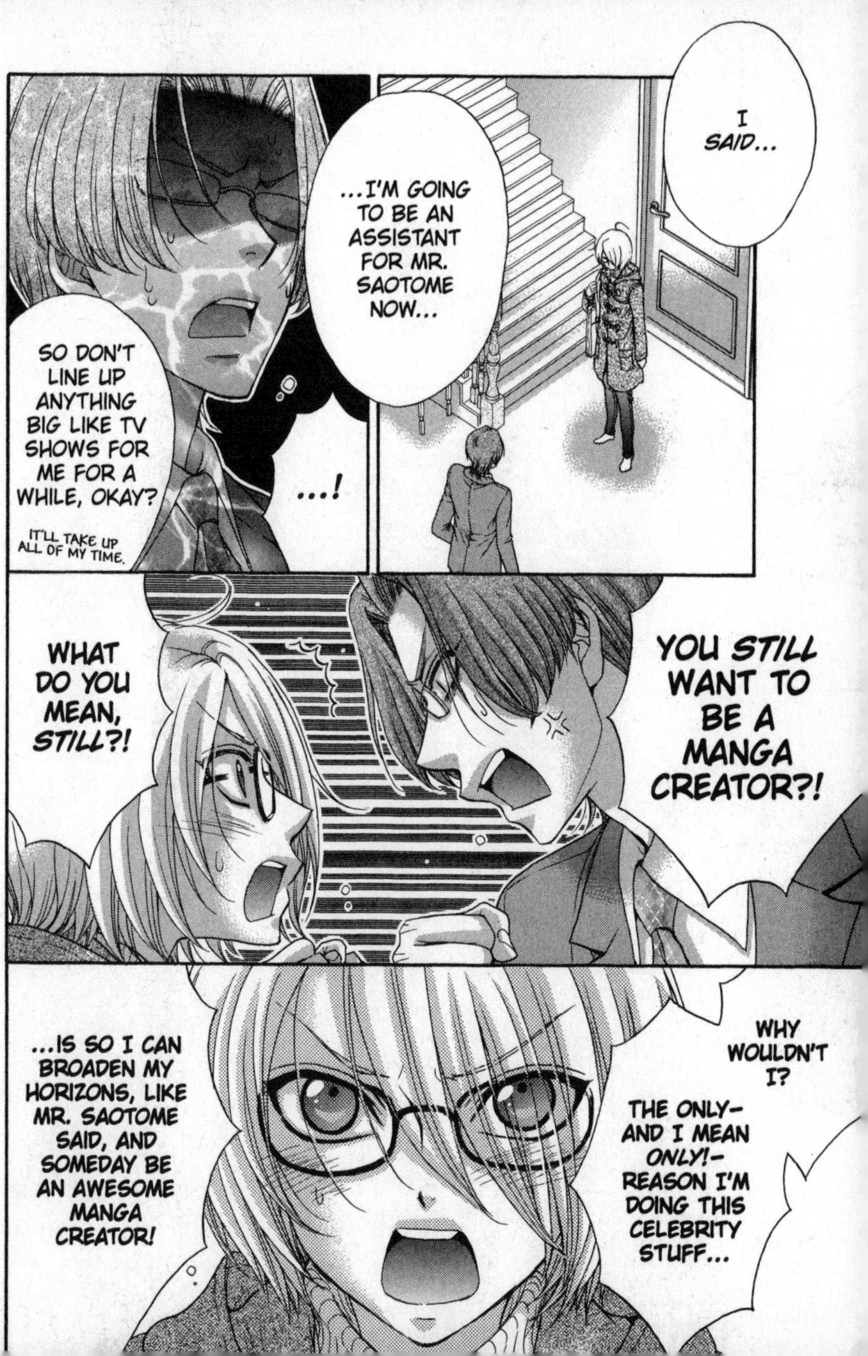
I SAID...
...I'M GOING TO BE AN ASSISTANT FOR MR. SAOTOME NOW...
SO DON'T LINE UP ANYTHING BIG LIKE TV SHOWS FOR ME FOR A WHILE, OKAY?
IT'LL TAKE UP ALL OF MY TIME.
...!
YOU *STILL* WANT TO BE A MANGA CREATOR?!
WHAT DO YOU MEAN, *STILL*?!
WHY WOULDN'T I?
THE ONLY- AND I MEAN *ONLY*!- REASON I'M DOING THIS CELEBRITY STUFF...
...IS SO I CAN BROADEN MY HORIZONS, LIKE MR. SAOTOME SAID, AND SOMEDAY BE AN AWESOME MANGA CREATOR!

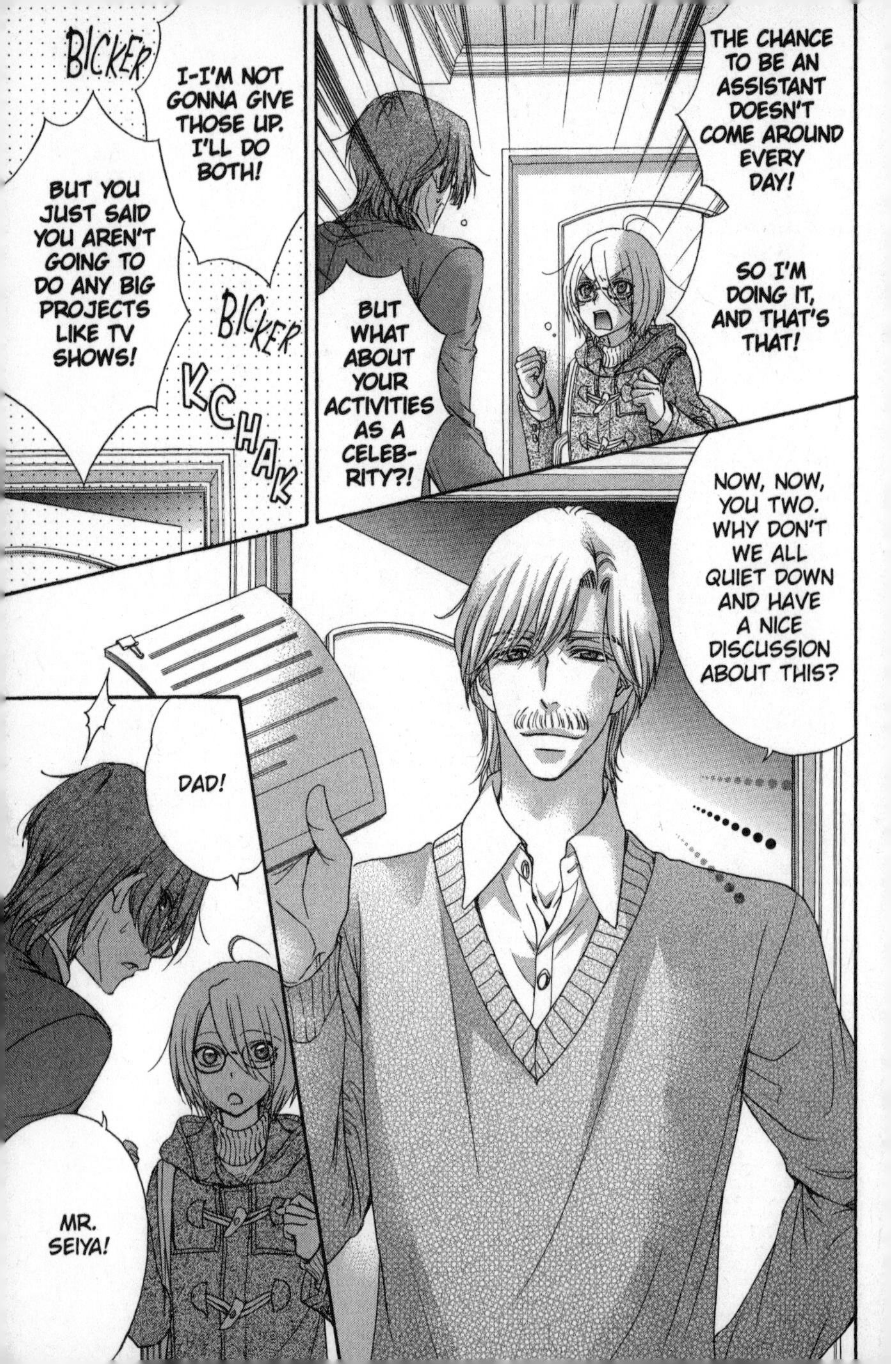
THE CHANCE TO BE AN ASSISTANT DOESN'T COME AROUND EVERY DAY!
SO I'M DOING IT, AND THAT'S THAT!
BUT WHAT ABOUT YOUR ACTIVITIES AS A CELEB-RITY?!
BICKER
I-I'M NOT GONNA GIVE THOSE UP. I'LL DO BOTH!
BUT YOU JUST SAID YOU AREN'T GOING TO DO ANY BIG PROJECTS LIKE TV SHOWS!
BICKER
KCHAK
NOW, NOW, YOU TWO. WHY DON'T WE ALL QUIET DOWN AND HAVE A NICE DISCUSSION ABOUT THIS?
DAD!
MR. SEIYA!

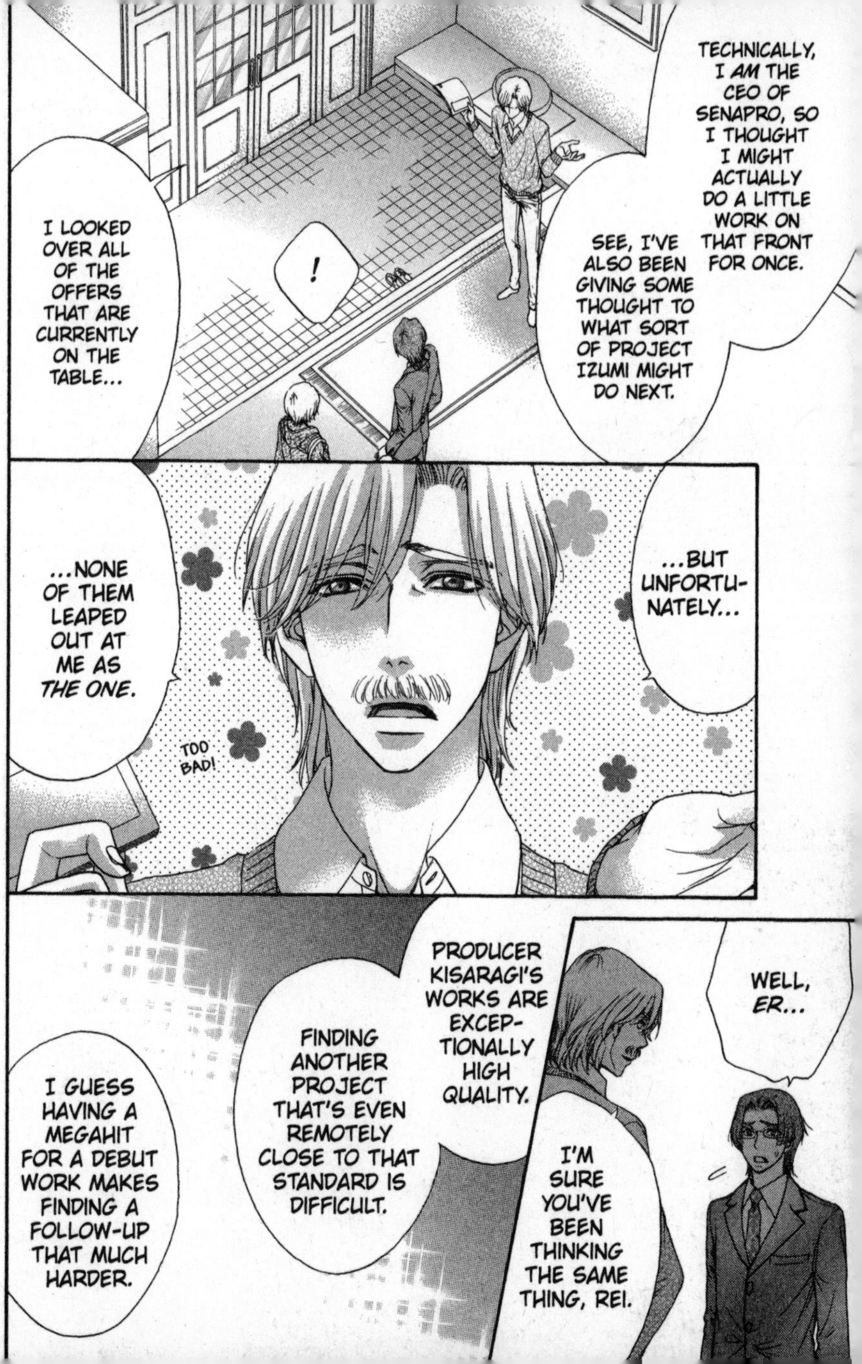
TECHNICALLY, I *AM* THE CEO OF SENAPRO, SO I THOUGHT I MIGHT ACTUALLY DO A LITTLE WORK ON THAT FRONT FOR ONCE.
SEE, I'VE ALSO BEEN GIVING SOME THOUGHT TO WHAT SORT OF PROJECT IZUMI MIGHT DO NEXT.
!
I LOOKED OVER ALL OF THE OFFERS THAT ARE CURRENTLY ON THE TABLE...
...BUT UNFORTUNATELY...
...NONE OF THEM LEAPED OUT AT ME AS *THE ONE*.
TOO BAD!
PRODUCER KISARAGI'S WORKS ARE EXCEPTIONALLY HIGH QUALITY.
FINDING ANOTHER PROJECT THAT'S EVEN REMOTELY CLOSE TO THAT STANDARD IS DIFFICULT.
I GUESS HAVING A MEGAHIT FOR A DEBUT WORK MAKES FINDING A FOLLOW-UP THAT MUCH HARDER.
I'M SURE YOU'VE BEEN THINKING THE SAME THING, REI.
WELL, ER...

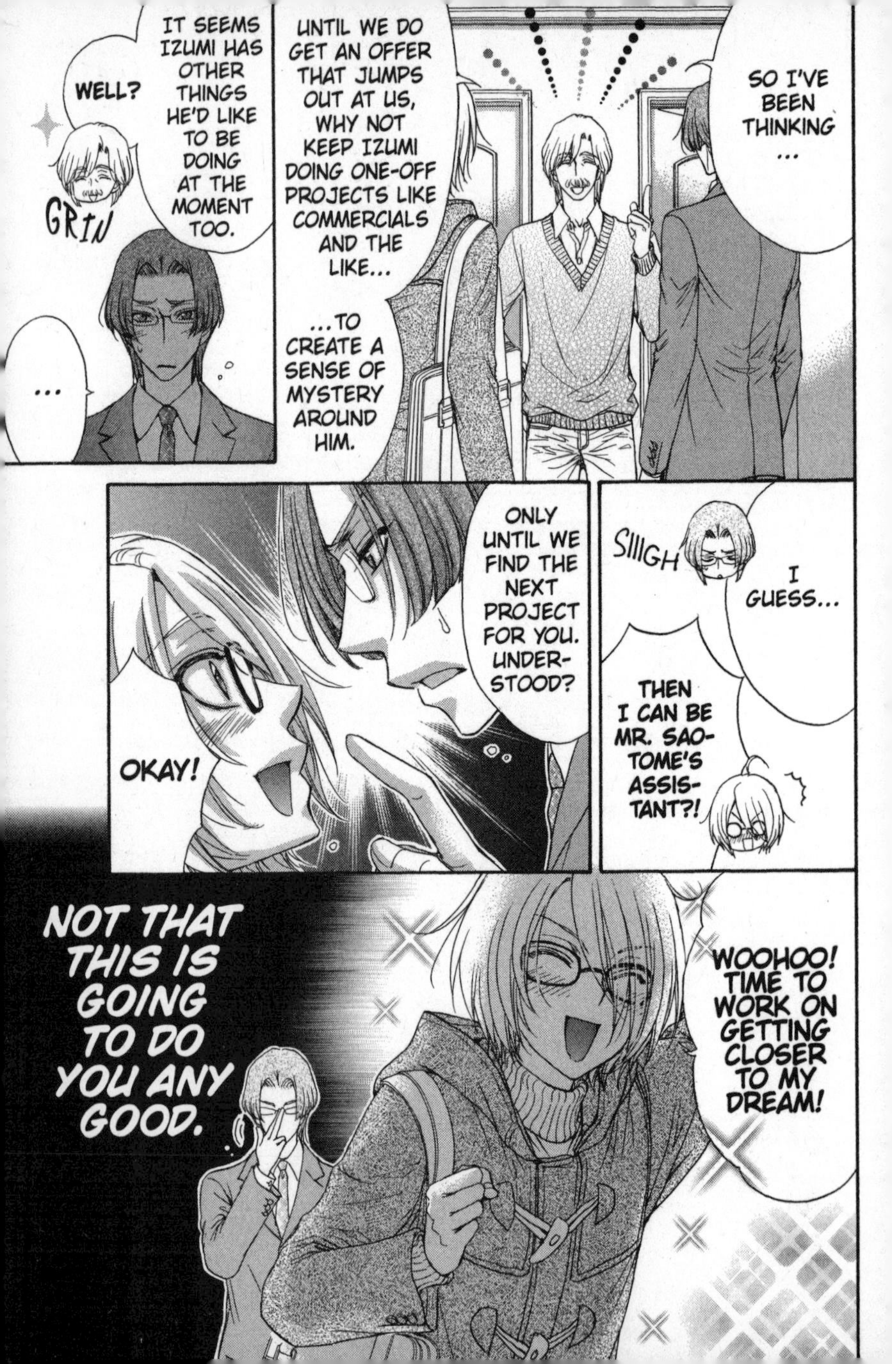
SO I'VE BEEN THINKING...
UNTIL WE DO GET AN OFFER THAT JUMPS OUT AT US, WHY NOT KEEP IZUMI DOING ONE-OFF PROJECTS LIKE COMMERCIALS AND THE LIKE...
...TO CREATE A SENSE OF MYSTERY AROUND HIM.
IT SEEMS IZUMI HAS OTHER THINGS HE'D LIKE TO BE DOING AT THE MOMENT TOO.
WELL?
GRIN
...
SIIIGH
I GUESS...
THEN I CAN BE MR. SAOTOME'S ASSISTANT?!
ONLY UNTIL WE FIND THE NEXT PROJECT FOR YOU. UNDERSTOOD?
OKAY!
WOOHOO! TIME TO WORK ON GETTING CLOSER TO MY DREAM!
NOT THAT THIS IS GOING TO DO YOU ANY GOOD.

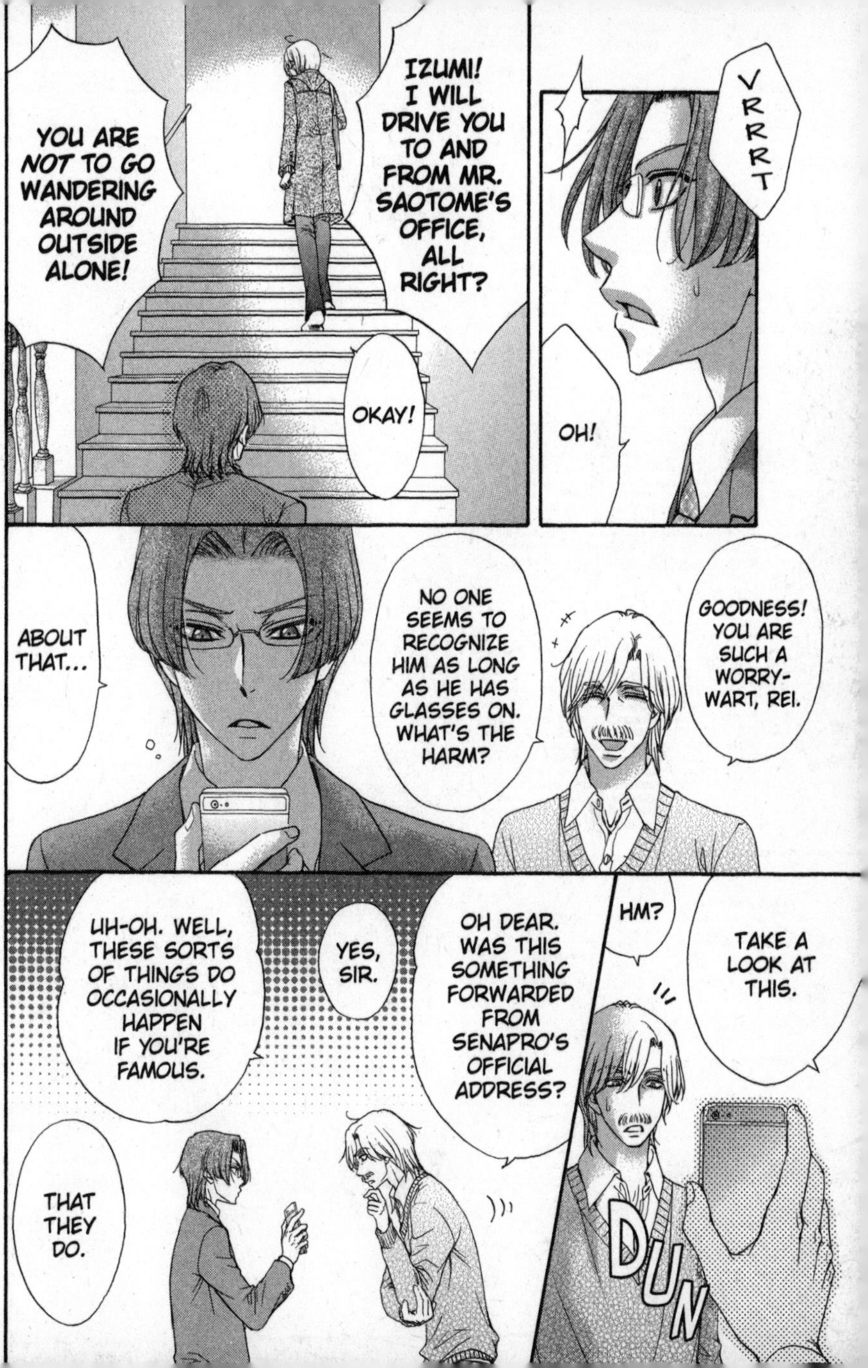
VRRRT
OH!
IZUMI! I WILL DRIVE YOU TO AND FROM MR. SAOTOME'S OFFICE, ALL RIGHT?
YOU ARE NOT TO GO WANDERING AROUND OUTSIDE ALONE!
OKAY!
GOODNESS! YOU ARE SUCH A WORRY-WART, REI.
NO ONE SEEMS TO RECOGNIZE HIM AS LONG AS HE HAS GLASSES ON. WHAT'S THE HARM?
ABOUT THAT...
HM?
TAKE A LOOK AT THIS.
DUN
OH DEAR. WAS THIS SOMETHING FORWARDED FROM SENAPRO'S OFFICIAL ADDRESS?
YES, SIR.
UH-OH. WELL, THESE SORTS OF THINGS DO OCCASIONALLY HAPPEN IF YOU'RE FAMOUS.
THAT THEY DO.

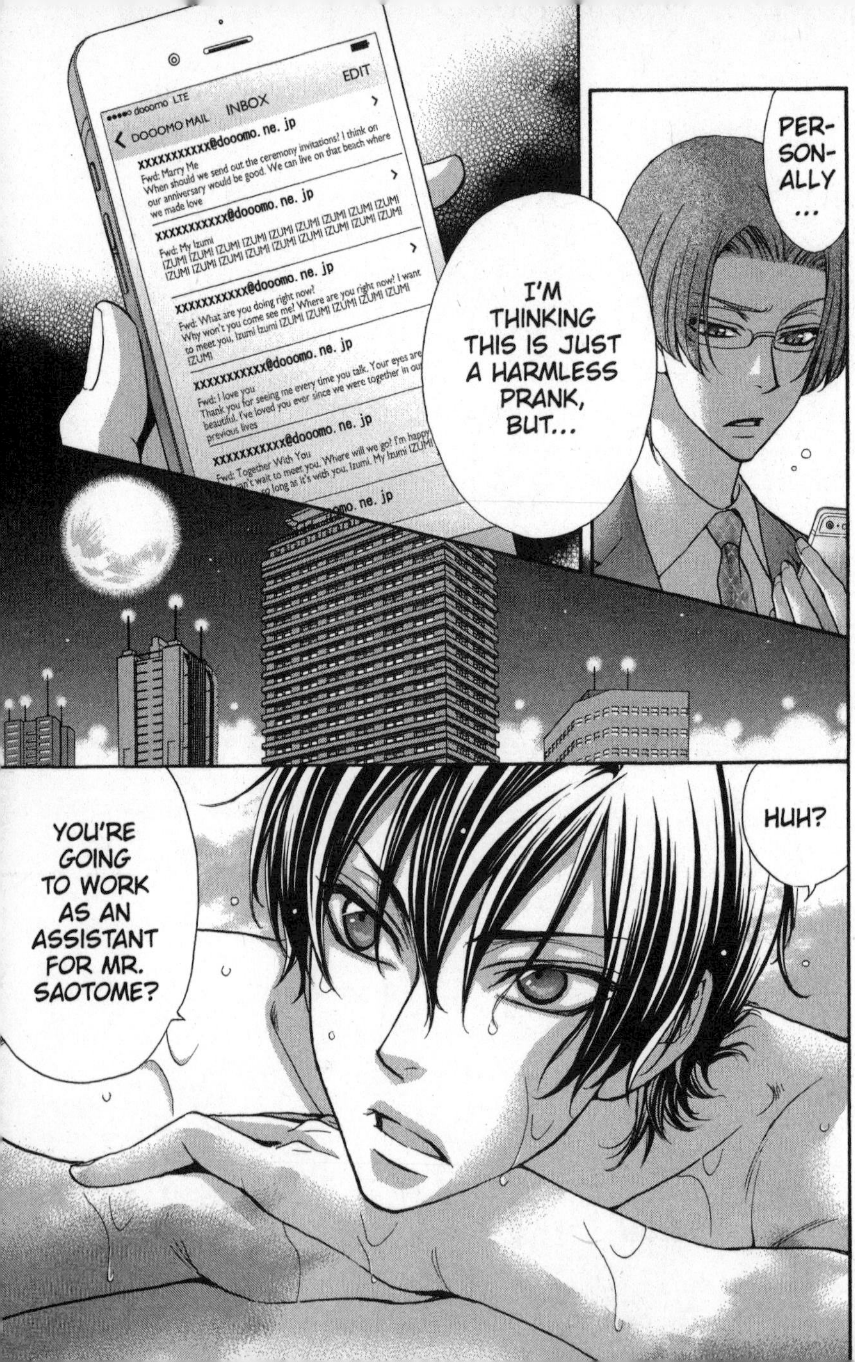
PER-SON-ALLY...
I'M THINKING THIS IS JUST A HARMLESS PRANK, BUT...
●●●●○ dooomo LTE
EDIT
DOOOMO MAIL
INBOX
xxxxxxxxxxx@dooomo. ne. jp
Fwd: Marry Me
When should we send out the ceremony invitations? I think on our anniversary would be good. We can live on that beach where we made love
xxxxxxxxxxx@dooomo. ne. jp
Fwd: My Izumi
IZUMI IZUMI IZUMI IZUMI IZUMI IZUMI IZUMI IZUMI IZUMI IZUMI IZUMI IZUMI IZUMI IZUMI IZUMI IZUMI IZUMI IZUMI IZUMI
xxxxxxxxxxx@dooomo. ne. jp
Fwd: What are you doing right now?
Why won't you come see me? Where are you right now? I want to meet you, Izumi Izumi IZUMI IZUMI IZUMI IZUMI IZUMI IZUMI IZUMI
xxxxxxxxxxx@dooomo. ne. jp
Fwd: I love you
Thank you for seeing me every time you talk. Your eyes are beautiful. I've loved you ever since we were together in our previous lives
xxxxxxxxxxx@dooomo. ne. jp
Fwd: Together With You
HUH?
YOU'RE GOING TO WORK AS AN ASSISTANT FOR MR. SAOTOME?

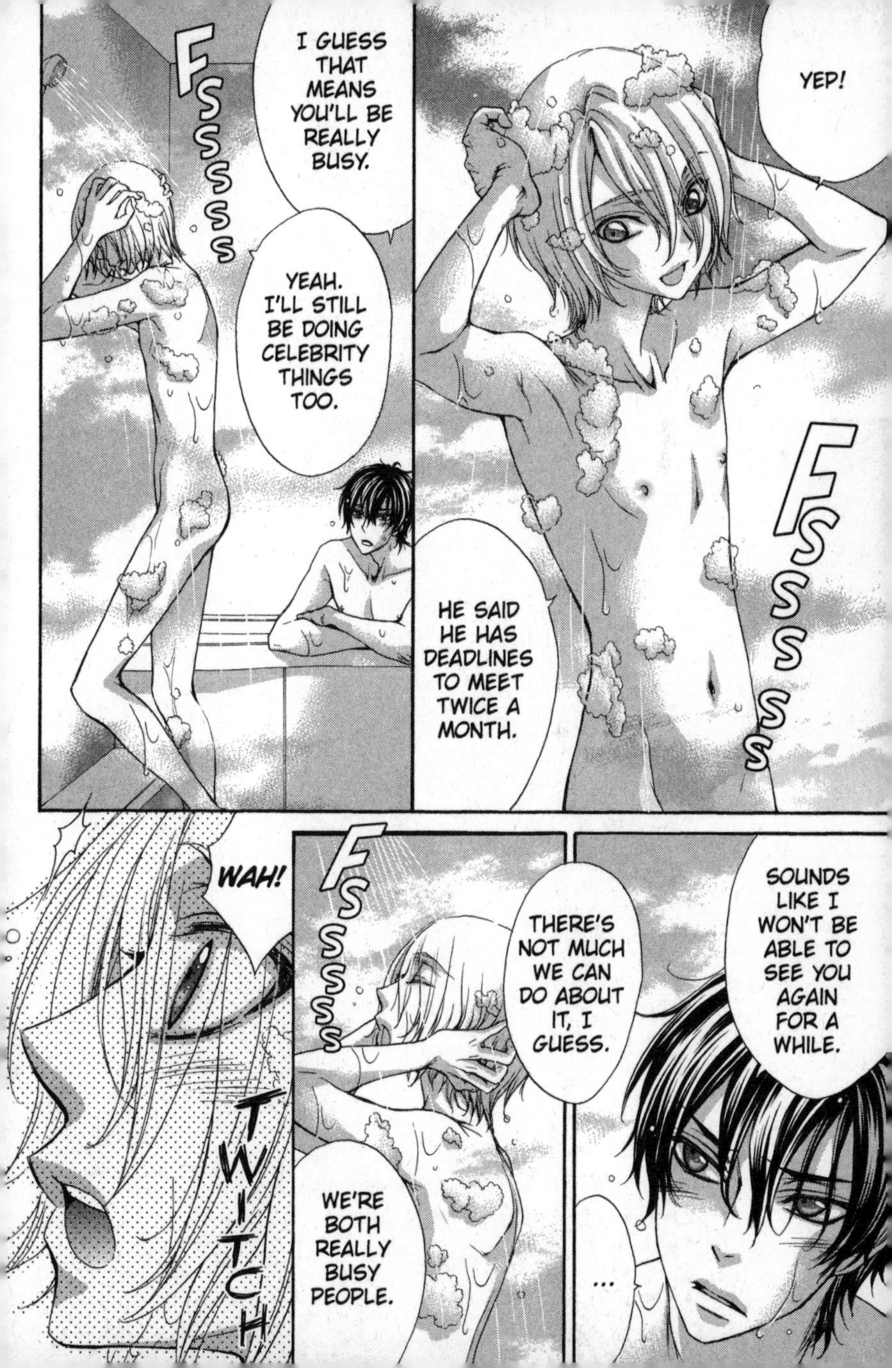
YEP!
HE SAID HE HAS DEADLINES TO MEET TWICE A MONTH.
FSSSSSS
I GUESS THAT MEANS YOU'LL BE REALLY BUSY.
FSSSSSS
YEAH. I'LL STILL BE DOING CELEBRITY THINGS TOO.
SOUNDS LIKE I WON'T BE ABLE TO SEE YOU AGAIN FOR A WHILE.
...
FSSSSS
THERE'S NOT MUCH WE CAN DO ABOUT IT, I GUESS.
WE'RE BOTH REALLY BUSY PEOPLE.
WAH!
TWITCH

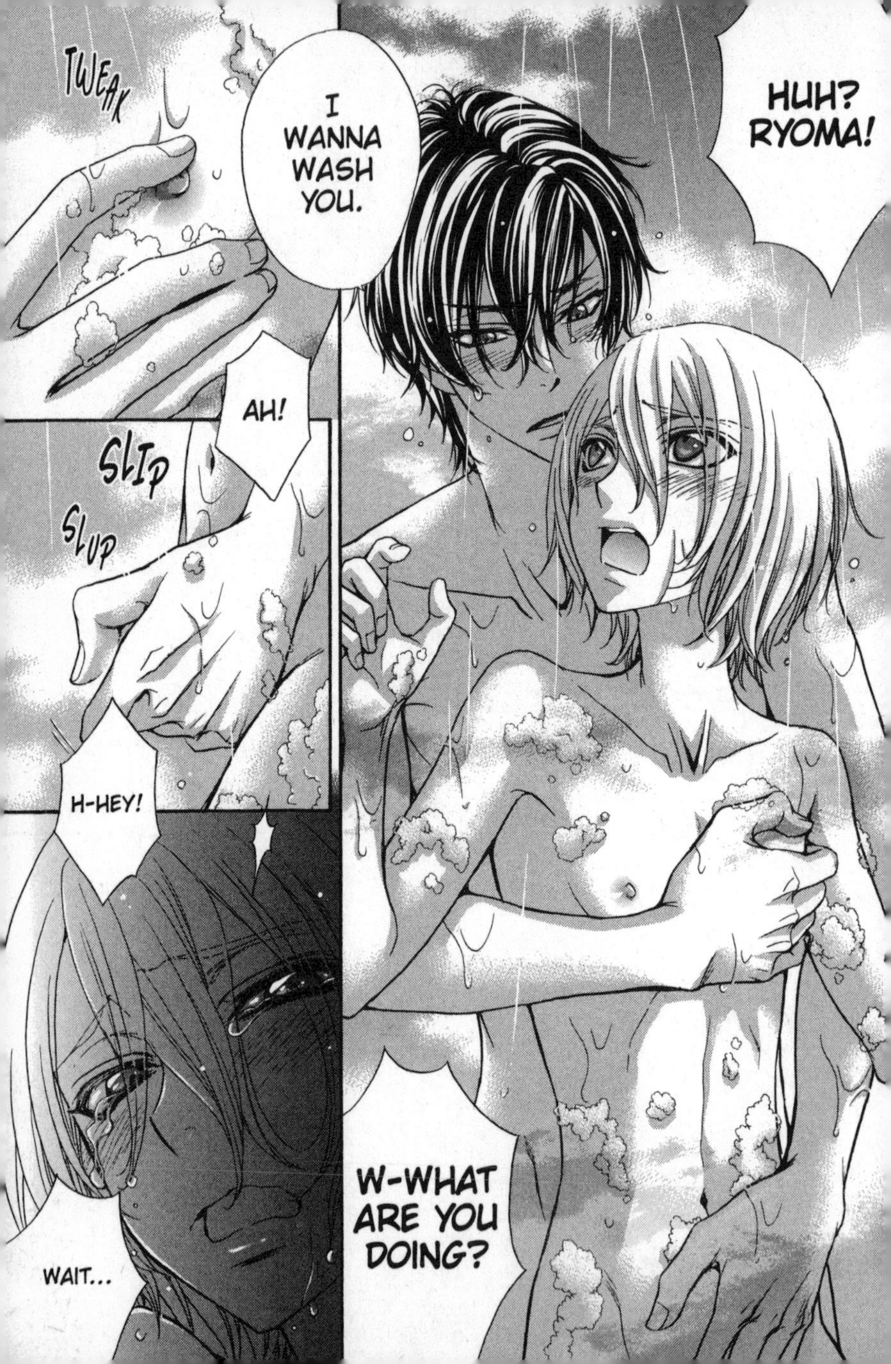
HUH? RYOMA!
I WANNA WASH YOU.
W-WHAT ARE YOU DOING?
TWEAK
AH!
SLIP
SLUP
H-HEY!
WAIT...

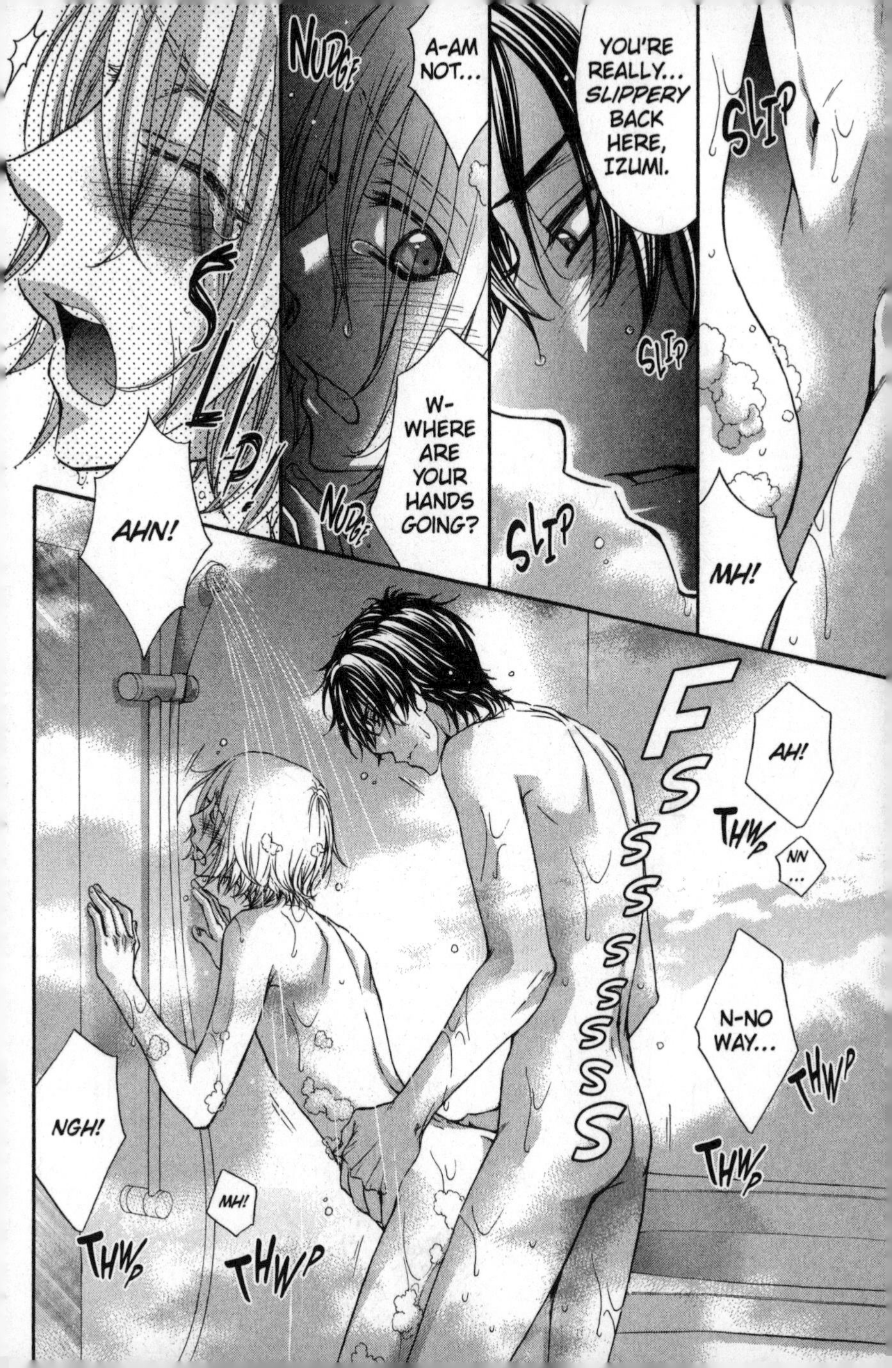
SLIP
MH!
YOU'RE REALLY... SLIPPERY BACK HERE, IZUMI.
SLIP
SLIP
NUDGE
A-AM NOT...
W-WHERE ARE YOUR HANDS GOING?
NUDGE
SLIP
AHN!
FSSSSSSSSS
AH!
THWP
NN...
N-NO WAY...
THWP
THWP
NGH!
MH!
THWP
THWP

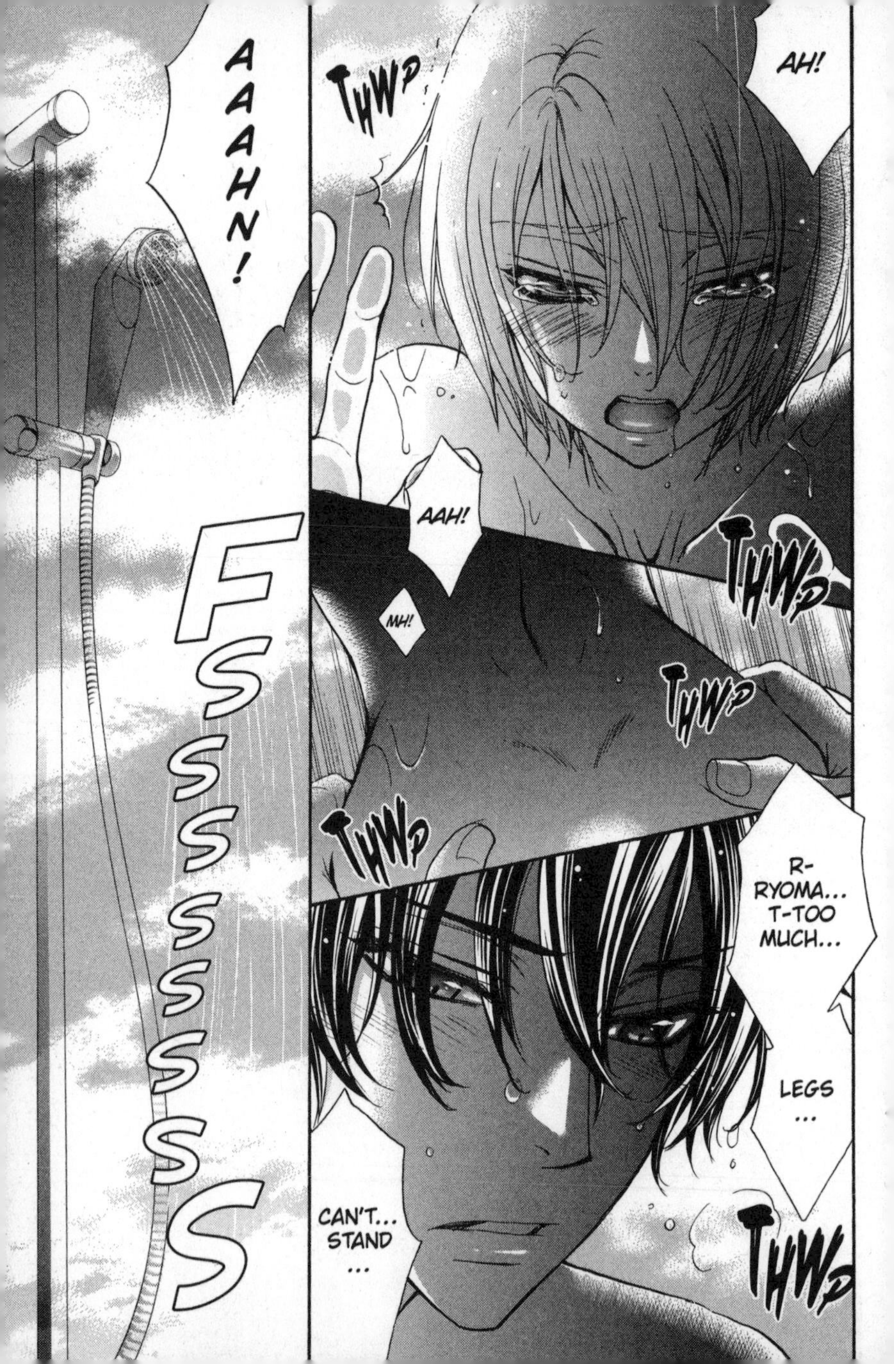
THWP
AH!
AAH!
THWP
MH!
THWP
THWP
R-RYOMA... T-TOO MUCH...
LEGS...
CAN'T... STAND...
THWP
AAAAHN!
FSSSSSSSS

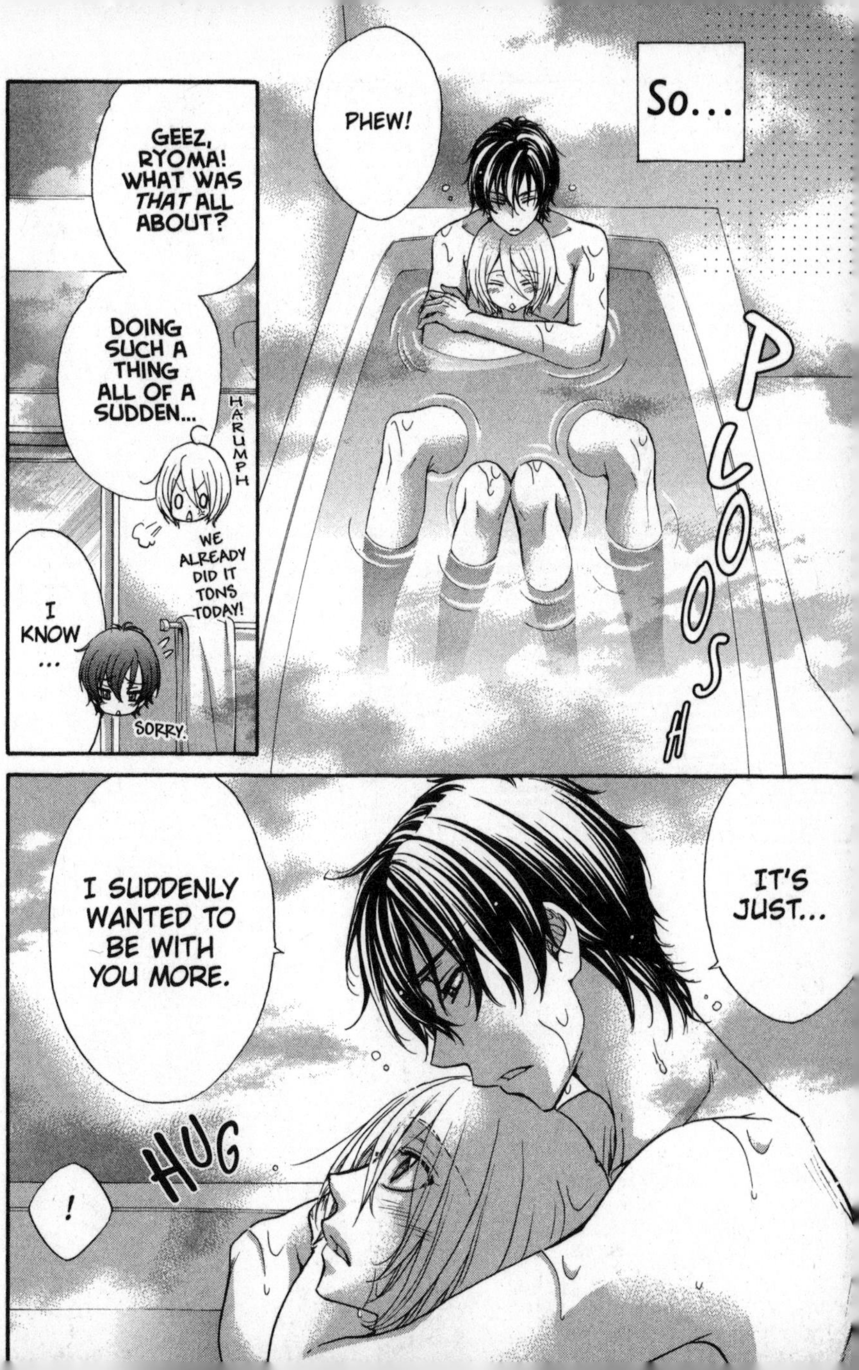
So...
PHEW!
PLOOSH
GEEZ, RYOMA! WHAT WAS *THAT* ALL ABOUT?
DOING SUCH A THING ALL OF A SUDDEN...
HARUMPH
WE ALREADY DID IT TONS TODAY!
I KNOW ...
SORRY.
IT'S JUST...
I SUDDENLY WANTED TO BE WITH YOU MORE.
HUG
!

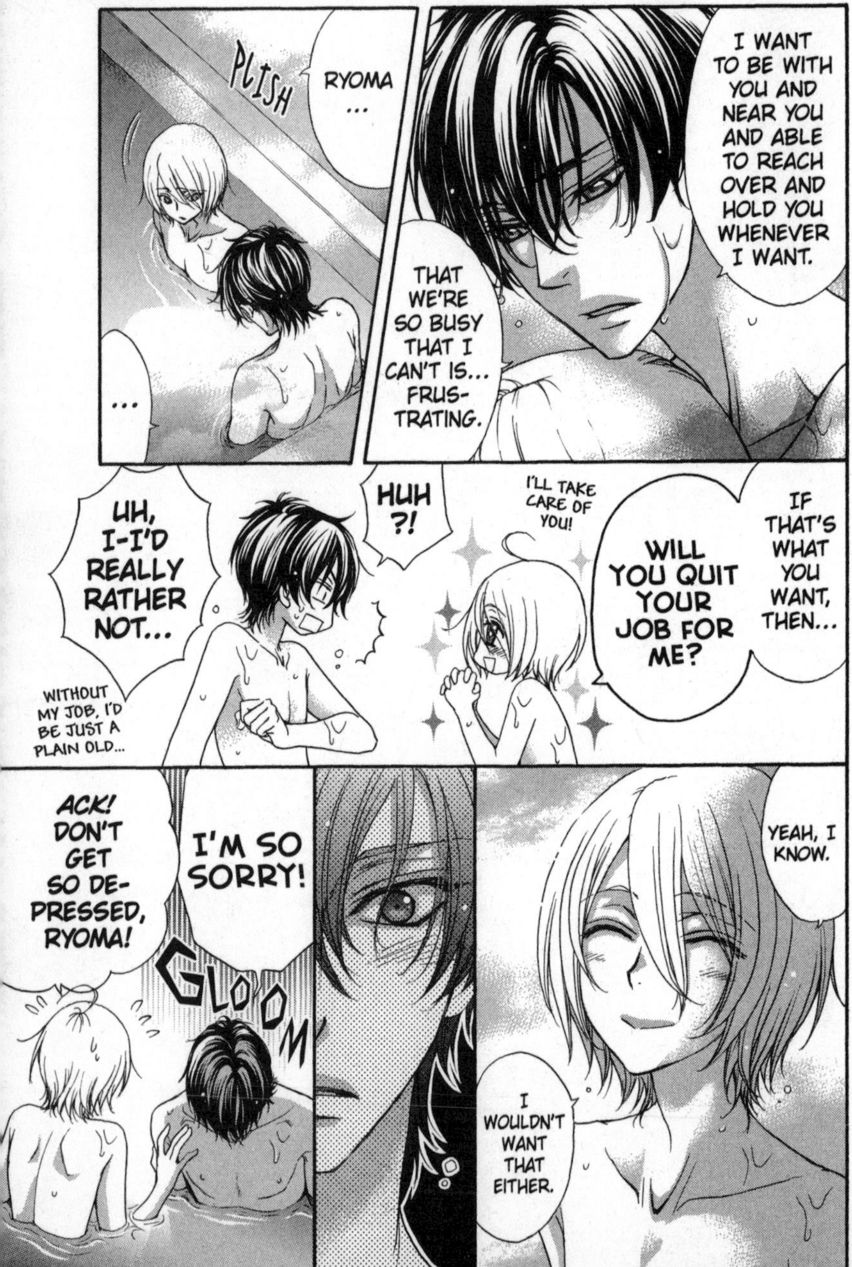
I WANT TO BE WITH YOU AND NEAR YOU AND ABLE TO REACH OVER AND HOLD YOU WHENEVER I WANT.
THAT WE'RE SO BUSY THAT I CAN'T IS... FRUS-TRATING.
PLISH
RYOMA ...
...
IF THAT'S WHAT YOU WANT, THEN...
WILL YOU QUIT YOUR JOB FOR ME?
I'LL TAKE CARE OF YOU!
HUH ?!
UH, I-I'D REALLY RATHER NOT...
WITHOUT MY JOB, I'D BE JUST A PLAIN OLD...
YEAH, I KNOW.
I WOULDN'T WANT THAT EITHER.
I'M SO SORRY!
ACK! DON'T GET SO DE-PRESSED, RYOMA!
GLOOM

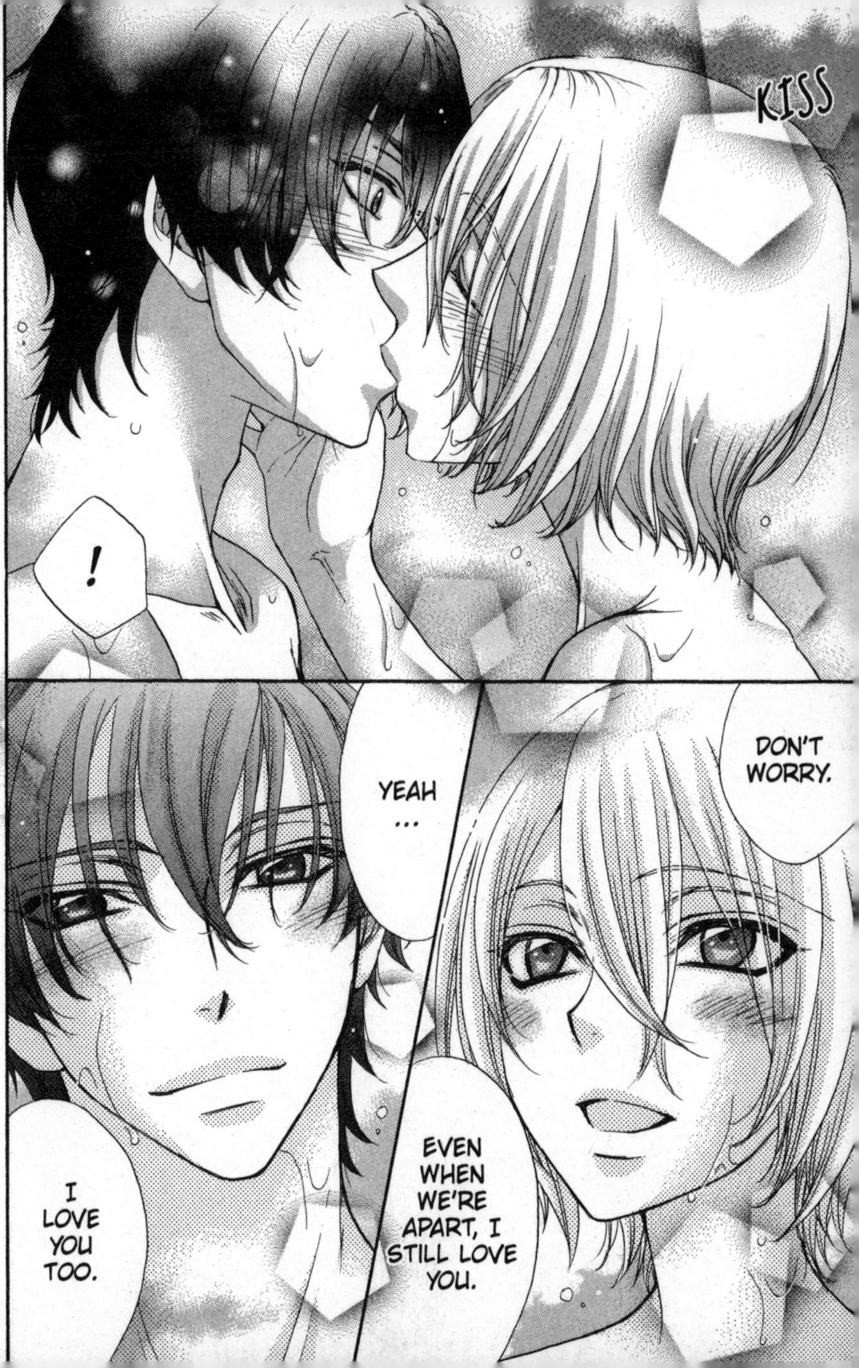
KISS
!
DON'T WORRY.
EVEN WHEN WE'RE APART, I STILL LOVE YOU.
YEAH ...
I LOVE YOU TOO.

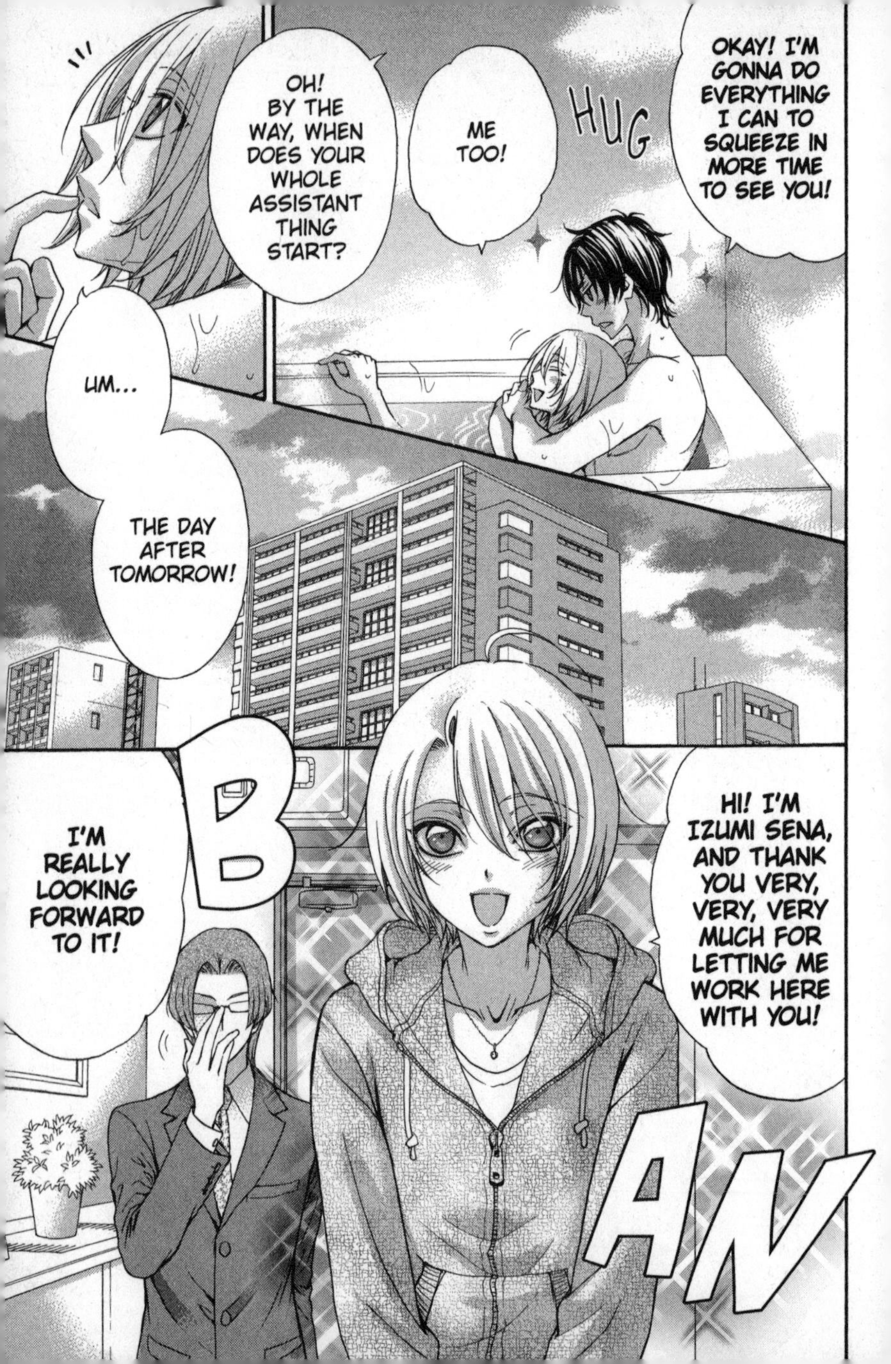

OKAY! I'M GONNA DO EVERYTHING I CAN TO SQUEEZE IN MORE TIME TO SEE YOU!
HUG
ME TOO!
OH! BY THE WAY, WHEN DOES YOUR WHOLE ASSISTANT THING START?
UM...
THE DAY AFTER TOMORROW!
HI! I'M IZUMI SENA, AND THANK YOU VERY, VERY, VERY MUCH FOR LETTING ME WORK HERE WITH YOU!
BAN
I'M REALLY LOOKING FORWARD TO IT!

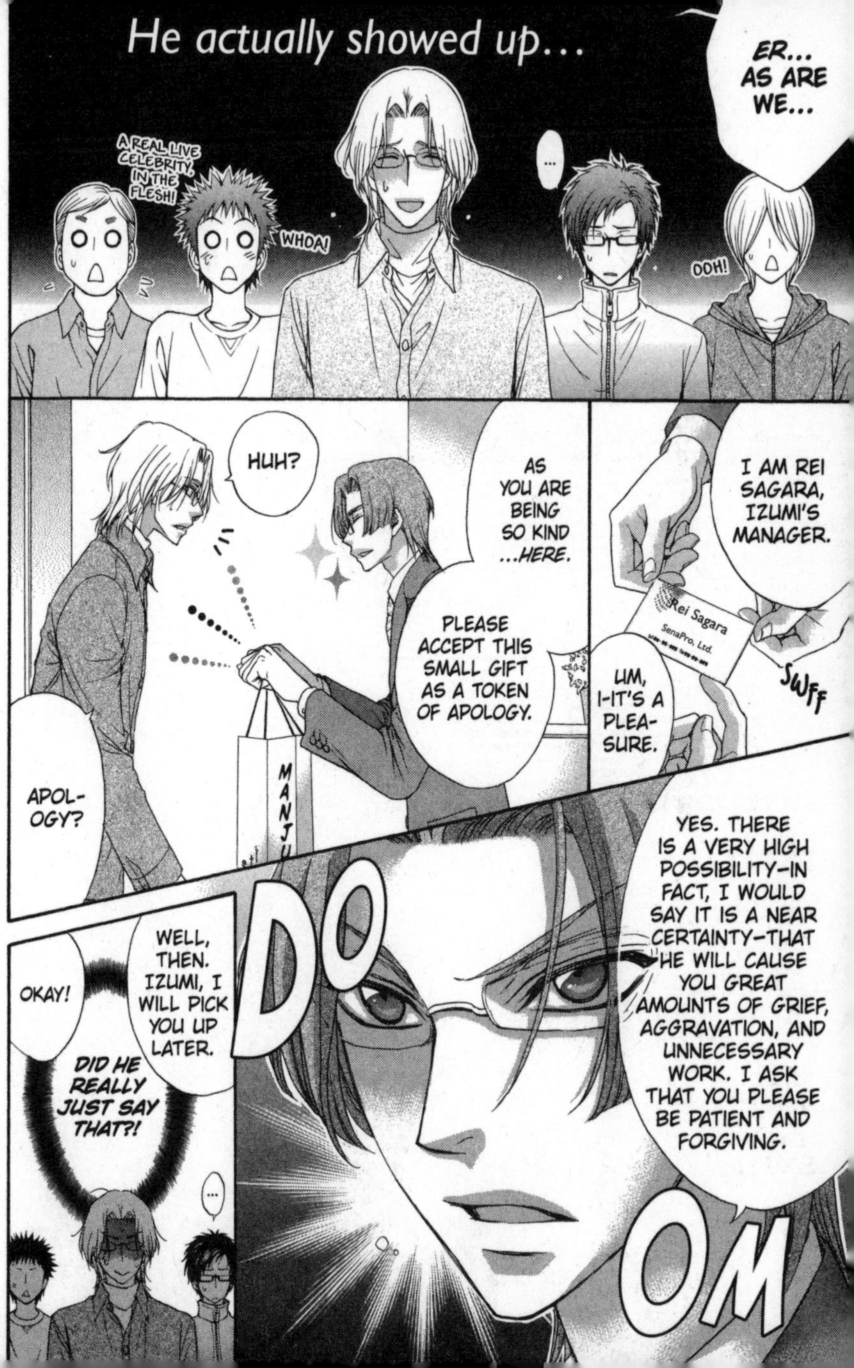
ER... AS ARE WE...
He actually showed up...
...
OOH!
A REAL LIVE CELEBRITY, IN THE FLESH!
WHOA!
I AM REI SAGARA, IZUMI'S MANAGER.
Rei Sagara
SenaPro, Ltd.
SWFF
UM, I-IT'S A PLEA-SURE.
AS YOU ARE BEING SO KIND ...HERE.
HUH?
PLEASE ACCEPT THIS SMALL GIFT AS A TOKEN OF APOLOGY.
APOL-OGY?
MANJU
YES. THERE IS A VERY HIGH POSSIBILITY—IN FACT, I WOULD SAY IT IS A NEAR CERTAINTY—THAT HE WILL CAUSE YOU GREAT AMOUNTS OF GRIEF, AGGRAVATION, AND UNNECESSARY WORK. I ASK THAT YOU PLEASE BE PATIENT AND FORGIVING.
DOOM
WELL, THEN. IZUMI, I WILL PICK YOU UP LATER.
OKAY!
DID HE REALLY JUST SAY THAT?!
...

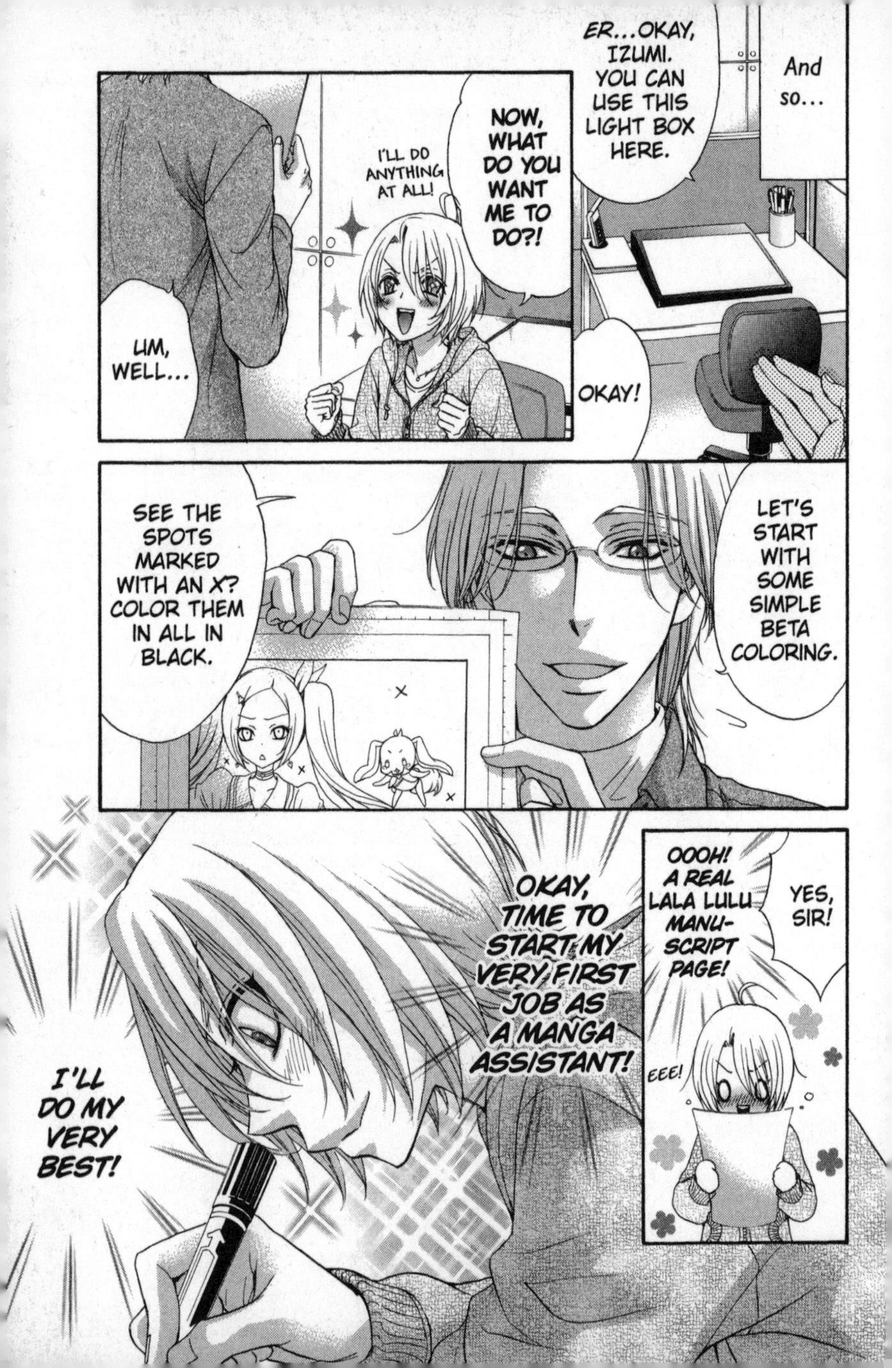
And so…
ER…OKAY, IZUMI. YOU CAN USE THIS LIGHT BOX HERE.
OKAY!
NOW, WHAT DO YOU WANT ME TO DO?!
I'LL DO ANYTHING AT ALL!
UM, WELL…
LET'S START WITH SOME SIMPLE BETA COLORING.
SEE THE SPOTS MARKED WITH AN X? COLOR THEM IN ALL IN BLACK.
YES, SIR!
OOOH! A REAL LALA LULU MANU-SCRIPT PAGE!
EEE!
OKAY, TIME TO START MY VERY FIRST JOB AS A MANGA ASSISTANT!
I'LL DO MY VERY BEST!

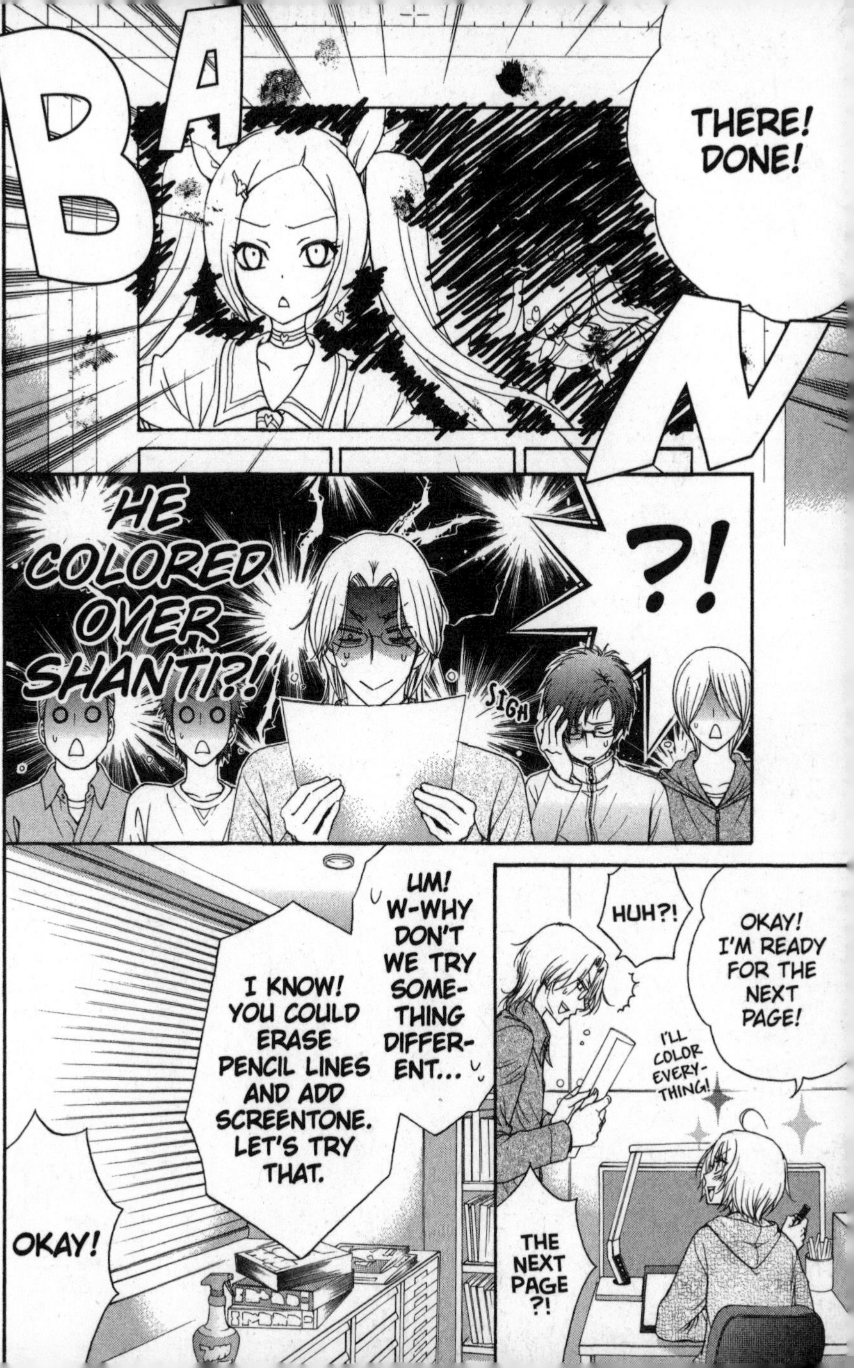
THERE! DONE!
?!
SIGH
HE COLORED OVER SHANTI?!
OKAY! I'M READY FOR THE NEXT PAGE!
I'LL COLOR EVERY-THING!
HUH?!
THE NEXT PAGE?!
UM! W-WHY DON'T WE TRY SOME-THING DIFFER-ENT...
I KNOW! YOU COULD ERASE PENCIL LINES AND ADD SCREENTONE. LET'S TRY THAT.
OKAY!

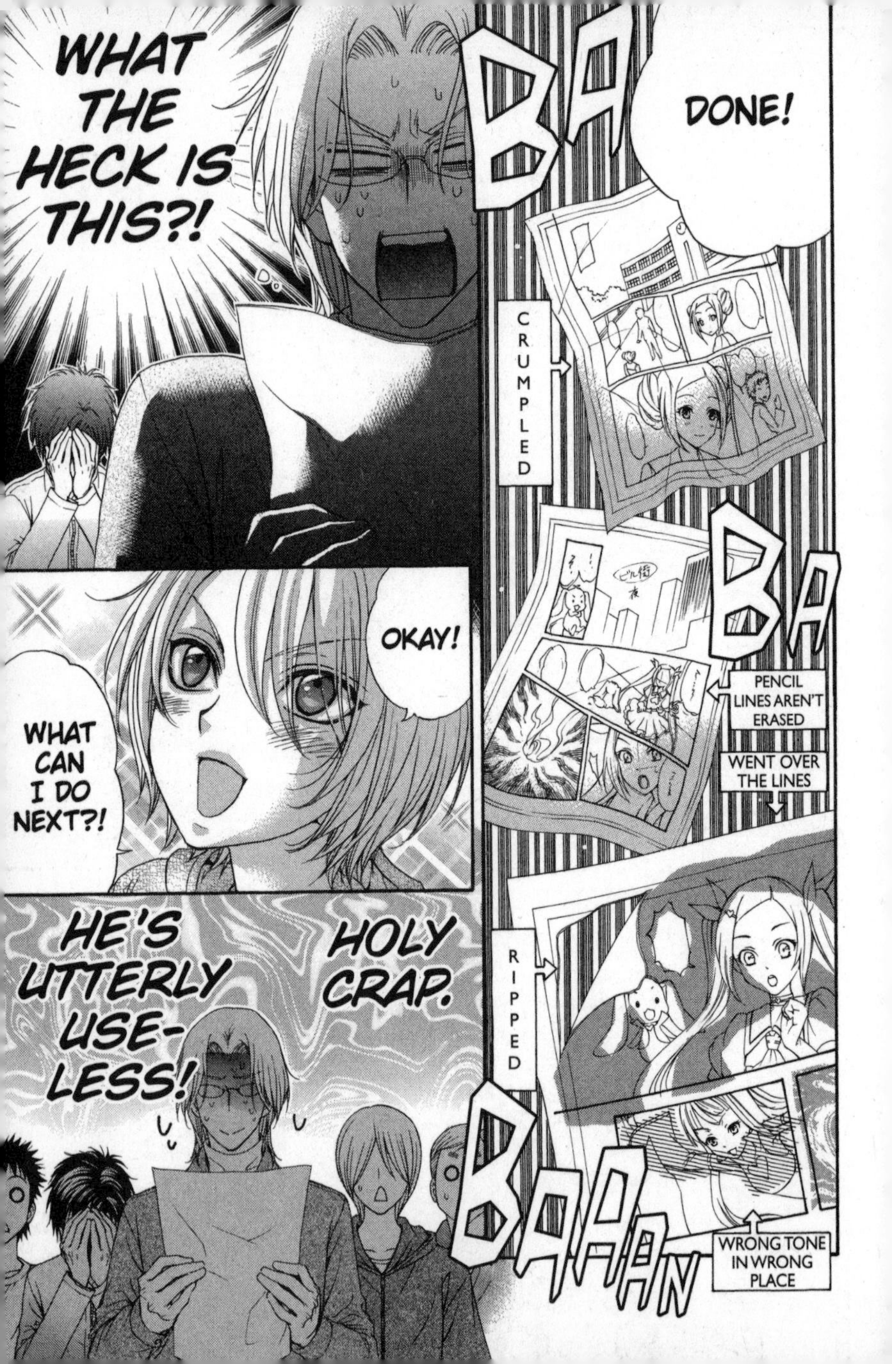
BA
DONE!
CRUMPLED
BA
BA
PENCIL LINES AREN'T ERASED
WENT OVER THE LINES
RIPPED
BAAAAN
WRONG TONE IN WRONG PLACE
WHAT THE HECK IS THIS?!
OKAY!
WHAT CAN I DO NEXT?!
HOLY CRAP.
HE'S UTTERLY USE-LESS!

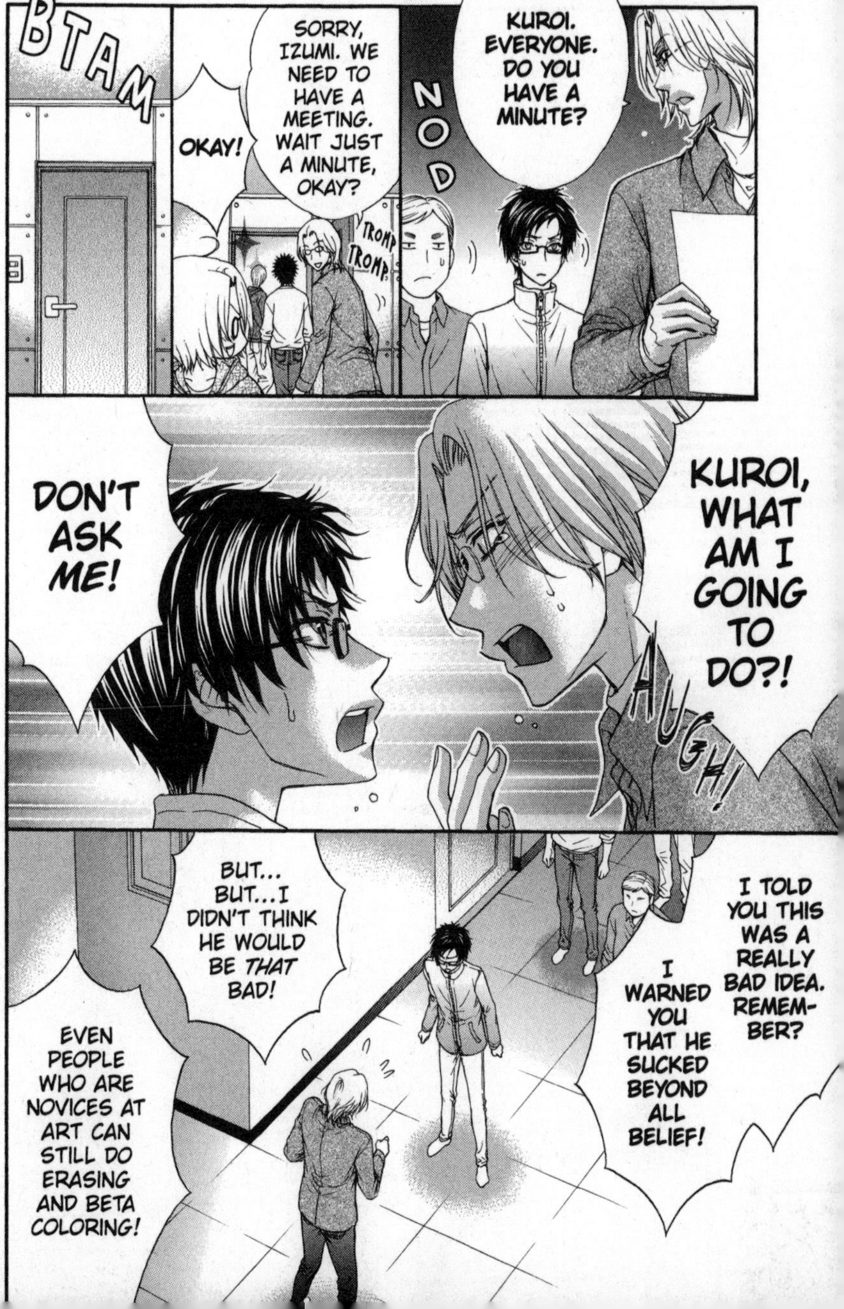
KUROI. EVERYONE. DO YOU HAVE A MINUTE?
NOD
SORRY, IZUMI. WE NEED TO HAVE A MEETING. WAIT JUST A MINUTE, OKAY?
OKAY!
TROMP TROMP
BTAM
KUROI, WHAT AM I GOING TO DO?!
AUGH!
DON'T ASK ME!
I TOLD YOU THIS WAS A REALLY BAD IDEA. REMEMBER?
I WARNED YOU THAT HE SUCKED BEYOND ALL BELIEF!
BUT... BUT...I DIDN'T THINK HE WOULD BE THAT BAD!
EVEN PEOPLE WHO ARE NOVICES AT ART CAN STILL DO ERASING AND BETA COLORING!

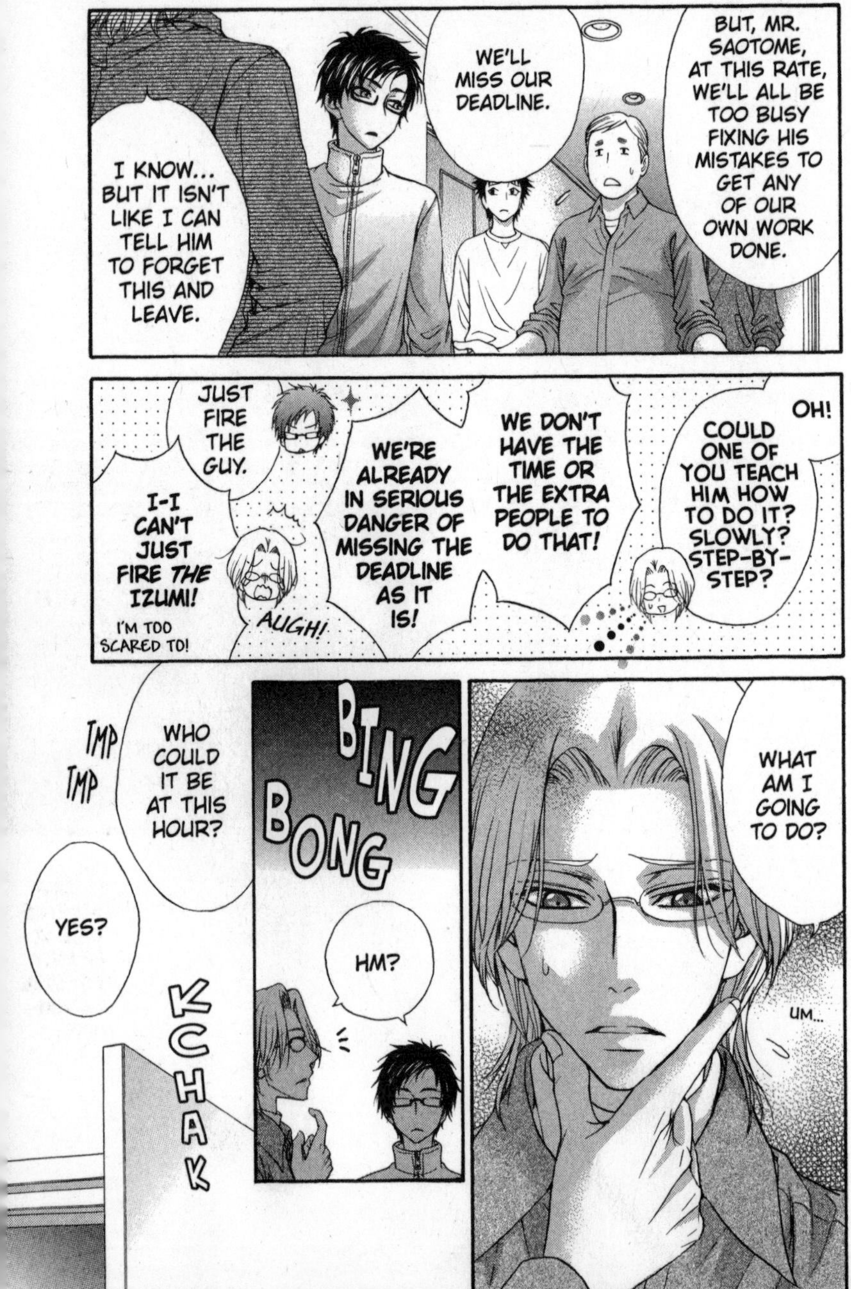
BUT, MR. SAOTOME, AT THIS RATE, WE'LL ALL BE TOO BUSY FIXING HIS MISTAKES TO GET ANY OF OUR OWN WORK DONE.
WE'LL MISS OUR DEADLINE.
I KNOW... BUT IT ISN'T LIKE I CAN TELL HIM TO FORGET THIS AND LEAVE.
OH!
COULD ONE OF YOU TEACH HIM HOW TO DO IT? SLOWLY? STEP-BY-STEP?
WE DON'T HAVE THE TIME OR THE EXTRA PEOPLE TO DO THAT!
WE'RE ALREADY IN SERIOUS DANGER OF MISSING THE DEADLINE AS IT IS!
JUST FIRE THE GUY.
I-I CAN'T JUST FIRE *THE* IZUMI!
AUGH!
I'M TOO SCARED TO!
WHAT AM I GOING TO DO?
UM...
BING BONG
HM?
TMP TMP
WHO COULD IT BE AT THIS HOUR?
YES?
KCHAK

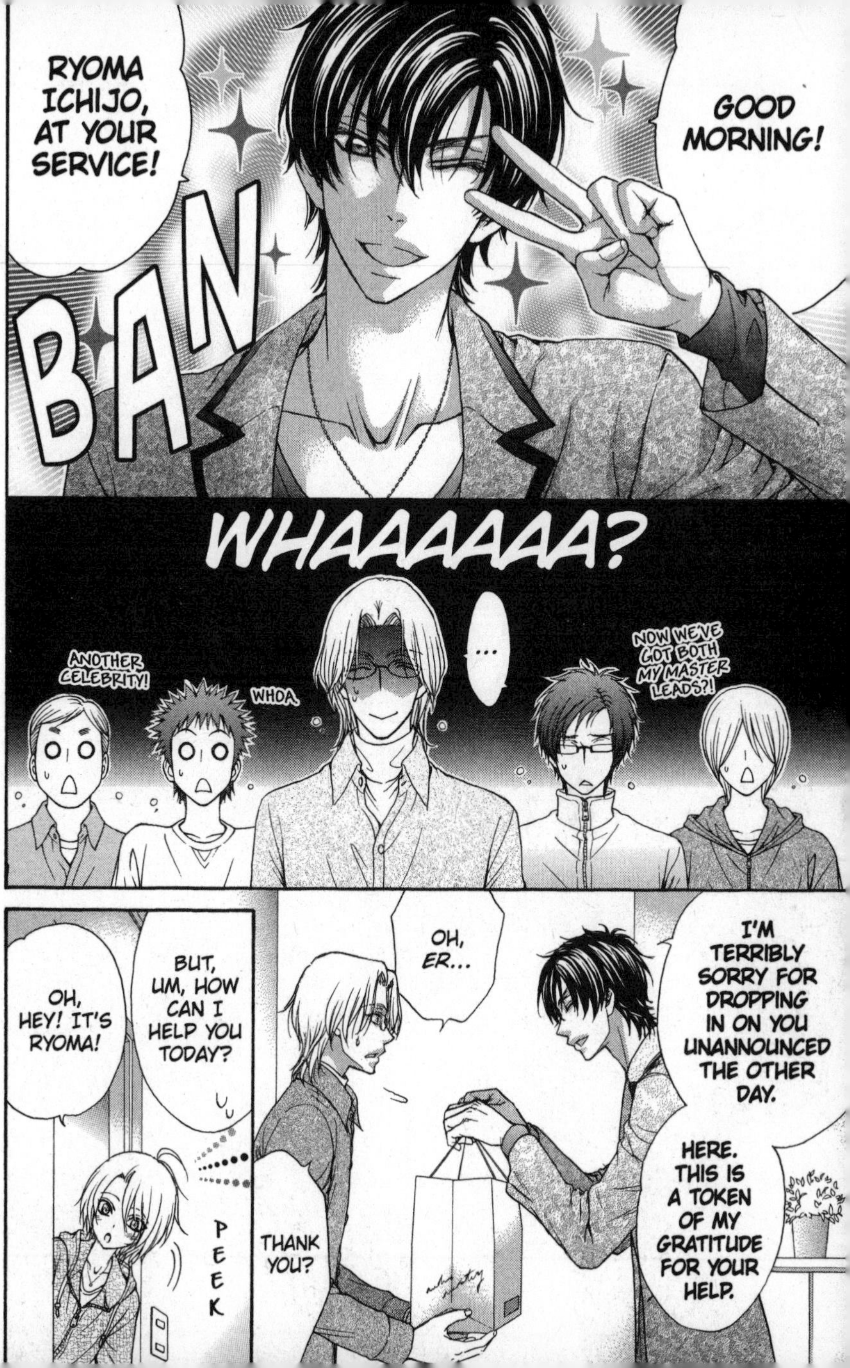
GOOD MORNING!
RYOMA ICHIJO, AT YOUR SERVICE!
BAN
WHAAAAAAA?
NOW WE'VE GOT BOTH MY MASTER LEADS?!
...
WHOA.
ANOTHER CELEBRITY!
I'M TERRIBLY SORRY FOR DROPPING IN ON YOU UNANNOUNCED THE OTHER DAY.
HERE. THIS IS A TOKEN OF MY GRATITUDE FOR YOUR HELP.
OH, ER...
THANK YOU?
BUT, UM, HOW CAN I HELP YOU TODAY?
OH, HEY! IT'S RYOMA!
PEEK

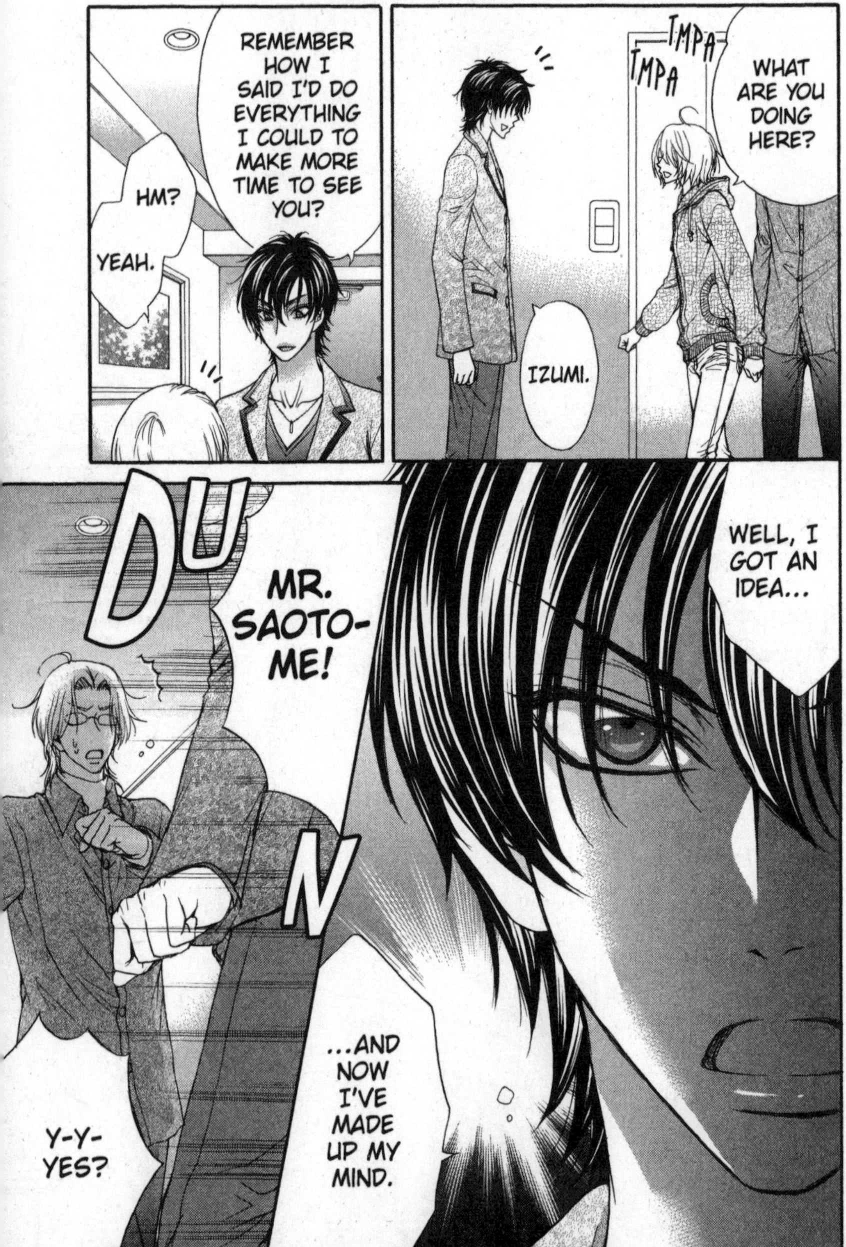
TMPA
TMPA
WHAT ARE YOU DOING HERE?
IZUMI.
REMEMBER HOW I SAID I'D DO EVERYTHING I COULD TO MAKE MORE TIME TO SEE YOU?
HM?
YEAH.
WELL, I GOT AN IDEA...
...AND NOW I'VE MADE UP MY MIND.
DUN
MR. SAOTO-ME!
Y-Y-YES?

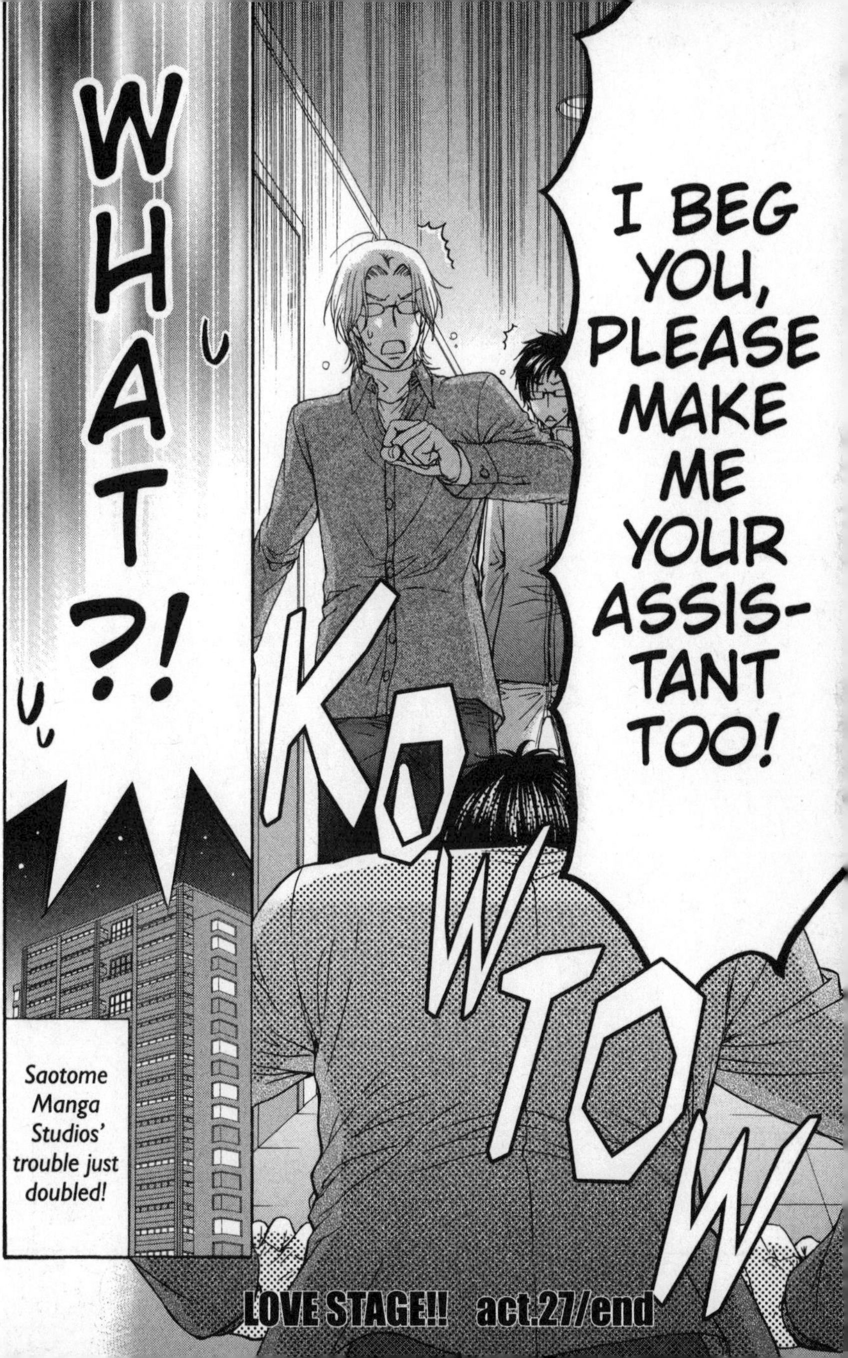
I BEG YOU, PLEASE MAKE ME YOUR ASSIS-TANT TOO!
KOWTOW
WHAT?!
Saotome Manga Studios' trouble just doubled!
LOVE STAGE!! act.27/end

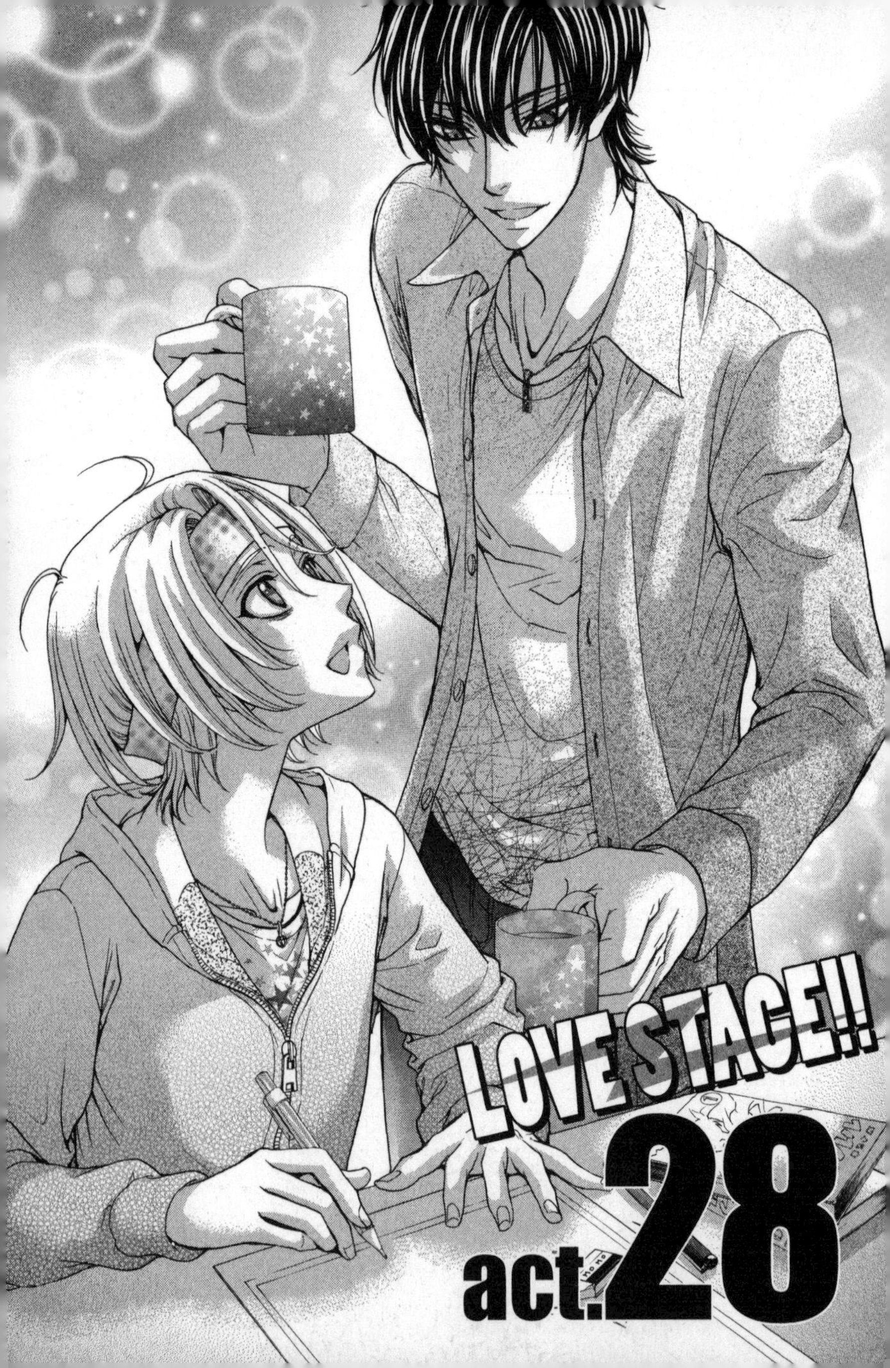
LOVE STAGE!!
act.28

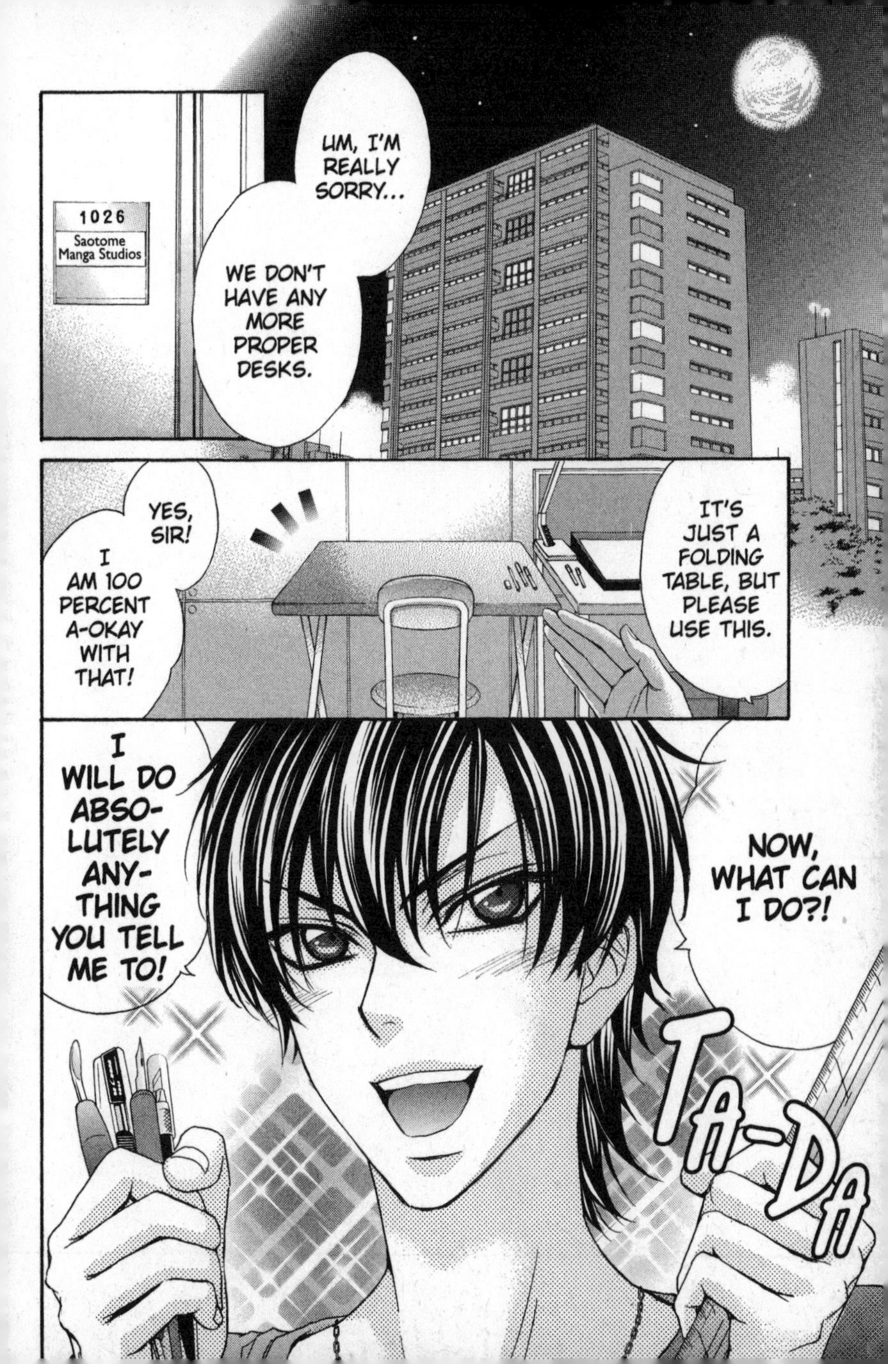

UM, I'M REALLY SORRY...
WE DON'T HAVE ANY MORE PROPER DESKS.
1026
Saotome Manga Studios
IT'S JUST A FOLDING TABLE, BUT PLEASE USE THIS.
YES, SIR!
I AM 100 PERCENT A-OKAY WITH THAT!
NOW, WHAT CAN I DO?!
I WILL DO ABSO-LUTELY ANY-THING YOU TELL ME TO!
TA-DA

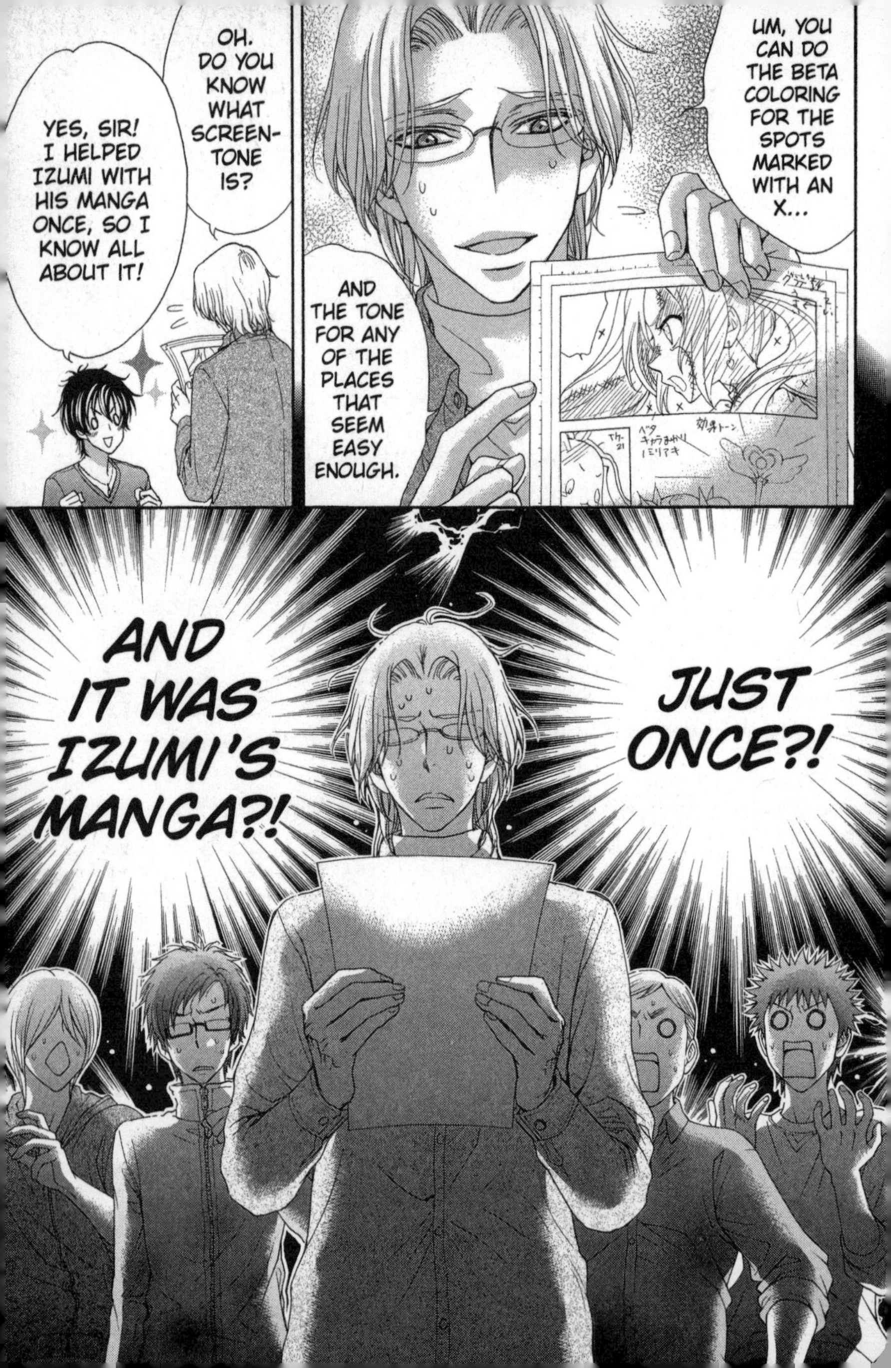
UM, YOU CAN DO THE BETA COLORING FOR THE SPOTS MARKED WITH AN X...
AND THE TONE FOR ANY OF THE PLACES THAT SEEM EASY ENOUGH.
OH. DO YOU KNOW WHAT SCREEN-TONE IS?
YES, SIR! I HELPED IZUMI WITH HIS MANGA ONCE, SO I KNOW ALL ABOUT IT!
JUST ONCE?!
AND IT WAS IZUMI'S MANGA?!

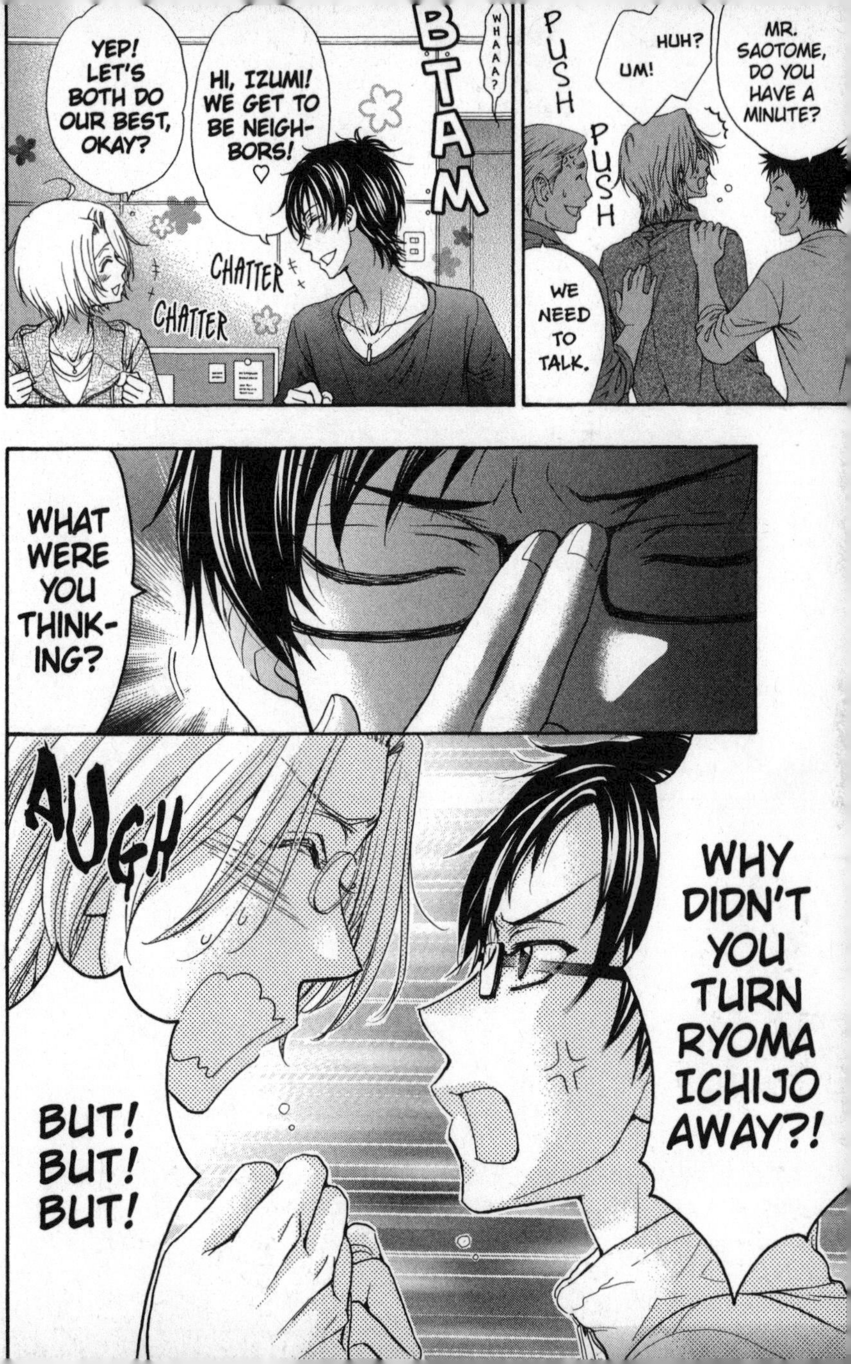
MR. SAOTOME, DO YOU HAVE A MINUTE?
HUH?
UM!
PUSH
PUSH
WE NEED TO TALK.
BTAM
WHAAA?
HI, IZUMI! WE GET TO BE NEIGHBORS! ♡
YEP! LET'S BOTH DO OUR BEST, OKAY?
CHATTER
CHATTER
WHAT WERE YOU THINKING?
WHY DIDN'T YOU TURN RYOMA ICHIJO AWAY?!
AUGH
BUT! BUT! BUT!

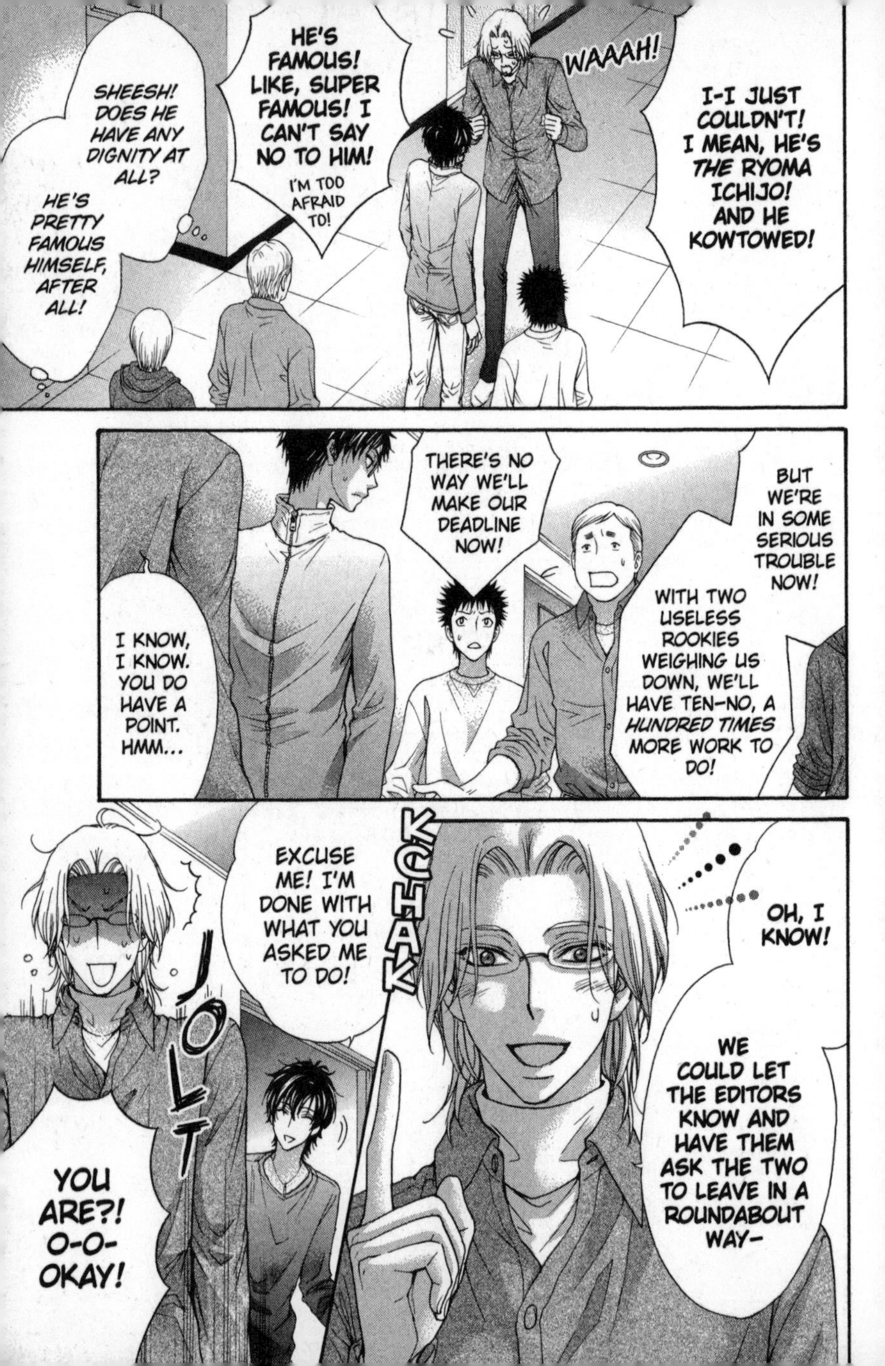
I-I JUST COULDN'T! I MEAN, HE'S *THE* RYOMA ICHIJO! AND HE KOWTOWED!
WAAAH!
HE'S FAMOUS! LIKE, SUPER FAMOUS! I CAN'T SAY NO TO HIM!
I'M TOO AFRAID TO!
SHEESH! DOES HE HAVE ANY DIGNITY AT ALL?
HE'S PRETTY FAMOUS HIMSELF, AFTER ALL!
BUT WE'RE IN SOME SERIOUS TROUBLE NOW!
WITH TWO USELESS ROOKIES WEIGHING US DOWN, WE'LL HAVE TEN–NO, A *HUNDRED TIMES* MORE WORK TO DO!
THERE'S NO WAY WE'LL MAKE OUR DEADLINE NOW!
I KNOW, I KNOW. YOU DO HAVE A POINT. HMM...
OH, I KNOW!
WE COULD LET THE EDITORS KNOW AND HAVE THEM ASK THE TWO TO LEAVE IN A ROUNDABOUT WAY–
KCHAK
EXCUSE ME! I'M DONE WITH WHAT YOU ASKED ME TO DO!
JOLT
YOU ARE?! O-O-OKAY!

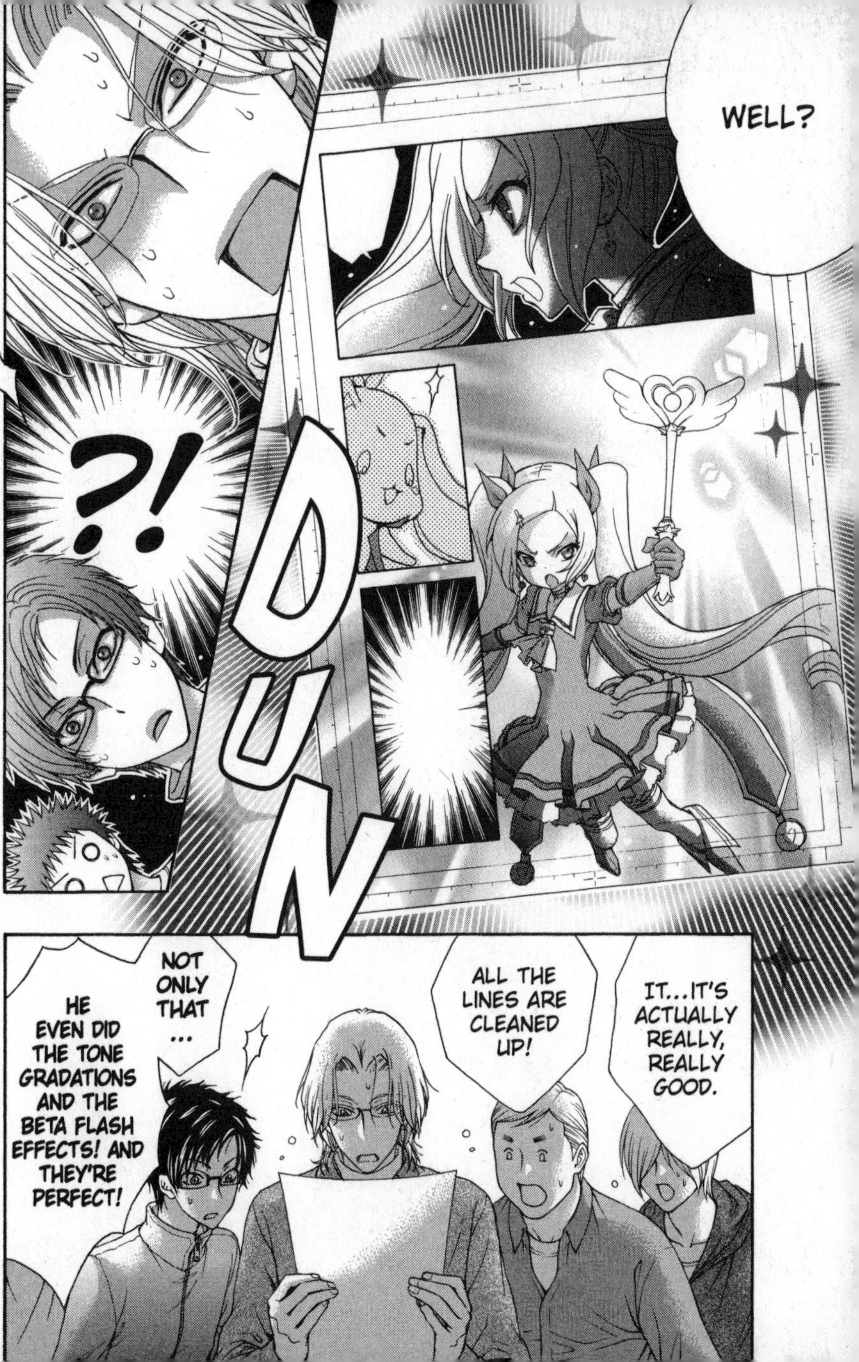
WELL?
DUN
?!
IT...IT'S ACTUALLY REALLY, REALLY GOOD.
ALL THE LINES ARE CLEANED UP!
NOT ONLY THAT ...
HE EVEN DID THE TONE GRADATIONS AND THE BETA FLASH EFFECTS! AND THEY'RE PERFECT!

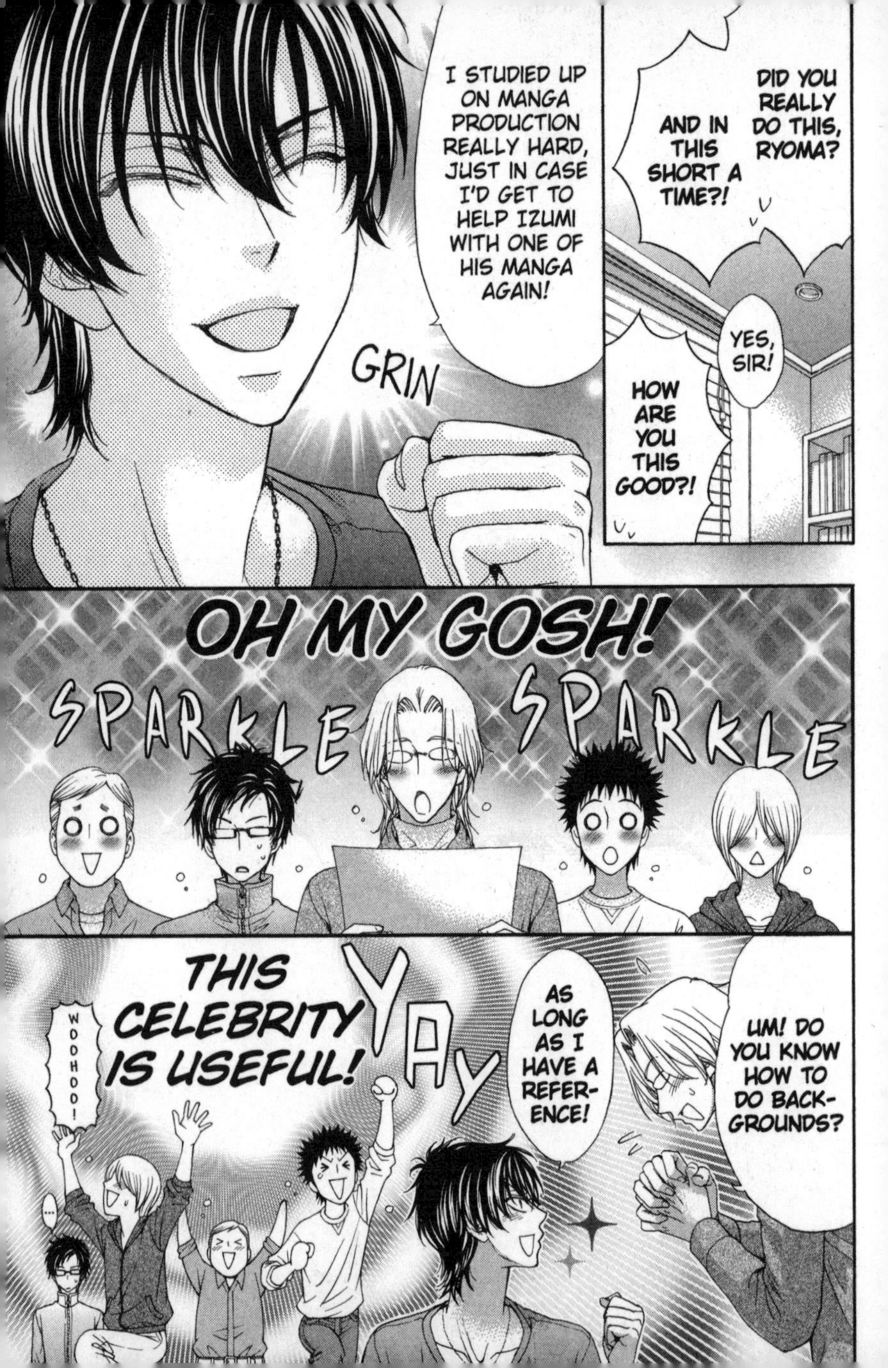
DID YOU REALLY DO THIS, RYOMA?
AND IN THIS SHORT A TIME?!
YES, SIR!
HOW ARE YOU THIS GOOD?!
I STUDIED UP ON MANGA PRODUCTION REALLY HARD, JUST IN CASE I'D GET TO HELP IZUMI WITH ONE OF HIS MANGA AGAIN!
GRIN
OH MY GOSH!
SPARKLE
SPARKLE
UM! DO YOU KNOW HOW TO DO BACK-GROUNDS?
AS LONG AS I HAVE A REFER-ENCE!
YAY
THIS CELEBRITY IS USEFUL!
WOOHOO!
...

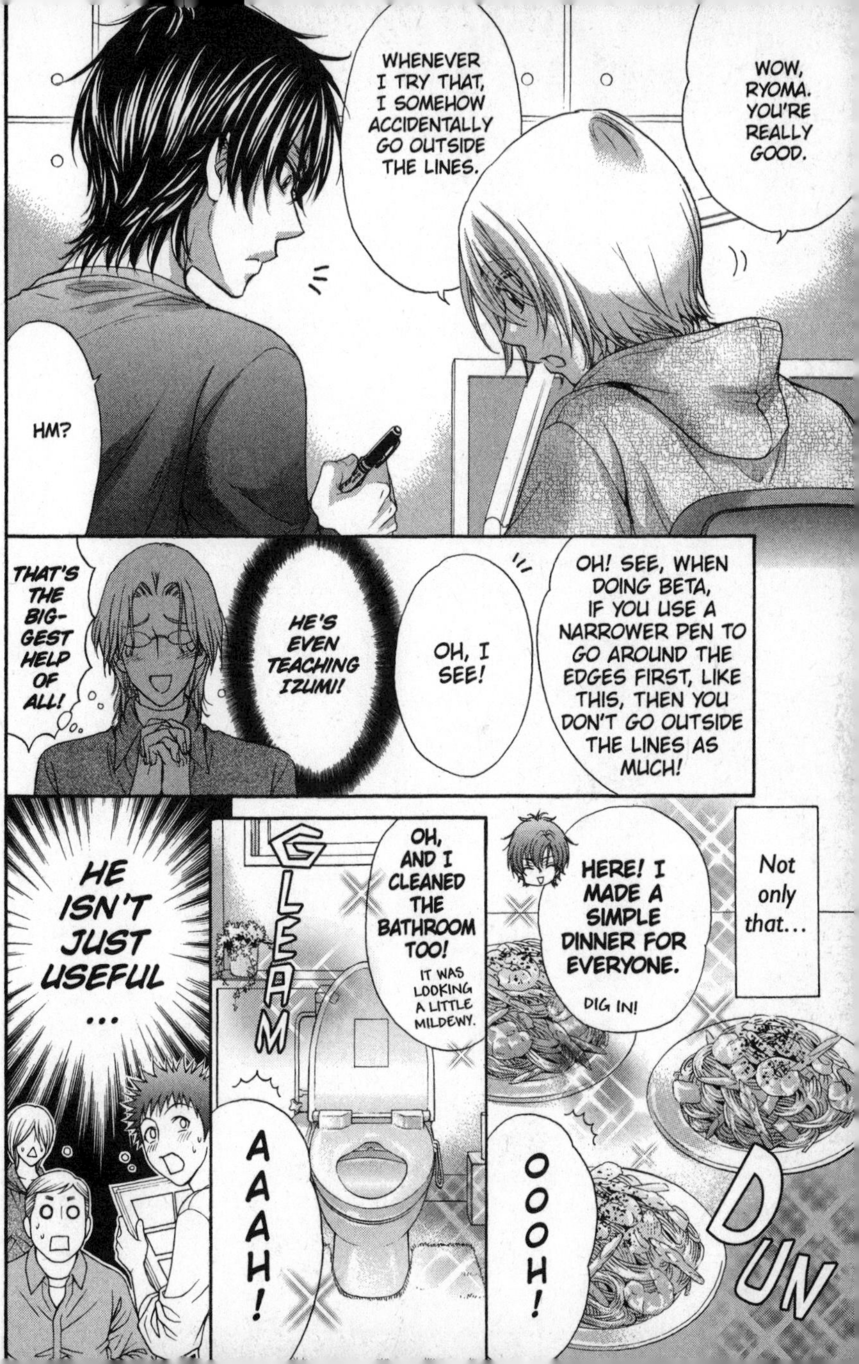
WOW, RYOMA. YOU'RE REALLY GOOD.
WHENEVER I TRY THAT, I SOMEHOW ACCIDENTALLY GO OUTSIDE THE LINES.
HM?
OH! SEE, WHEN DOING BETA, IF YOU USE A NARROWER PEN TO GO AROUND THE EDGES FIRST, LIKE THIS, THEN YOU DON'T GO OUTSIDE THE LINES AS MUCH!
OH, I SEE!
HE'S EVEN TEACHING IZUMI!
THAT'S THE BIG-GEST HELP OF ALL!
Not only that…
HERE! I MADE A SIMPLE DINNER FOR EVERYONE.
DIG IN!
OOOOH!
DUN
OH, AND I CLEANED THE BATHROOM TOO!
IT WAS LOOKING A LITTLE MILDEWY.
GLEAM
AAAAH!
HE ISN'T JUST USEFUL...

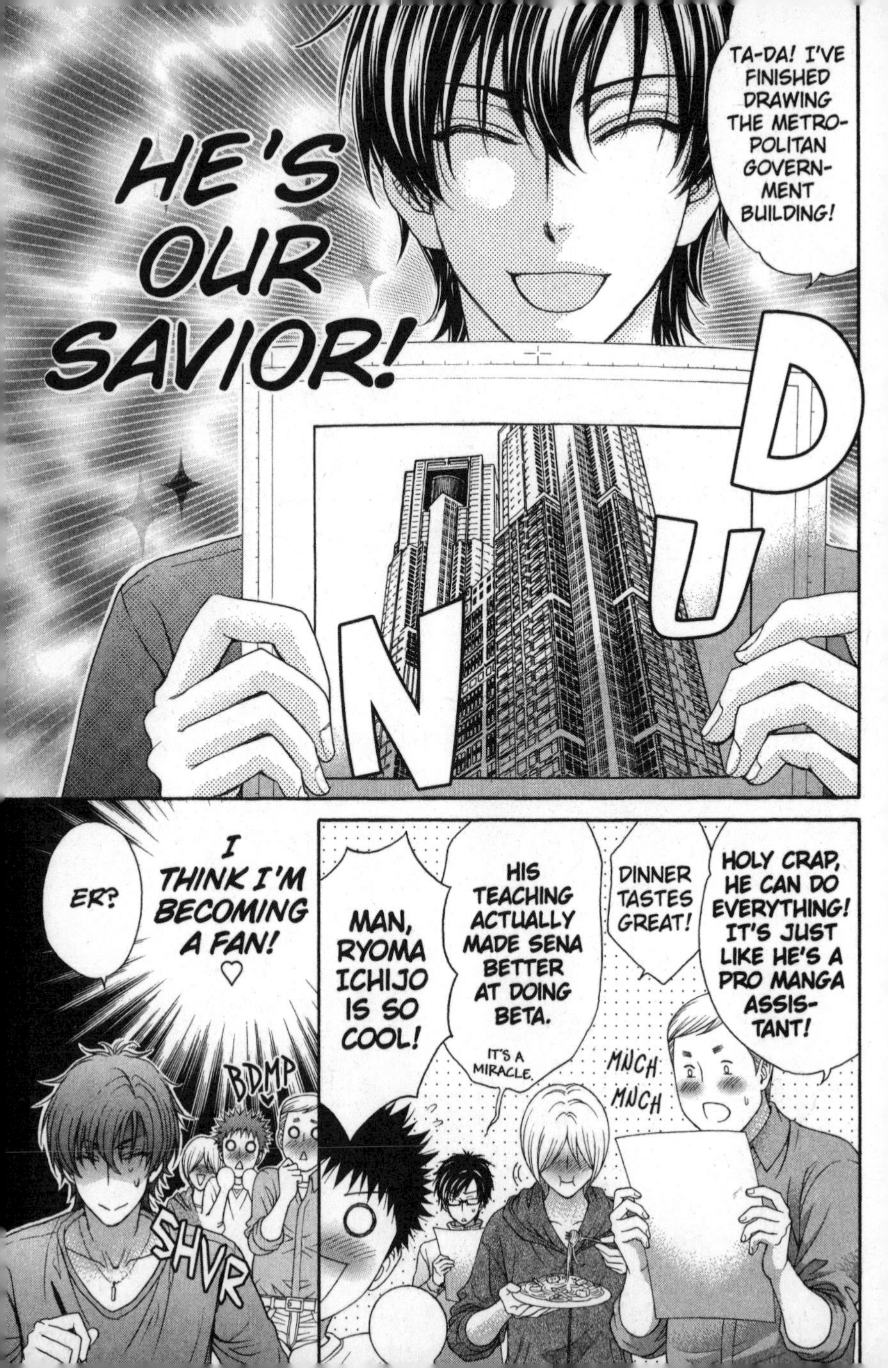
TA-DA! I'VE FINISHED DRAWING THE METRO-POLITAN GOVERN-MENT BUILDING!
HE'S OUR SAVIOR!
DUN
HOLY CRAP, HE CAN DO EVERYTHING! IT'S JUST LIKE HE'S A PRO MANGA ASSIS-TANT!
DINNER TASTES GREAT!
HIS TEACHING ACTUALLY MADE SENA BETTER AT DOING BETA.
IT'S A MIRACLE.
MNCH MNCH
MAN, RYOMA ICHIJO IS SO COOL!
I THINK I'M BECOMING A FAN! ♡
ER?
BDMP
SHVR

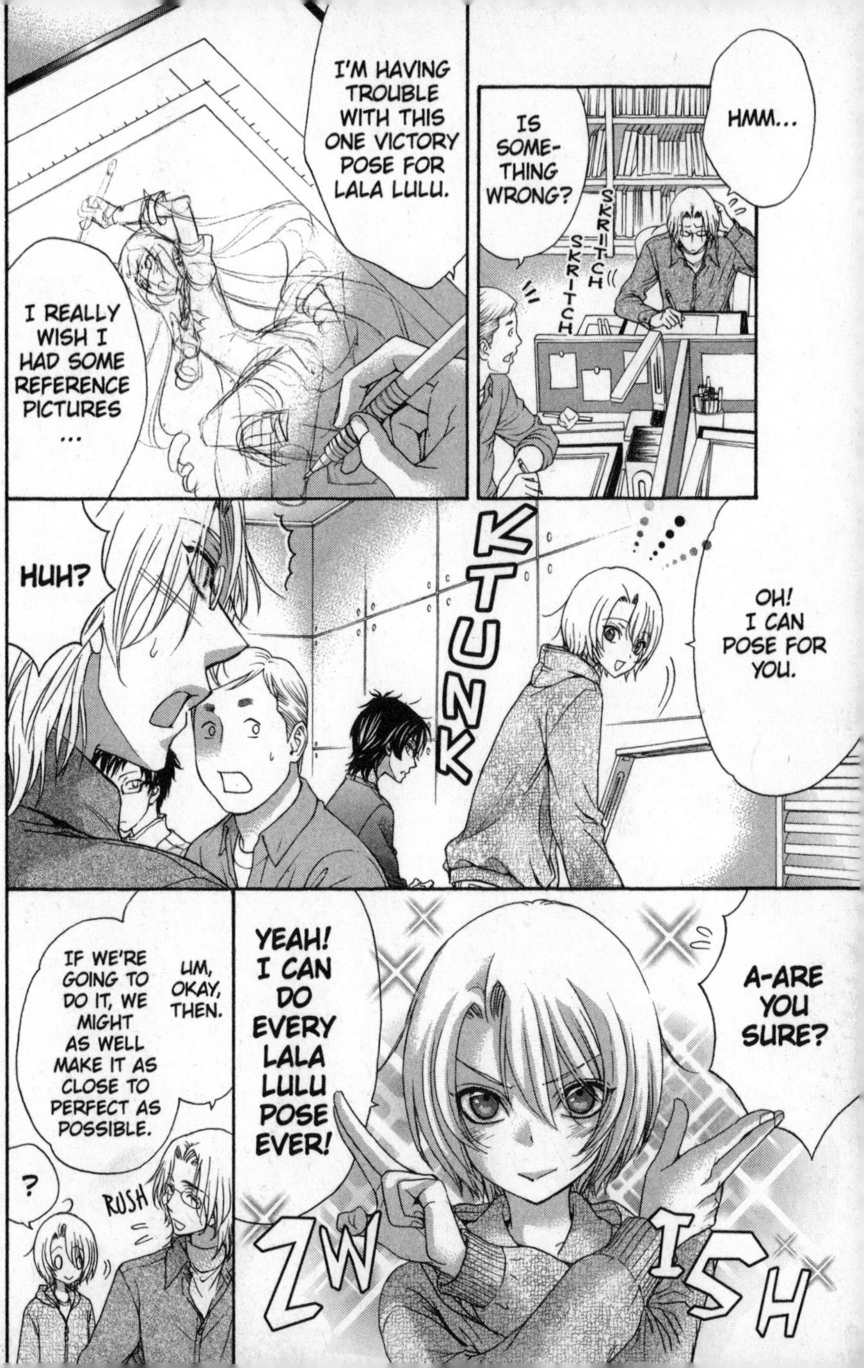
HMM...
IS SOME-THING WRONG?
SKRITCH SKRITCH
I'M HAVING TROUBLE WITH THIS ONE VICTORY POSE FOR LALA LULU.
I REALLY WISH I HAD SOME REFERENCE PICTURES...
OH! I CAN POSE FOR YOU.
KTUNK
HUH?
A-ARE YOU SURE?
YEAH! I CAN DO EVERY LALA LULU POSE EVER!
ZWISH
UM, OKAY, THEN.
IF WE'RE GOING TO DO IT, WE MIGHT AS WELL MAKE IT AS CLOSE TO PERFECT AS POSSIBLE.
RUSH
?

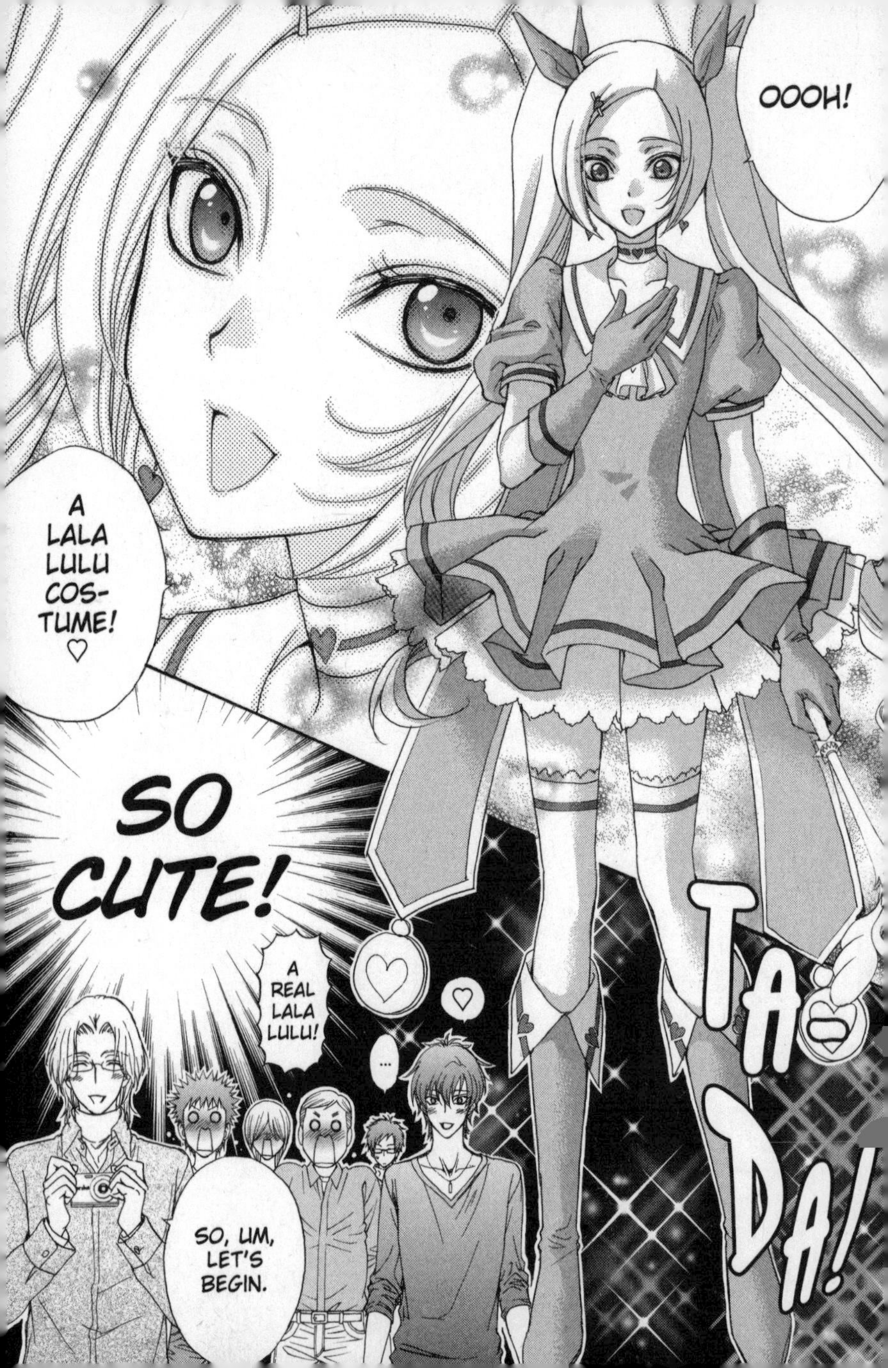
OOOH!
TA-DA!
A LALA LULU COS-TUME! ♡
SO CUTE!
A REAL LALA LULU!
♡
...
SO, UM, LET'S BEGIN.

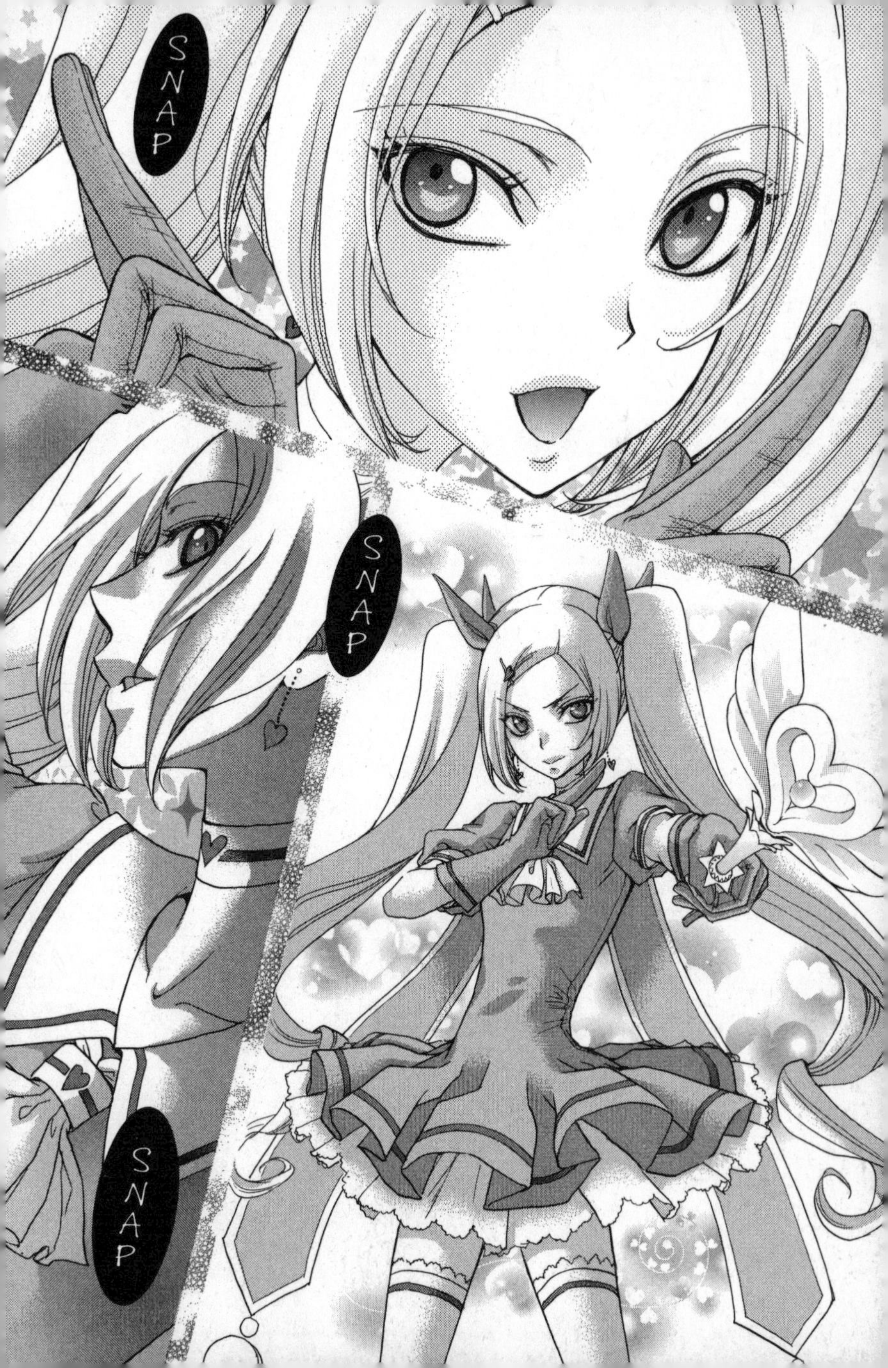
SNAP
SNAP
SNAP

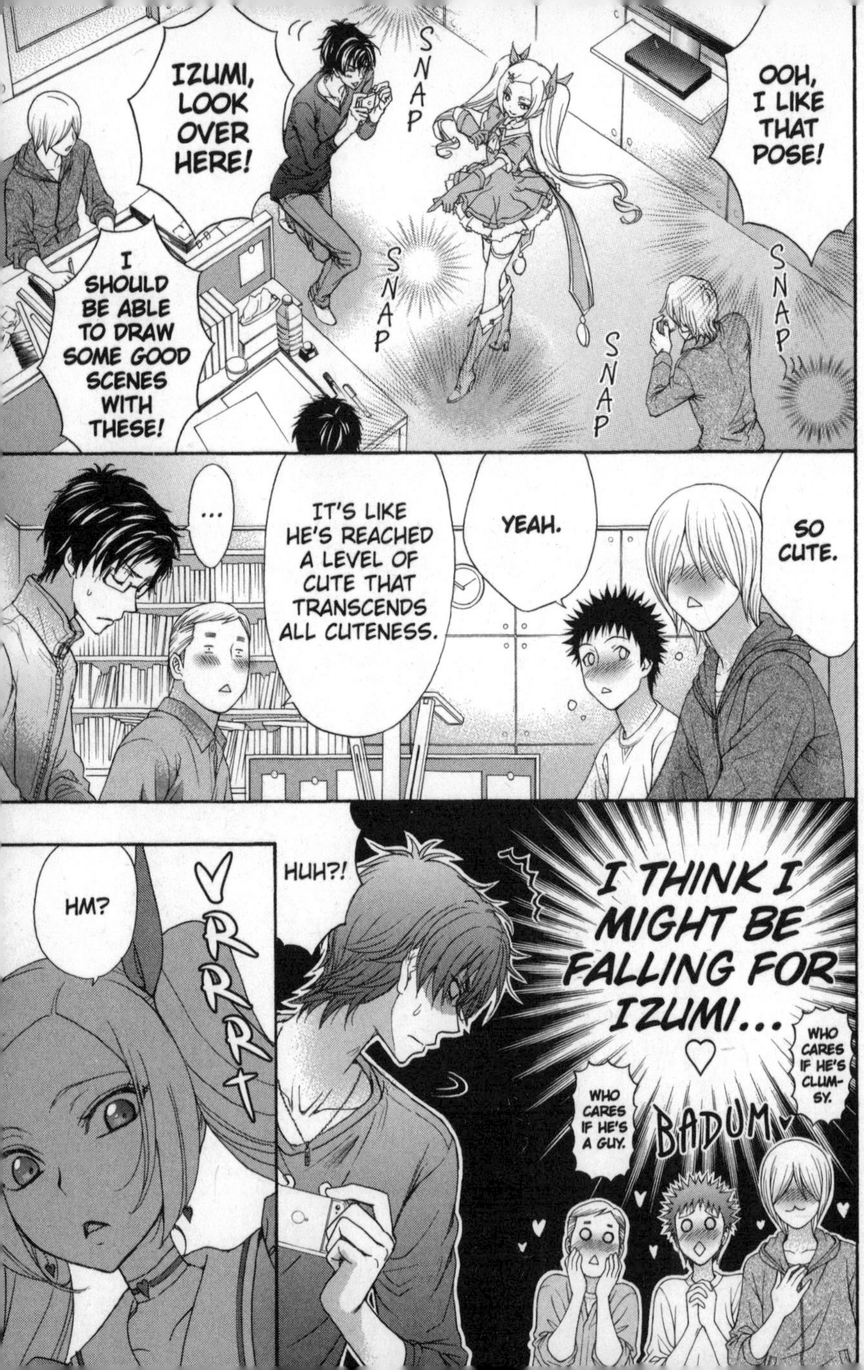
OOH, I LIKE THAT POSE!
SNAP
SNAP
SNAP
IZUMI, LOOK OVER HERE!
SNAP
SNAP
I SHOULD BE ABLE TO DRAW SOME GOOD SCENES WITH THESE!
SO CUTE.
YEAH.
IT'S LIKE HE'S REACHED A LEVEL OF CUTE THAT TRANSCENDS ALL CUTENESS.
...
I THINK I MIGHT BE FALLING FOR IZUMI...
WHO CARES IF HE'S CLUMSY.
WHO CARES IF HE'S A GUY.
BADUM
HUH?!
VRRRT
HM?

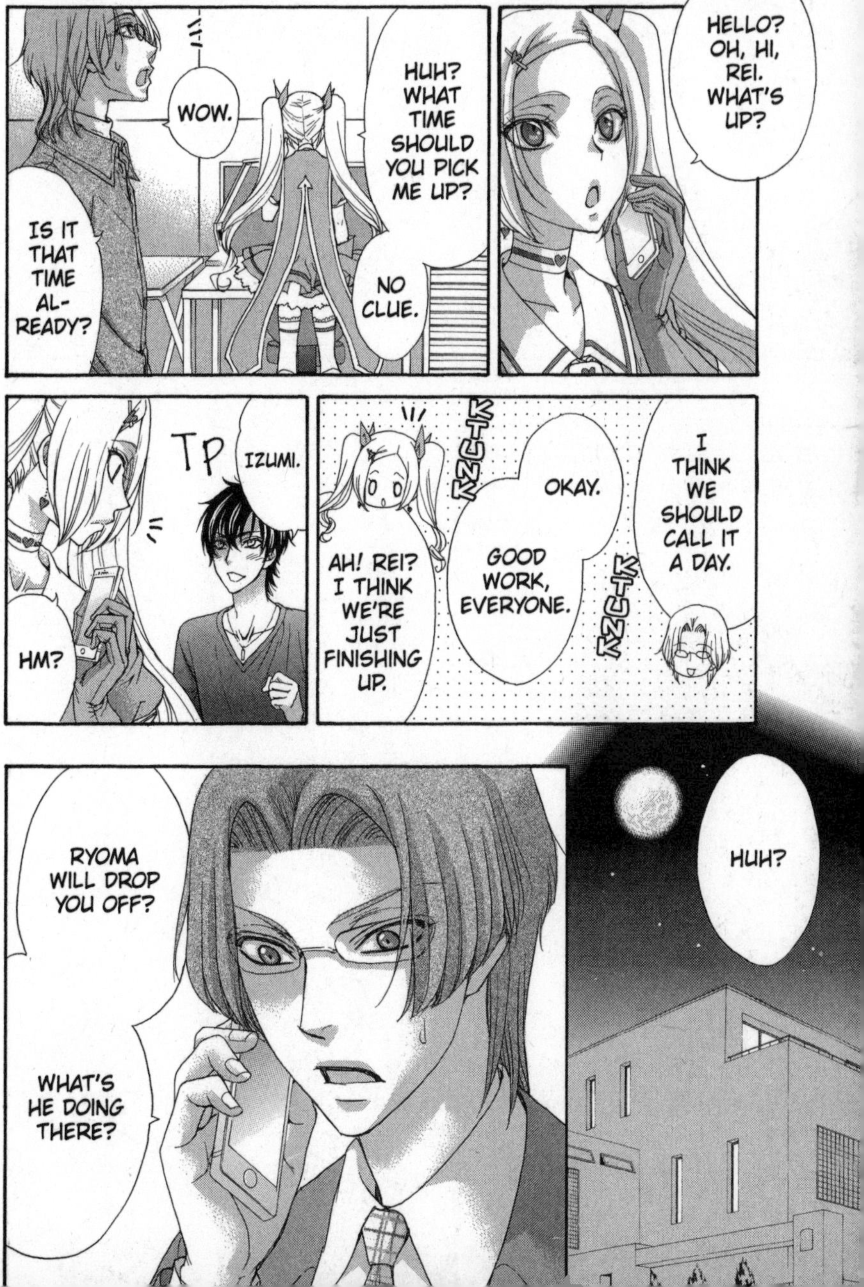
HELLO? OH, HI, REI. WHAT'S UP?
HUH? WHAT TIME SHOULD YOU PICK ME UP?
WOW.
NO CLUE.
IS IT THAT TIME AL-READY?
I THINK WE SHOULD CALL IT A DAY.
KTUNK
OKAY.
GOOD WORK, EVERYONE.
KTUNK
AH! REI? I THINK WE'RE JUST FINISHING UP.
IZUMI.
TP
HM?
HUH?
RYOMA WILL DROP YOU OFF?
WHAT'S HE DOING THERE?

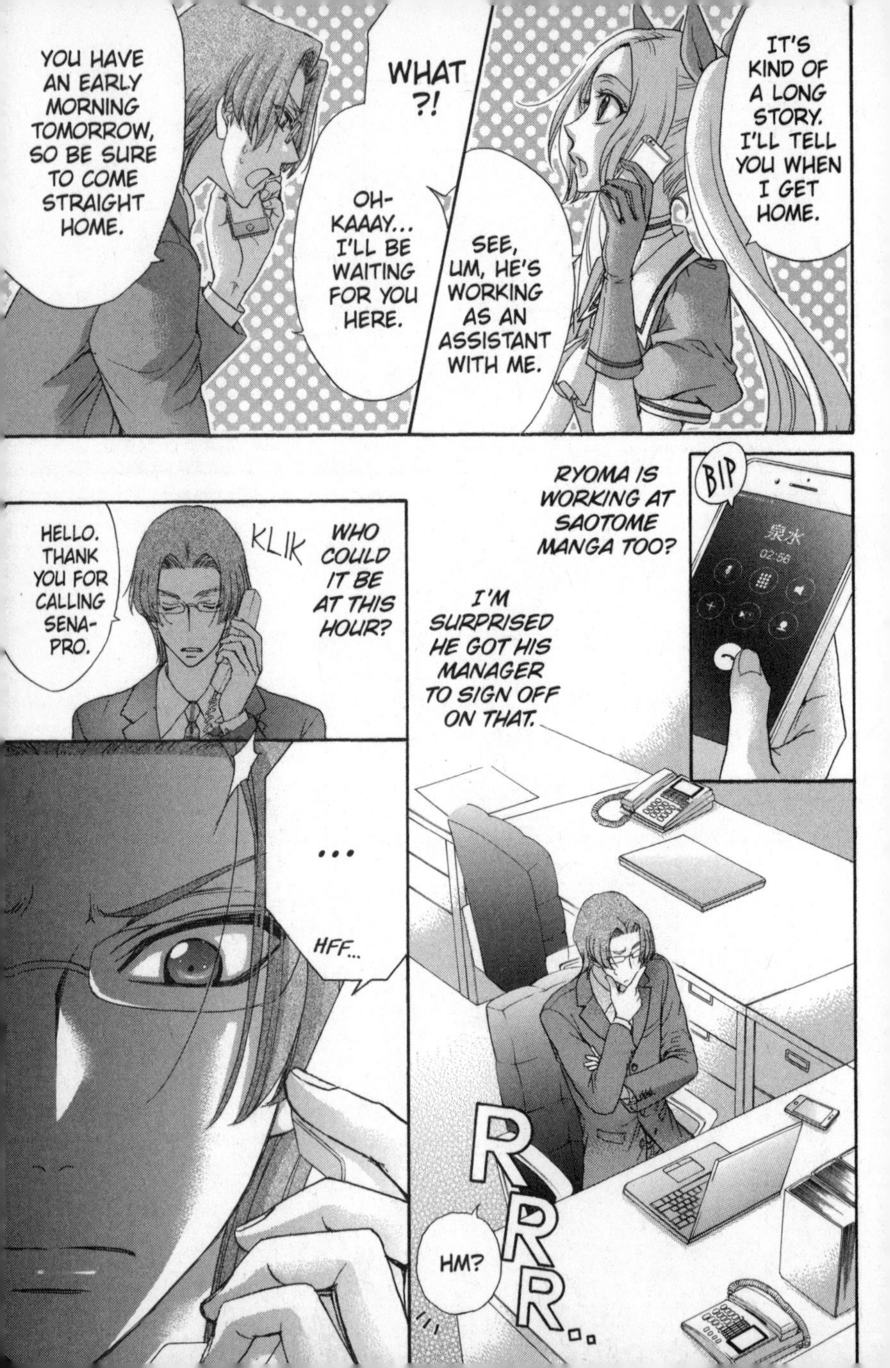
IT'S KIND OF A LONG STORY. I'LL TELL YOU WHEN I GET HOME.
SEE, UM, HE'S WORKING AS AN ASSISTANT WITH ME.
WHAT ?!
OH-KAAAY... I'LL BE WAITING FOR YOU HERE.
YOU HAVE AN EARLY MORNING TOMORROW, SO BE SURE TO COME STRAIGHT HOME.
BIP
泉水
02:56
RYOMA IS WORKING AT SAOTOME MANGA TOO?
I'M SURPRISED HE GOT HIS MANAGER TO SIGN OFF ON THAT.
RRRR..
HM?
WHO COULD IT BE AT THIS HOUR?
KLIK
HELLO. THANK YOU FOR CALLING SENA-PRO.
...
HFF...

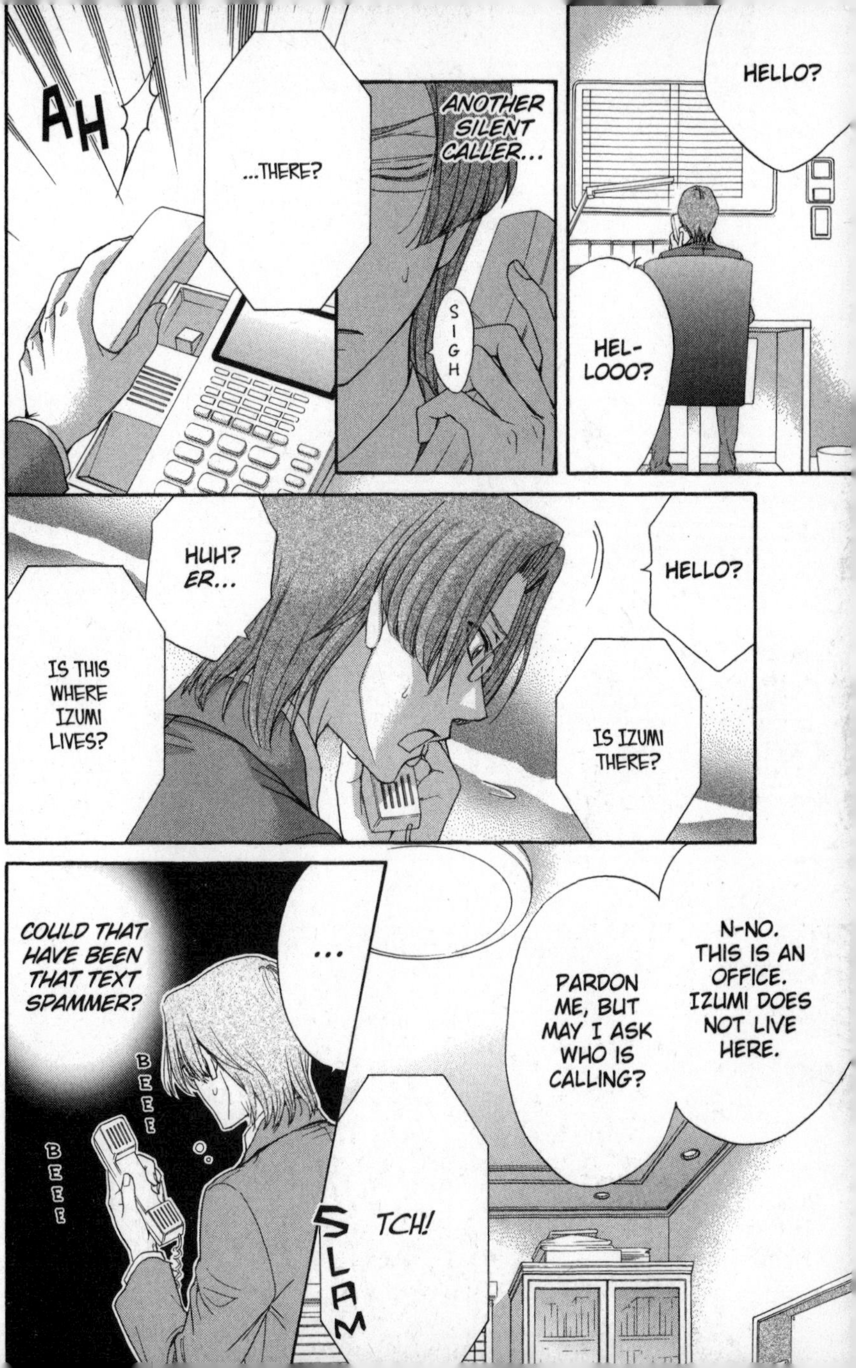
HELLO?
HEL-LOOO?
ANOTHER SILENT CALLER...
SIGH
...THERE?
AH
HELLO?
IS IZUMI THERE?
HUH? ER...
IS THIS WHERE IZUMI LIVES?
N-NO. THIS IS AN OFFICE. IZUMI DOES NOT LIVE HERE.
PARDON ME, BUT MAY I ASK WHO IS CALLING?
...
TCH!
SLAM
COULD THAT HAVE BEEN THAT TEXT SPAMMER?
BEEE
BEEE

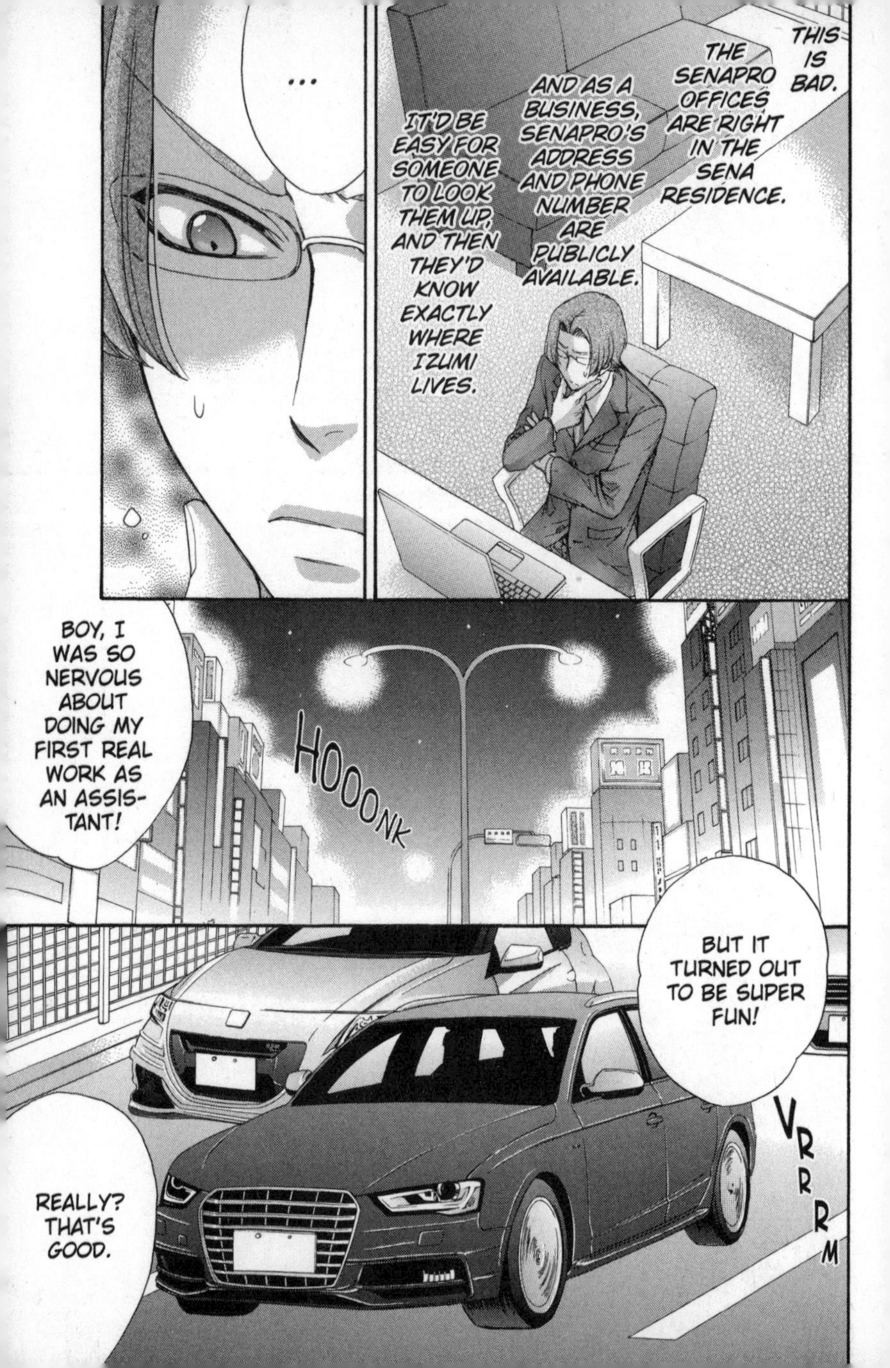
THIS IS BAD.
THE SENAPRO OFFICES ARE RIGHT IN THE SENA RESIDENCE.
AND AS A BUSINESS, SENAPRO'S ADDRESS AND PHONE NUMBER ARE PUBLICLY AVAILABLE.
IT'D BE EASY FOR SOMEONE TO LOOK THEM UP, AND THEN THEY'D KNOW EXACTLY WHERE IZUMI LIVES.
...
HOOONK
BOY, I WAS SO NERVOUS ABOUT DOING MY FIRST REAL WORK AS AN ASSIS-TANT!
BUT IT TURNED OUT TO BE SUPER FUN!
VRRRRM
REALLY? THAT'S GOOD.

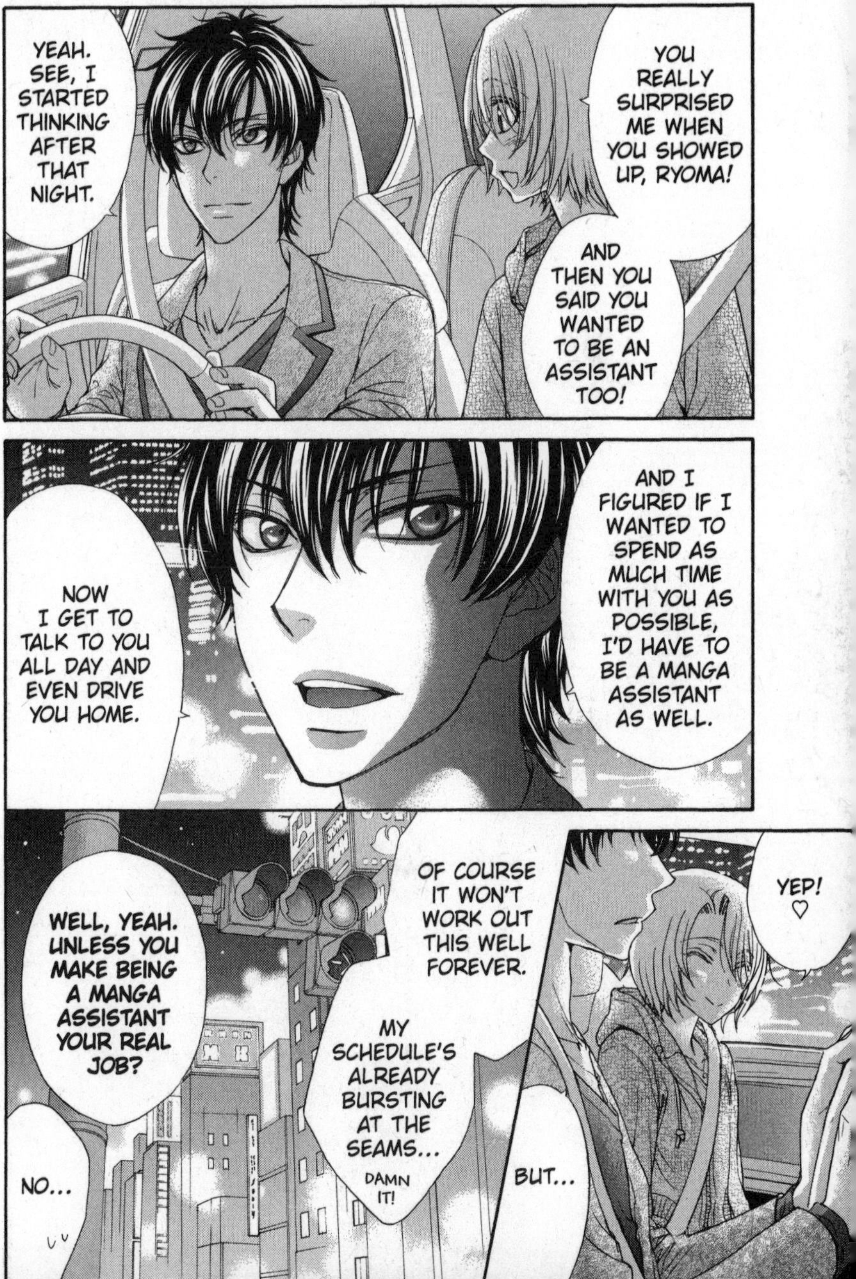
YOU REALLY SURPRISED ME WHEN YOU SHOWED UP, RYOMA!
AND THEN YOU SAID YOU WANTED TO BE AN ASSISTANT TOO!
YEAH. SEE, I STARTED THINKING AFTER THAT NIGHT.
AND I FIGURED IF I WANTED TO SPEND AS MUCH TIME WITH YOU AS POSSIBLE, I'D HAVE TO BE A MANGA ASSISTANT AS WELL.
NOW I GET TO TALK TO YOU ALL DAY AND EVEN DRIVE YOU HOME.
YEP! ♡
BUT...
OF COURSE IT WON'T WORK OUT THIS WELL FOREVER.
MY SCHEDULE'S ALREADY BURSTING AT THE SEAMS...
DAMN IT!
WELL, YEAH. UNLESS YOU MAKE BEING A MANGA ASSISTANT YOUR REAL JOB?
NO...

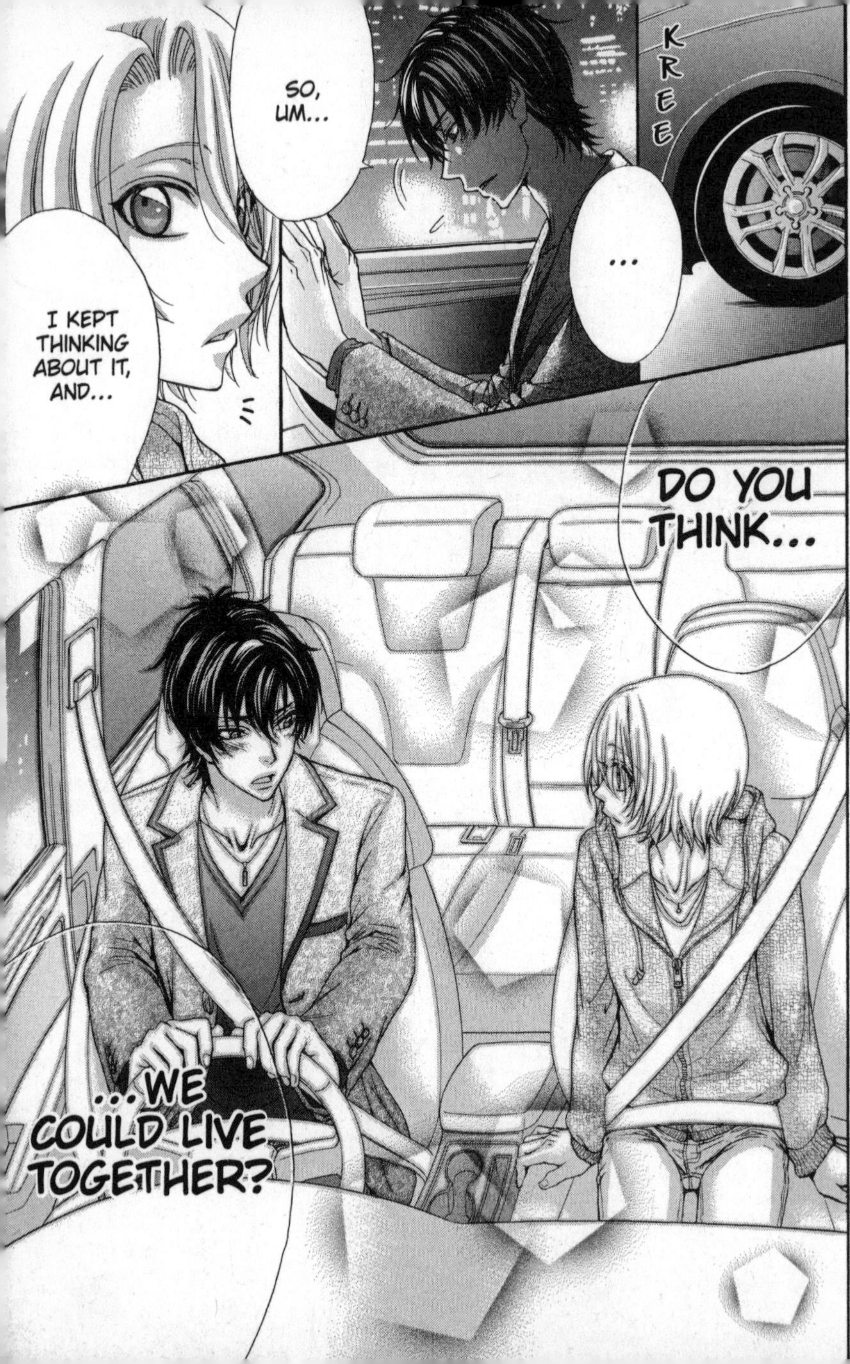
KREE
...
SO, UM...
I KEPT THINKING ABOUT IT, AND...
DO YOU THINK...
...WE COULD LIVE TOGETHER?

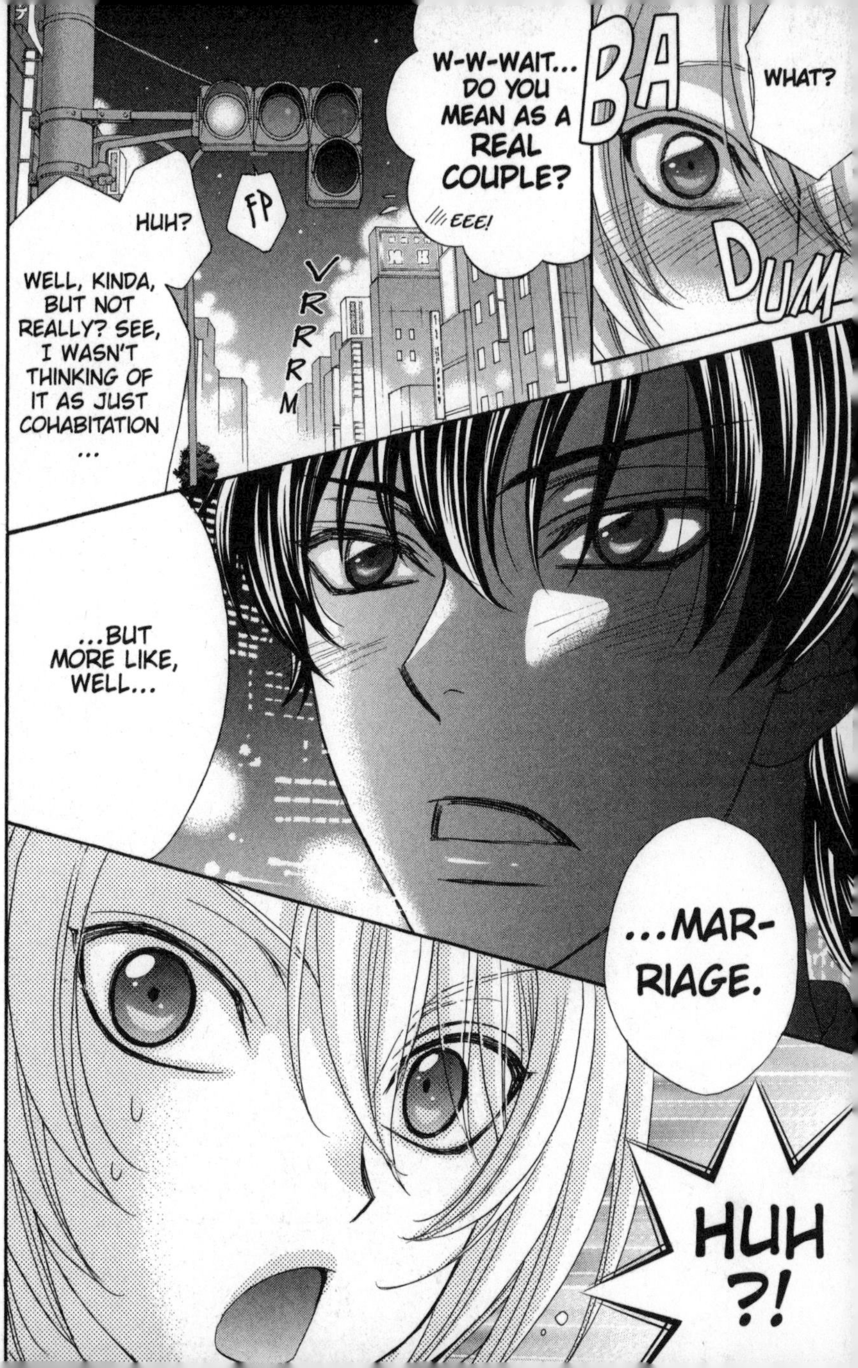
WHAT?
BA
DUM
W-W-WAIT... DO YOU MEAN AS A REAL COUPLE?
EEE!
FP
VRRRM
HUH?
WELL, KINDA, BUT NOT REALLY? SEE, I WASN'T THINKING OF IT AS JUST COHABITATION ...
...BUT MORE LIKE, WELL...
...MAR-RIAGE.
HUH ?!

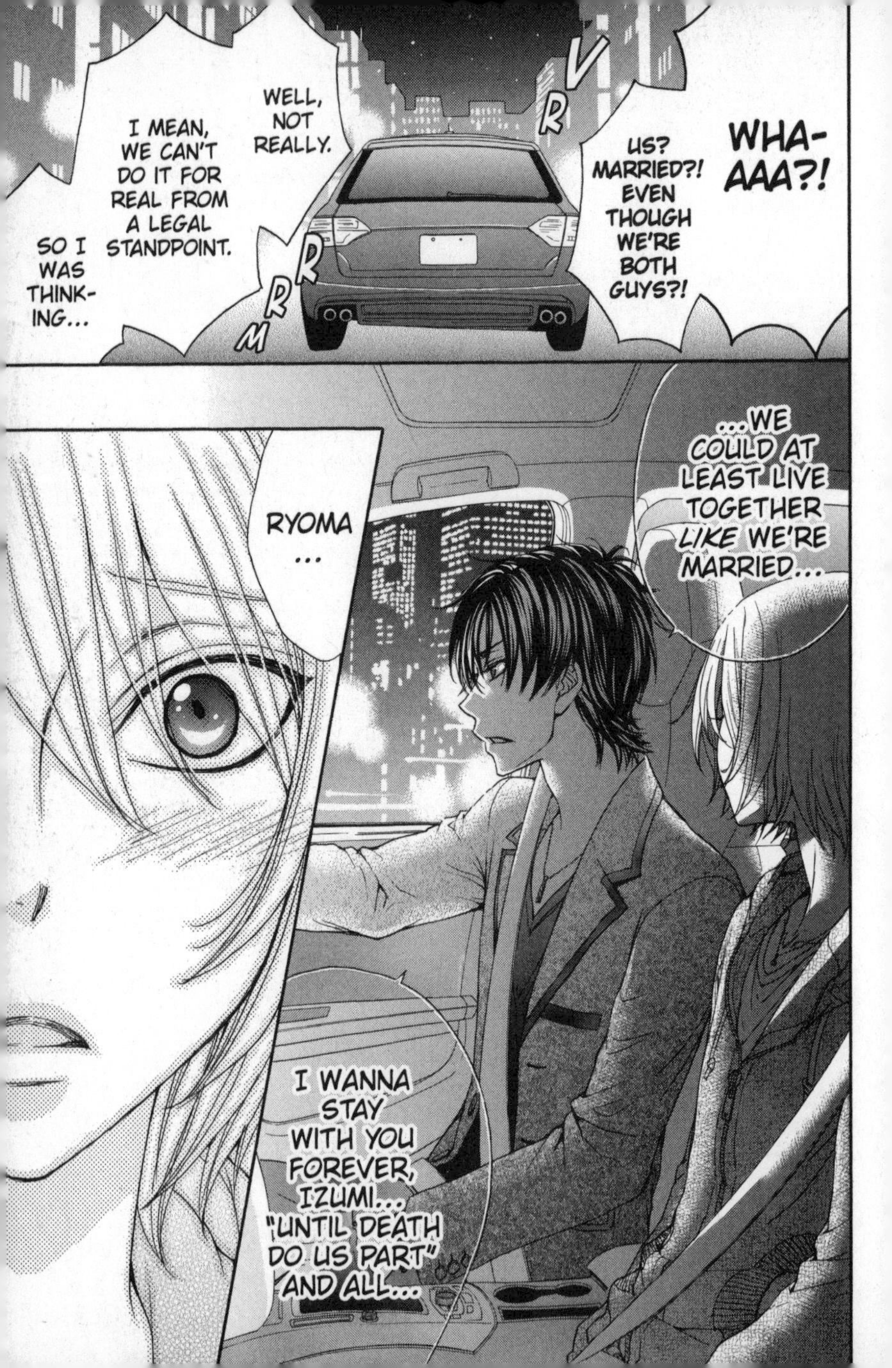
WHA-AAA?!
US? MARRIED?! EVEN THOUGH WE'RE BOTH GUYS?!
VRRRM
WELL, NOT REALLY.
I MEAN, WE CAN'T DO IT FOR REAL FROM A LEGAL STANDPOINT.
SO I WAS THINKING...
...WE COULD AT LEAST LIVE TOGETHER *LIKE* WE'RE MARRIED...
I WANNA STAY WITH YOU FOREVER, IZUMI... "UNTIL DEATH DO US PART" AND ALL...
RYOMA...

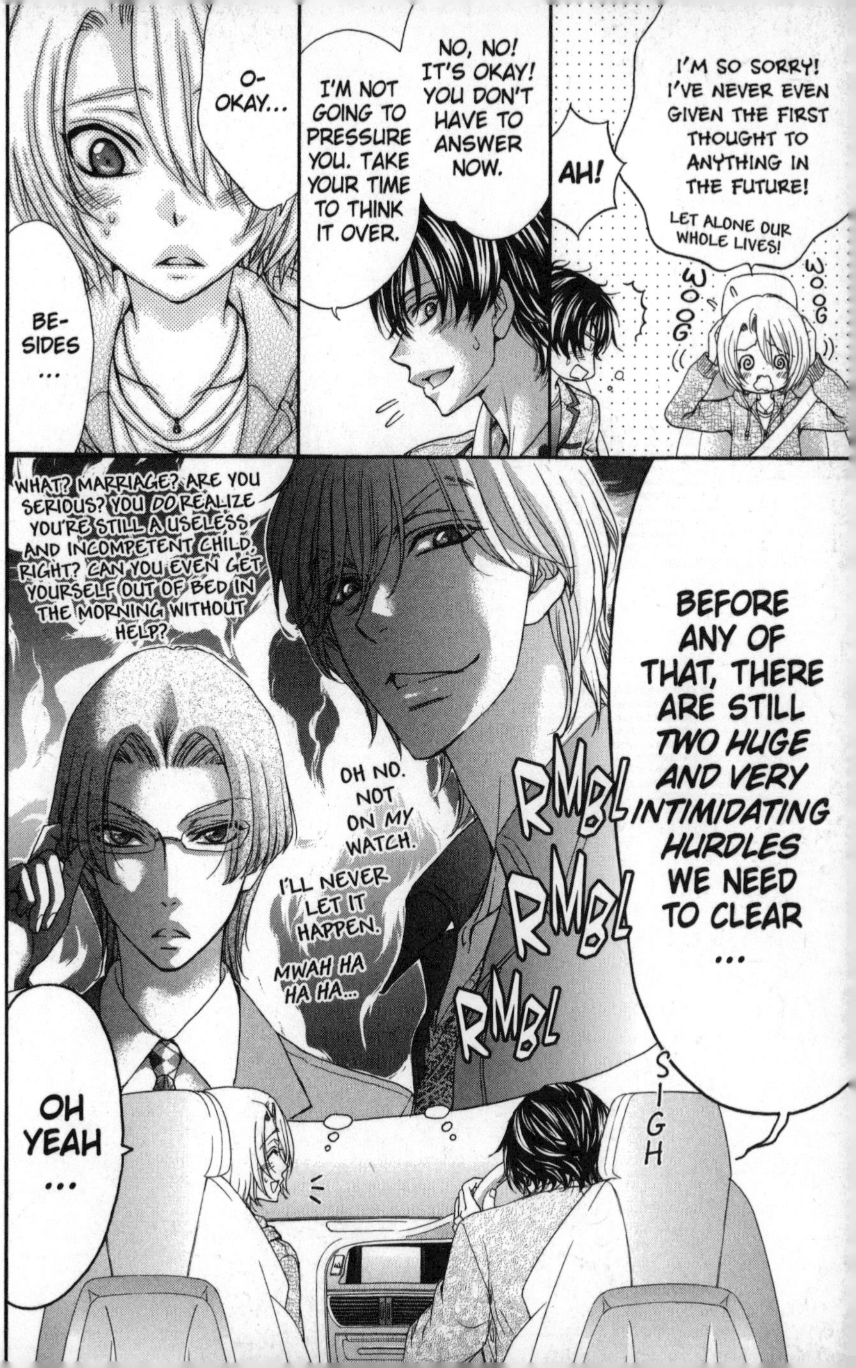
I'M SO SORRY! I'VE NEVER EVEN GIVEN THE FIRST THOUGHT TO ANYTHING IN THE FUTURE!
LET ALONE OUR WHOLE LIVES!
WOOG
WOOG
AH!
NO, NO! IT'S OKAY! YOU DON'T HAVE TO ANSWER NOW.
I'M NOT GOING TO PRESSURE YOU. TAKE YOUR TIME TO THINK IT OVER.
O-OKAY...
BE-SIDES...
BEFORE ANY OF THAT, THERE ARE STILL TWO HUGE AND VERY INTIMIDATING HURDLES WE NEED TO CLEAR...
RMBL
RMBL
RMBL
OH NO. NOT ON MY WATCH.
I'LL NEVER LET IT HAPPEN.
MWAH HA HA HA...
WHAT? MARRIAGE? ARE YOU SERIOUS? YOU DO REALIZE YOU'RE STILL A USELESS AND INCOMPETENT CHILD, RIGHT? CAN YOU EVEN GET YOURSELF OUT OF BED IN THE MORNING WITHOUT HELP?
SIGH
OH YEAH...

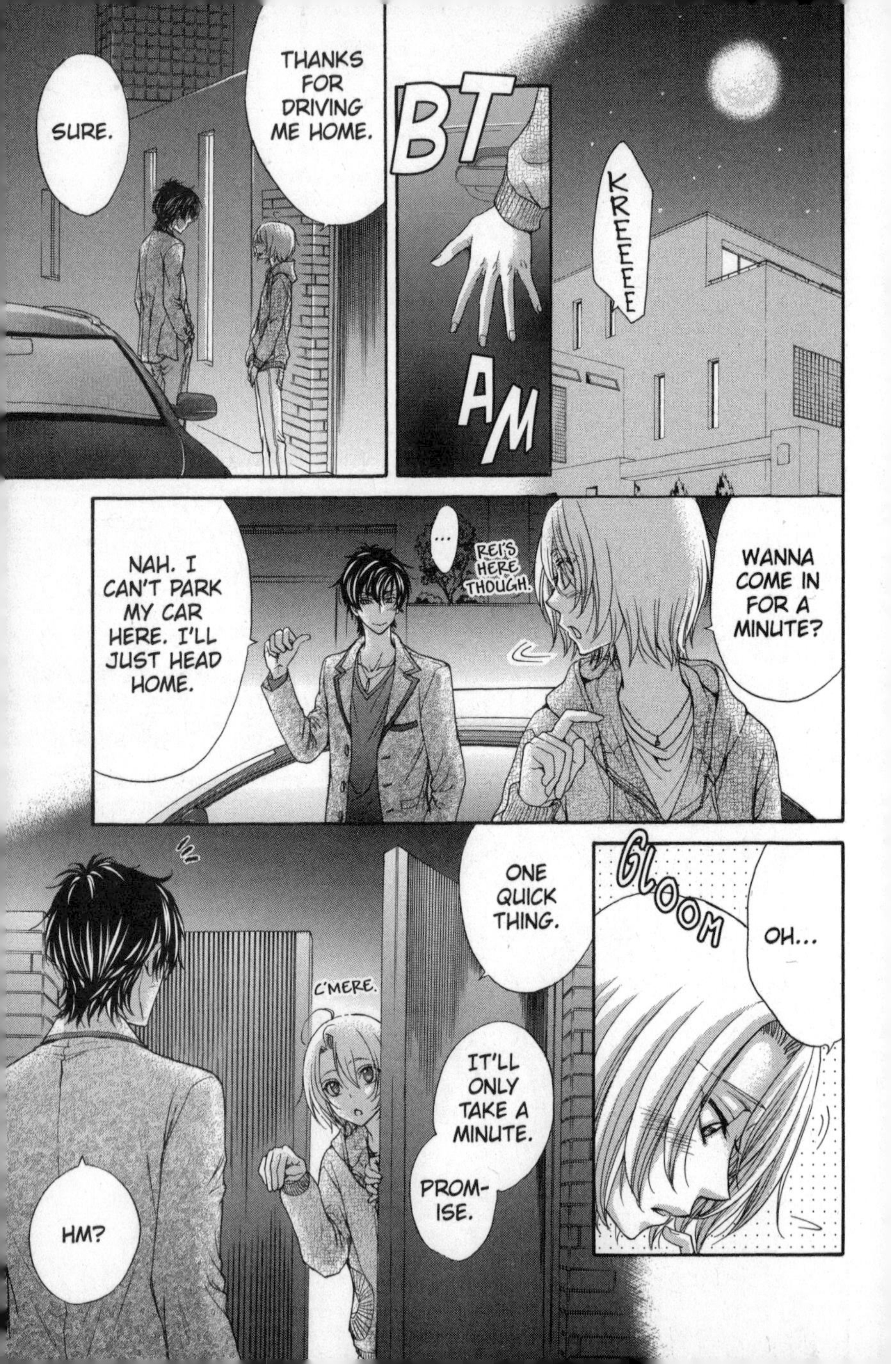
KREEEEE
BT
AM
THANKS FOR DRIVING ME HOME.
SURE.
WANNA COME IN FOR A MINUTE?
...
REI'S HERE THOUGH.
NAH. I CAN'T PARK MY CAR HERE. I'LL JUST HEAD HOME.
GLOOM
OH...
ONE QUICK THING.
IT'LL ONLY TAKE A MINUTE.
PROMISE.
C'MERE.
HM?

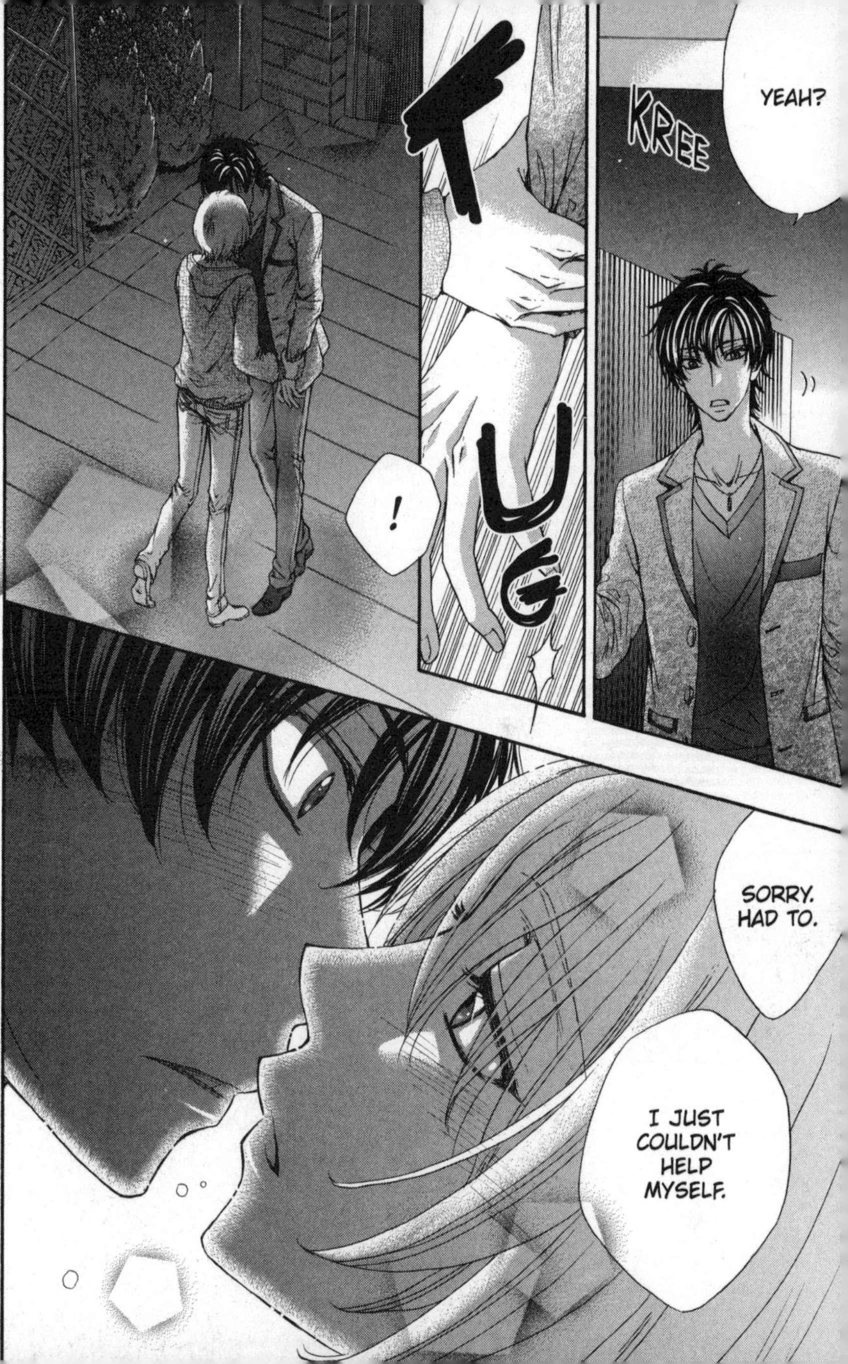
YEAH?
KREE
TUG
!
SORRY. HAD TO.
I JUST COULDN'T HELP MYSELF.

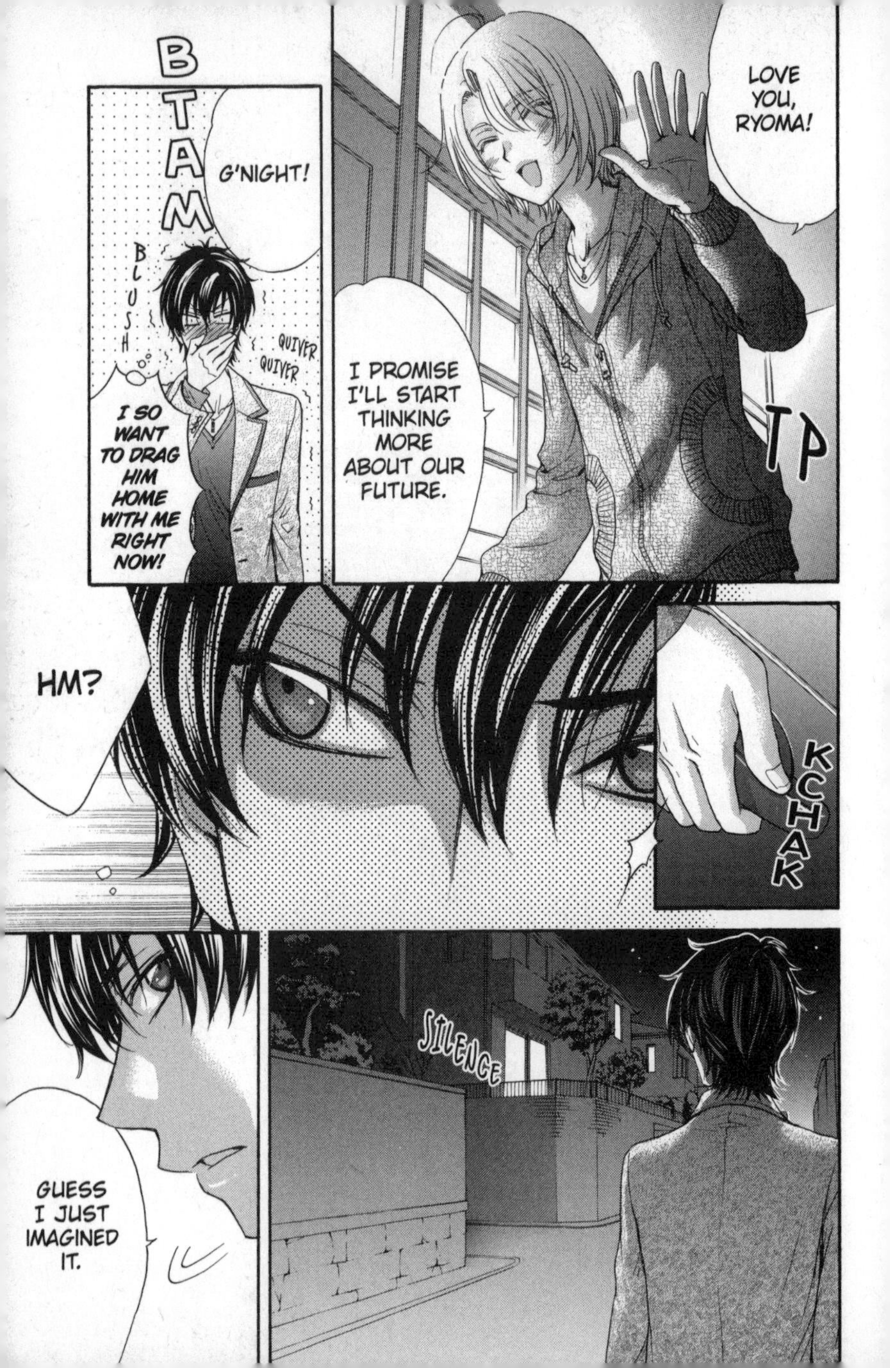
LOVE YOU, RYOMA!
I PROMISE I'LL START THINKING MORE ABOUT OUR FUTURE.
TP
BTAM
G'NIGHT!
BLUSH
QUIVER QUIVER
I SO WANT TO DRAG HIM HOME WITH ME RIGHT NOW!
KCHAK
HM?
SILENCE
GUESS I JUST IMAGINED IT.

PEEK

VRRRM-

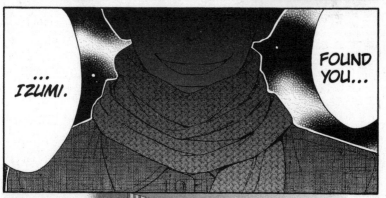

...IZUMI.

FOUND YOU...

LIVING TOGETHER...

...FOR THE REST OF OUR LIVES...

SHOOP

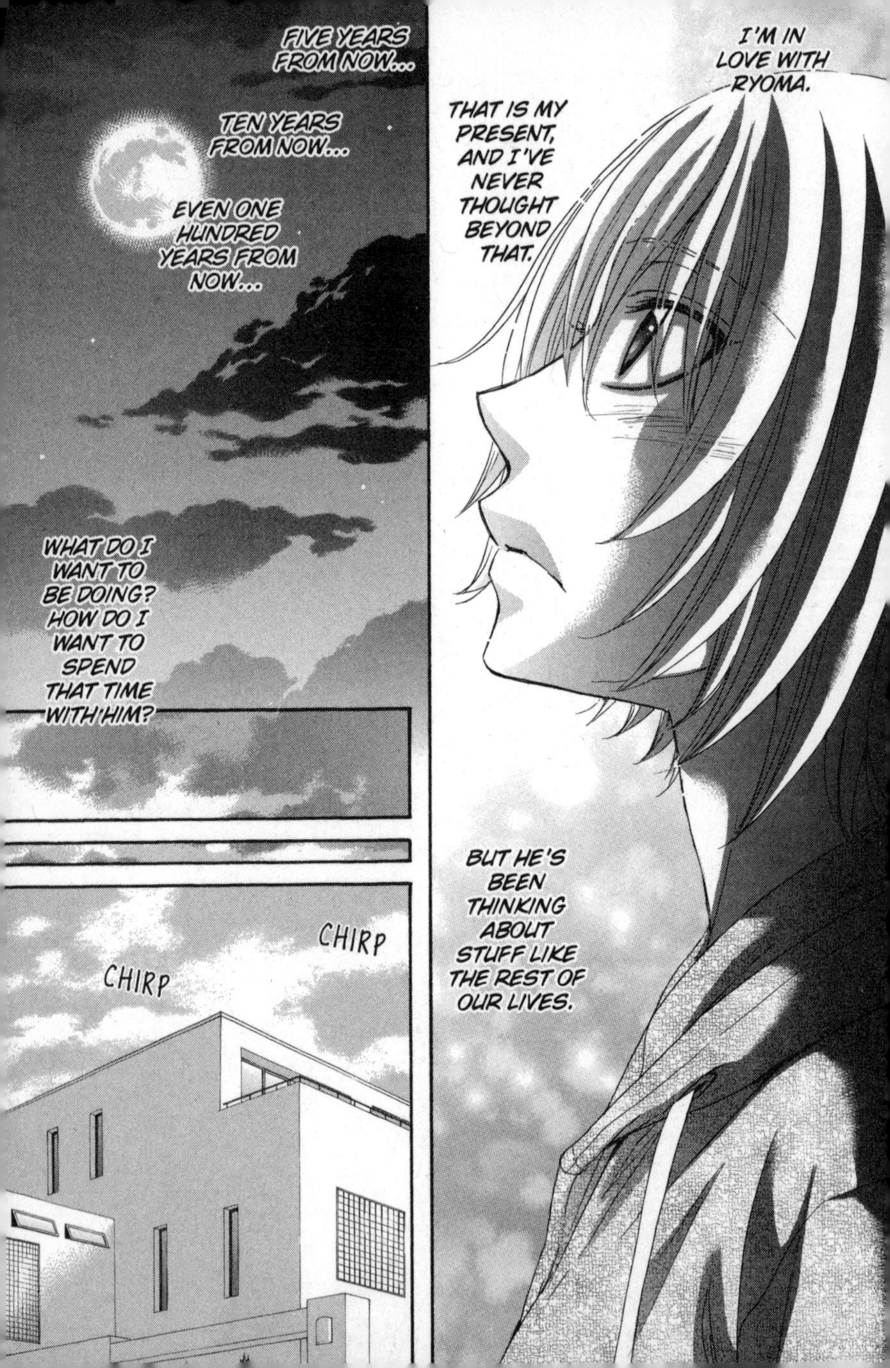
I'M IN LOVE WITH RYOMA.
THAT IS MY PRESENT, AND I'VE NEVER THOUGHT BEYOND THAT.
BUT HE'S BEEN THINKING ABOUT STUFF LIKE THE REST OF OUR LIVES.
FIVE YEARS FROM NOW...
TEN YEARS FROM NOW...
EVEN ONE HUNDRED YEARS FROM NOW...
WHAT DO I WANT TO BE DOING? HOW DO I WANT TO SPEND THAT TIME WITH HIM?
CHIRP
CHIRP

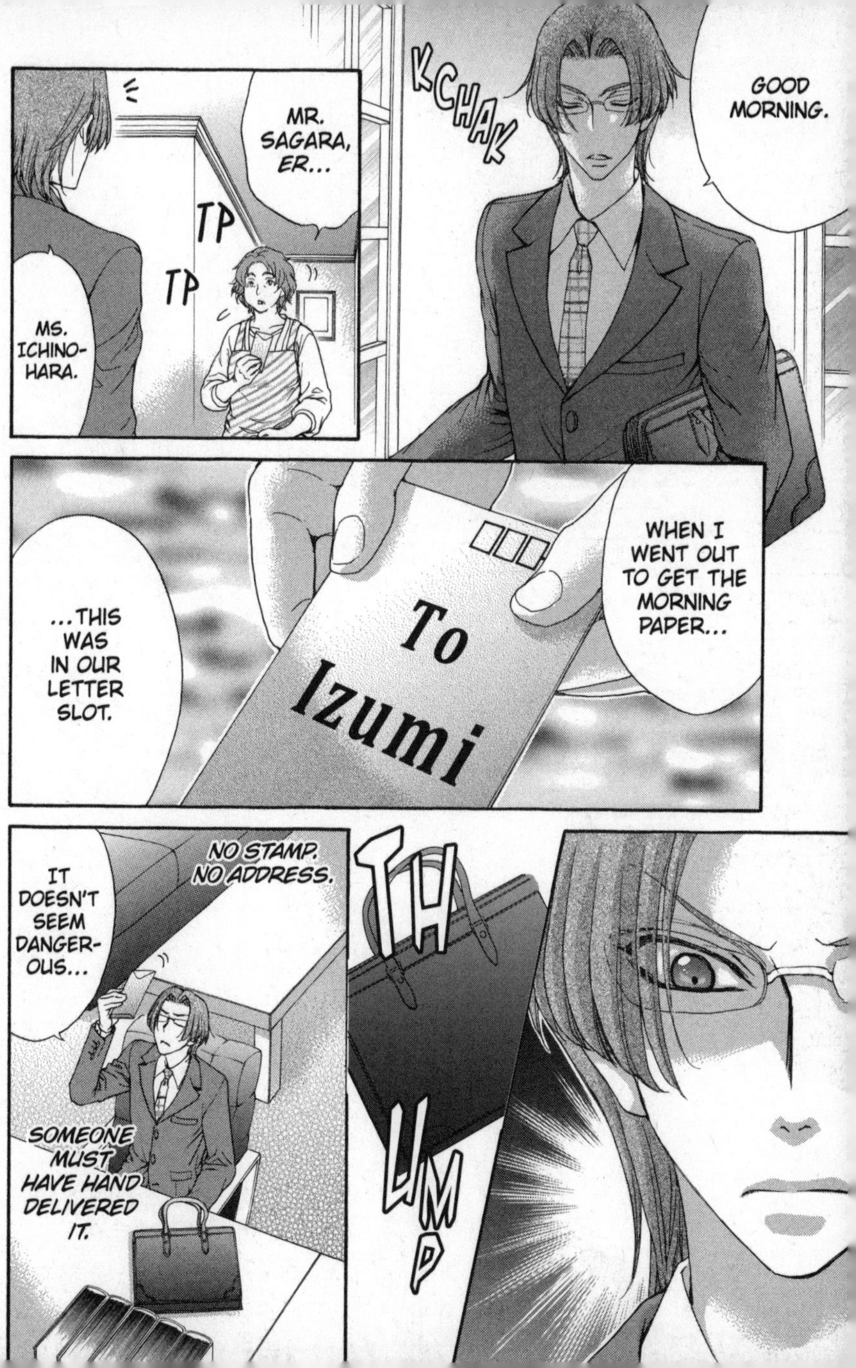
KCHAK
GOOD MORNING.
MR. SAGARA, ER...
TP
TP
MS. ICHINO-HARA.
WHEN I WENT OUT TO GET THE MORNING PAPER...
To Izumi
...THIS WAS IN OUR LETTER SLOT.
THUMP
NO STAMP. NO ADDRESS.
IT DOESN'T SEEM DANGER-OUS...
SOMEONE MUST HAVE HAND DELIVERED IT.

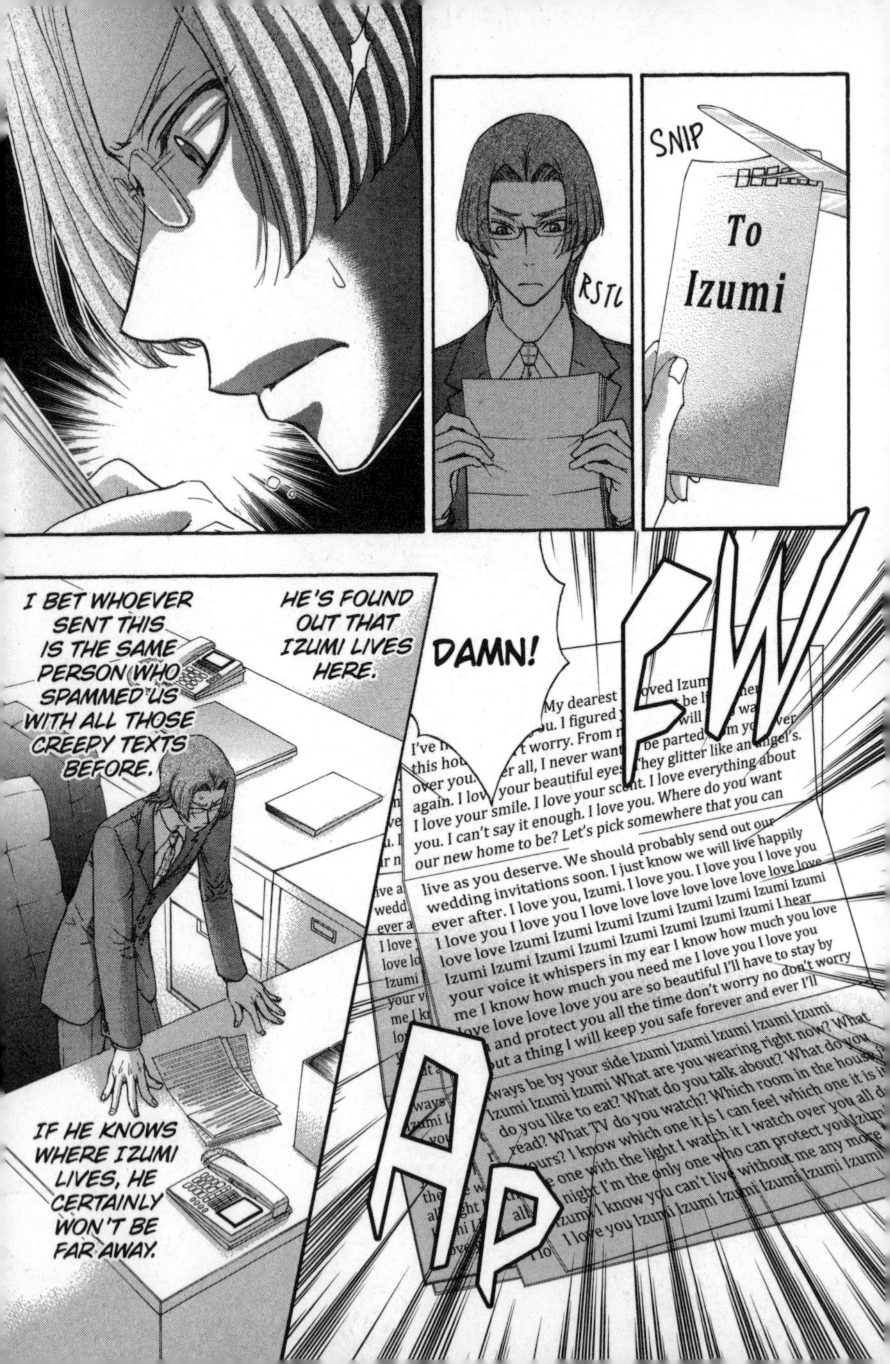
SNIP
To Izumi
RSTL
DAMN!
FWAP
I love your smile. I love your scent. I love everything about
you. I can't say it enough. I love you. Where do you want
our new home to be? Let's pick somewhere that you can
live as you deserve. We should probably send out our
wedding invitations soon. I just know we will live happily
ever after. I love you, Izumi. I love you. I love you I love you
I love you I love you I love love love love love love love
love love Izumi Izumi Izumi Izumi Izumi Izumi Izumi Izumi
Izumi Izumi Izumi Izumi Izumi Izumi Izumi I hear
your voice it whispers in my ear I know how much you love
me I know how much you need me I love you I love you
HE'S FOUND OUT THAT IZUMI LIVES HERE.
I BET WHOEVER SENT THIS IS THE SAME PERSON WHO SPAMMED US WITH ALL THOSE CREEPY TEXTS BEFORE.
IF HE KNOWS WHERE IZUMI LIVES, HE CERTAINLY WON'T BE FAR AWAY.

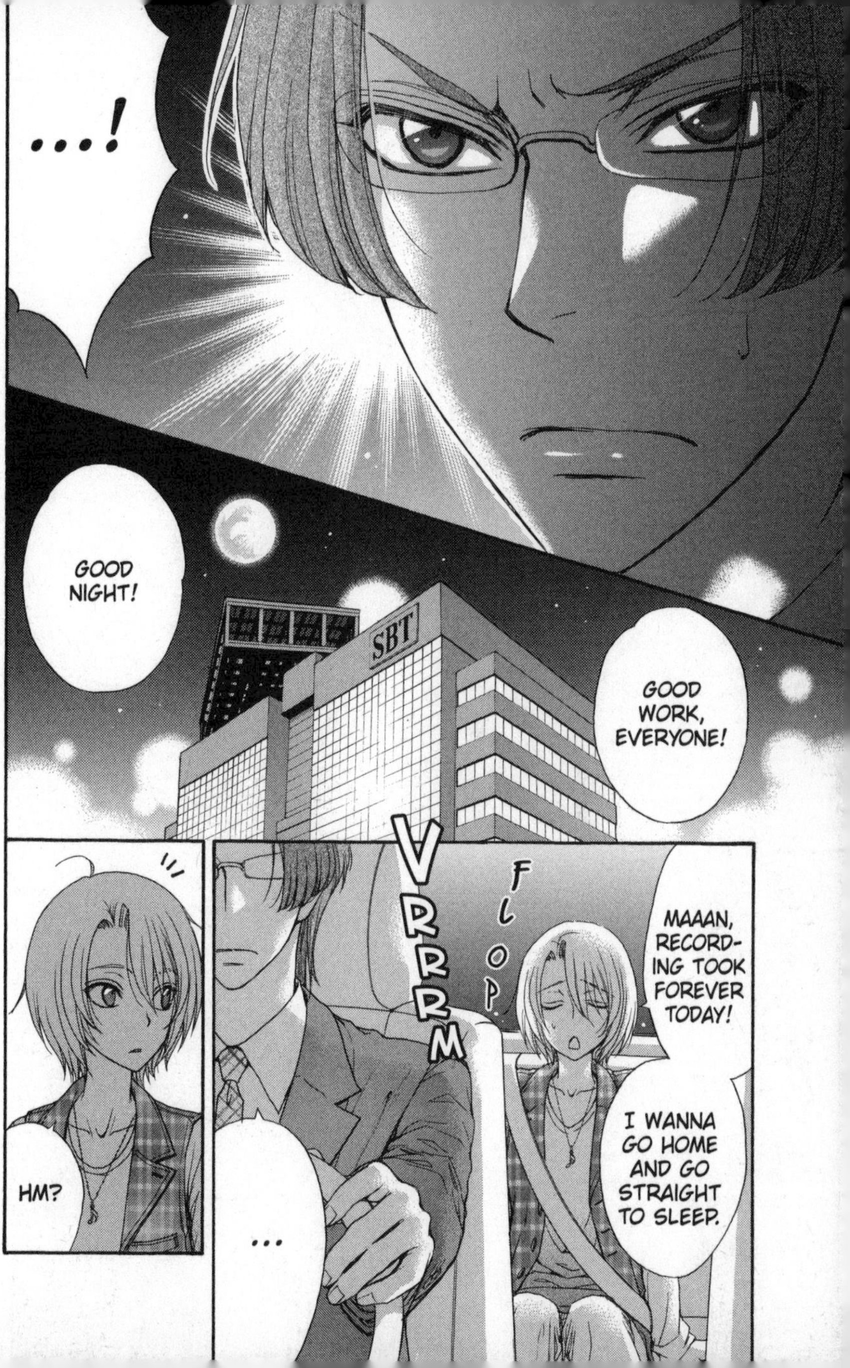
...!
GOOD WORK, EVERYONE!
GOOD NIGHT!
VRRRM
FLOP
MAAAN, RECORDING TOOK FOREVER TODAY!
I WANNA GO HOME AND GO STRAIGHT TO SLEEP.
...
HM?

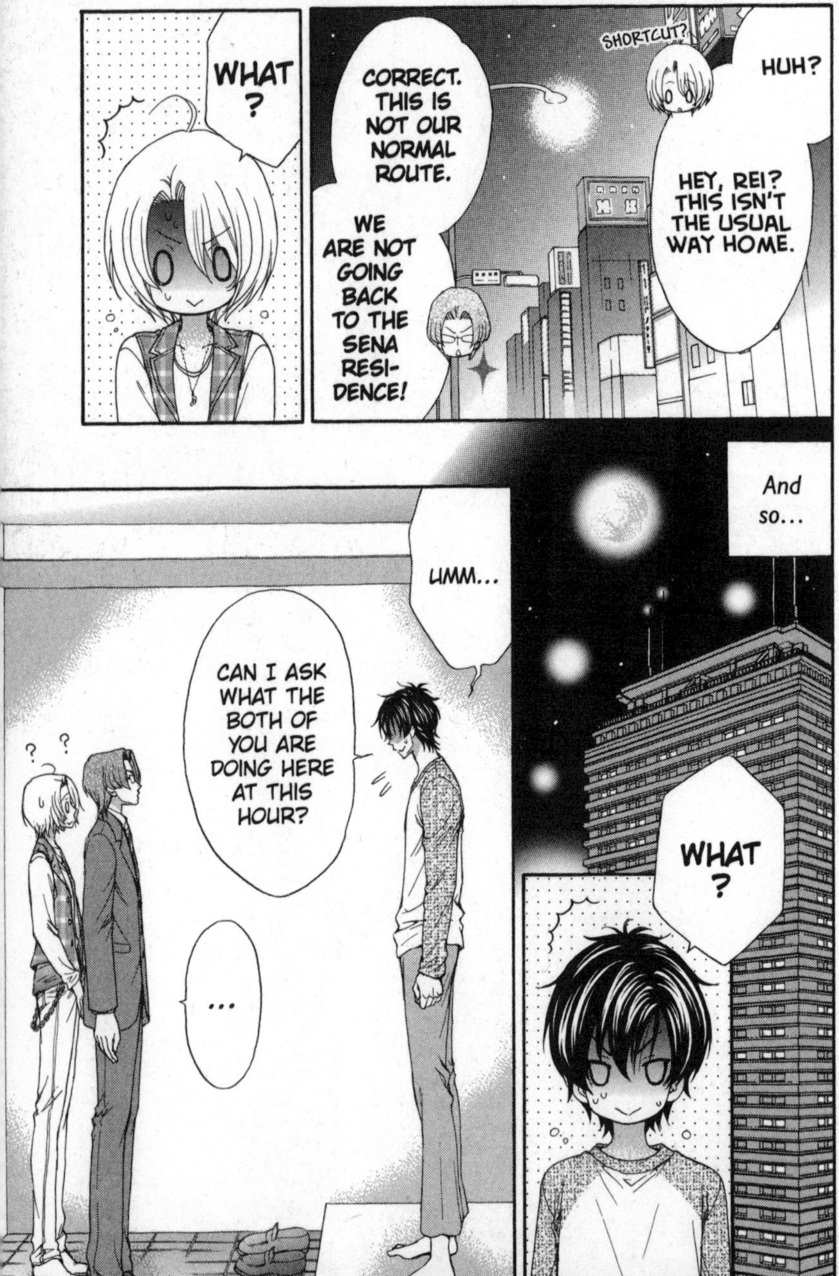
HUH?
HEY, REI? THIS ISN'T THE USUAL WAY HOME.
SHORTCUT?
CORRECT. THIS IS NOT OUR NORMAL ROUTE.
WE ARE NOT GOING BACK TO THE SENA RESI-DENCE!
WHAT?
And so...
WHAT?
UMM...
CAN I ASK WHAT THE BOTH OF YOU ARE DOING HERE AT THIS HOUR?
...

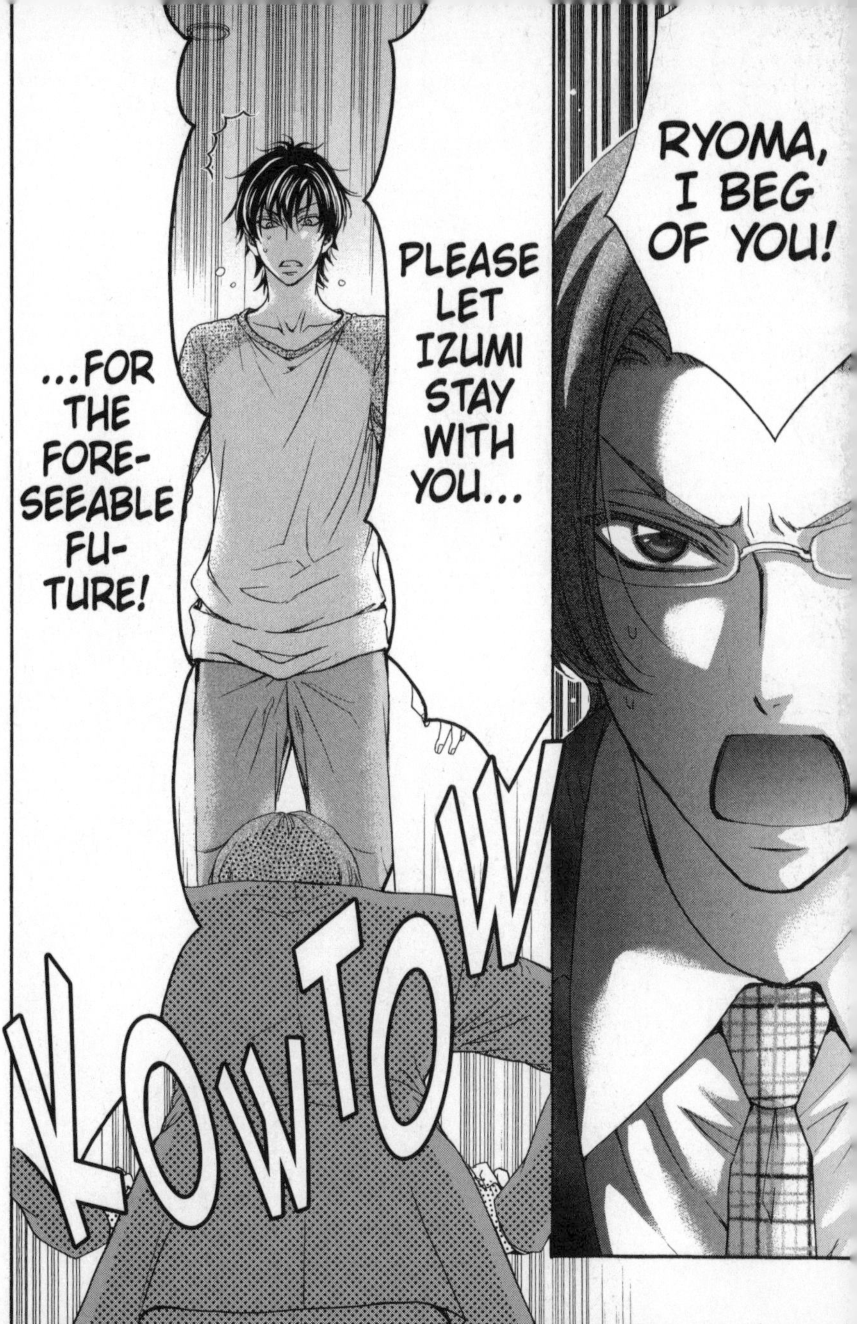
RYOMA, I BEG OF YOU!
PLEASE LET IZUMI STAY WITH YOU...
...FOR THE FORE-SEEABLE FU-TURE!
KOWTOW

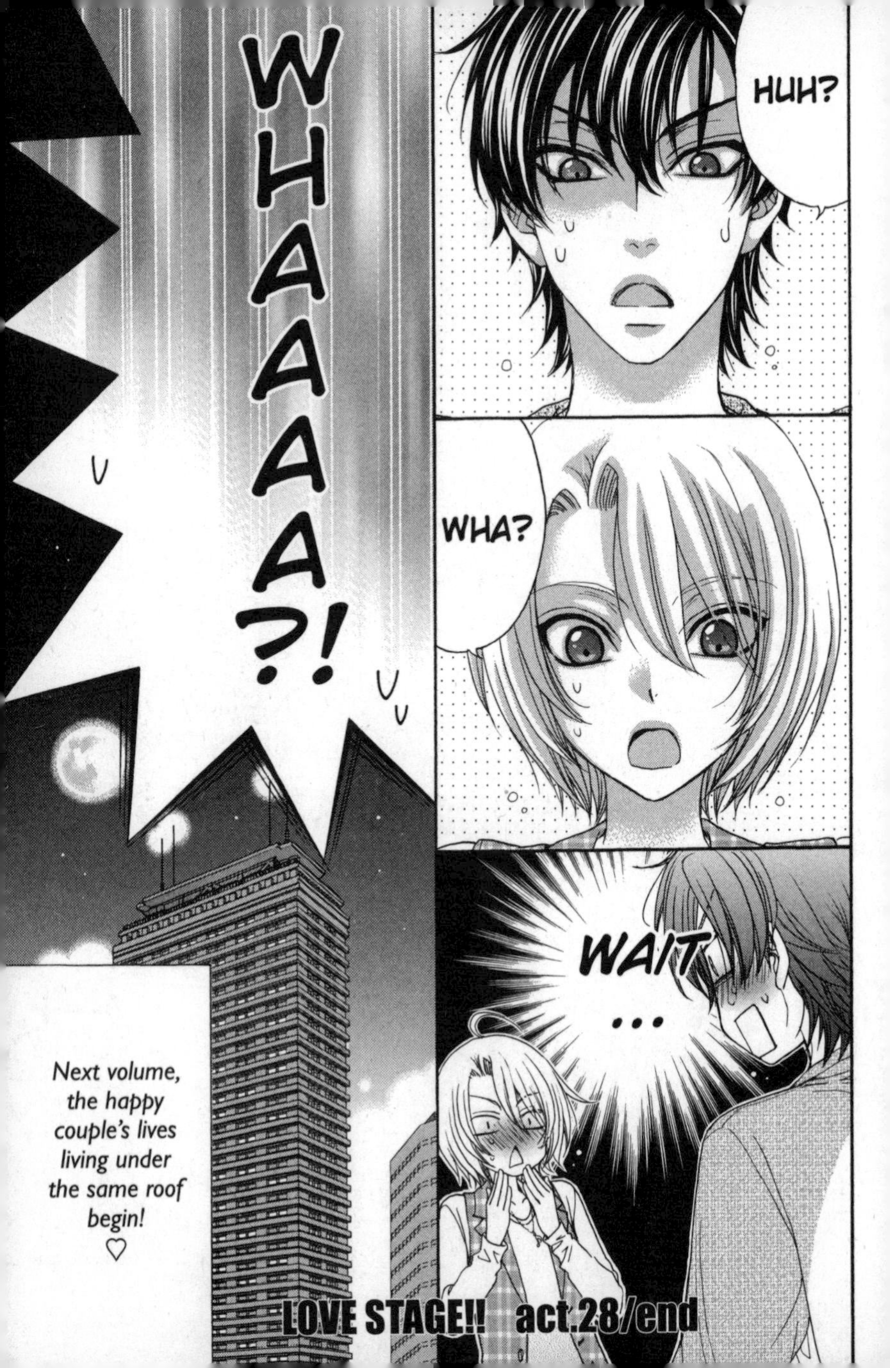
HUH?
WHA?
WAIT ...
WHAAAA?!
Next volume, the happy couple's lives living under the same roof begin! ♡
LOVE STAGE!! act.28/end

LOVE STAGE!!

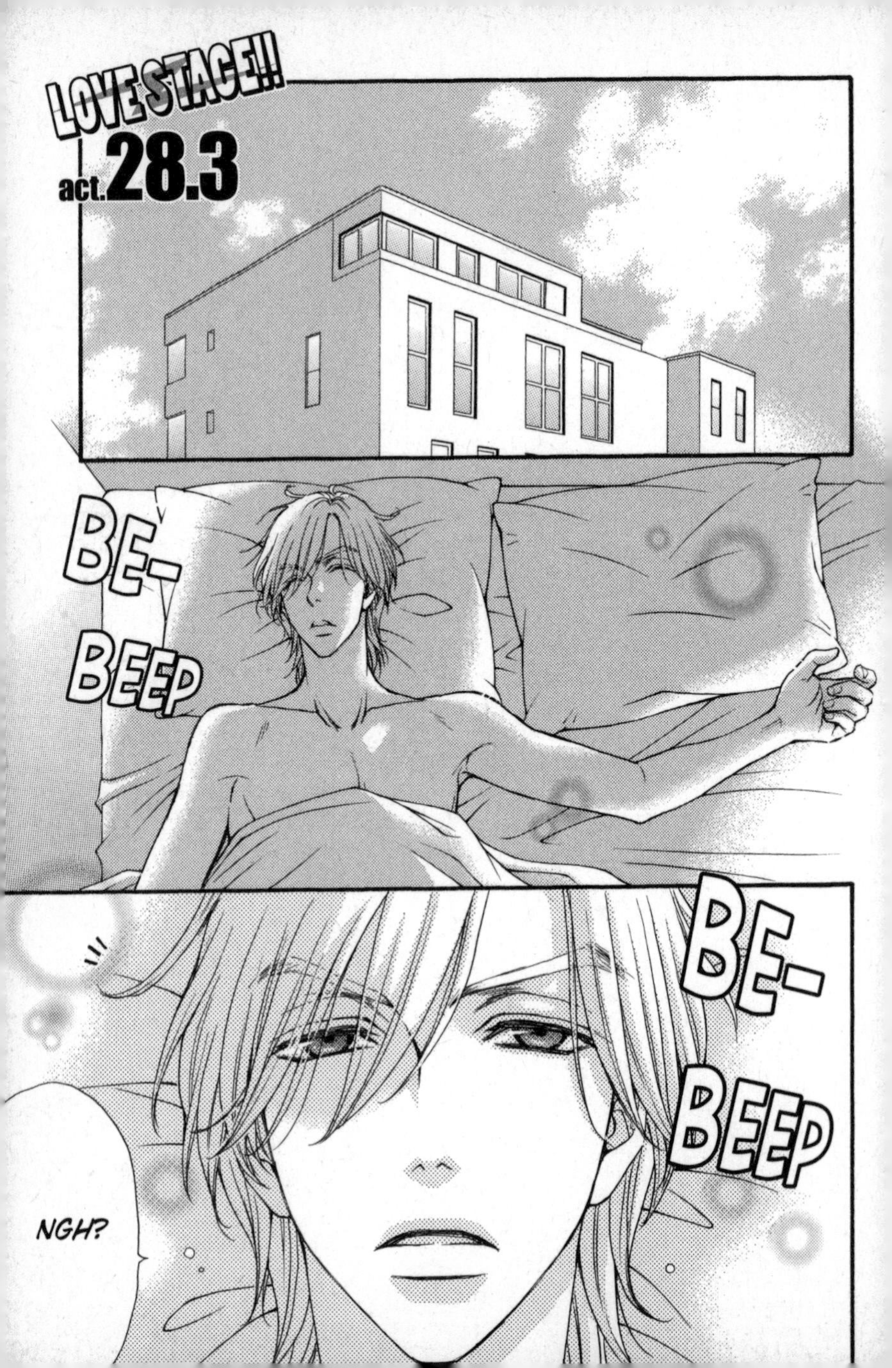
LOVE STAGE!!
act.28.3
BE-BEEP
BE-BEEP
!!
NGH?

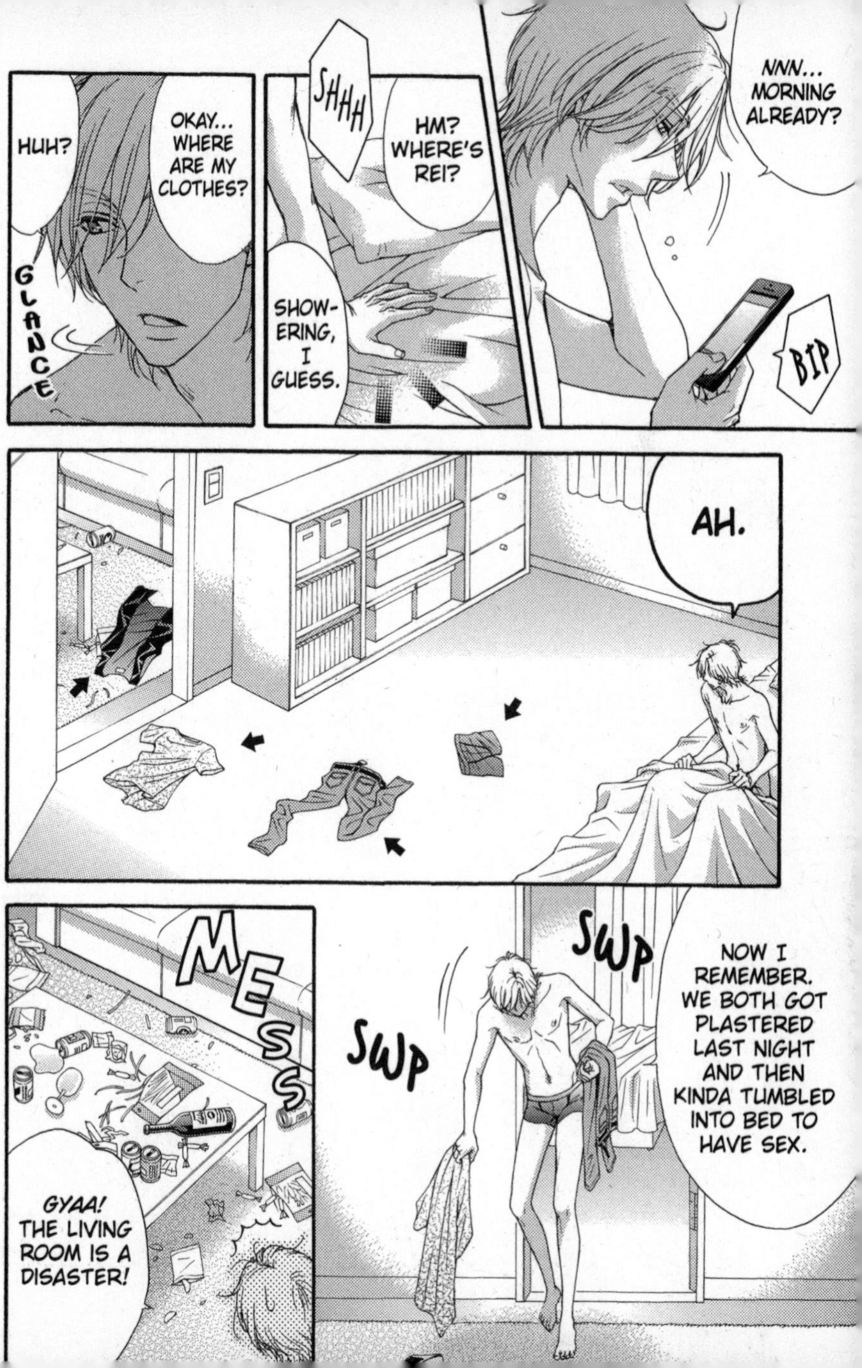
NNN... MORNING ALREADY?
BIP
SHHH
HM? WHERE'S REI?
SHOW-ERING, I GUESS.
OKAY... WHERE ARE MY CLOTHES?
HUH?
GLANCE
AH.
SWP
SWP
NOW I REMEMBER. WE BOTH GOT PLASTERED LAST NIGHT AND THEN KINDA TUMBLED INTO BED TO HAVE SEX.
MESS
GYAA! THE LIVING ROOM IS A DISASTER!

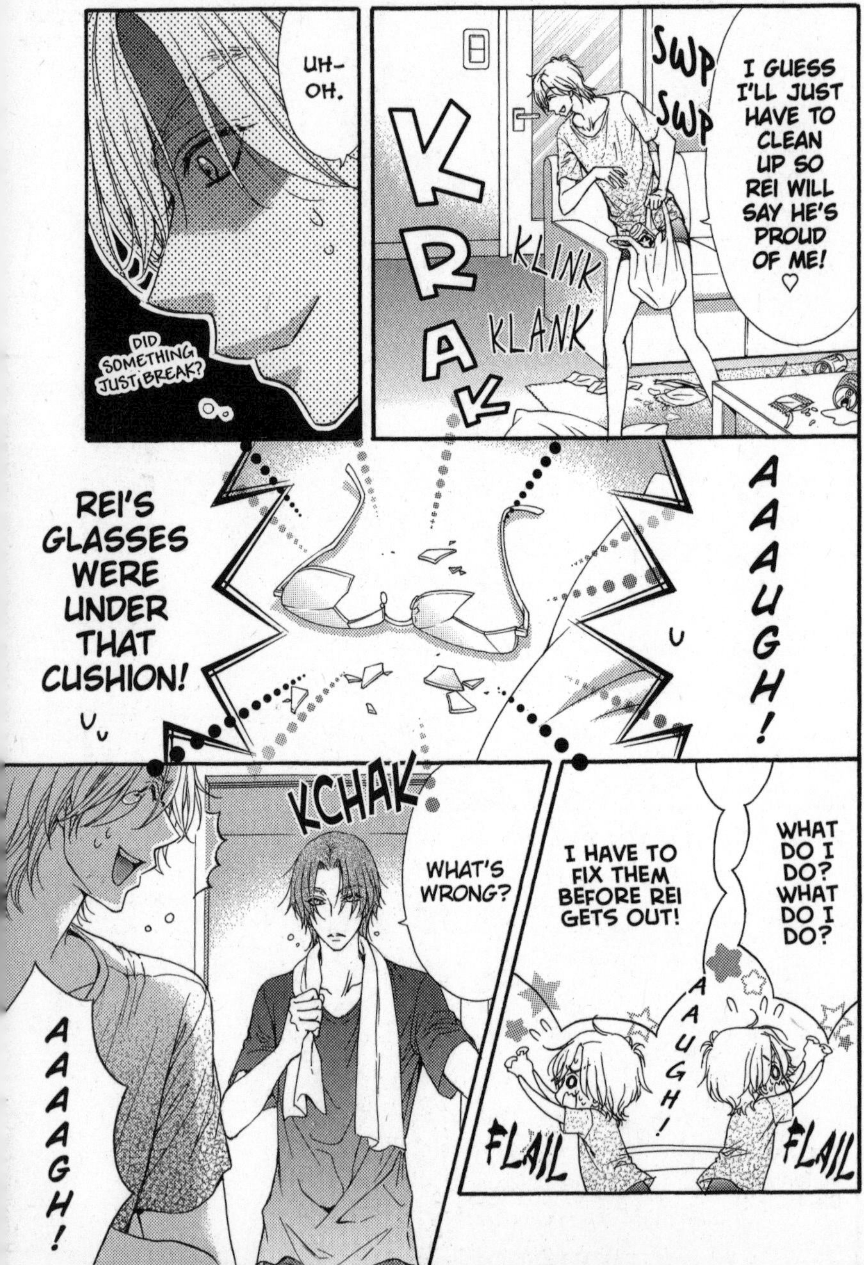

SWP SWP
I GUESS I'LL JUST HAVE TO CLEAN UP SO REI WILL SAY HE'S PROUD OF ME! ♡
KRAK
KLINK
KLANK
UH-OH.
DID SOMETHING JUST BREAK?
AAAAUGH!
REI'S GLASSES WERE UNDER THAT CUSHION!
WHAT DO I DO? WHAT DO I DO?
I HAVE TO FIX THEM BEFORE REI GETS OUT!
AAUGH!
FLAIL
FLAIL
KCHAK
WHAT'S WRONG?
AAAAAGH!

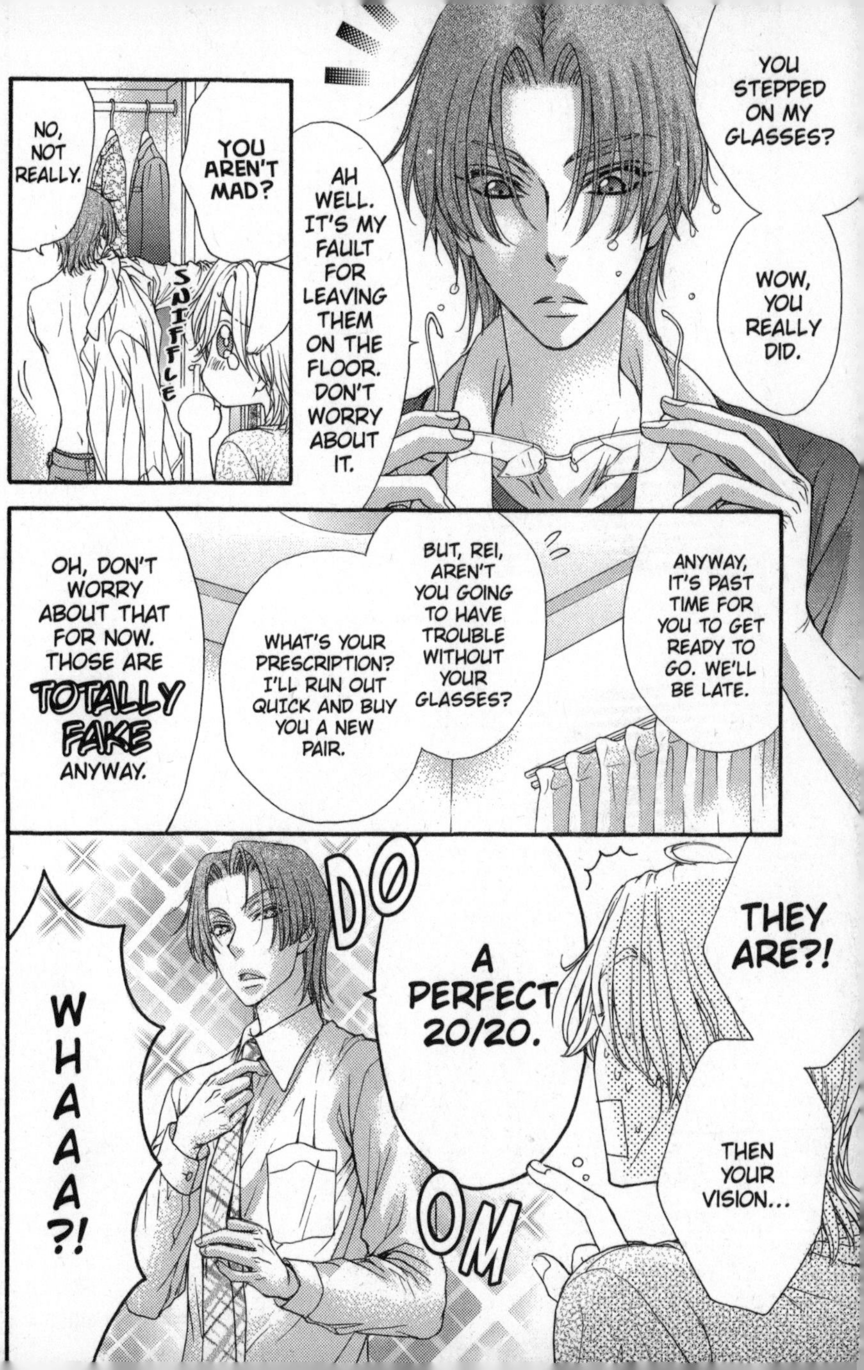
YOU STEPPED ON MY GLASSES?
WOW, YOU REALLY DID.
AH WELL. IT'S MY FAULT FOR LEAVING THEM ON THE FLOOR. DON'T WORRY ABOUT IT.
YOU AREN'T MAD?
NO, NOT REALLY.
SNIFFLE
ANYWAY, IT'S PAST TIME FOR YOU TO GET READY TO GO. WE'LL BE LATE.
BUT, REI, AREN'T YOU GOING TO HAVE TROUBLE WITHOUT YOUR GLASSES?
WHAT'S YOUR PRESCRIPTION? I'LL RUN OUT QUICK AND BUY YOU A NEW PAIR.
OH, DON'T WORRY ABOUT THAT FOR NOW. THOSE ARE TOTALLY FAKE ANYWAY.
THEY ARE?!
THEN YOUR VISION...
A PERFECT 20/20.
DOOM
WHAAAA?!

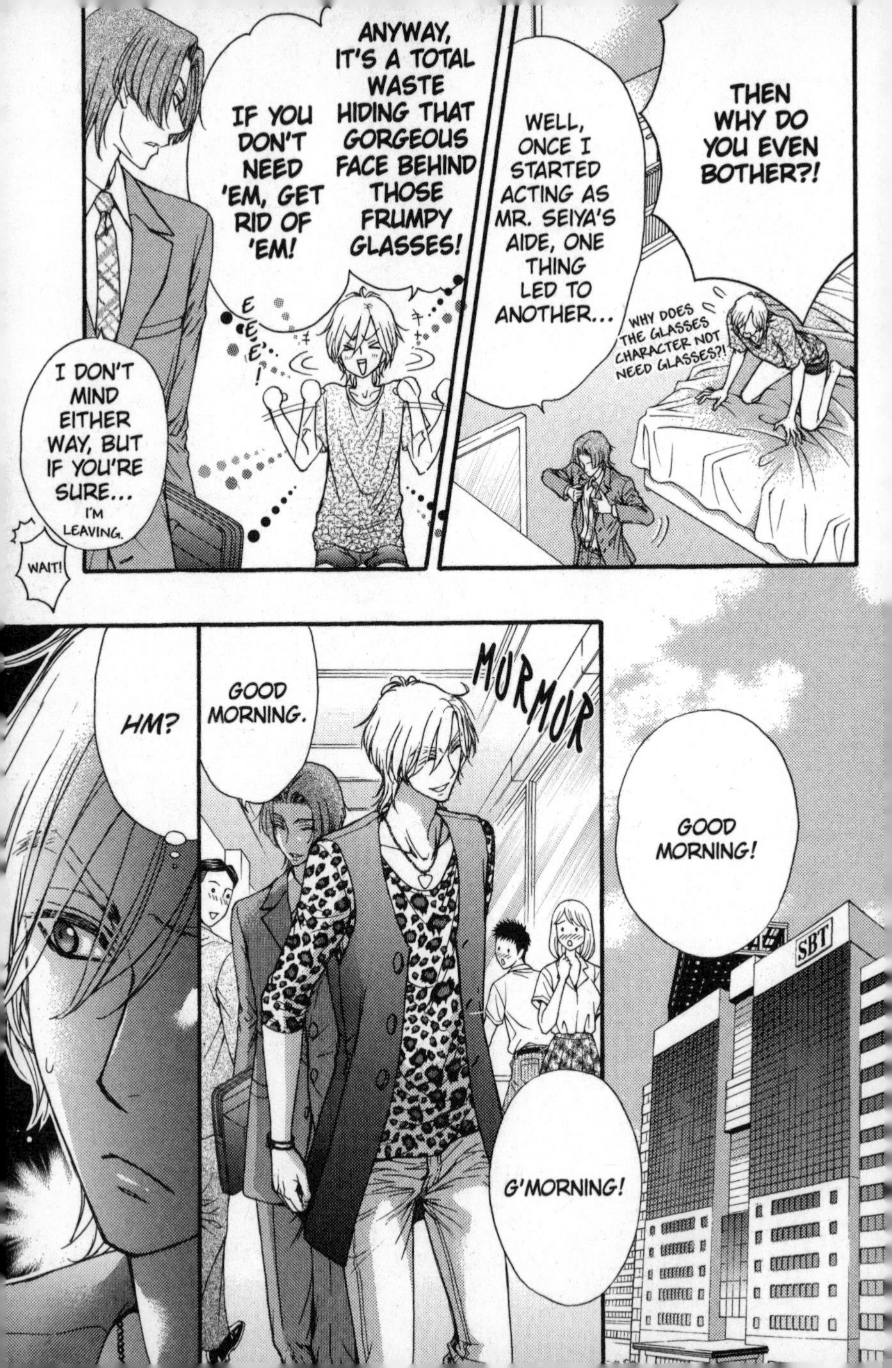
THEN WHY DO YOU EVEN BOTHER?!
WELL, ONCE I STARTED ACTING AS MR. SEIYA'S AIDE, ONE THING LED TO ANOTHER...
WHY DOES THE GLASSES CHARACTER NOT NEED GLASSES?!
ANYWAY, IT'S A TOTAL WASTE HIDING THAT GORGEOUS FACE BEHIND THOSE FRUMPY GLASSES!
IF YOU DON'T NEED 'EM, GET RID OF 'EM!
EEE!
I DON'T MIND EITHER WAY, BUT IF YOU'RE SURE...
I'M LEAVING.
WAIT!
GOOD MORNING!
G'MORNING!
SBT
MURMUR
GOOD MORNING.
HM?

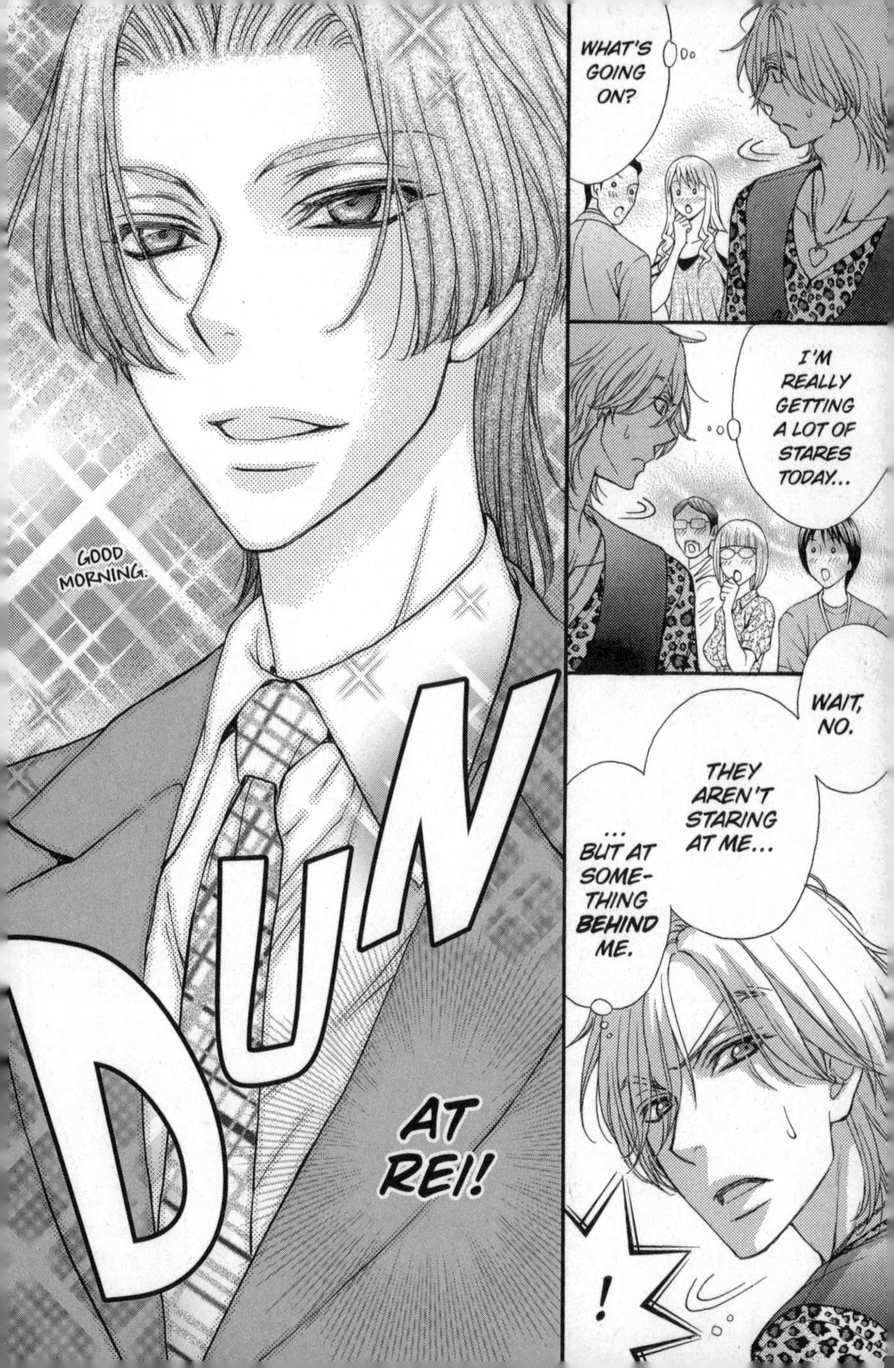
WHAT'S GOING ON?
I'M REALLY GETTING A LOT OF STARES TODAY...
WAIT, NO.
THEY AREN'T STARING AT ME...
... BUT AT SOME-THING BEHIND ME.
!
GOOD MORNING.
DUN
AT REI!

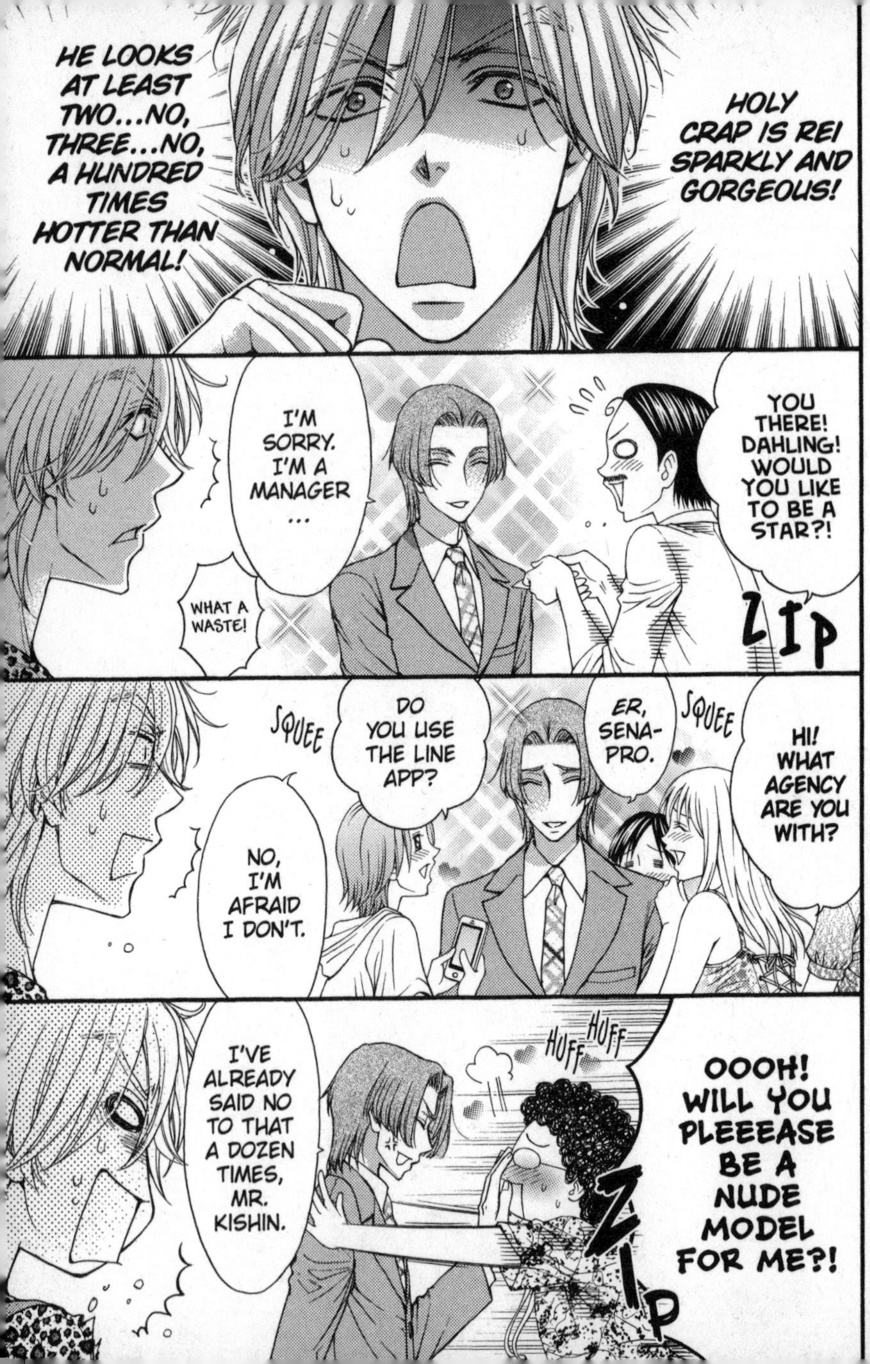
HOLY CRAP IS REI SPARKLY AND GORGEOUS!
HE LOOKS AT LEAST TWO...NO, THREE...NO, A HUNDRED TIMES HOTTER THAN NORMAL!
YOU THERE! DAHLING! WOULD YOU LIKE TO BE A STAR?!
ZIP
I'M SORRY. I'M A MANAGER...
WHAT A WASTE!
HI! WHAT AGENCY ARE YOU WITH?
SQUEE
ER, SENA-PRO.
DO YOU USE THE LINE APP?
SQUEE
NO, I'M AFRAID I DON'T.
OOOH! WILL YOU PLEEEASE BE A NUDE MODEL FOR ME?!
ZIP
HUFF HUFF
I'VE ALREADY SAID NO TO THAT A DOZEN TIMES, MR. KISHIN.

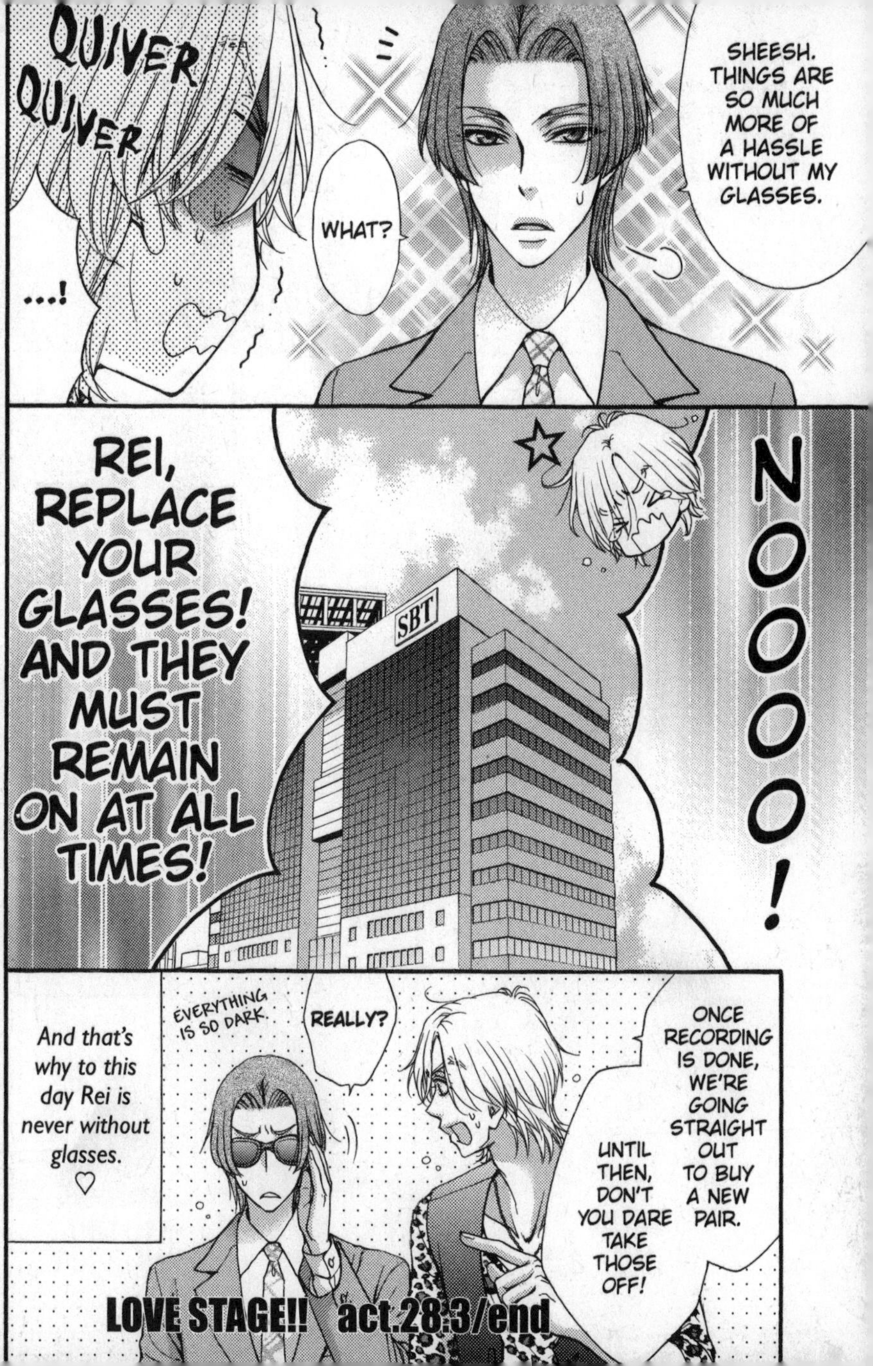
SHEESH. THINGS ARE SO MUCH MORE OF A HASSLE WITHOUT MY GLASSES.
WHAT?
QUIVER QUIVER
...!
NOOOO!
REI, REPLACE YOUR GLASSES! AND THEY MUST REMAIN ON AT ALL TIMES!
SBT
ONCE RECORDING IS DONE, WE'RE GOING STRAIGHT OUT TO BUY A NEW PAIR.
UNTIL THEN, DON'T YOU DARE TAKE THOSE OFF!
REALLY?
EVERYTHING IS SO DARK.
And that's why to this day Rei is never without glasses. ♡
LOVE STAGE!! act.28.3/end

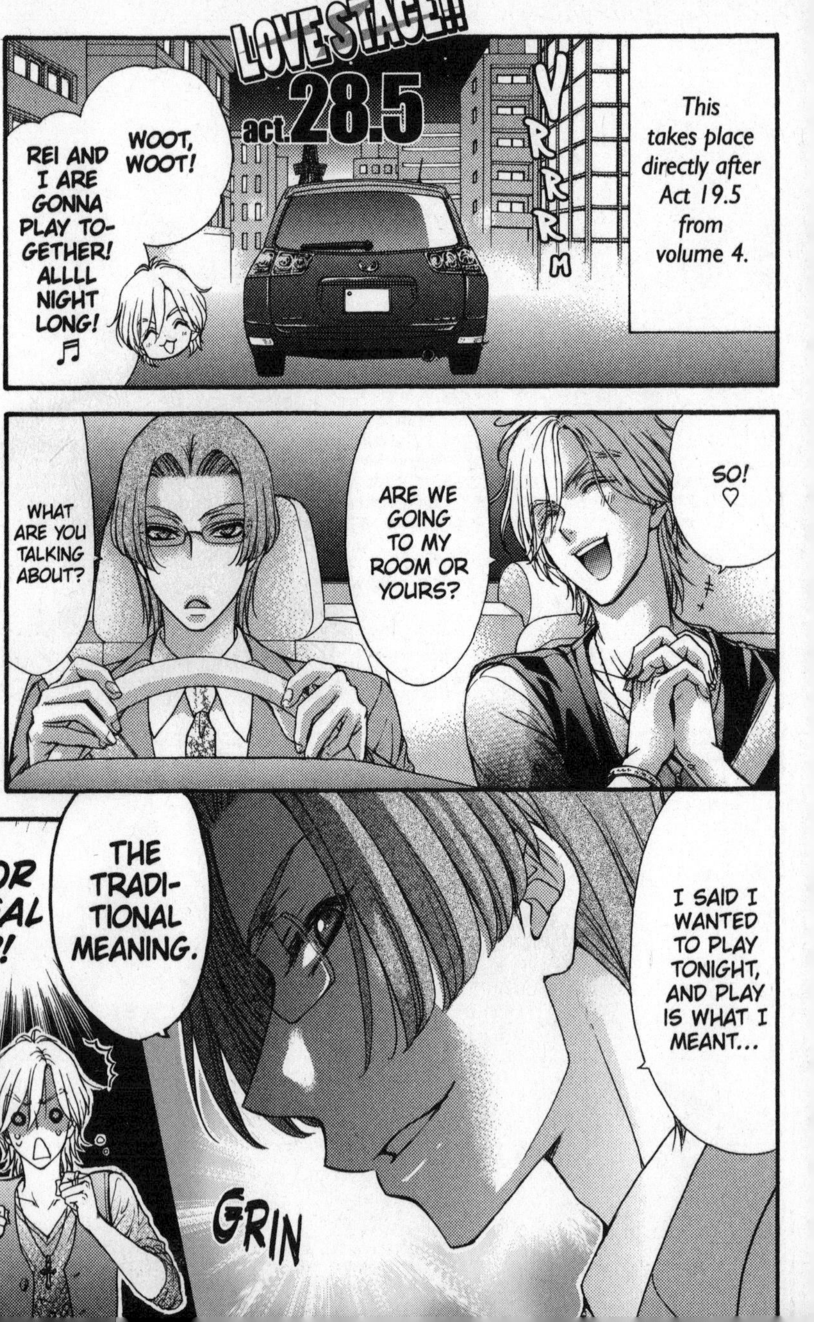
This takes place directly after Act 19.5 from volume 4.
VRRRRM
LOVE STAGE!!
act.28.5
WOOT, WOOT!
REI AND I ARE GONNA PLAY TO-GETHER! ALLLL NIGHT LONG! ♬
SO! ♡
ARE WE GOING TO MY ROOM OR YOURS?
WHAT ARE YOU TALKING ABOUT?
I SAID I WANTED TO PLAY TONIGHT, AND PLAY IS WHAT I MEANT...
THE TRADI-TIONAL MEANING.
FOR REAL ?!
GRIN

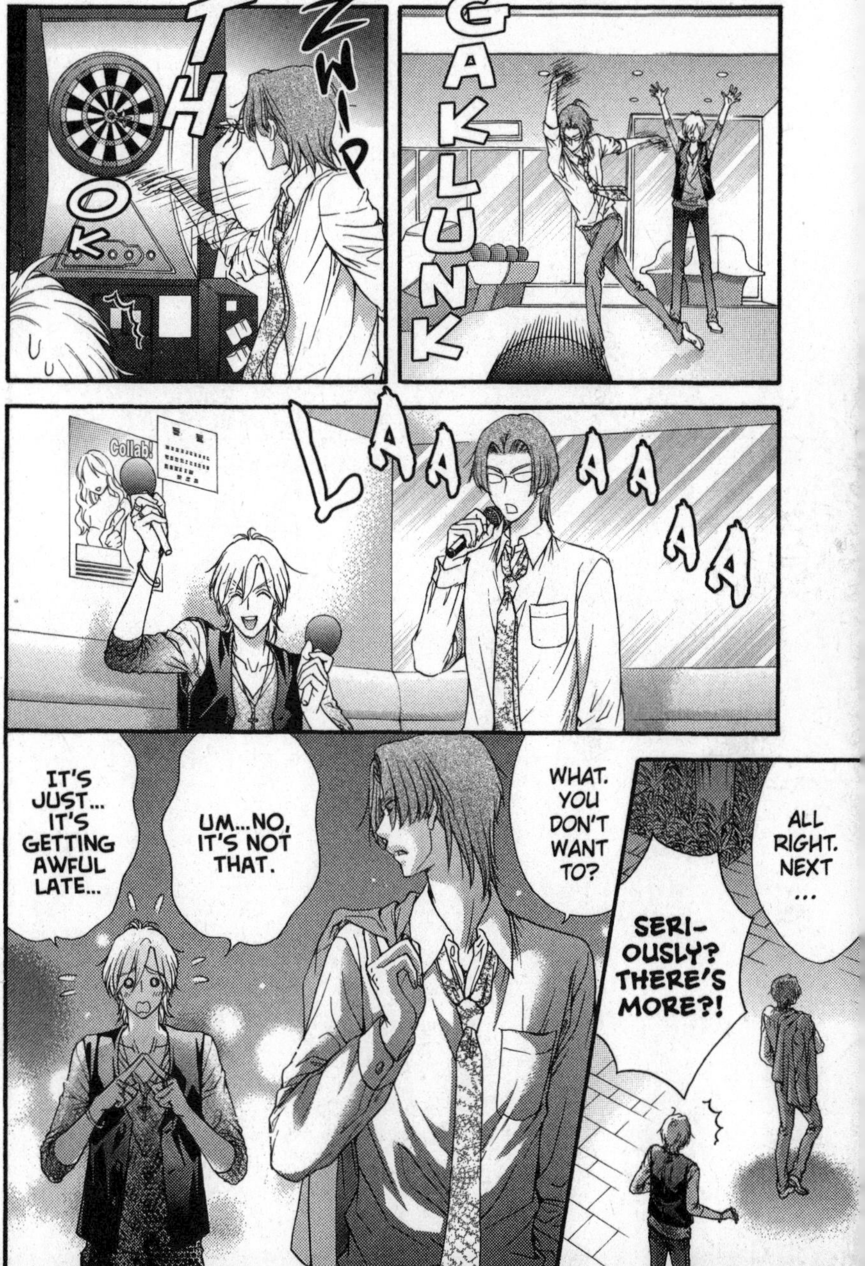
GAKLUNK
ZWIP
THOK
LAAAAAAA
Collab!
ALL RIGHT. NEXT...
SERI-OUSLY? THERE'S MORE?!
WHAT. YOU DON'T WANT TO?
UM...NO, IT'S NOT THAT.
IT'S JUST... IT'S GETTING AWFUL LATE...

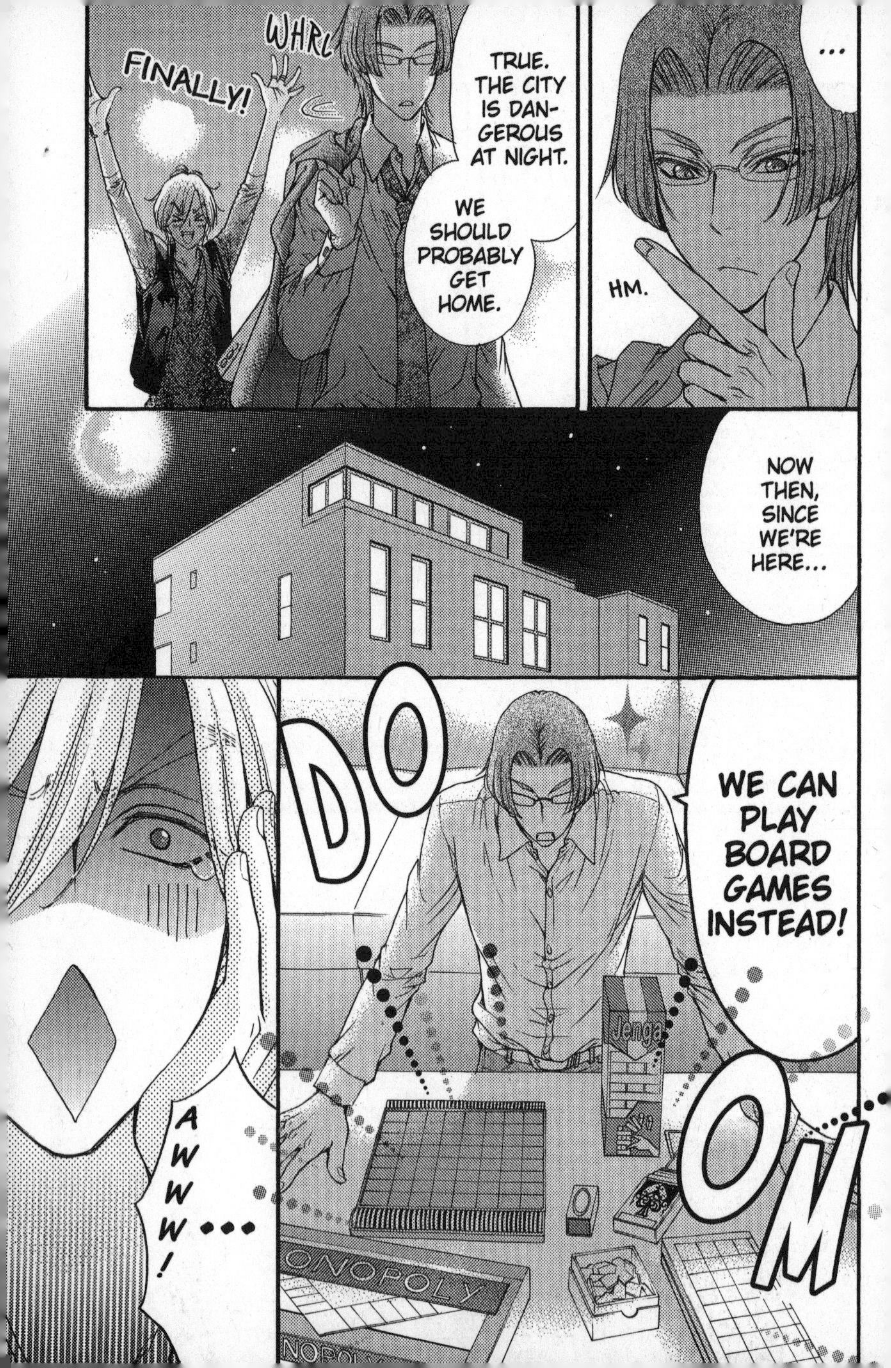
...
HM.
TRUE. THE CITY IS DAN-GEROUS AT NIGHT.
WHRL
FINALLY!
WE SHOULD PROBABLY GET HOME.
NOW THEN, SINCE WE'RE HERE...
WE CAN PLAY BOARD GAMES INSTEAD!
DO
OM
Jenga
ONOPOLY
NOPOLY
AWWW...!

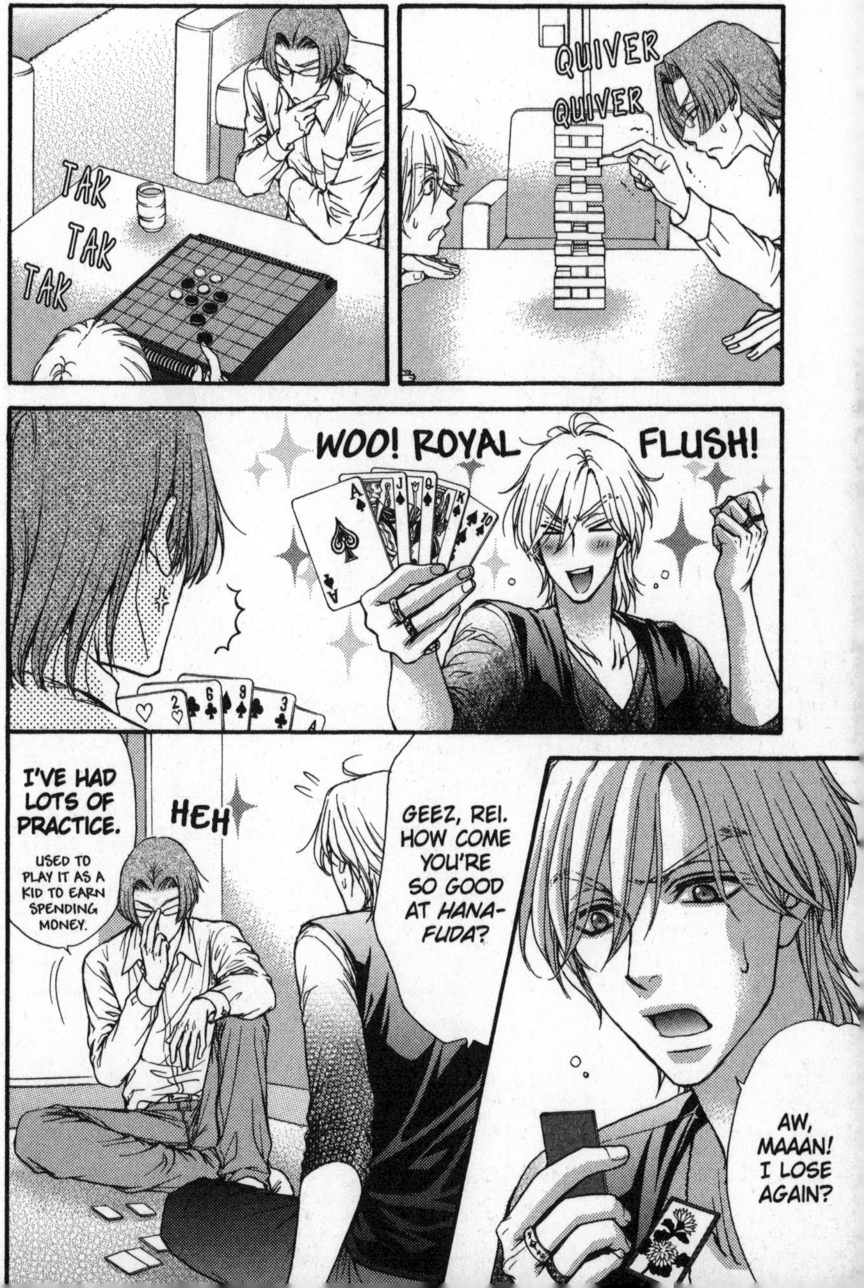
QUIVER
QUIVER
TAK
TAK
TAK
WOO! ROYAL
FLUSH!
AW, MAAAN! I LOSE AGAIN?
GEEZ, REI. HOW COME YOU'RE SO GOOD AT HANA-FUDA?
HEH
I'VE HAD LOTS OF PRACTICE.
USED TO PLAY IT AS A KID TO EARN SPENDING MONEY.

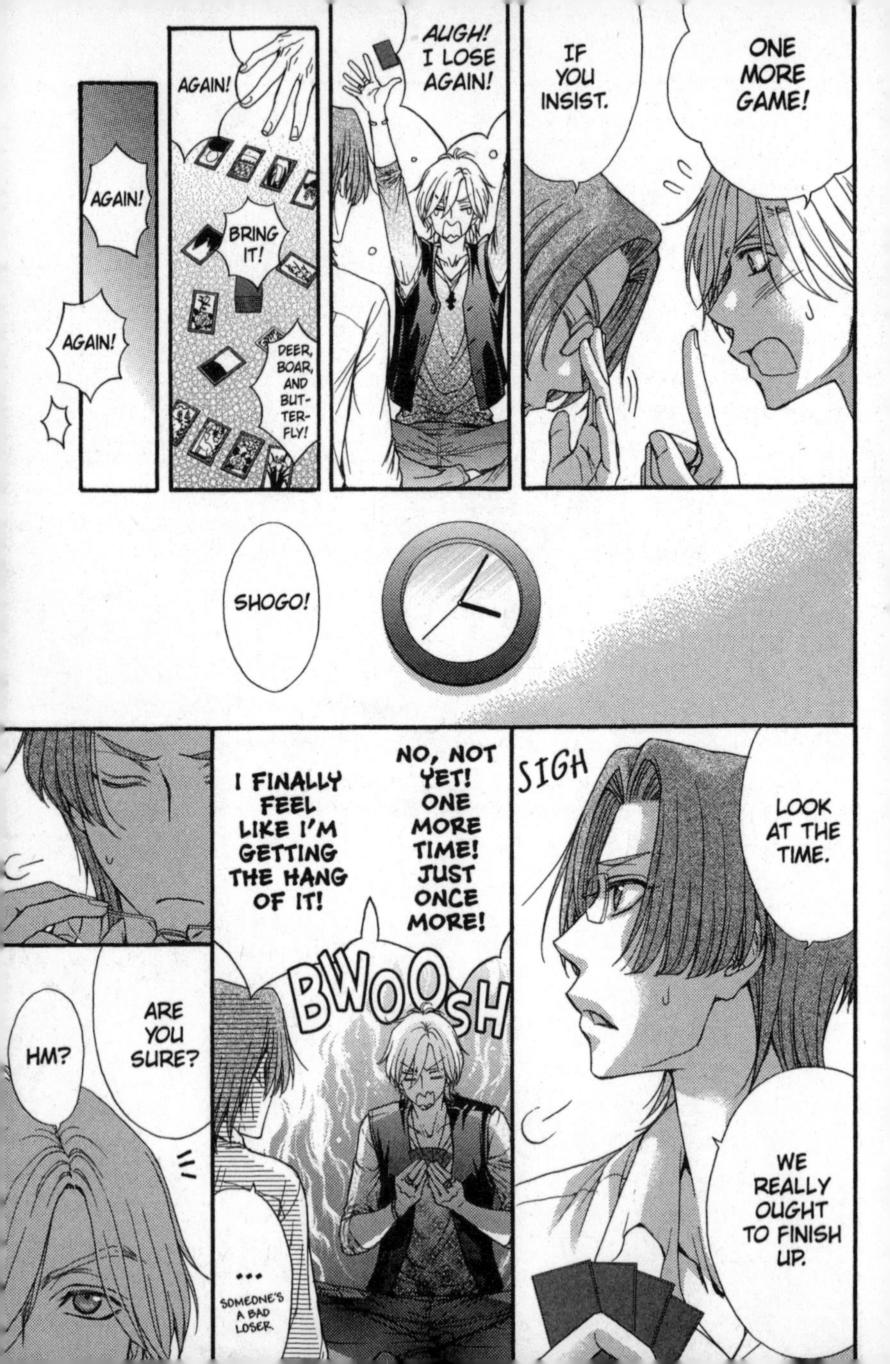
ONE MORE GAME!
IF YOU INSIST.
AUGH! I LOSE AGAIN!
AGAIN!
BRING IT!
DEER, BOAR, AND BUT-TER-FLY!
AGAIN!
AGAIN!
SHOGO!
SIGH
LOOK AT THE TIME.
WE REALLY OUGHT TO FINISH UP.
NO, NOT YET! ONE MORE TIME! JUST ONCE MORE!
I FINALLY FEEL LIKE I'M GETTING THE HANG OF IT!
BWOOSH
...
SOMEONE'S A BAD LOSER
ARE YOU SURE?
HM?

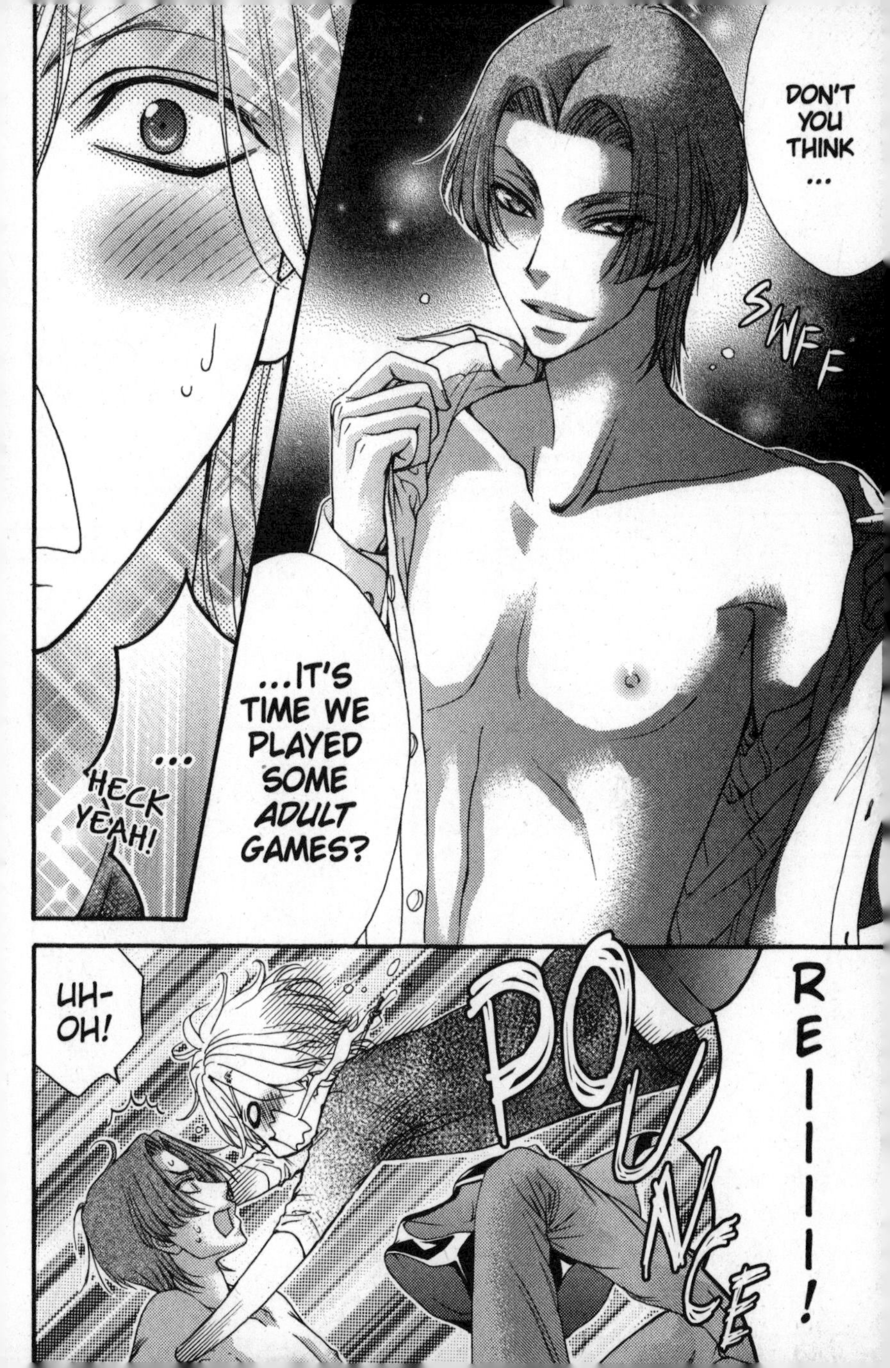
DON'T YOU THINK ...
SNFF
...IT'S TIME WE PLAYED SOME ADULT GAMES?
... HECK YEAH!
RE-----!
POUNCE
UH-OH!

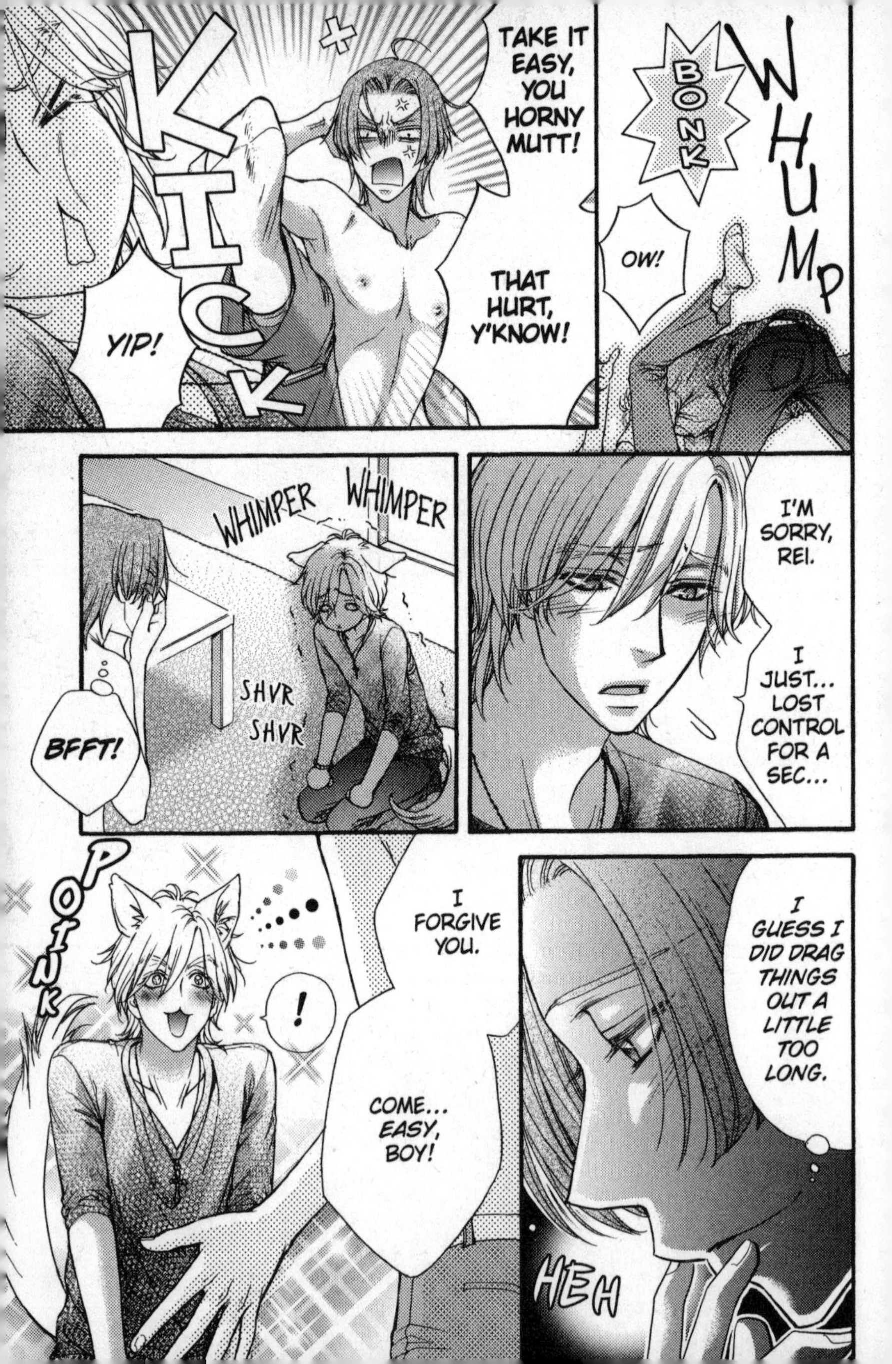
WHUMP
BONK
OW!
TAKE IT EASY, YOU HORNY MUTT!
KICK
THAT HURT, Y'KNOW!
YIP!
I'M SORRY, REI.
I JUST... LOST CONTROL FOR A SEC...
WHIMPER WHIMPER
SHVR SHVR
BFFT!
I GUESS I DID DRAG THINGS OUT A LITTLE TOO LONG.
HEH
I FORGIVE YOU.
!
POINK
COME... EASY, BOY!

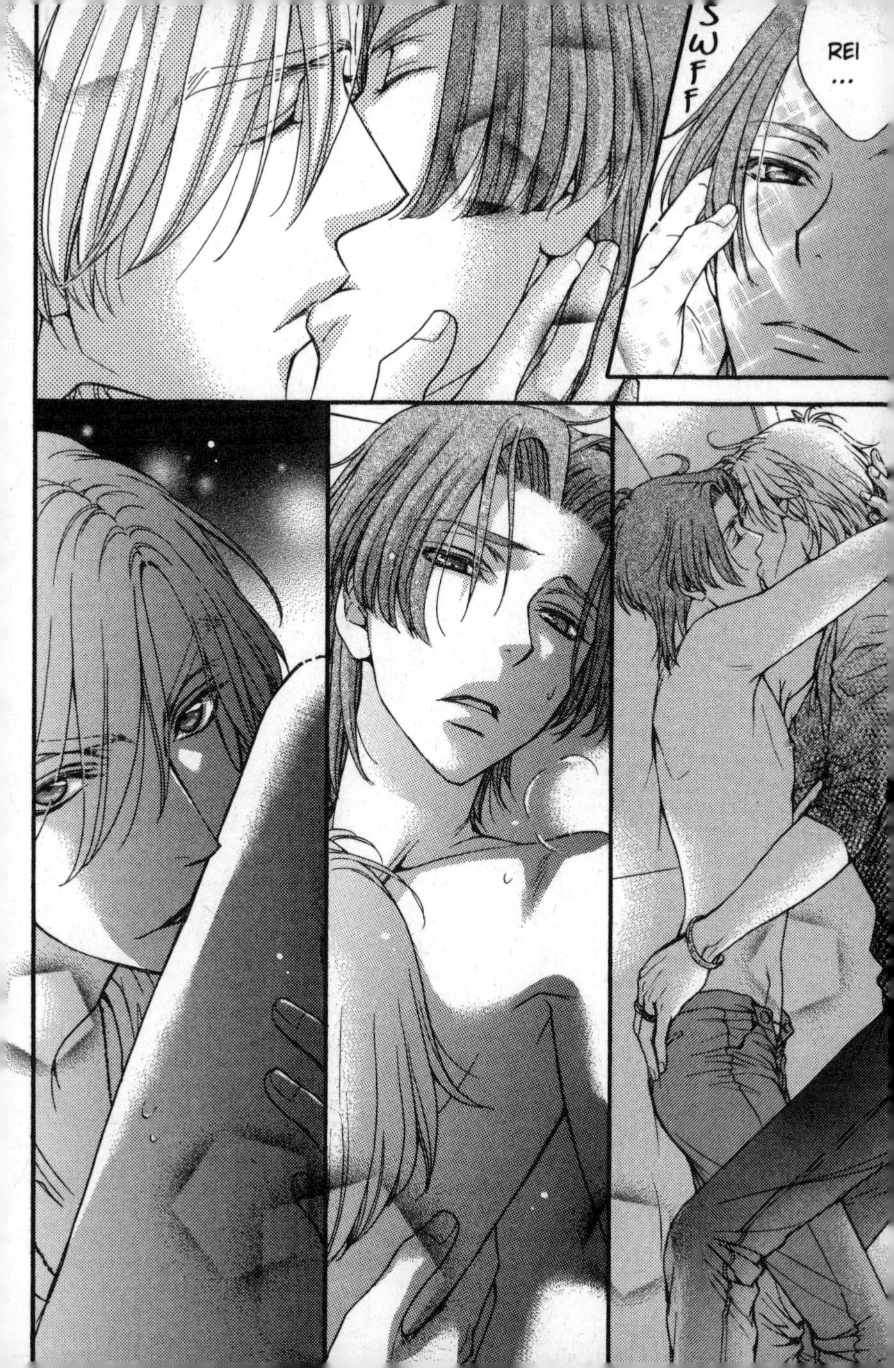
REI ...
SWFF

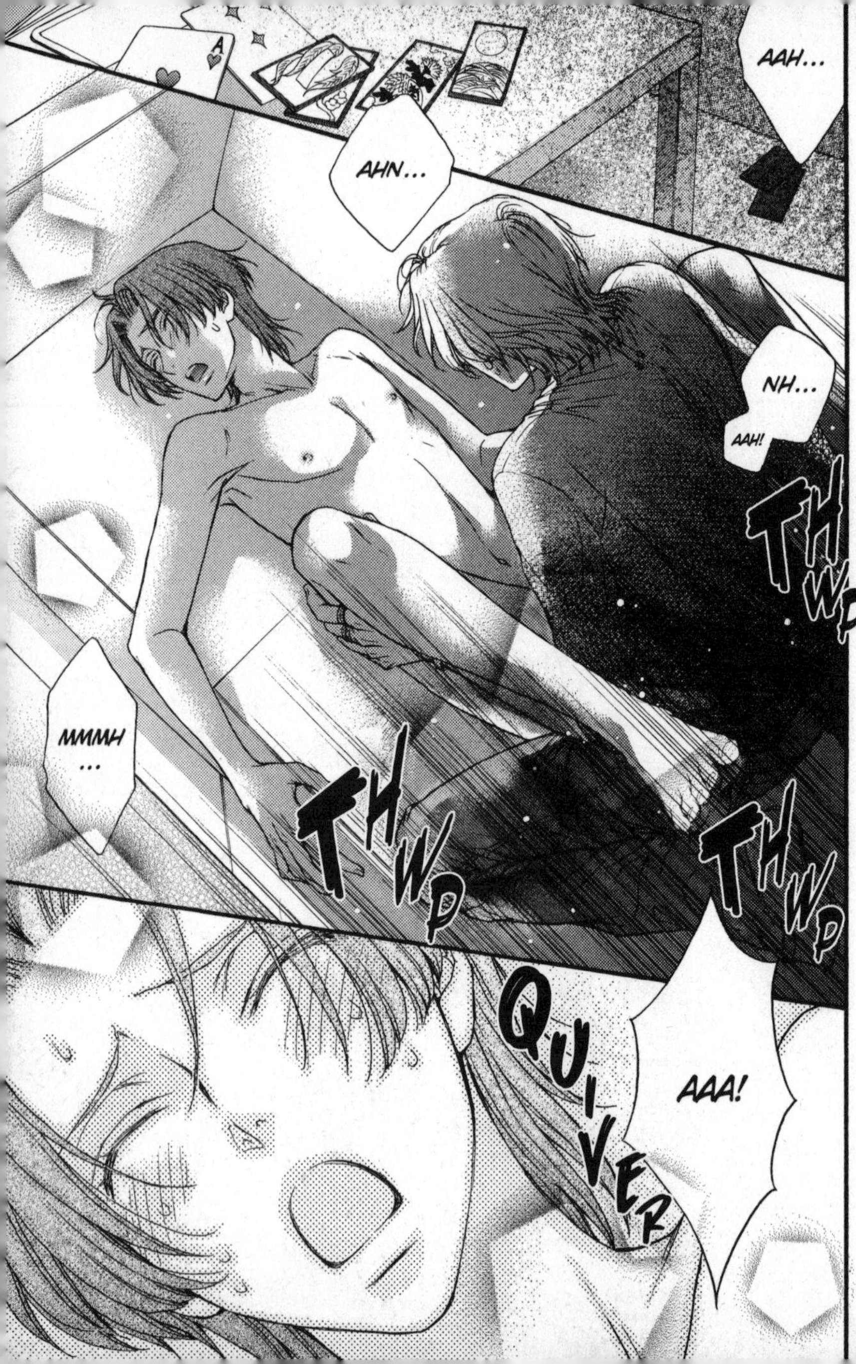
AAH...
AHN...
NH...
AAH!
THWP
THWP
MMMH ...
THWP
QUIVER
AAA!

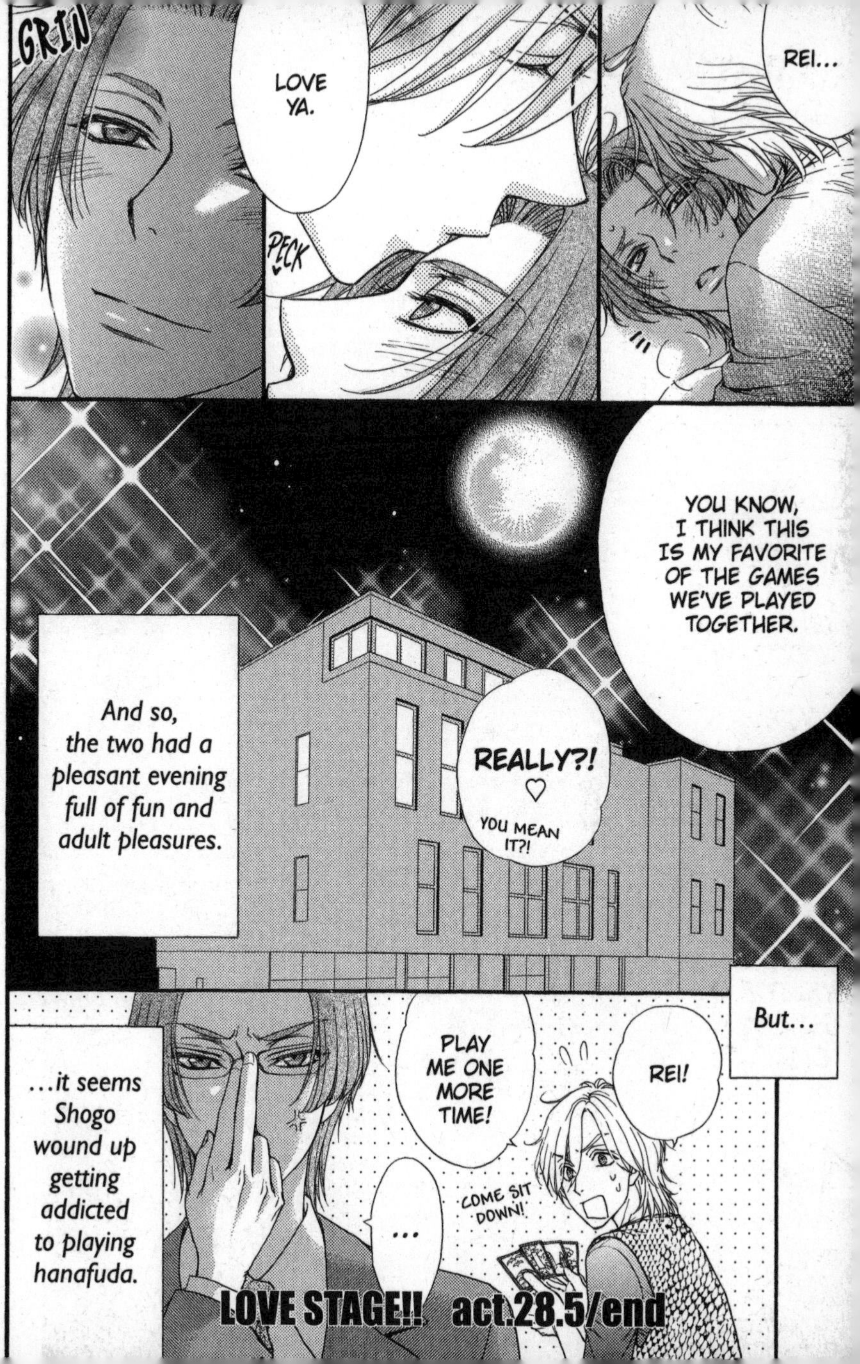
REI...
LOVE YA.
PECK
GRIN
YOU KNOW, I THINK THIS IS MY FAVORITE OF THE GAMES WE'VE PLAYED TOGETHER.
REALLY?! ♡
YOU MEAN IT?!
And so, the two had a pleasant evening full of fun and adult pleasures.
But...
REI!
COME SIT DOWN!
PLAY ME ONE MORE TIME!
...
...it seems Shogo wound up getting addicted to playing hanafuda.
LOVE STAGE!! act.28.5/end

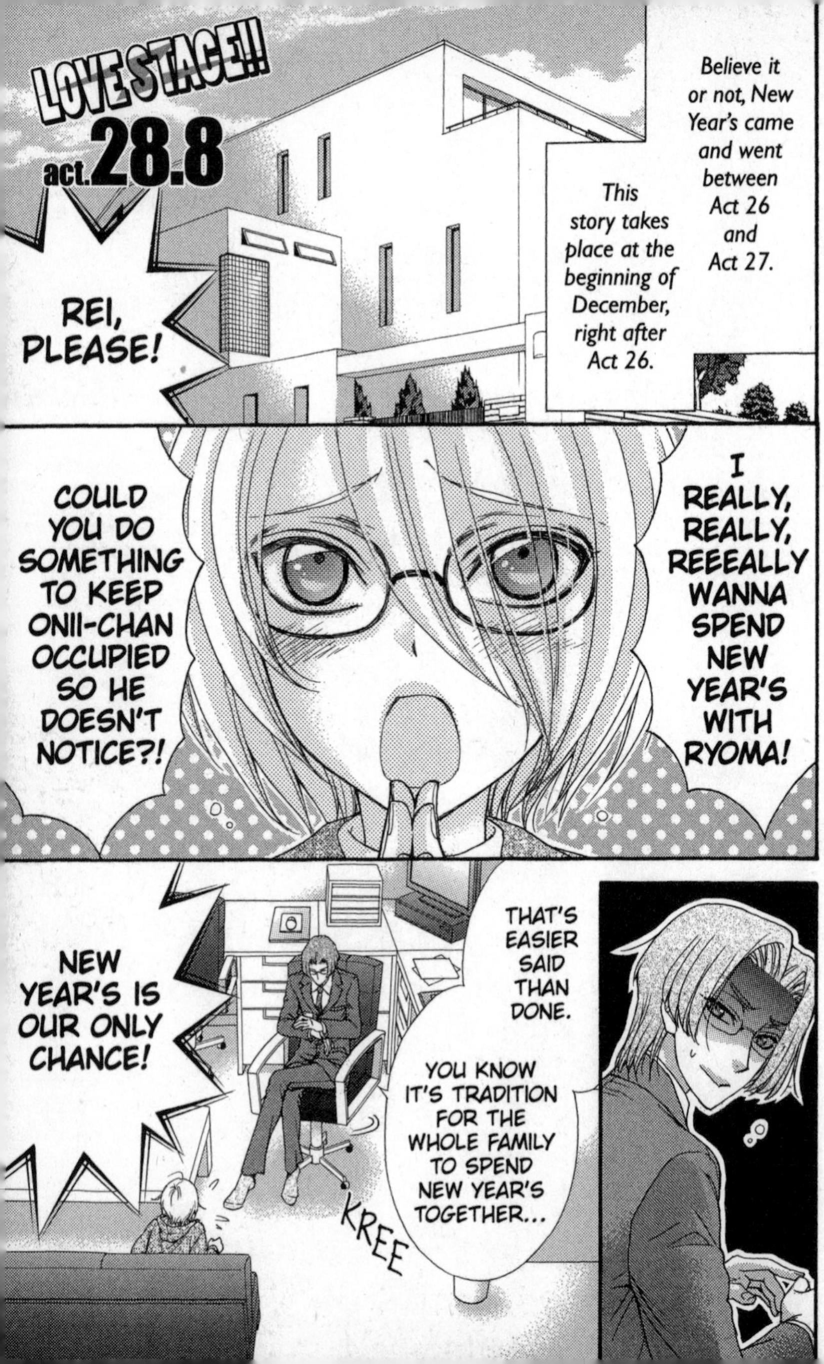
LOVE STAGE!!
act.28.8
Believe it or not, New Year's came and went between Act 26 and Act 27.
This story takes place at the beginning of December, right after Act 26.
REI, PLEASE!
I REALLY, REALLY, REEEALLY WANNA SPEND NEW YEAR'S WITH RYOMA!
COULD YOU DO SOMETHING TO KEEP ONII-CHAN OCCUPIED SO HE DOESN'T NOTICE?!
THAT'S EASIER SAID THAN DONE.
YOU KNOW IT'S TRADITION FOR THE WHOLE FAMILY TO SPEND NEW YEAR'S TOGETHER...
NEW YEAR'S IS OUR ONLY CHANCE!
KREE

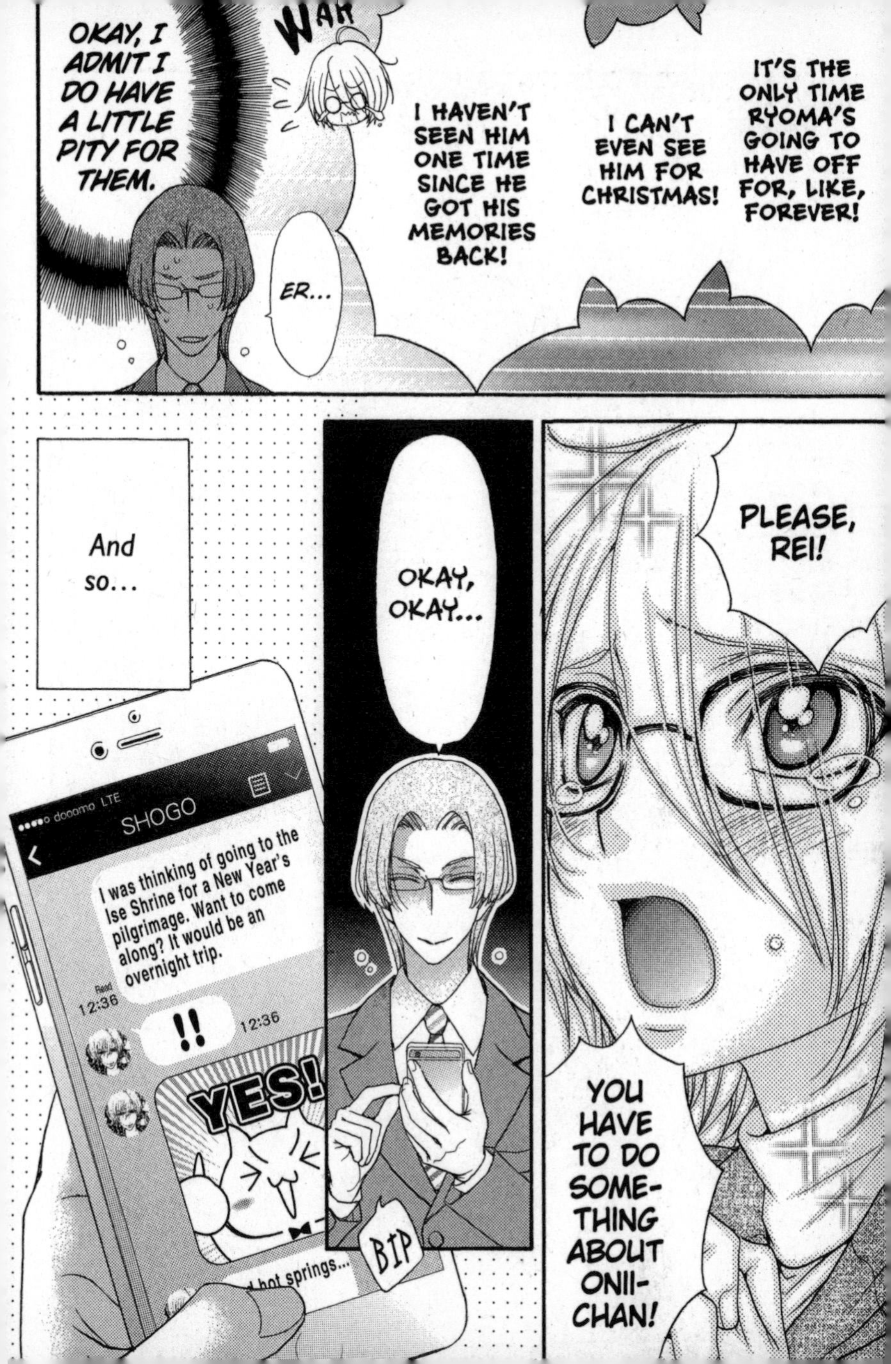
IT'S THE ONLY TIME RYOMA'S GOING TO HAVE OFF FOR, LIKE, FOREVER!
I CAN'T EVEN SEE HIM FOR CHRISTMAS!
I HAVEN'T SEEN HIM ONE TIME SINCE HE GOT HIS MEMORIES BACK!
WAH
ER...
OKAY, I ADMIT I DO HAVE A LITTLE PITY FOR THEM.
PLEASE, REI!
YOU HAVE TO DO SOME-THING ABOUT ONII-CHAN!
OKAY, OKAY...
BIP
And so...
SHOGO
I was thinking of going to the Ise Shrine for a New Year's pilgrimage. Want to come along? It would be an overnight trip.
Read
12:36
!!
12:36
YES!
hot springs...

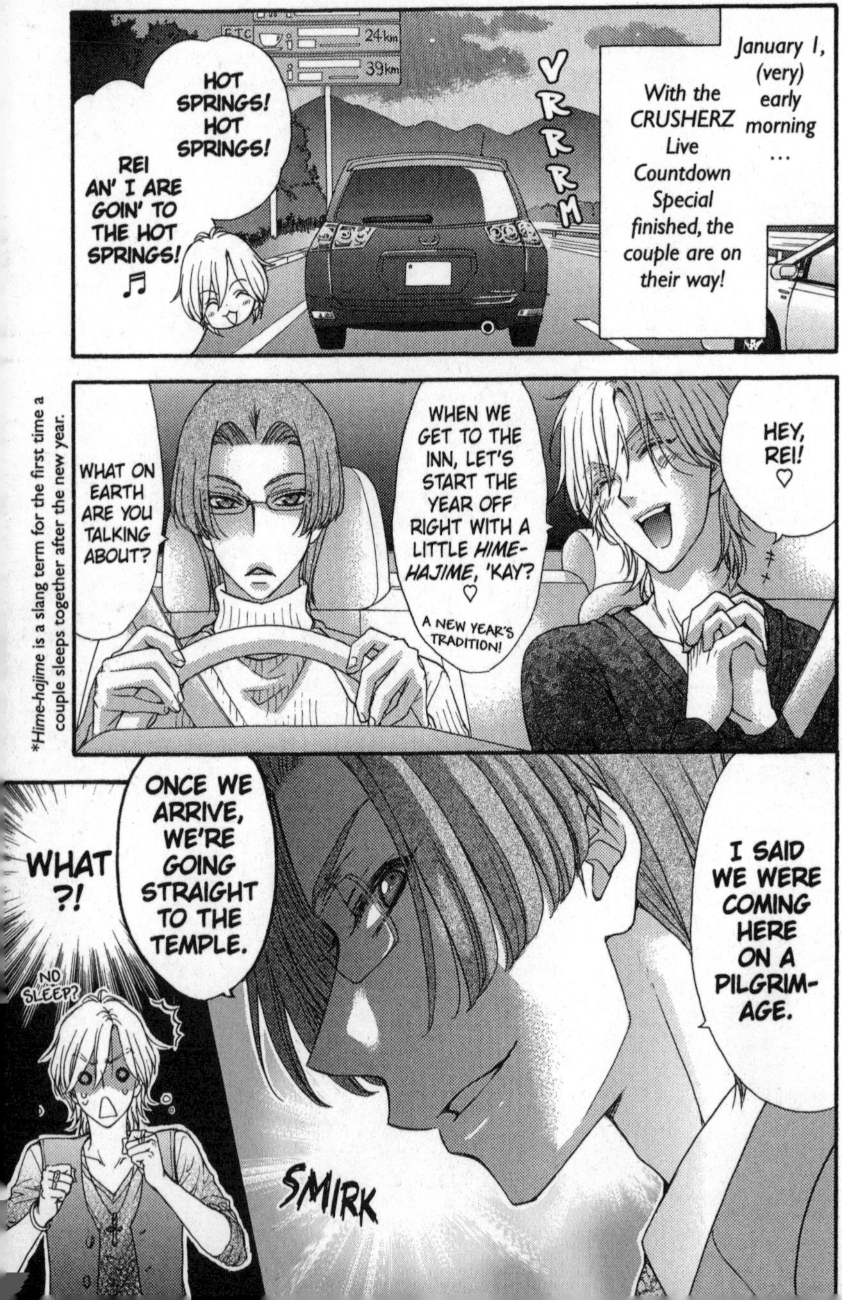
January 1, (very) early morning…
With the CRUSHERZ Live Countdown Special finished, the couple are on their way!
VRRRM
24km
39km
HOT SPRINGS! HOT SPRINGS!
REI AN' I ARE GOIN' TO THE HOT SPRINGS! ♬
HEY, REI! ♡
WHEN WE GET TO THE INN, LET'S START THE YEAR OFF RIGHT WITH A LITTLE *HIME-HAJIME*, 'KAY? ♡
A NEW YEAR'S TRADITION!
WHAT ON EARTH ARE YOU TALKING ABOUT?
I SAID WE WERE COMING HERE ON A PILGRIMAGE.
SMIRK
ONCE WE ARRIVE, WE'RE GOING STRAIGHT TO THE TEMPLE.
WHAT?!
NO SLEEP?

**Hime-hajime* is a slang term for the first time a couple sleeps together after the new year.

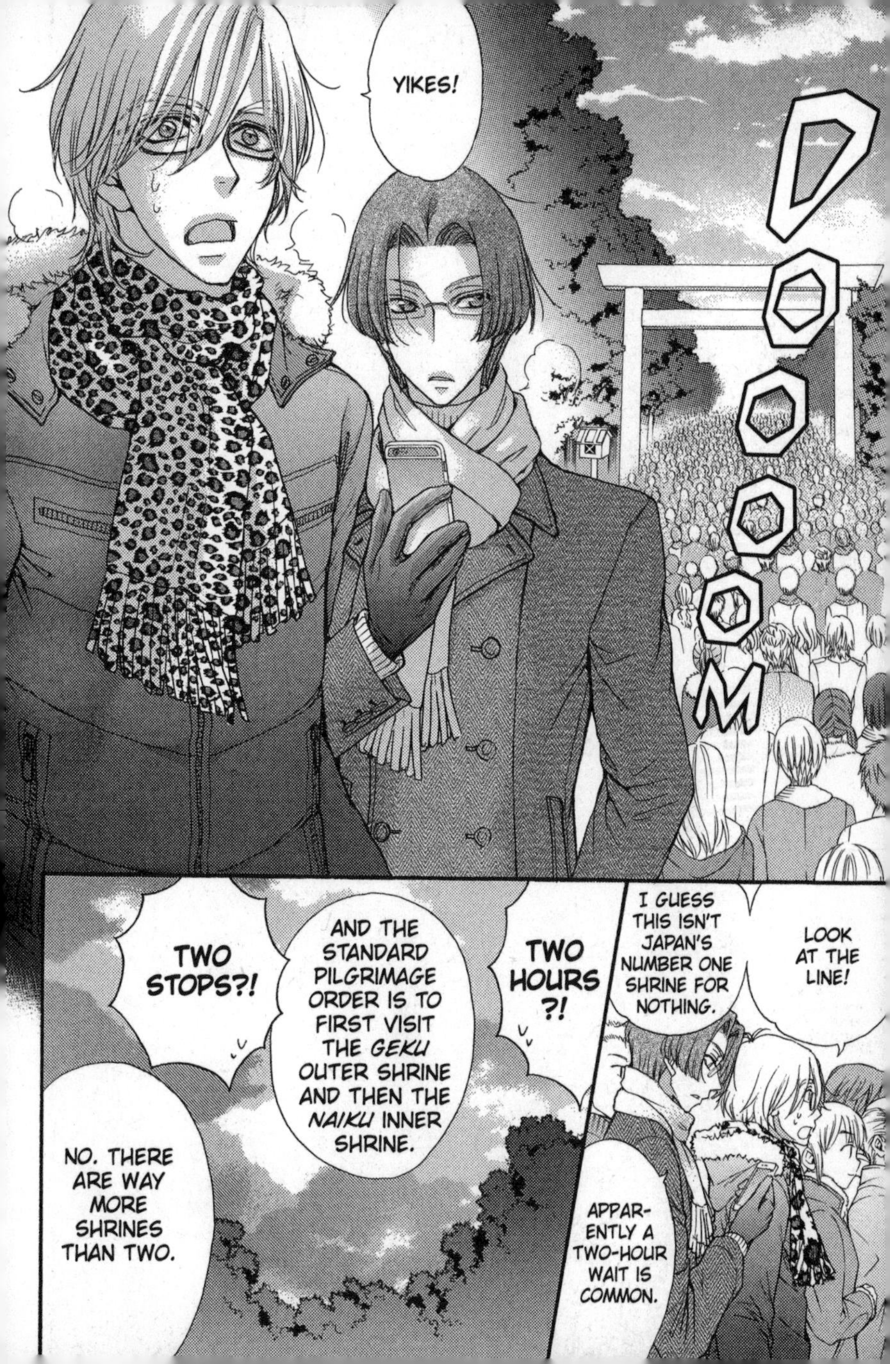
DOOOOOM
YIKES!
LOOK AT THE LINE!
I GUESS THIS ISN'T JAPAN'S NUMBER ONE SHRINE FOR NOTHING.
APPARENTLY A TWO-HOUR WAIT IS COMMON.
TWO HOURS?!
AND THE STANDARD PILGRIMAGE ORDER IS TO FIRST VISIT THE *GEKU* OUTER SHRINE AND THEN THE *NAIKU* INNER SHRINE.
TWO STOPS?!
NO. THERE ARE WAY MORE SHRINES THAN TWO.

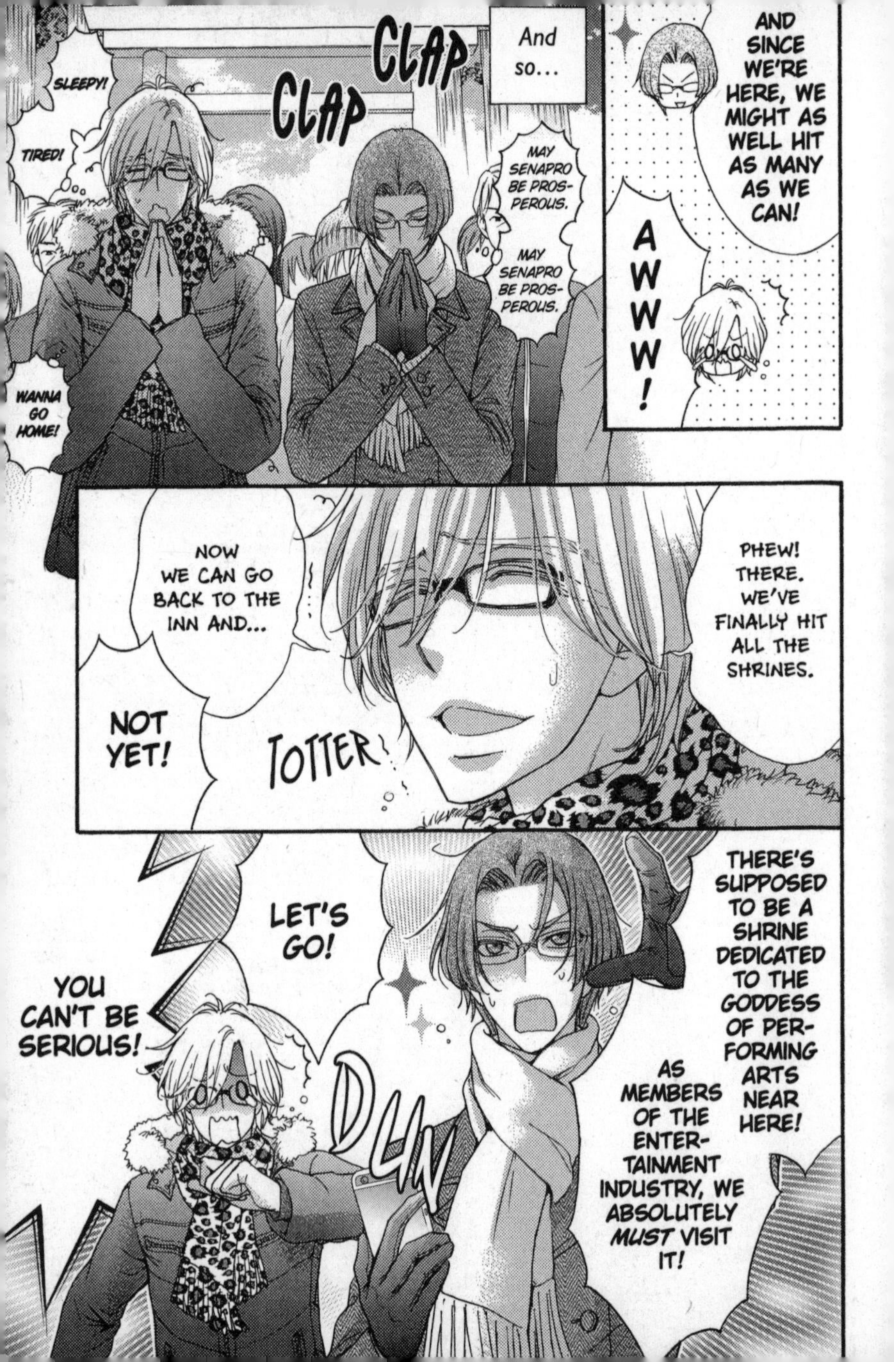
AND SINCE WE'RE HERE, WE MIGHT AS WELL HIT AS MANY AS WE CAN!
AWWW!
And so...
CLAP
CLAP
MAY SENAPRO BE PROSPEROUS.
MAY SENAPRO BE PROSPEROUS.
SLEEPY!
TIRED!
WANNA GO HOME!
PHEW! THERE. WE'VE FINALLY HIT ALL THE SHRINES.
NOW WE CAN GO BACK TO THE INN AND...
TOTTER
NOT YET!
THERE'S SUPPOSED TO BE A SHRINE DEDICATED TO THE GODDESS OF PERFORMING ARTS NEAR HERE!
AS MEMBERS OF THE ENTERTAINMENT INDUSTRY, WE ABSOLUTELY *MUST* VISIT IT!
LET'S GO!
DUN
YOU CAN'T BE SERIOUS!

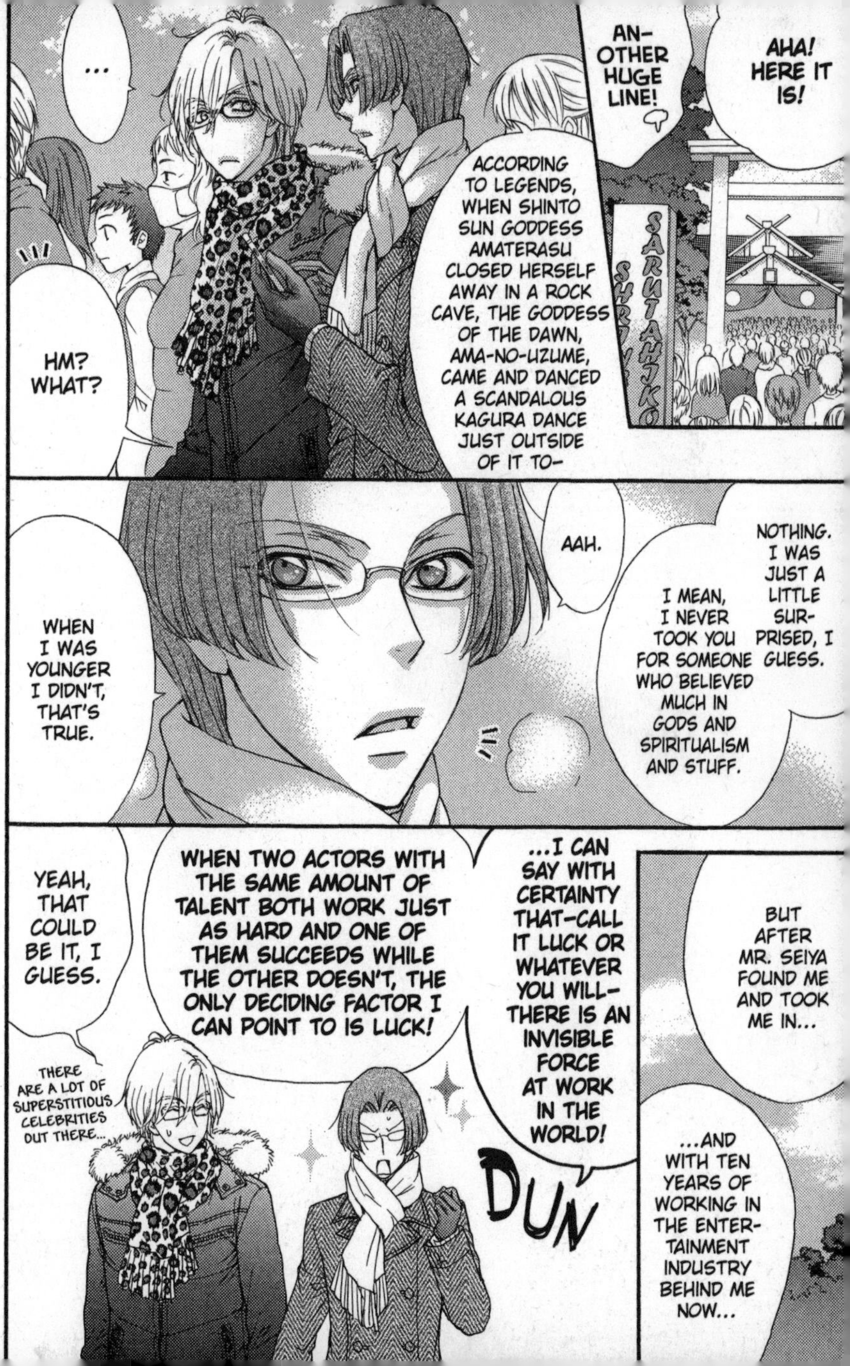
AHA! HERE IT IS!
ANOTHER HUGE LINE!
SARUTAHIKO
ACCORDING TO LEGENDS, WHEN SHINTO SUN GODDESS AMATERASU CLOSED HERSELF AWAY IN A ROCK CAVE, THE GODDESS OF THE DAWN, AMA-NO-UZUME, CAME AND DANCED A SCANDALOUS KAGURA DANCE JUST OUTSIDE OF IT TO—
...
HM? WHAT?
NOTHING. I WAS JUST A LITTLE SURPRISED, I GUESS.
I MEAN, I NEVER TOOK YOU FOR SOMEONE WHO BELIEVED MUCH IN GODS AND SPIRITUALISM AND STUFF.
AAH.
WHEN I WAS YOUNGER I DIDN'T, THAT'S TRUE.
BUT AFTER MR. SEIYA FOUND ME AND TOOK ME IN...
...AND WITH TEN YEARS OF WORKING IN THE ENTERTAINMENT INDUSTRY BEHIND ME NOW...
...I CAN SAY WITH CERTAINTY THAT—CALL IT LUCK OR WHATEVER YOU WILL—THERE IS AN INVISIBLE FORCE AT WORK IN THE WORLD!
WHEN TWO ACTORS WITH THE SAME AMOUNT OF TALENT BOTH WORK JUST AS HARD AND ONE OF THEM SUCCEEDS WHILE THE OTHER DOESN'T, THE ONLY DECIDING FACTOR I CAN POINT TO IS LUCK!
DUN
YEAH, THAT COULD BE IT, I GUESS.
THERE ARE A LOT OF SUPERSTITIOUS CELEBRITIES OUT THERE...

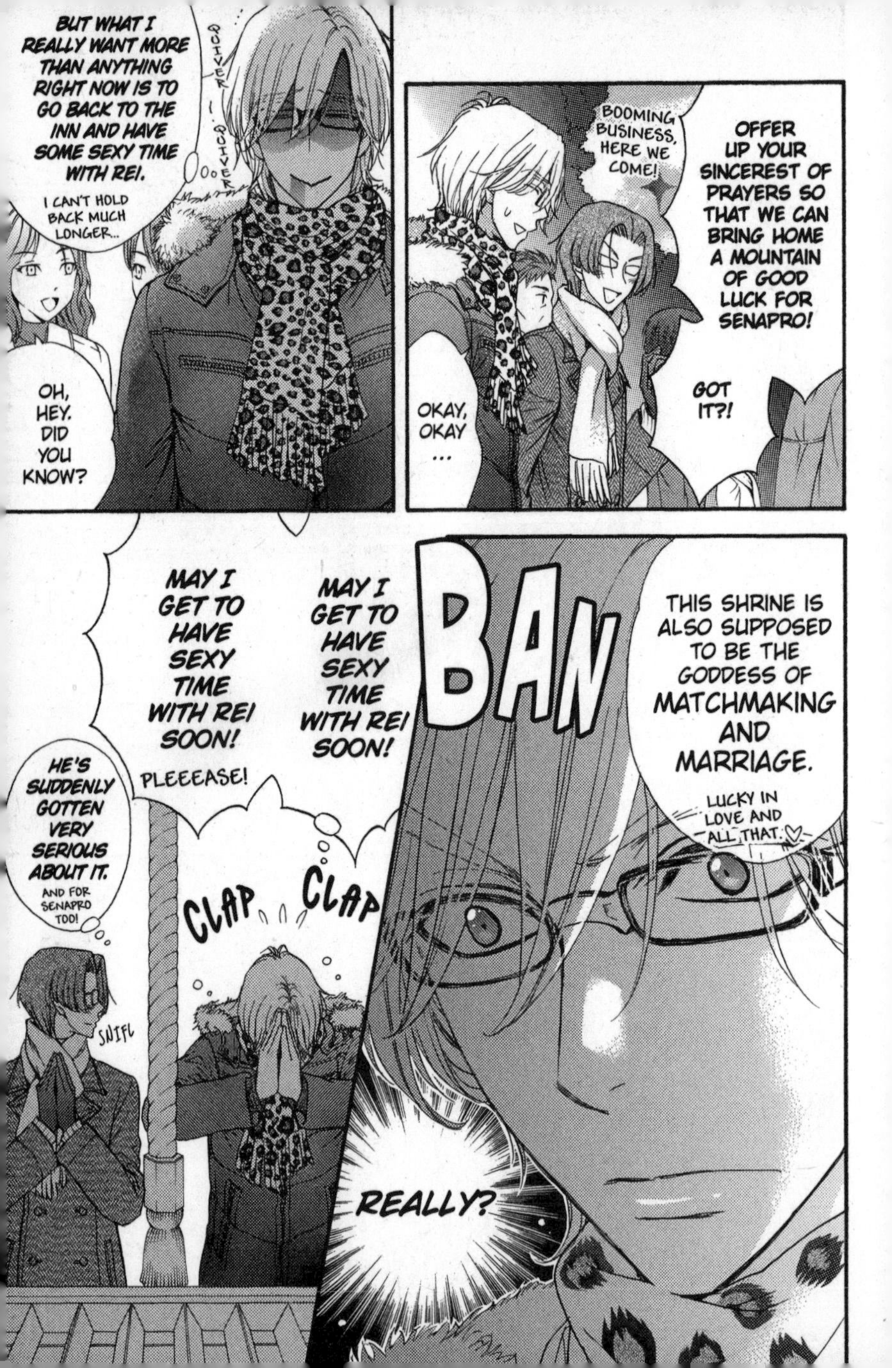
OFFER UP YOUR SINCEREST OF PRAYERS SO THAT WE CAN BRING HOME A MOUNTAIN OF GOOD LUCK FOR SENAPRO!
BOOMING BUSINESS, HERE WE COME!
GOT IT?!
OKAY, OKAY ...
BUT WHAT I REALLY WANT MORE THAN ANYTHING RIGHT NOW IS TO GO BACK TO THE INN AND HAVE SOME SEXY TIME WITH REI.
QUIVER QUIVER
I CAN'T HOLD BACK MUCH LONGER...
OH, HEY. DID YOU KNOW?
BAN
THIS SHRINE IS ALSO SUPPOSED TO BE THE GODDESS OF MATCHMAKING AND MARRIAGE.
LUCKY IN LOVE AND ALL THAT.♡
REALLY?
MAY I GET TO HAVE SEXY TIME WITH REI SOON!
MAY I GET TO HAVE SEXY TIME WITH REI SOON!
PLEEEASE!
CLAP
CLAP
HE'S SUDDENLY GOTTEN VERY SERIOUS ABOUT IT.
AND FOR SENAPRO TOO!
SNIFL

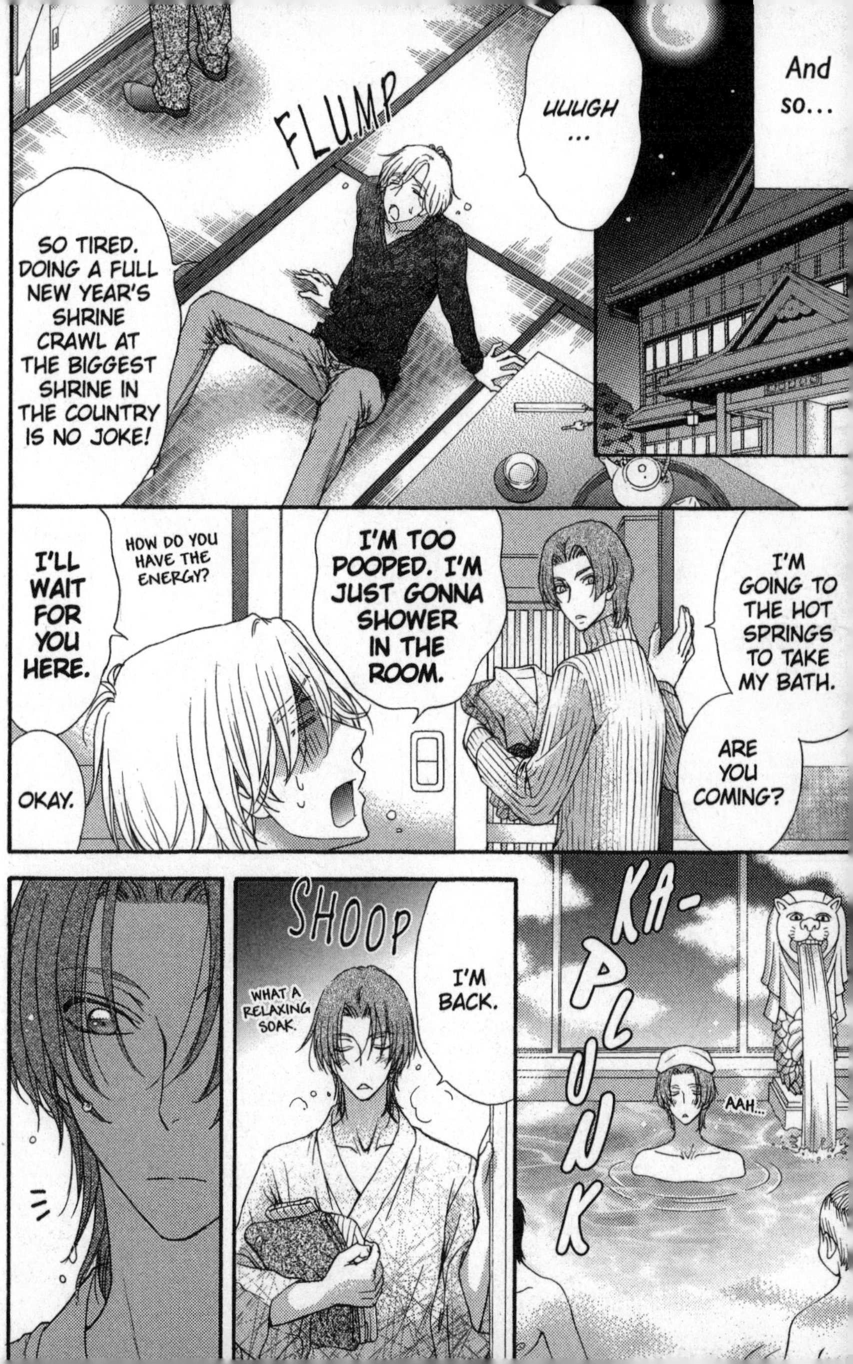
And so…
UUUGH …
FLUMP
SO TIRED. DOING A FULL NEW YEAR'S SHRINE CRAWL AT THE BIGGEST SHRINE IN THE COUNTRY IS NO JOKE!
I'M GOING TO THE HOT SPRINGS TO TAKE MY BATH.
ARE YOU COMING?
I'M TOO POOPED. I'M JUST GONNA SHOWER IN THE ROOM.
HOW DO YOU HAVE THE ENERGY?
I'LL WAIT FOR YOU HERE.
OKAY.
KA-PLUNK
AAH…
SHOOP
I'M BACK.
WHAT A RELAXING SOAK.

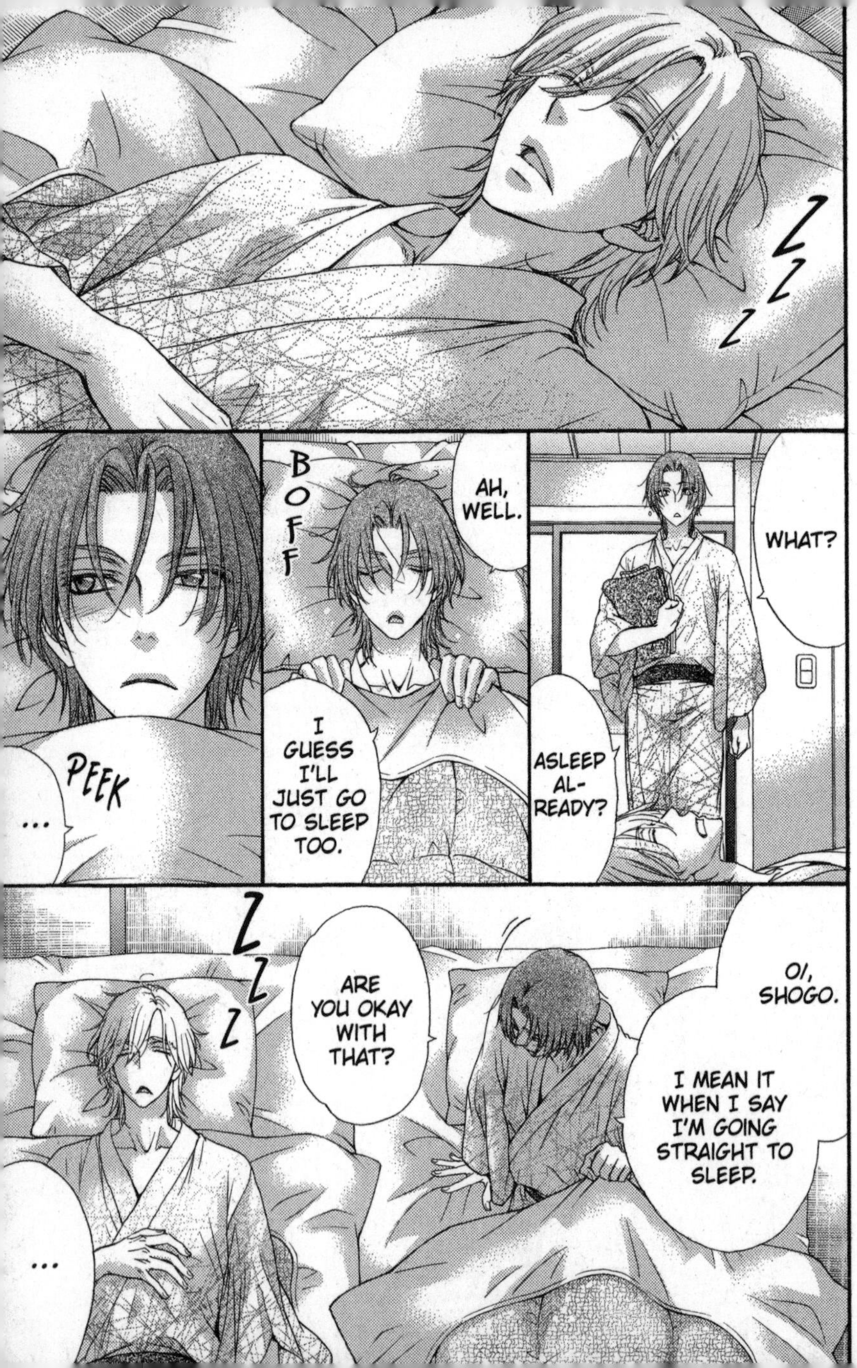
Z Z Z
WHAT?
ASLEEP AL-READY?
AH, WELL.
BOFF
I GUESS I'LL JUST GO TO SLEEP TOO.
PEEK
...
OI, SHOGO.
I MEAN IT WHEN I SAY I'M GOING STRAIGHT TO SLEEP.
ARE YOU OKAY WITH THAT?
Z Z Z
...

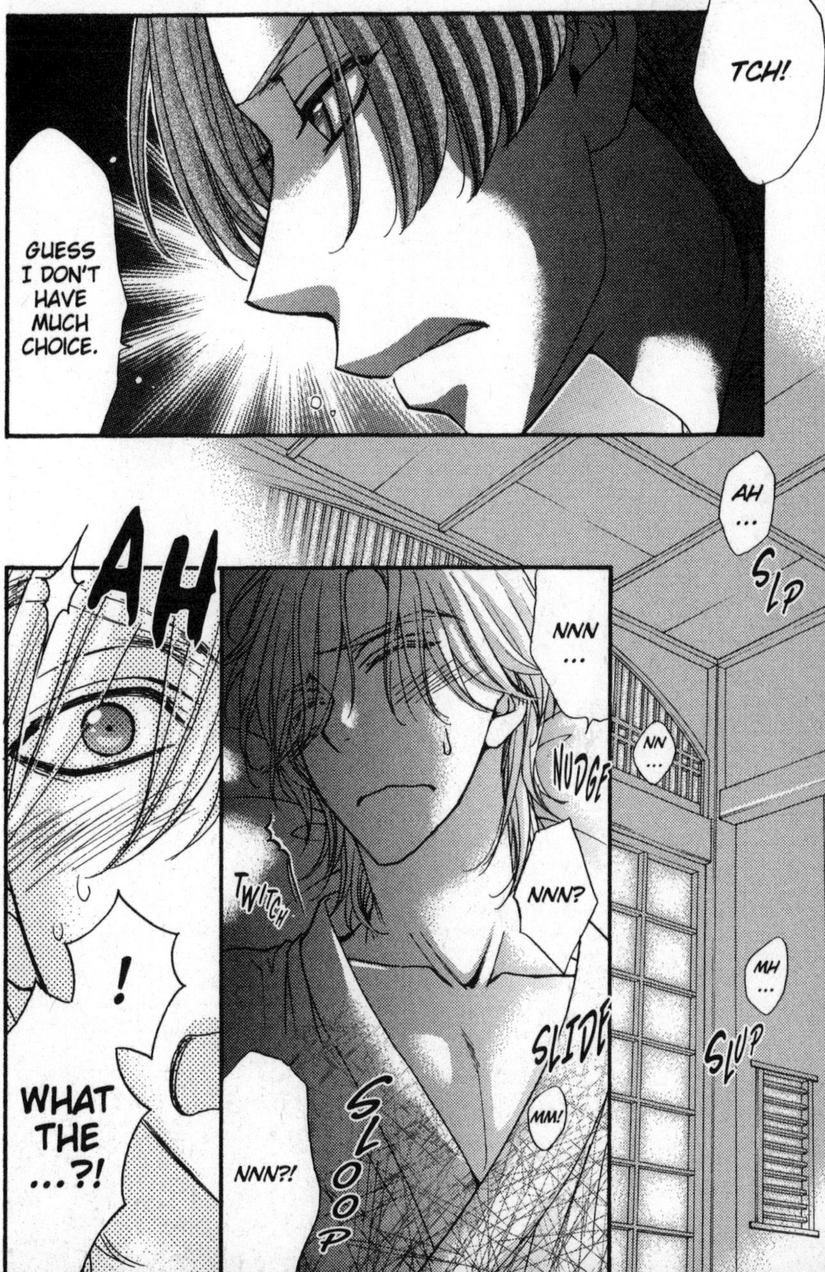
TCH!
GUESS I DON'T HAVE MUCH CHOICE.
AH ...
SLIP
NN ...
MH ...
SLUP
NNN ...
NUDGE
NNN?
TWITCH
SLIDE
MM!
SLOOOP
NNN?!
AH
!
WHAT THE ...?!

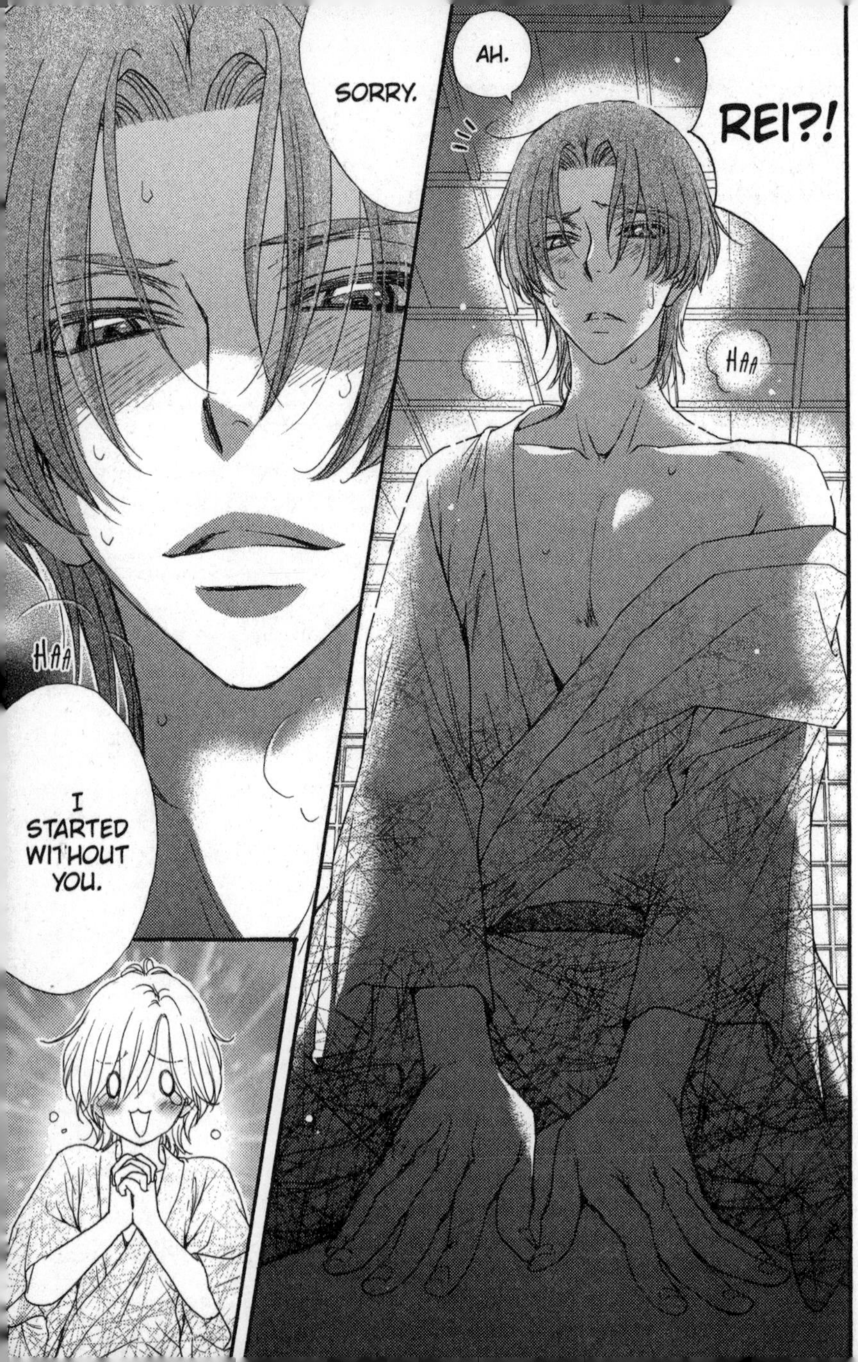
REI?!
AH.
HAA
SORRY.
HAA
I STARTED WITHOUT YOU.

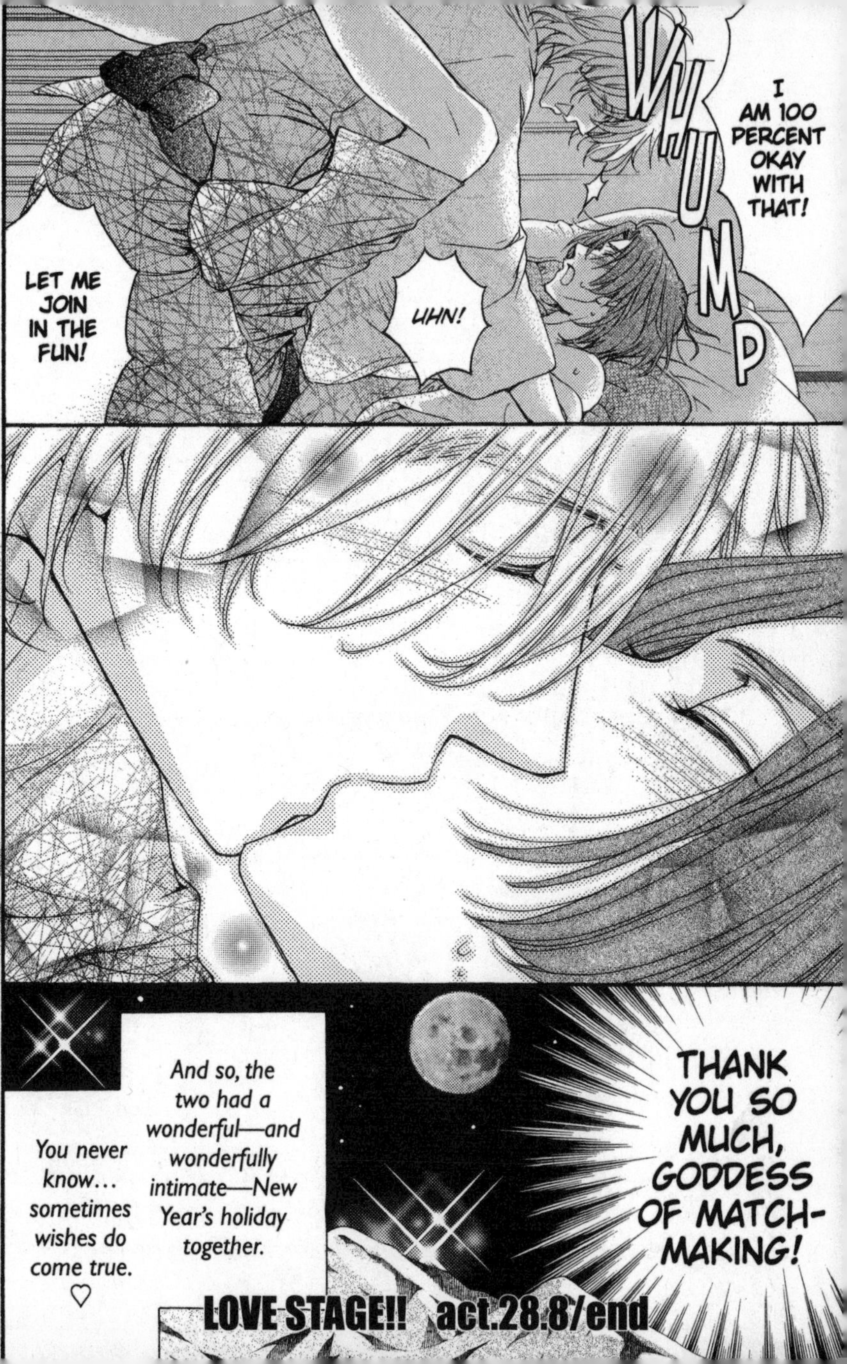
I AM 100 PERCENT OKAY WITH THAT!
WHUMP
UHN!
LET ME JOIN IN THE FUN!
THANK YOU SO MUCH, GODDESS OF MATCH-MAKING!
And so, the two had a wonderful—and wonderfully intimate—New Year's holiday together.
You never know… sometimes wishes do come true. ♡
LOVE STAGE!! act.28.8/end

AFTERWORD

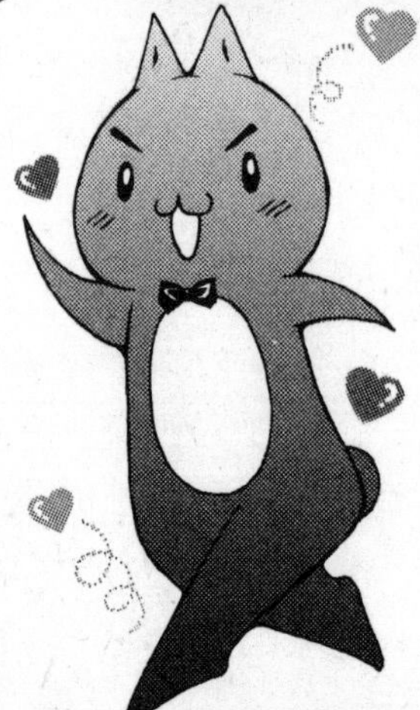

Hi! This is scriptwriter Eiki Eiki! Ta-da! It's *Love Stage* volume 6. The TV-show arc has finally come to a close. It feels like that would have been a nice place to wrap up the series, but there are still a few things I have yet to write. And so I present to you the manga/living-together arc! ♡ Mr. Saotome and Kuroi finally get their day in the spotlight!

We got to add into this volume a short Shogo and Rei one-off I did for the anthology, so I decided to stay in that vein and add more Shogo/Rei stories for this volume's bonus content. I kinda agree with Rei. Looking at what goes on around me, I think there must be some unknown, unseen force at work in the world.

Now then, *Love Stage*'s story is finally reaching its climax! I hope you'll stick around to the very end. I'm forever thankful for the support that you and all the other readers out there give to us!

Eiki Eiki LOVE xxx

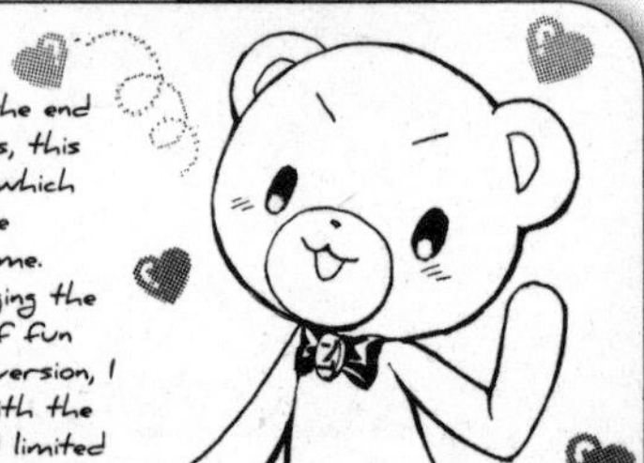

Hello! This is artist Taishi Zaou! This volume saw the end of the TV-show arc. Unlike some of the other arcs, this one involved the characters being in costume a lot, which was almost like having them in uniform. So once the designs were set, the drawing got pretty easy for me. And since they're a great tool for completely changing the atmosphere of a composition, I got to have a lot of fun doing the covers for this volume! For the normal version, I had both of them in almost artsy outfits to go with the manga arc. But for the Animate special edition and limited edition covers, I decked out both Izumi and Ryoma in their TV-show costumes—a rich young man and his butler! That one turned out looking a lot different from the standard *Love Stage* cover, so I'd love it if you would check it out.

Well then, now that the TV-show arc is over, it's time to start a new one! I get the feeling there's going to be a lot of cosplaying in someone's future. I can hardly wait! *Love Stage* isn't technically a cosplay series, but oh well! ☆ Mwah ha ha...

Taishi Zaou PEACE xxx

Eiki Eiki is the creator of numerous yaoi and shojo manga. Her previous English-language releases include *Train★Train*, *Millennium Prime Minister*, and *The Art of Loving*. Born on December 6th, she is a Sagittarius with an A blood type.

Taishi Zaou's works have been published in English, French, and German. Her previous English-language releases include *Green Light*, *Fevered Kiss*, *Living For Tomorrow*, *Mysterious Love*, and *Electric Hands*. She was born a Capricorn on January 10th and has an O blood type.

About the Creators

Their hit series *Love Stage!!* has been adapted into a drama CD and a television anime series. Eiki Eiki and Taishi Zaou also publish *doujinshi* (independent comics) under the name "Kozouya." You can find out more about them at their website, http://www.kozouya.com/.